ISRAELI FOREIGN POLICY

Perspectives on Israel Studies

S. Ilan Troen, Natan Aridan, Donna Divine, David Ellenson, Arieh Saposnik, and Jonathan Sarna, editors

Sponsored by
The Ben-Gurion Research Institute for the Study of Israel and Zionism of the Ben-Gurion University of the Negev
and the
Schusterman Center for Israel Studies of Brandeis University

ISRAELI FOREIGN POLICY

A People Shall Not Dwell Alone

Uri Bialer

Indiana University Press

This book is a publication of

Indiana University Press
Office of Scholarly Publishing
Herman B Wells Library 350
1320 East 10th Street
Bloomington, Indiana 47405 USA

iupress.indiana.edu

Manufactured in the United States of America

Cataloging information is available from the Library of Congress.

ISBN 978-0-253-04620-8 (hardback)
ISBN 978-0-253-04621-5 (paperback)
ISBN 978-0-253-04622-2 (web PDF)

1 2 3 4 5   25 24 23 22 21 20

"Behold, it is a people that shall dwell alone, and shall not reckon itself among the nations."

—Numbers 23:9

Contents

Acknowledgments

THIS BOOK REPRESENTS an effort to summarize a multifaceted academic activity that began in the late 1980s. While working in this field of study over the course of more than three decades, I have gained immensely from the advice, criticism, and encouragement of many. I owe deep thanks to Shlomo Avineri, Avraham Sela, Yoseph Heller, Gadi Heimann, Raymond Cohen, Gabi Sheffer, Kobi Metzer (Hebrew University); Tuvia Frueling and Natan Aridan (Ben-Gurion University); Itamar Rabinovitch, Motti Golani, Yaacov Roi, Aharon Klieman, and David Vital (Tel Aviv University); Zach Levey (Haifa University); Stuart Cohen (Bar Ilan University); Yoav Gelber (Interdisciplinary Center); Yehoshua Freundlich, Yemima Rosenthal, and Gilad Livne (Israel State Archives); Baruch Tor-Raz (Israel Labor Party Archive); Yoram Mayorek (Central Zionist Archives); Yitzhak Minerbi, Arie Levin, Binyamin Navon, Yosef Lamdan, Shimon Stein, Nimrod Barkan, Haim Koren, and Yaacov Amitai (Israeli Foreign Ministry); Mordechai Ben-Porath and Shlomo Hillel (Mossad LeAliyah Beth); Elad Van Gelder (Israeli Prime Minister's Office); Yair Tzaban (Israeli Cabinet); and Ben Cohen.

Donna Robinson Divine, Alan Dowty, and Robert Freedman offered thoughtful and perceptive comments as readers of the draft book. Merav Datan provided considerable help as a highly professional translator. Dee Mortensen and Ashante Thomas of Indiana University Press greatly assisted in preparing the typescript for print. The book was published with the support of the Israel Science Foundation (Grant No. 1/18). The Schusterman Center at Brandeis University and the Israel Institute offered moral and generous financial help, which facilitated the research and production of the book.

Last but not least, I owe the deepest gratitude to Ilan Troen of Brandeis University and Ben-Gurion University, who presented me with the very rewarding challenge of writing this book and whose insightful criticism, advice, and constant support throughout its writing have made it all happen.

The book is dedicated to my grandchildren—Guy, Tal, Alma, Eden, Adam, Amos, Imri, Alona, Zohar, and Keshet—whose grandfather's strange endeavors have naturally been far beyond their grasp. Yet they are so close to my heart.

Let them never dwell alone.

Jerusalem, January 2019

ISRAELI FOREIGN POLICY

Introduction

My interest in the history of Israel's foreign policy is informed by four sources. The first was a class taught by Professor Michael Brecher in 1970, which I attended as a master's student at the Hebrew University. Professor Brecher was among the first in Israel and in the world to address this issue as an academic subject. In two books published in the ensuing four years, *The Foreign Policy System of Israel: Setting, Images, Process* (1972) and *Decisions in Israel's Foreign Policy* (1974), he laid the foundations for the discipline, and these foundations are still standing today. The topic inspired me—one of his first students—to write a master's thesis under his supervision on the roles of David Ben-Gurion and Moshe Sharett in the decision-making process that led to Israel's 1948 declaration of statehood. During this time I met personally on several occasions with Israel's first (and by then former) prime minister, who granted me access to classified state documents in his possession. In 1971, while still a master's student, I published my first academic article based on this research.

The second source that drew me to study this issue, four years later, was my service of several years as a founder and senior researcher in the Foreign Ministry's Department of Research and Policy Planning, established in the aftermath of the Yom Kippur War. The work exposed me to the making of Israeli foreign policy in real time. Shortly thereafter I joined the International Relations Department of the Hebrew University, the third source of my interest, where I gained access to Israeli state documents that had just become available thanks to a law permitting the disclosure of government documents thirty years after an event. Consequently, I abandoned my research on Britain's foreign and defense policy during the two world wars, which I had been pursuing since the days of my doctoral studies at the University of London. The new material fascinated me and has since become the core of my academic work, a focus of my publications, and a central theme of the courses I have taught.[1] At my initiative, the subject became a required course for BA students in international relations at the Hebrew University, which for years I have taught jointly with my colleague and friend Professor Avraham Sela. The fourth source of my interest was my service of more than twenty-five years as a reserves officer in the Strategic Planning Division of the Israel Defense Forces (IDF). The experience opened my eyes to the realities of Israel's foreign and defense policy and greatly enriched my insights into the history of this policy.

My research to date has centered on unknown aspects of this subject within clearly defined and relatively brief historical periods, drawing almost exclusively on primary sources and newly available documents. These studies were published, for the most part, in three books: *Between East and West: Israel's Foreign Policy Orientation, 1948–1956* (1990), *Oil and the Arab Israeli Conflict, 1948–63* (1999), and *Cross on the Star of David: The Christian World in Israel's Foreign Policy, 1948–1967* (2005).

This book, in contrast, offers a synthesis of existing literature as well as a broader chronological expanse. As such, it represents my first attempt at writing in this genre. The book is based primarily on the works of many other authors and aims to present my personal, partial selection of findings from the rich literature that already exists regarding this subject.

For numerous complex reasons, Israel's foreign policy is a relatively recent field of historical study, so a few historiographical comments are necessary at the outset. During its first years of statehood, Israel retained many patterns of secrecy that had been characteristic of the *Yishuv* (the Jewish community in Palestine during the British Mandate), when the use of code names was a very common practice. It is hardly surprising, therefore, to come across a little-known book by Gershon Rivlin and Aliza Rivlin, *The Stranger Cannot Understand* (1998 [in Hebrew]), where hundreds pages of code names used in the Yishuv appear. After independence, it was natural for Israel to continue its prestate political behavior, and there were several reasons for maintaining secrecy: political and institutional inertia were rife in the country; the same people remained active participants in public affairs before and after 1948; and, most important, the young state was surrounded by hostile neighbors. The inherent tendency to secrecy with regard to internal political matters and especially foreign affairs was expressed in the quality and quantity of documentary material available to the public in the state's archives. The government's obvious interest in avoiding publicity on certain sensitive aspects of the Arab-Israeli conflict—and the close cooperation it enjoyed with the press at the time—meant that the question of Palestinian refugees, for example, remained almost completely outside the public debate. Other areas of Israeli foreign policy, such as immigration, oil resources, and the procurement of arms, were hushed up for similar reasons.

During the first years of the state's existence, the tendency to secrecy meant that little was written on issues of foreign policy, except for dramatic events and issues that the government could not keep classified, such as the War of Independence, the reparations from Germany, the Sinai Campaign, and the 1967 war. Further, Israel adopted the "thirty year" formula as an iron rule for declassifying state documents. In other words, only by the end of the 1970s was it possible to begin researching the War of Independence based on Foreign Ministry material, and only in the early 1980s was documentation available on the origins of the

Reparations Agreement with Germany. The 1948–56 period thus became available for academic historical research only in the late 1980s. Considering the time involved from the start of formal research to the published results, it becomes obvious why most historical studies on which the present book is based started to be published only during the 1990s.

The basic difficulty surrounding the source material for research on Israeli foreign policy has not abated. In theory, Foreign Ministry documents dealing with this period have been opened to researchers—and many have actually been published in the ongoing government series *Documents on the Foreign Policy of Israel* (Jerusalem, 1979–present)—but the declassification process is far from over. Major lacunae remain due to administrative difficulties, and serious gaps exist in government, Defense Ministry, and military records. Since a considerable amount of Israeli foreign policy is contained in the last two bodies, today's research suffers from the unavailability of material and can reconstruct only a fragmented picture. The disclosure of documents was not absolute for yet another reason. Not only did the state decide that only some of its military documents would be made accessible to researchers, but the security services—the Mossad and Shin Bet—continue to this day to resist the state law obligating them to disclose official documents. Significant delays in the disclosure of archival material also stem from the state archives' slow digitization process. As a result, only 550 thousand out of the three million documents deposited at present at the Israeli State Archive are open for study, and the contents of one million files are not known. The situation is worse at the Israel Defense Forces Archive, where only fifty thousand of over one million documents have been declassified. Finally, the Israeli Foreign Ministry lacked a tradition of methodic internal reporting, a defect that is obvious in the quantity and quality of documents in the state archives. The aggregate result of these obstacles has meant that a significant number of areas in the history of Israel's foreign policy have not received systematic academic treatment. Nevertheless, the fruit of the extant research has provided a basis for the following analysis and has laid a solid foundation on which a proper historiography will eventually rise.

Interestingly, many insights regarding Israeli foreign policy have been derived from publications about and by states with which Israel has political relations—publications based on official documents of those states, and demonstrated in works by Doron Itzchakov, P. R. Kumaraswamy, Eva Taterova, and Kata Bohus.[2] Often these documents, such as those in the American series *Foreign Relations of the United States*, are of greater scope and depth than the material declassified by Israel, especially as some of the declassified Israeli documents were never intended for publication. A fascinating instance of such information on Israel from an external perspective recently came to light: on July 22, 1946, the Irgun Zva'i Leumi (the National Military Organization in the Land of Israel—ETZEL, or "the Irgun"—a Zionist paramilitary organization that operated in Mandate Palestine) attacked the main secretariat of the Mandate government at the King David Hotel in Jerusalem. The attack and its aftermath motivated the high commissioner to have essential documents from the central archives of CID (Committee of Imperial Defence) photographed. Accordingly, roughly half a million documents were "transferred" to hundreds of reels of film, which were unearthed a few years ago at an Israeli defense facility. Originally they were stored in sealed metal containers, apparently in order to be shipped overseas, but presumably were forgotten during the upheaval surrounding the British withdrawal upon termination of the Mandate. Today this material provides a wealth of information for researchers, although, for understandable reasons, such researchers are still unable to make full use of the Jordanian documentation captured by Israel after its 1967 conquest of East Jerusalem or of Palestinian documents acquired by the IDF when it occupied parts of Beirut in 1982. These sources undoubtedly contain vital information about Israel that still awaits review by historians.

It is noteworthy in this context that the State of Israel has engaged in a cooperative endeavor with the governments of Russia and Poland to release compilations of documents from the three governments' archives that shed light on their relations during Israel's early years.[3] In addition, some years ago the Czech Republic and Romania released documents regarding their own relations with Israel.[4] Finally, it is worth noting that much of the discourse on Israeli foreign policy has deviated from the customary historical context by engaging sociologists and political scientists who added new focal points and comparative perspectives, thereby contributing to the diversity of the discipline.[5] Israeli Foreign Ministry retirees also helped enrich this field of study when they published two large volumes containing the retrospective viewpoints of those involved with the foreign affairs.[6] The area of study has likewise been boosted by the recent publication of three bulky volumes of the collected speeches of Moshe Sharett, Israel's first foreign minister.[7]

The new historiography of Israel's foreign relations rests largely, as noted, on gradually released official documentation that allows us to cast an ever-wider thematic net and discover previously unknown aspects of these relations. I have selected certain portions (the wine) using four containers, or parts, comprising eleven analytical chapters (the bottles). Part I covers events, experiences, lessons learned, objectives, and modes of operation that transpired or took shape before the founding of the state and had reverberations long after 1948. In other words, this part aims to excavate the historical legacy that Israel's foreign policy shapers inherited after the founding of the state. The findings appear in chapters 1–4, which address Jewish diplomacy, the foreign relations of the Yishuv under the British Mandate, the state in the making, and the War of Independence. Part II (chapters 5–7) analyzes three main goals of Israeli foreign policy that remain unchanged to this day and describes the means of their pursuit: the struggle for recognition, the importation of oil, and the encouragement of immigration. Part III (chapters 8–10) illustrates these issues in detail by discussing the key elements of Israel's relations with two states and one bloc of states: France, sub-Saharan Africa, and the United States. The final part (chapter 11) examines Israel's diplomatic efforts after 1979 to actualize its peace treaty with Egypt and make it substantively meaningful. The book concludes with an epilogue, which offers some insights on the long road Israel had taken in the international arena from the UN resolution of November 1947 to the controversial agreement with the Palestinians signed in September 1993.

The core analysis offered here focuses on the objectives of Israel's foreign policy and their actualization. My main thesis is that the supreme goal of this policy, from the outset and to this day, has been to build a state and to ensure its existence; its political, economic, and social fortitude; and its security. A review of declassified minutes from cabinet meetings makes this goal manifestly evident. Israel's foreign policy was aimed at establishing and maintaining bilateral and multilateral relations, yet these relations can be understood as one of the many "products" vital for Israel's physical existence—products in which it was lacking and for the sake of which Israeli diplomats were enlisted. Yet diplomats were not the only ones, and often not the most important ones, who bore this burden. This book highlights many figures who had no defined diplomatic role but played a critical, influential part.

In this context, if one takes the content of cabinet meetings as an indicator of an issue's centrality, it appears that relations with Arab states, or the lack thereof, were not always a salient concern among the state's leaders. Admittedly, one cannot understand Israeli foreign policy if one ignores this dimension. At the same time, a common and no less significant mistake (particularly prevalent among American researchers with a political science orientation) is to view this dimension as the most significant factor and to ignore or minimize the importance of other existential objectives that have preoccupied policy makers in Jerusalem since 1948. Ultimately, resolution of the conflicts with Arab states and with Palestinians is indeed an *end* but more so a *means* to a more important existential goal. The book reflects this fact in its division of topics into chapters that highlight issues in which the Arab-Israeli conflict was neither a sole nor a central factor.

Israel's struggle to secure existential resources and build a state through its foreign relations was one of its primary endeavors from 1948 to the 1990s, the period addressed in this book. Undoubtedly, that struggle is still paramount, and it is difficult to imagine that this situation will change in the future. Accordingly, the book lays a foundation for understanding the principal aspects of Israeli foreign policy throughout the state's existence.

Finally, I would like to clarify that it is not my intention to present an exhaustive discourse on all facets of this issue, nor could I do so within the technical confines of a book of this length. I have chosen to focus on those matters I find particularly interesting and to offer subsequent researchers a new and complementary analytical approach to the subject.

The endnotes in this volume are reserved for direct quotes and references. Suggested further readings are provided for each chapter.

Notes

1. See Uri Bialer, "Al HaMismakhim BaMartef VeMekhkar Histori—Mabat Ishi" [On documents in the basement and historical research—a personal perspective], in *Perspectivot Khadashot Al HaHistoria Shel HaYakhasim HaBenleumi'im* [New perspectives on the history of international relations], ed. Gadi Heiman, The Leonard Davis Institute (Jerusalem, 2012), 91–102.

2. See Doron Itzchakov, "Iran-Israel Relations, 1948–1963: The Iranian Perspective" (PhD diss., Tel Aviv University, 2012); P. R. Kumaraswamy, *India's Israel Policy* (New York: Columbia University Press, 2010); Eva Taterova, "Czechoslovakia and Israel in Cold War: From Friendship to Hostility" (PhD diss., Mendel University Brno, 2017); and Kata Bohus, "Jews, Israelites, Zionists: The Hungarian States' Policies on Jewish Issues in a Comparative Perspective (1956–1968)" (PhD diss., Central European University, 2013).

3. Gabriel Gorodetsky et al., eds., *Documents on Israeli-Soviet Relations, 1941–1953*, 2 vols. (London, Frank Cass, 2000); Marcos Silber and Szymon Rudnicki, eds., *Polish Israeli Diplomatic Relations, a Selection of Documents (1945–1967)* (Warsaw, 2009 [in Polish]; Jerusalem, Government Printer, 2009 [in Hebrew]).

4. *Ministerul Afacerilor Externe, Directia Archivelor Diplomatice, Romania-Israel 50 De Ani Relatii Diplomatice*, vol. 1, *1948–1969* (Bucharest, Ministerul Afacerilor Externe, 2000); *Cekoslovensko a Izrael v letech 1945–1956—Dokumenty* (Ústav pro soudobé dějiny AV ČR ve spolupráci s Historickým ústavem České armády a se Státním ústředním archivem, Praha, 1993).

5. See, for example, Michael Barnett, "Culture, Strategy and Foreign Policy Change: Israel's Road to Oslo," *European Journal of International Relations* 5, no. 1 (1999): 5–36; and, Fatemeh Shafiee Sarvestani, Saied Reza Ameli, and Foad Izadi, "Israeli Public Diplomacy toward the United States: A Network and Narrative Approach," *Asian Journal of Communication* 29, no. 2 (2019): 181–200.

6. Moshe Yegar, Yosef Govrin, and Arye Oded, eds., *Ministry for Foreign Affairs: The First Fifty Years* [in Hebrew] (Jerusalem, Keter, 2002).

7. Yaakov Sharett and Rina Sharett, eds., *Speaking Out, 1948, 1949, 1950* [in Hebrew] (Tel Aviv, Moshe Sharett Heritage Society, 2013, 2016, 2018).

PART I
THE HISTORICAL LEGACY

1 Jewish Diplomacy

VARIOUS DISCIPLINES HAVE axioms to explain causal relations between that which exists and that which develops. Botanists have recognized that plant growth is affected by dynamic mutuality between the plant's basic attributes and the climate and land in which it is located. Researchers in the field of intelligence have long held that intellectual potential is both innate and acquired. Historians, for their part, have always emphasized the phenomenon of historical periods leaving at least an initial impression on later periods. This is a trite but incontrovertible truth. One cannot understand the French Revolution unless one is familiar with the political and economic system that preceded it. It is also hard to understand the American Civil War if one ignores the basic characteristics of American society in earlier eras. Understanding developments in international relations in Europe from 1870 is a precondition for analyzing World War I.

The Israeli case is no exception. The State of Israel did not emerge out of the clear blue one fine morning in the late spring of 1948. Its leaders during that fateful time brought with them a multidimensional historical heritage that shaped developments before independence and continued to do so long afterward. Accordingly, any discussion of Israel's foreign policy requires familiarity with its historical and contextual heritage, which includes Jewish diplomacy in nineteenth-century Europe and even earlier, the Mandate-era diplomacy of the Zionist movement and the Yishuv, and prestate geostrategic and political realities. Let us therefore review the *innate* and then the *acquired* elements of the state's external politics, bearing in mind that space permits only the most cursory discussion.

The Jewish Lobby

The architects of Israel's foreign policy were influenced by a legacy with deep roots that remained intact even after Israel achieved sovereignty. Borrowing from the Hebrew, one might metaphorically refer to this legacy as a historical mound (*tel histori*) to indicate its layered complexity and enduring presence. Familiarity with this "historical mound" provides not only historical information about the prestate era but also an understanding of Israel's style and modes of diplomatic activity in subsequent years. These stemmed from two unique characteristics of Jewish existence over the centuries, which remained unchanged in certain aspects even after Israel was founded. The first characteristic was the fact that

Jews have maintained their solidarity as a nation despite nearly two millennia of dispersion. As Ilan Troen explained it, "The bonds that hold modern Jewry together have proved vital in the commitment of a dispersed people to reach out over vast geographical distances and across diverse political systems. The commitment to act on behalf of fellow Jews has its roots in the centuries-old traditions that have always been part of the diaspora experience."[1]

The second characteristic of this reality was weakness resulting not only from the lack of state sovereignty but primarily from existential dependence on others. As such, Jewish communities—mainly in Europe but elsewhere as well—practiced a form of diplomacy aimed primarily at convincing the powerful not to inflict harm on the weak among them, while also demonstrating survivability. This diplomatic activity was carried out by shtadlanim, from the Hebrew root verb *shidel*—to persuade or pressure. For our purposes, they served as lobbyists, a modern term but an apt description of their historical role. These lobbyists were often and for various reasons described in unflattering terms: court Jews, back-door diplomats, occasional philanthropists, unappointed or undelegated representatives, machers (Yiddish for influential and possibly corrupt agents who have access to bureaucracies and act as mediators), and especially, diplomats without a state.[2]

Ultimately, the lobbyist was a diplomat in almost every sense. The unabridged *Webster's Dictionary* defines *diplomacy* as "adroitness or artfulness in securing advantages without arousing hostility" (New York 1996) and "the skillful or successful settlement of differences between peoples." It defines *diplomatic* as "employing tact and conciliation," *diplomat* as a "liaison officer," and *diplomatist* as "one who is dexterous, tactful or artful in meeting situations without arousing antagonism."

This is an accurate description of Jewish lobbyists' sometimes successful efforts to mediate between those who were weak and lacked sovereignty, on the one hand, and a powerful government, on the other. Some representatives drew their authority from official recognition by the sovereign, while others earned status by providing financial or medical services that gave them access to the ruling elite. Among their key qualifications was a fluency and expressiveness in languages requiring extensive education. Financial success was also an important condition for access to the courts of power, as were loyalty and a recognized, proven patriotism. Other essential skills undoubtedly included familiarity with the local and international political systems, negotiating skills, tact, and cumulative wisdom characterized by, among other factors, an awareness that politics is the art of the possible. In later times, beginning with the French Revolution and the Enlightenment, other important lobbying tools included Jewish engagement in the intellectual and political lives of their countries and their exit-out of the ghetto into the open political forum.

Jewish lobbying (*shtadlanut*) emerged from a harsh existential reality characterized by inferiority, weakness, and extreme vulnerability. Given the nature of its formative years, it was necessarily based on unmediated contact (whenever possible) between the lobbyist and the sovereign. In this context there developed two belief systems that nearly always reflected the weaker party's cautious optimism. The first was faith in the power of persuasion and explanation based on logic, which grew out of an ancient cultural tradition of Talmudic study, and the second was an enduring expectation of influence through moral arguments of justice alongside materialistic arguments. This type of diplomacy and the hope that contact at this level would allow influence through the power of explanation and persuasion drawing heavily on matters of principle were salient characteristics of Jewish lobbying in Europe before the French Revolution. This style of lobbying left a legacy that lasted for centuries, even after the founding of a sovereign Jewish state.

The complete history of the local activity of Jewish lobbyists in premodern Europe has yet to be unearthed, and it deserves an in-depth, comprehensive comparative analysis. Nevertheless, existing studies on two dramatic events—in the seventeenth and nineteenth centuries—do shed significant light on the nature of lobbying during those periods. What distinguishes these events is that they shifted the sphere of operations from localized, community-based individual lobbying to the state and international levels through the informed use of the modern tools of transnational political action. The lobbyists demonstrated styles, modes of operation, and dynamics that left their mark on Zionist diplomacy and the diplomacy of Israel throughout the twentieth century.

The first and lesser-known event related to an edict issued on December 18, 1744, by Hapsburg empress Maria Theresa, banishing Jews from Prague and prohibiting them from settling anywhere in the empire. The full set of motives behind this edict remains unclear, but it was evidently linked, at least in part, to wars of imperial succession during which Prague was captured twice by anti-Hapsburg forces—first in 1741 by the Bavarian-Saxons and the French, and three years later by the Prussians. The Jews, who were accused of supporting these foreign forces, became the target of violent demonstrations in the city, and it seemed their fate was sealed. But history proved otherwise. Leaders of the Jewish community immediately turned to eight other Jewish communities in Europe with a moving request for help aimed specifically at suspension of the edict (which seemed more feasible than a repeal). Recipients of the request conveyed it to others, and within two weeks of the imperial edict's issue, dozens of Jewish communities throughout Europe joined efforts with the Jews of Prague. Their responsive lobbying efforts were equally prompt, as each community turned to figures who had ties of one sort or another with Jews, no doubt fearing the potential banishment of Jews throughout the continent. Jews could be facing a danger exceeding the expulsion from Spain in 1492, in the words of a message sent to heads of Jewish communities in Altona.³ The main themes of the request for suspension are reflected in the appeal issued by leaders of the Amsterdam community in late December, citing considerations of "justice, mercy, and benefit"⁴ (Mevorach op. cit., 135, which is the source of the following analysis until otherwise cited). The last of these was explained without embellishment and directed, among others, at the Saxon crown prince, underscoring that the state's commercial interests would suffer if the Jews were expelled from Prague. Not all the efforts were fruitful, but many requests did yield successful contacts with high-ranking officials, ambassadors, clergymen, and businessmen and even the king of England, who was "shocked by the terrible injustice perpetuated against innocent people" and instructed his ambassador in Vienna to take the matter to the imperial court. The king of Denmark had a similar reaction, and the Ottoman sultan made a direct request to Maria Theresa that she repeal the edict. The Vatican instructed nuncios in Venice to express its disapproval of the expulsion order, and the Saxon crown council and senate of Venice voiced similar sentiments.

The suspension and eventual repeal of the edict on May 12, 1745, resulted, according to Baruch Mevorach, from a combination of political and international factors related to cessation of the war of imperial succession, and only some of these factors related directly to Jewish lobbying efforts. Still, the lobbyists' activities reflected an understanding of their political reality and an effort to align their interests with those of the imperial throne in Vienna. Moreover, the activities demonstrated an impressive ability to consolidate Jewish solidarity locally and internationally, a remarkably effective communications network, and the formation and exploitation of ties with centers of political and economic power across the continent. The sophistication and success of these lobbying activities are, according to Shlomo Avineri, impressive even to contemporary observers. The affair certainly demonstrated the diplomatic abilities of the Jews as a public despite lack of official organization, not to mention political sovereignty. It was also a clear display of the tools and types of action they were able to employ.

About a century later, these and other capabilities were put to the test in what came to be known as the Damascus affair, which began with Christian blood libel accusations against Jews in Damascus in 1840. An Italian monk and his servant disappeared after visiting the city's Jewish market. His monastery then turned to the Muslim authorities, accusing the Jews of murdering the two to make matzah of their blood. The French consul upheld the charge. An investigation led to the arrest of many members of Damascus's Jewish community, one of whom eventually succumbed to torture and agreed to confess. After his false confession, several leaders of the community were arrested, including Chief Rabbi Jacob Antebi, who became the main suspect. Two of those arrested were put to death, one converted to Islam, and others "confessed" under extreme torture. The affair sparked a furor in Europe and eventually ended through the intervention of Jewish public figures as well as political leaders in the West. The primary motivation for Jewish intervention was anxiety regarding the impact of the libel on their political, economic, and social integration into liberal European societies, which seemed to be in full swing. The lobbying efforts have been researched and analyzed by many historians, prominent among whom was Jonathan Frankel. The activities differed from those related to the Prague expulsion order in terms of scope, techniques, and the salience of economic factors, and they made extensive use of the press for the first time in history. In addition, after 1840 Jewish diplomacy had to cope not only with the affair's impact on what had been a local, internal political mechanism but also with the European political publicity that had exposed it and its financial workings, Rothschild's (a well-known Jewish banker and philanthropist) involvement became apparent for all to see. It is not surprising that *The Protocols of the Elders of Zion* (a fabricated antisemitic text purporting to describe a Jewish plan for global domination) appeared following this time and henceforth served as a double-edged sword for Jewish diplomacy: on the one hand, it was a blatant indictment, but on the other hand, the myth could serve diplomatic purposes by enhancing perceptions of Jewish power.

In any event, Jewish diplomacy did not come to a standstill. Beginning in the mid-nineteenth century, it evolved into what Daniel Gutwein termed "all-Jewish diplomacy"[5] (activities aimed at improving conditions for Jews in countries where they faced hardship in terms of personal security and legal status, by directing efforts at the relevant authorities and appealing to Western governments that could exert influence. This definition of diplomacy highlights intercommunal solidarity and coordination among Jewish figureheads and organizations. Many of the activities for which we have historical accounts took place during the years 1891–1906, at a time when individual members of the Jewish financial elite in Western countries sought to exert their economic and political power to persuade the tsarist government to change its policy toward Russian Jews. Salient examples include efforts by the Rothschilds in Paris and London and by Jacob Schiff in New York during the Russo-Japanese War and subsequent revolution and reforms. In addition, the very popular Moses Montefiore became a familiar symbol of Jewish diplomacy around this time.

Montefiore, a Jewish philanthropist and activist from England, devoted his life to assisting Jews in various countries and came to be known as Sir Moses Montefiore, or in Hebrew, "Sar" in the original sense—an honorific title for a highly respected public figure as well as an attempt to translate the title granted to him by Queen Victoria in 1846. As Abigail Green noted in her monumental study of Montefiore, his prolific endeavors "through the realms of court and ghetto, tsar and sultan, synagogue and stock exchange" made him "one of the first truly global celebrities."[6] Among the participants in these public activities were international Jewish organizations established during the latter half of the nineteenth century that made it their mission to assist Jews suffering persecution. Examples include the Alliance Israélite Universelle and Hilfsverein der Deutschen Juden. These organizations were based in Western Europe and North America, and their target audiences were mainly in the Middle East and Eastern Europe.

Theodore Herzl also appeared on the scene during those years and has since become the best-known Zionist diplomat. It is unclear how familiar he was with Jewish history and Jewish lobbying surrounding the Damascus affair and the expulsion of Jews from Prague. Nonetheless, his diplomatic activity demonstrated many traditional aspects of diplomacy. He established personal ties with influential political figures (holding meetings with Sultan Abdul Hamid, Kaiser Wilhelm II, King Victor Emmanuel of Italy, and Pope Pius X, for example). He sought alliances with leaders of Jewish communities as a way of gaining legitimacy (the Jewish Congresses beginning in 1897), building a power base, and developing a network and diplomatic argumentation. In parallel he solicited the support of Jewish financiers (Baron Hirsch and Baron Rothschild), made extensive use of the press, and drew on humanitarian as well as realpolitik arguments to persuade monarchs and rulers on issues of concern to Jews, such as proposals for Jewish homelands in El Arish and Uganda that were backed by facts such as the plight of the Jews, their financial skills, the status of Jews in European society, and the geopolitical fate of the historical Land of Israel. He was gifted with personal charm, a pleasing appearance, and skills of expression—attributes he exploited and that bring to mind the classic characteristics of Jewish lobbying. His charisma contributed greatly to his influence among Jewish supporters.

Author Mordechai Ben-Ami described the impressiveness of Herzl's presence at the opening ceremony of the First Zionist Congress (Basel, August 1897): "Herzl casually enters the stage. My eyes devour him. What is this? This is not the Herzl I have known, the one I saw just last night. Before us stands the glorious image of a son of kings with a deep, focused gaze, proud yet solemn. This was not that refined Herzl from Vienna, but a member of the House of David who had suddenly risen from the grave in his entire legendary splendor. . . . It seemed to me that our people's dream of two thousand years was now realized, and our Messiah stood before us."[7]

In spite of these characteristics, his external diplomacy failed to achieve any of its concrete objectives. His hope of enlisting the sultan proved illusory, and the concept of German-English cooperation in shaping international policy and sponsoring an autonomous Jewish entity or state had no basis in reality. At the same time, Herzl's originality (and in this respect, success) is reflected in his creation of a permanent, institutionalized political Zionist organization operating on behalf of the entire Jewish public, and especially in his identification of the organization's goals. Avineri's characterization thus expresses a historiographic axiom: "[Through] his spiritual outlook, unremitting energy, and political insight and perspective [Herzl contributed more than anyone to transforming the Zionist idea from aspiration to a political, dynamic, institutionalized, and organized reality."[8]

At the individual level, we can point to some of Herzl's successors during the twentieth century as lobbyists of sorts, including Chaim Weizmann (for his activity in the English arena) and Nahum Goldmann (for forging ties with the Soviet Union and formulating the reparations agreement with Germany). Their personalities, worldviews, individual styles, and Jewish connections reflected classic Jewish lobbying. In his activities as Israel's first foreign minister, Moshe Sharett also represented some of these qualities. On October 9, 1948, he met with Soviet deputy foreign minister Andrey Vyshinsky at Israel's first summit meeting since attaining statehood. In his report to colleagues in Israel, Sharett described points that emerged in the course of their dialogue. The minutes of their meeting, however, tell a different story. Evidently, after opening niceties Sharett seized the floor and for nearly an hour delivered a lecture on Israeli policy, primarily in the context of Jewish immigration from Eastern Europe, with a long series of morally based arguments. Vyshinsky could not or did not want to utter a word, but this did not deter Sharett from reporting that he had successfully "enlightened" his interlocutor. Another example of lobbying, at the organizational level, is the World Jewish Congress, whose activities today still maintain some form of the centuries-old legacy of Jewish diplomacy.

Not everyone would agree with the general argument presented here. Sasson Sofer, for example, asserts in his book on the roots of Israel's foreign policy that "within two generations, the familiar figures of the Jewish 'fixer' and the emissary of the Zionist pioneering movement were obliged to shed their shabby raiment and don the formal garb of the diplomat."[9] On the other hand, Aharon Klieman, a prominent scholar of Israeli diplomacy, argues, "What better proof of the continuity of Diaspora diplomacy than the term *shdula*? Used in modern colloquial Hebrew to denote special interest groups, political action committees and lobbies, it, too, like *shtadlan* and *shtadlanut*, is a derivative form of the root *sh-d-l*."[10]

In any event, it is evident that during the early and especially the mid-nineteenth century, the classic form of lobbying was sidelined after Israel achieved sovereignty. Yet its raison d'être—the need of the relatively weaker Jews to cope politically with the stronger, hostile countries surrounding them by creating a positive international predisposition toward themselves—remained an existential cornerstone of political Zionism and Israeli democracy.

Herzl and His Successors

Herzl's diplomatic activity was based on a plan for self-motivated collective Jewish entry into the world of international politics. No longer would Jews focus on eclectic efforts to prevent or minimize the effects of local decrees. Rather, their

Zionist Organization would enlist the entire international system in a focused effort to find a comprehensive resolution of the Jewish problem through the establishment of a Jewish state and by overcoming Jewish reluctance to engage in political tests of power. Herzl also strongly believed that a state of Jews was a global, not just Jewish, need. His political program was intended not only to liberate the Jewish people or construct a new, functional society but also to offer a solution to Europe as a whole: the liberation of European society from anti-Semitism, on the one hand, and from Jewish revolutionaries, on the other, by removing the Jews from the continent. The basic idea necessitated a massive, proactive mobilization of Jews to engage in global politics and diplomacy and renounce their isolation of thousands of years. In Herzl's view, the concept of excellence as an entry ticket into history for a people isolated within the international system should replace the concept of choice for a people persecuted in Europe. Excellence was required in many different areas: in economic activity, as a model society, and in the arts and sciences, medicine, technology, the humanities, and the social sciences. His revolutionary theses were not easily accepted. Moreover, his political and diplomatic failings were compounded by a very limited ability to enlist the support of Jews, a majority of whom did not support Zionism as a goal. His approach to diplomacy was also completely at odds with that of most Jewish leaders at the time, who preferred self-containment and the long-standing tradition of passivity. Indeed, the vision of an independent Jewish state was far from heartwarming for many Jews. The elderly Lord Nathaniel Mayer Rothschild, patriarch of the British Rothschild family, wrote to Herzl on August 18, 1902, "Basically, I view the plans for the establishment of a Jewish colony with trepidation; such a Jewish colony would be a ghetto within a ghetto, with all the prejudices of the ghetto. It would be a small, petty Jewish state, Orthodox and not liberal, which would exclude non-Jews and Christians."[11]

Herzl's intellectual and political development is the subject of ongoing historiographic debate between historians and philosophers, a debate that gained momentum after the publication in 1999 of Amos Elon's biography based on Herzl's diaries containing his writings on Jews. Similarly, academic interpretations of Herzl's image shifted in emphasis from "defining radicalism to adaptive marginality," in Gutwein's words.[12] Nonetheless, the legacy of Herzl's activity left a mark whose importance cannot be overstated on the diplomacy of the Zionist movement during the first half of the twentieth century and on Israeli diplomacy ever since. The question, therefore, is this: What legacy did the founder of the political Zionist movement bequeath to David Ben-Gurion, Moshe Sharett, Golda Meir, and Levi Eshkol?

The grand objective of Herzlian Zionism was to offer a solution to the Jewish problem in its entirety by establishing a national home in Palestine. Herzl was not the first to propose this idea, but thanks to him and the resolutions of the

First Zionist Congress, it became a recognized, agreed-upon goal that remains fundamentally unassailable to this day. This state was to be a place of refuge for all Jews. It was expected to offer sanctuary for all who sought it and to help them reach it. In operative terms, this was a far-reaching holistic political plan never before presented to Jewish lobbyists. Its reach spanned the entire world geographically and all Jewish populations demographically. Advancing these objectives required simultaneous action on the part of Jewish communities and on behalf of the Jewish state. From the outset, Zionist diplomacy was intended to be global, as even a cursory examination indicates. The conceptual gap between Zionist diplomacy and the traditional Jewish diplomacy that preceded it is monumental. It transformed the Jews from a relatively passive population politically to an extremely active one focused wholly on Palestine.

The main concrete objective of Herzlian diplomacy was to secure political recognition in the form of a charter sponsored by one or more great powers, which would recognize the right of the Jewish people to a state of its own and could serve as a practical tool in pursuit of the goal. From the outset, the Zionist movement affirmed this objective and did not alter it at any point before or after the founding of the state. A guarantee of external political support was critical in light of two existential facts that remained unchanged long after the First Zionist Congress in 1897.

The first and more basic fact was the political, economic, and strategic weakness of the Zionist movement. In the first volume of his trilogy on the Zionist revolution, David Vital notes that in contrast to the prevailing myth, the movement's financial resources during its early days were so limited that it could sponsor only a small number of families to settle in Ottoman Palestine. Moreover, the Jewish communities, of which only very small portions were willing to join the Zionist movement, were scattered throughout Europe, and Zionist activities were prohibited by law in tsarist Russia, their main stronghold. In addition, very few wealthy Jews or prominent philanthropists and businesspersons were willing to back the Herzlian plan financially. Most rejected the proposal, preferring to assist in alleviating hardship among Jews on a local basis rather than pursue a comprehensive solution for Jews everywhere. The second existential fact was the need for a charter of great powers to pave the way diplomatically for the Zionist movement to pursue other international political courses. A charter was critical specifically in order to unseal the locked gates into Ottoman Palestine and permit Jewish settlement. External political advantage was therefore vital in an operative sense.

International recognition remained a central aim despite failures to achieve it, and it remained a goal of the Zionist movement even after Herzl's departure. For various reasons the focus shifted from Russia, Germany, and the Ottoman Empire to Britain, where the efforts led to resounding success. The Balfour Declaration of 1917 granted the movement an English patron who, by virtue of the

League of Nations Covenant, had official, internationally recognized control over Palestine. The historical importance of this achievement cannot be overstated.

The roots of this declaration are complex, but undoubtedly, part of the British argumentation, to which Weizmann's diplomacy contributed, corresponded with a somewhat racist view that greatly overstated the Jews' political power and collective economic capability, especially in the war context. Arthur Balfour, whose sympathy toward Jews was honest and deeply ingrained, felt that they "undoubtedly constitute[d] a most formidable power whose manifestations [were] not by any means always attractive."[13] In February 1916 Lord Robert Cecil wrote that "[it is not] easy to exaggerate the international power of the Jews."[14]

In any event, through a diplomacy undeniably built on Herzlian elements, the Zionist movement not only secured its longed-for charter as well as critical political assistance, economic support, and military backing. It also received highly significant and virtually unassailable approval of the main thesis promoted by Herzl ("the visionary of the state") and a green light for future diplomatic activity. Britain's contribution to diplomatic activity over the next three decades was pivotal. It combined unconditional acceptance of the principles of the Mandate with unceasing diplomatic efforts to improve conditions. Diplomacy and existence were symbiotically bound in a way Herzl certainly could not have foreseen.

The Herzlian legacy presented one overriding political end and a key diplomatic instrument. After the establishment of the British Mandate, there naturally emerged an optimistic belief in this instrument as a way of ensuring strategic operative achievements. There was also a widespread consensus that the instrument should be used as an existential element of future activity. This perspective was virtually axiomatic, which is perhaps why (paradoxically), as Jehuda Reinharz argued, little has been written about it.[15] However, it did not disappear after 1948.

Notes

1. Ilan Troen and Benjamin Pinkus (eds.) "Introduction," in *Organizing Rescue: National Jewish Solidarity in the Modern Period* (London, Frank Cass1992): 3.

2. See *Encyclopedia Otzar Israel*, ed. Julius David Eisenstein (New York, 1951), s.v. "shtadlan."

3. Shlomo Avineri, "Prague 1744—Lake Success 1947: Jewish Statecraft without a State," in *Jewish Studies at the CEU: Yearbook IV* (Budapest, 2005), 15.

4. See Baruch Mevorach, "Ma'asei Hishtadlut BeEropa U-Meni'at Geirusham shel Yehudi Bohemia VeMoravia" [Hishtadlut activities in Europe in prevention of the expulsion of Bohemia's and Moravia's Jews], *Tzion* 15 (1963): 125–64. See also Avineri, "Prague 1744."

5. Gutwein 1991, 23.

6. Abigail Green, *Moses Montefiore: Jewish Liberator, Imperial Hero* (Boston, Belknap Press, 2010), book cover.

7. Mordechai Ben-Ami, *HaSneh Bo'er VeUkal* [The bush is burned and consumed]. (Jerusalem, The Zionist Library, 2016), 8.

8. Shlomo Avineri, *Herzl* (London, Weidenfeld, 2013), 220.

9. Sasson Sofer, *Zionism and the Foundation of Israel* (Cambridge, Cambridge University Press, 2007), 380.

10. Aharon Klieman, "Shtadlanut as Statecraft by the Stateless," *Israel Journal of Foreign Affairs* 2 (2008): 3.

11. Quoted in Gabi Sheffer, "Ish Mizdaken U-Mfursam" [A famous, aging man], *Haaretz*, October 22, 2001 (a review of Michael Heymann and Josef Wenkert, eds., *Theodor Herzl: The Jewish Cause—Diaries, 3, April 1902–May 1904* [Jerusalem, 2001]).

12. Daniel Gutwein, "HaKhavaya HaKhozeret al Atzma shel Dmuto shel Herzl BaZikaron HaKibutzi HaIsraeli: MeRadicalism Me'atzev LeShuliyut Mistagelet" [The reconstruction of Herzl's image in Israeli collective memory: From formative radicalism to an adapting fringe], *Iyunim Bitkumat Israel* 12 (2002): 29–73.

13. Brian Klug, *Being Jewish and Doing Justice: Bringing Argument to Life* (London, Vallentine Mitchell, 2011), 199–210.

14. James Renton, *The Zionist Masquerade: The Birth of the Anglo-Zionist Alliance, 1914–1918* (London, Palgrave, 2007), 24.

15. Jehuda Reinharz, "Zionism and the Great Powers: A Century of Foreign Policy," *Leo Baeck Memorial Lecture 38* (New York, Leo Baeck Institute, 1994).

2 The Foreign Relations of the Yishuv

The Overall Strategy

The British Mandate era constituted the most important formative period for Israeli diplomacy and foreign relations. During the twenty-six years of the Mandate, the Jewish Yishuv and Zionist leadership focused their attention on laying the critical foundations of a national home. Diplomatic activity toward this end centered mainly on political dialogue with the British with the aim of ensuring the homeland's establishment, growth, and security. As this dialogue proceeded, the initially somewhat passive predisposition of the Zionist movement toward the English evolved into a hard-line platform with new political objectives and diplomatic tools. The transformation occurred mainly because of British constraints that seemed to cast doubt on the future course of the national home and that, from a Zionist perspective, even threatened its very existence. Most painful was the issue of aliyah (Jewish immigration). At the start of the Mandate era, the Yishuv numbered eighty thousand Jews, whereas the Arab population totaled nearly six hundred thousand. The implications of this demographic situation were widely recognized by supporters of the Jews. Thus, Czech president Thomas Masaryk shared with Hugo Bergmann (the Czech Jewish philosopher who later became dean of the Hebrew University) his impressions of his visit to Palestine in 1927 and emphasized that "it is interesting and magnificent to see what Jews are doing there and it has all the prospects of success because it is not only about enthusiasm but also about having enough funds at hand. However, I find a difficult problem in that the Jews will hardly ever have a majority in the country. Against the numerical predominance of the Arabs there is hardly ever anything that can be done."[1]

For the Zionist movement, this situation went from undesirable to unacceptable as a result of two simultaneous processes that began shortly after the start of the Mandate. First, the ever-growing pressure of world Jewry for a refuge in Palestine had started to emerge in the mid-1920s and peaked with the Nazi rise to power in the early 1930s. Second, Arab militancy was on the rise, as the riots of 1929 and 1936 blatantly demonstrated. The riots constituted not only an immediate physical danger but also, in Jewish eyes, a writing on the wall, a warning that compromise with the Arabs would not be possible.

The British response to these developments included restrictions on aliyah and military clashes with the Arabs, as well as radical (though short-lived) proposals to resolve the question of Palestine by revoking the Mandate and dividing the land between Arabs and Jews. These measures gave rise to a sense of urgency and crisis among the Zionist leadership given that, in the words of the Jewish Agency's chairman, "We are about to be denied the option of saving the Zionism we had until now."[2] The new stance adopted by the Zionist leadership, as Joseph Heller has analyzed, demonstrated a willingness to engage openly in political struggle with the British on matters of aliyah and land purchases, on the one hand, and a reluctant acceptance in principle of the concept of partition, on the other.[3] The leadership recognized that "the actualization of Zionism requires fully exploiting historical opportunities," in the words of Moshe Sharett, head of the Jewish Agency's Political Department.[4] At the same time, these developments clarified the supreme political objective of the Jews, as expressed in the 1942 Biltmore Program: no more striving to maintain a Jewish national home, no more playing around with the idea of equal division of rule with the Arabs (the "parity" plan), but rather, the establishment of a sovereign Jewish state. When World War II broke out, the Yishuv decided to support the British war effort and therefore briefly suspended the formulation and implementation of its new diplomacy. But two years after the war ended, it reinstated this diplomacy with full vigor, following the British affirmation in 1945 of the 1939 "White Paper" that severely restricted Zionist aliyah and land-acquisition activities. One year later, however, Britain announced its intention to terminate the Mandate, placing the issue on the agenda of the United Nations. The urgency seemed to be mounting as the magnitude of the Holocaust started coming to light and refugees from Europe came knocking on the closed doors of Palestine—developments that further shook up the Zionist leadership.

The leadership's reaction included a new strategy and diplomacy, key elements of which would influence Israel's future leaders as well. The first of these was the prioritization of statehood as a matter of urgency. Suspending the Biltmore Program may have been acceptable in 1942, but five years later the program's goal became an immediate necessity. The second element was self-fortification, primarily through aliyah (the May 1945 plan aimed to absorb the "first" million Jews from Europe) and defiance of British policy—that is, engaging in clandestine aliyah. Notably, Ben-Gurion decreed that the struggle against the British be conducted only along the Mandatory border, not within Palestine, so as to deny Britain any basis for claims that the Yishuv leadership was disrupting law and order and should therefore be disarmed. The third element was a willingness to compromise, in the form of an agreement on the partition of Palestine, without acquiescing in advance to any border demarcation plan. The aim here was to achieve the ultimate objective of Zionism as soon as possible and to gain diplomatic credibility with the United States. In other words, the Zionist movement at the time adopted both the principle of compromise and the principle of sovereignty, but translating these principles into action meant that a refusal to compromise on sovereignty necessitated a compromise on territory. And thus emerged the formula, as Sharett framed it, that the smaller the territory, the greater the sovereignty. Or as Ben-Gurion prosaically argued, sovereignty would provide the tools to control aliyah and purchase land, thus giving the Jews enough land to settle new immigrants within the framework of a sustainable state.

This pragmatic policy began to take shape in the mid-1930s and gained ground immediately after the war, when the harsh implications of any alternative strategies became apparent to the Zionist leadership. In August 1946 the leadership officially accepted the concept of partition. Stephen Wise, a prominent American Zionist, shared the anguish this question caused him with the Jewish Agency Executive: "I have not changed my mind about the evil of partition," he asserted. "But after what happened in Europe I must confess that I am tormented by guilt. I have often thought that if we had been more willing to accept partition [during the 1930s], we would have had a state and could have issued permits and saved many lives. . . . Perhaps now, if we have a small state of our own . . . we can save half of the survivors." At the same forum, Wise also shared what Theodor Herzl had told him during the April 1904 gathering of the Zionist General Council, while they strolled through the streets of Vienna: "I won't live to see the Jewish state, but you will, at least some of it."[5] Herzl died three months later. Accepting partition was a painful decision, with detractors on both the left (HaShomer HaTza'ir) and the right (Revisionist Zionists) of the Yishuv leadership, but it enabled the Jewish Agency to conduct a successful political campaign during the United Nations Special Committee on Palestine (UNSCOP) in 1947 to search for a solution to the problem of Palestine.

The greatest challenge to the concept of "a state now" took place during the final two months of the British Mandate, after the (temporary) withdrawal of US support for partition. Foreign diplomats suggested other alternatives to the Jewish Agency Executive so as to avoid military confrontation: trusteeship, truce, and postponement of the declaration of independence. These ideas even drew some internal political support in the Yishuv. But Ben-Gurion and his associates rejected all of them. Sharett voiced a salient view at a meeting with the Nuncio in Athens during a stopover while flying home from New York, when the Nuncio offered refuge for future Jewish refugees from war in Palestine. Sharett politely declined the offer, explaining that whether the Yishuv wins or loses, "there will not be any more Jewish refugees."[6] Later, on May 12, 1948, speaking before the Central Committee of MAPAI (Workers' Party in the Land of Israel, the dominant political party before statehood and for two decades thereafter), Sharett argued that "we have no choice but to proceed."[7]

These elements of the Jewish leadership's overall strategy during the Mandate era inevitably shaped Israeli diplomatic activity after 1948, but other elements contributed as well.

The Search for Allies

The Zionist movement devoted much effort to fortifying its national homeland through diplomatic relations with the British, and it maintained this approach until 1946. At the same time, however, most of its attention at the operational level was devoted to land acquisition and demographic, political, social, economic, and—secretly—military buildup. Strength was seen as the main way to realize the Zionist vision and, after 1948, ensure the state's existence. In a 1933 article published in *HaPo'el HaTza'ir* (The young laborer—mouthpiece of MAPAI's precursor), Ben-Gurion explained pointedly,

> There is no greater delusion, in my view, than to believe that the Jewish People are a global political factor that shapes the course adopted by major states such as England. We were never such a factor and probably never will be. But there are some matters in which we are even stronger than some of the major states. . . . Regarding Eretz Israel [the Land of Israel]—which does not pose a question of life for the English People or the Arab People, but does pose the question of existence and of life and death for the entire Jewish People, not only in the abstract historical sense but also in the real and actual sense—the strength of the Jewish People, the will and ability of the Jewish People are decisive and determinative. This is, in my view, the foundation of Zionist policy and the only approach we should take for the Zionist enterprise.

Ben-Gurion cited himself extensively when, twenty-one years later, he drew the attention of the editorial board of *Davar* to his resolve on this matter, emphasizing that "if I had to address this matter today, I would not change one word of the above quotations, though I would delete a few extraneous particles [referring to changes in Hebrew grammar]." Six months later, in a letter to his friend Ari Ankorion, who had suggested various political alternatives to ease Israel's international difficulties, the "Old Man" (Ben-Gurion's nickname) argued that the three-part solution to these problems was "internal fortification, internal fortification, and internal fortification."[8]

The British facilitated this process by providing monetary and military support to buttress the Yishuv, thereby freeing it from concerns about law and order, external military civilian security, and infrastructure such as roads. As a result, the Yishuv could focus all its attention on settlement, construction, and immigration. These pursuits also received substantial assistance from Jewish capital in the form of massive investments in Palestine, particularly in the urban sector, as Jacob Metzer has described.[9] Consequently, most documents in the Central Zionist Archives in Jerusalem address matters such as "another goat and another hen," while only a minority deal with high-level diplomacy. Evidently, the Yishuv placed great emphasis on "practical Zionism" and minimized "diplomatic Zionism." The Jews had their charter and now needed to act on it by devoting themselves to the physical construction of a national homeland.

Does this mean that diplomatic activity lost its centrality? May we conclude that, indeed, to cite Ben-Gurion again, "what matters is what the Jews do, not what the Gentiles say"?[10] The historical answer, in terms of the Mandate's legacy, is complex. At the moment of independence, in May 1948, the leaders of the new state would have had to admit, looking back, that the Mandate years were critical for achieving a Jewish population of six hundred thousand (matching the Arab population) as well as a widespread network of settlements, large-scale economic activity, military strength, and institutional and political consolidation. At the same time, nearly all leaders were united in the view that these achievements would not have been possible without the British security net, maintained through continuous dialogue. Moreover, in November 1947 the Zionist movement received the most important charter of its history: a UN resolution on the establishment of a Jewish state (alongside an Arab state) in Palestine. Several factors led to this achievement, but there can be no doubt that Zionist diplomacy was remarkably successful during the preceding years and can explain the events that followed. The leaders of the state-in-the-making witnessed how, as with the Balfour Declaration, diplomacy could yield major, even historical, achievements. That success reinforced the position of Zionist leaders who were attuned to "what the Gentiles say." Thus, the debate between those who emphasized action over foreign diplomacy and those who saw international support as an existential cornerstone naturally carried over from the Yishuv era to the political history of Israel after 1948.

The dispute between diplomacy and physical industry was not the only one to become more polarized during the Mandate era. Another internal debate had emerged by the end of this era: the question of the great power or great powers on which the Zionist movement, and later Israel, could rely in place of Britain. Besides the decision to pull out of Palestine, from the Zionist perspective, Britain had also adopted a categorically hostile and uncompromising stance after the Labour Party came to power in 1945. Indeed, in February 1947, Foreign Secretary Ernest Bevin, the architect of the decision to pull out of Palestine, explaining his support for Jewish autonomy rather than statehood in a speech to Parliament, argued that the Jews are a religious community, not a nation, and should not be granted a partitioned state, let alone an entire state. Conversely, he expressed sympathy for the position of Arabs who, according to him, objected to the intervention of the "foreign" and US-funded Jewish Agency in the affairs of Palestine, shaping the fate of its Arab residents of two thousand years.[11] It seemed that after decades of continuous diplomatic endeavors in Britain, which bore fruit during the 1920s and early 1930s, Zionists and the British Jewish community had lost any sway over public opinion and government circles. The means of influence and channels of communication with policy makers were blocked, some since the early 1930s when the pro-Zionist group that supported the Balfour Declaration and "national home" policy had withdrawn from political life. Labour's rise to power further widened the gap. Any old ties with the conservative government that still existed were severed, and the new leaders were unknown and inaccessible to Chaim Weizmann and his associates. Likewise, the hopes of forging unmediated ties with the Labour government on the basis of socialist-democratic fraternity were dashed. Indeed, internal British documents from this period indicate an interest in terminating the Mandate. Over the years, growing numbers of policy makers in London had come to believe that the harm caused by the Mandate outweighed its benefits. The anti-Zionist Miles Lampson, longtime British ambassador to Egypt, stated in early 1945 that the Mandate had always been a "yoke around our neck," while the pro-Zionist Churchill asserted in July 1945, "I am not aware of the slightest advantage which has ever accrued to Great Britain from this painful and thankless task."[12]

Ben-Gurion, for his part, delivered his diagnosis and prognosis to the MAPAI bureau in October 1946: "The Anglo-centric chapter of our foreign relations policy has come to a close. . . . It is time for a policy of Jewish independence . . . with everything that term implies."[13] Ben-Gurion had no illusions that the Yishuv could force the British Empire's hand, but he advised the Zionist leadership at the time to act up, or as Amitzur Ilan described it, "to act like that clever child who knows his parents are slightly hysterical and is willing to scream until he's blue in the face to get what he wants."[14]

Despite all of the above, the British decision to turn to the UN came as a complete shock to the Yishuv. Given this situation, the question of an international "orientation" was not merely academic. It was a matter of realpolitik. The state-in-the-making was not strong enough to pursue independence without strategic foreign backing. Moreover, the Soviets and Americans had supported the establishment of the state in UN debates leading up to November 1947. The future state therefore had a few options: forging a strategic alliance with the United States and the West, cultivating ties with the Soviet Union, or asserting Zionism's neutrality in the emerging Cold War confrontation. The questions of "our place in the world" and "whom to rely on" that surfaced in Jerusalem in the post–World War II political vacuum were therefore very real. In this respect, we cannot ignore the general direction toward which at least Ben-Gurion had been leaning since the early days of the war. In mid-October 1941, he voiced the opinion that "whether the United States joins the war—as it almost certainly will—or not, I believe that the United States is now the center of gravity for our political activity. At the end of the war America will have a major role, perhaps the main one, for the simple reason that it will be less exhausted than the other major fighting forces: Europe's welfare will depend largely on US economic assistance; and the maintenance of peace—almost certainly the victorious powers' main concern—will depend more than ever on America's participation in new post-war arrangements."[15]

This realization had actually begun to take shape two years earlier. Ben-Gurion originally decided on a Western orientation in March 1939, immediately after the St. James Conference. He tried to act on it during his first wartime visit to the United States, with only partial success, and with greater success during his second visit in the context of the Biltmore Conference. As Tuvia Frilling has demonstrated, he tried at the time and through his associates to persuade the heads of US intelligence, Allen Dulles and William Donavan, that the Zionist movement had important assets to sell them, but without success.[16] Ultimately, the specific decision on an international orientation—in the practical terms of Herzl's objective—came a decade later, when the sovereign State of Israel officially and independently set out on the bumpy international road taken by many others.

Jews and Arabs

The purpose of the Zionist movement was to offer a comprehensive solution to the Jewish problem by establishing a national home in Palestine. Its originators had certain expectations of the relationship between the Diaspora and Jewish residents of Palestine: on the one hand, the enterprise would provide much-needed refuge and safety, and on the other, world Jewry would have an ongoing role, providing political, economic, and demographic support for the establishment of this refuge. These expectations intensified with the onset of World War II. "At the end of the war," Ben-Gurion predicted in late March 1941, "there will be two questions that require a solution . . . the fate of Jewry and the fate of the Land [of Israel]. . . . We must first prevent an anti-Zionist solution to the question of Eretz Israel. We can prevent this in two ways: 1. Through the power of settlement, and 2. Through the power of world Jewry—the moral political power of Jewry throughout the world. . . . Before we win the heart of the Anglo-Saxon world and the world as a whole, we must win over the soul of the Jewish People."[17] Political support, economic aid, and aliyah remained salient operational objectives of the Yishuv vis-à-vis world Jewry after 1945, but beyond that, they constituted central political goals of the State of Israel in later years. The Jewish connection became critical during the military struggle for the establishment of the state and was a supremely important political and economic resource during its formative years. While this orientation was generally acceptable, other issues that emerged during the Yishuv era generated difficult disputes.

One of these disputes resulted from the regional situation in the Middle East at the time and relations with Arabs: What was the impact of thirty years of shared existence in Palestine? What did the dialogue between the two sides during that period yield? What basic positions regarding the Arab-Jewish conflict took hold then? In 1907 the pioneering educator Yitzhak Epstein, one of the Hebrew language revivalists and a First Aliyah immigrant, published a paper titled "The Hidden Question." The paper, based on a lecture he delivered at the

Seventh Zionist Congress in 1905, drew attention to the question of relations with Arabs. Its ironic title reflects his criticism of the Zionist movement. In his view, relations with the Arabs constituted an existential question that would determine the fate of Zionism, but Zionism had opted to ignore the matter, thus making it a "hidden question." Even if there was only some truth to this claim at the time, these relations undoubtedly became a central issue later. Reality compelled the Zionist movement to devote a great deal of effort to the matter. Consequently, as historian Neil Caplan demonstrates in *Futile Diplomacy*,[18] it was not ignorance of one another that characterized Jewish-Arab relations during the Mandate era but rather their close familiarity. It was an accurate mutual understanding—not a misunderstanding—of each other that paradoxically generated pessimism among the Zionist leadership by the mid-1930s. As early as November 1929, Ben-Gurion wrote that there was no need to try to turn Arabs into Zionists, because that would never happen. "The Arab of Eretz Israel does not need to be and cannot be a Zionist. He cannot wish for a Jewish majority. Therein lies the real contradiction. The political contradiction between us and the Arabs is that [both] we and they want to be a majority."[19]

Arthur Ruppin, a proponent of the binational solution, had already arrived at the conclusion that "what we can get [from the Arabs]—we do not need. And what we need—we cannot get. At most, the Arabs are willing to give us the rights of a national minority in an Arab state, following the format of national rights in Eastern Europe. . . . The fate of the Jewish minority would depend on the goodwill of the Arab majority. . . . Any form of Zionism that is willing to reach such a compromise with the Arabs would not earn the support of East European Jews and would quickly become Zionism without Zionists."[20] Two salient events confirmed this fatalistic and pessimistic thesis in the eyes of the Yishuv. The first was the bloody riots of 1929 in Palestine, whose repercussions went far beyond affirming the categorical, violent, and inevitable conflict with Arabs. According to Hillel Cohen, author of the recent, comprehensive book on the subject (*1929: Year Zero of the Arab-Israeli Conflict*), these events also made the ethos of the fighter a central motif in Jewish society and starkly highlighted the consequent domestic priorities: In the eyes of the Yishuv, the internal political struggle within the Yishuv was the be all and end all. It embodied deep historical and ideological divisions reflecting the party's roots in Europe and subsequent transition in Mandate-era Palestine, which culminated in a split. Cohen notes that besides this seemingly existential struggle, the gap between Labor and the Revisionists was monumental, and the struggle between the secular and ultraorthodox of the old Yishuv appeared catastrophic. Indeed, "all these rifts fueled hundreds upon thousands of words and deeds. In 1929, [however,] a single drop below the surface of the water transformed the People of Israel into a united, consolidated People working towards one goal—the establishment of a Jewish state."[21]

The second event was the failure of Ben-Gurion's attempts during the 1930s to reach agreements with moderate Palestinians, in particular through extensive exchanges with Musa Alami, a prominent Palestinian nationalist and politician. In Ben-Gurion's view, this failure proved that agreement, even with moderates, was impossible. The chairman of the Jewish Agency Executive had even been prepared, at the time, to concede the matter of a Jewish state and accept integration of the Yishuv into an Arab-majority state—with representation conditional on unrestricted Jewish immigration (a central consideration, of course, during the Nazi rise to power). Ben-Gurion incorporated this proposal into the Zionist movement's willingness to assist the Arab Nationalist Movement in liberating itself from Western imperialist rule. Alami and other Arab leaders rejected these proposals because they understood that the demand for unrestricted Jewish immigration was ultimately aimed at achieving a Jewish majority. The respective positions therefore remained unbridgeable.

In short, from the early days of the British Mandate, Chaim Weizmann and his associates in the Zionist leadership believed that the Palestinian national movement viewed relations with Jews as a zero-sum game. The Palestinian leadership and Arab states' rejection of the British Peel Commission's 1937 recommendation for partition further reinforced their line of thought. Yet not everyone shared this pessimism. In *Zionism and the Arabs, 1882–1948: A Study of Ideology*, Yosef Gorny identifies four ideological outlooks regarding the Arab question in the Zionist movement before 1948: integrative, separatist, liberal, and constructive socialist.[22] At the emotional level, according to Gorny, the pessimism and embarrassment that characterized MAPAI's discussions contrasted starkly with the brutal resolve, national-religious extremism, moral piety, or belief in progress that characterized the other movements and parties. All were united, however, in feeling that a nearly unbridgeable gulf existed between the Zionist aims and enterprise, on the one hand, and the Arab position, on the other.

MAPAI's embarrassment resulted mainly from its leadership role. In contrast to the other parties, MAPAI had to deal with social and political problems at a practical level. In this context the Zionist movement confronted one of its major paradoxes regarding the Arab issue. Initially the Zionist movement operated on the assumption that the country could accommodate both peoples and that peace and friendship would benefit both. At the same time, the movement was unwilling to relinquish its main objectives—aliyah and settlement—even if it was willing to concede to the regime of certificates that restricted aliyah and to the constraints that dictated the famous N-shaped pattern of settlement (mainly along the coastal strip, Jezreel Valley, Jordan Valley, and Hula Valley). In any event, aliyah and settlement could not have taken place without a strong measure of optimism. Yet as Gorny persuasively argues, the entity that systematically guided the complex processes of aliyah and settlement became, over time, pessimistic regarding the possibility of living together. Its pessimism increased during the late 1920s, the mid-1930s, and the final years of the British Mandate. The lessons it drew from the Holocaust and discussions with Arab leaders were harsh and generated a great deal of doubt among Yishuv leaders. In late August 1947, Ben-Gurion presented the following diagnosis to the Zionist General Council: "No one here should presume that the destruction of the Yishuv is *a priori* impossible. We should not ignore the fact that such an aspiration exists among our Arab friends. The leaders who control Arab public opinion . . . view such destruction as the only solution to the problem of Palestine, because they see no other possibility of making Palestine Arab. In their opinion—maybe rightly so—there cannot be an Arab state that is one-third Jews, [let alone] Jews like *these*."[23] This outlook necessitated the establishment of a political and military power capable of armed struggle, but simultaneously it paved the way to acceptance of partition as the least of all evils.

Did the Yishuv's political architects extend their pessimism to the entire Arab world? Did they view the hope of political agreement with *any* Arab states as futile? The historical answer to this question is complex. For the glass-half-empty camp, the answer was categorically affirmative: the position of Arabs living in Mandatory Palestine applied to the entire Arab world as well. The Zionist leadership was well aware of the extremist positions held by most Arab Palestinian leaders. It closely monitored the events of the 1930s and their effects on Arabs as well as Jews. This historical period generated one of the greatest tragedies to befall the Arabs of Palestine. Their leaders' decision to launch an armed revolt against Britain resulted in the annihilation of large segments of their population. This decision also led to fierce internal fighting and massive bloodshed, including the execution of thousands of Palestinians who were accused of treason and collaboration with the Zionists. Many of those persecuted fled the country, fearing for their lives. Long afterward, Palestinian society continued to suffer the consequences of these events, according to Yuval Arnon-Ohana.[24] The revolt also created a critical dependence on Arab states. Moreover, the Palestinians' demographic, political, and economic weakness, in contrast to the Jews' prosperity during the 1930s, only radicalized their position.

The Arab rebellion led to cooperation between what remained of its leadership and Nazi Germany. Indeed, Haj Amin al-Husseini, the grand mufti of Jerusalem, resided in Hitler's Germany during World War II. The cumulative effect of the leadership's misguided decisions and absolute intransigence was that during the crucial decade preceding Israel's independence, the Palestinian national movement was absent from the political arena. Its absence played nicely into the Zionists' hands in one sense, as it greatly weakened their major rivals. Yet it also shattered any hopes for the emergence of a new Palestinian leadership that would be willing to propose, not to mention implement, a compromise. Furthermore, the mufti's wartime activity in Berlin seemed to validate the stance of the Jewish Agency Executive and confirm the equivalence of two major, and now united, enemies of the Jews. Shortly after the end of World War II, the Jewish Agency Intelligence managed to acquire private papers of the mufti, which include the following message from Heinrich Himmler, dated November 2, 1943: "Since its beginning, Greater Germany's National-Socialist Movement has maintained its struggle against world Jewry as its banner. For this reason, it closely monitors the struggle of freedom-loving Arabs—especially in Palestine—against the Jewish invaders. Our shared recognition of the enemy and our joint struggle against it are the source of the strong foundation between Germany and freedom-loving Muslims throughout the world. In this spirit, on the anniversary of the accursed Balfour Declaration, I am pleased to offer you warm wishes in your continuing struggle, until the great victory."[25] Presumably, therefore, Ben-Gurion was not surprised when local Arab dignitary Awni Abd al-Hadi informed him, as they sat on the terrace of the latter's Jerusalem home in late August 1946, that the Arabs were determined to fight to the end: "We also have youth who are willing to sacrifice themselves. . . . All countries are now pursuing the secret of the atom bomb. Why shouldn't the Arabs be able to build atom bombs in time?"[26]

The Zionist pessimism of this era was, however, tempered by a guarded hope of compromise in principle with Arab states at large. We should bear in mind that from the outset Arab states were a secondary arena for Zionist diplomacy, notwithstanding isolated attempts to make contact with Arab leaders and explore possibilities for a Jewish-Arab understanding. Research on these efforts has drawn increasing interest in recent years. According to Yoav Gelber, however, the interest in them is inversely proportional to their importance at the time, as the Zionist leadership believed that the future of its enterprise would be determined in Berlin or London, followed by Washington and New York, and not in Damascus, Baghdad, or Cairo.[27] Accordingly, the Zionist leadership and Yishuv institutions, as well as the Jewish Agency and its Political Department, directed most of their activities in neighboring countries, first and foremost, to the gathering of information about developments therein. They did, however, also seek to forge connections in order to circumvent Palestinian opposition to the Zionist enterprise and to buttress political Zionist efforts in the West, the main arena.

Thus, the glass-half-full perspective led to a number of attempts to "de-Palestinize" the Arab-Jewish conflict—that is, to bypass local barriers by reaching an agreement with Arab leaders outside of Palestine and engaging other powers. Diplomatic contacts with these parties began after World War I. These include the famous agreement signed in London on January 3, 1919, between Chaim Weizmann on behalf of the Zionist movement and Emir Faysal, son of the king of Hijaz, on behalf of the Kingdom of Hijaz. The agreement would have established relations between the Zionist movement and a united Arab kingdom, which was supposed to emerge after World War I and the Arab Revolt instigated and funded by Britain during that war. Talks on implementing the agreement led nowhere. The Zionist movement lacked enthusiasm because the agreement did not promise the establishment of a Jewish state in Palestine, although the movement did not categorically oppose the notion of a federative Arab state that would ease Arab pressure on Jewish Palestine and permit the creation of a national home for the Jewish people. The latter consideration was another reason why the Zionist movement continued trying to circumvent Arab Palestinian opposition by chipping away at regional hostility. In the mid-1930s, when Arab states came out in firm opposition to the British partition plan, the Zionist movement sought new means of furthering its cause through de-Palestinization. It focused its efforts on enlisting the support of the United States, Britain, and Saudi Arabia in establishing an Arab federation in the Fertile Crescent and Arabian Peninsula, under the rule of King Ibn Saud of Saudi Arabia. Through the concept of a federation, its architects, who included Chaim Weizmann, hoped to achieve unrestricted aliyah and possibly the transfer of Palestine's Arab population. The concept ended in failure, once again dashing hopes of enlisting Arab states in the creation of a joint Arab-Zionist platform. For a long time, the Zionists failed to understand that public legitimization of their cause required Arab states to withdraw openly from the all-Arab consensus, which was politically impossible. Moreover, any compensation that might come from the Jewish Agency's little facility on Keren HaYesod Street in Jerusalem lacked real value.

The cumulative effect of these events was a deep sense of fatalism regarding the possibility of reaching a political agreement between the Zionist movement and the Arabs of Palestine and neighboring Arab states. During the final six months of the British Mandate, this fatalism proved accurate on two occasions. As noted, the Palestinians and Arab states did not accept the proposal for partition approved by the UN General Assembly in November 1947. They waged a fierce political campaign against the establishment of a Jewish state, which, according to Elad Ben-Dror, might have been successful had it not been so poorly run: "It was based on predictions, wrong assessments and a downright ignorance of reality and suffered from a lack of consolidated leadership, and eventually it contributed crucially to the support of most UNSCOP delegates for the pro-Zionist plan."[28]

In any event, as soon as they realized their campaign had failed, with the passage of the UN resolution, Palestine was destined for civil war. The Jewish Agency Executive naturally considered it absurd to entertain any thoughts of strategic dialogue with Palestinian leaders who supported the mufti, and they rightly regarded any hopes of fruitful talks with his opponents as delusional. Furthermore, any expectations that King Abdullah and King Farouk would ultimately refrain from invading Israel were dashed when these two, alongside the leaders of Syria, Lebanon, and Iraq, began military maneuvers and launched incursions. In mid-May 1948, the Jews' worst-case scenario of the Arab response materialized in full force.

Consequently, and unsurprisingly, the diagnosis and prognosis for the Arab question that underpinned Zionist strategy toward the end of the Mandate continued to guide Israeli policy on the Jewish-Arab conflict for decades to come. To this day, their influence is manifest in the Israeli government's thinking and policy.

Did Ben-Gurion and associates see any glimmer of light in this regional political gloom? Had they exhausted all options for avoiding perpetual conflict? The answer lies along the eastern border of Palestine, in the form of the Kingdom of Transjordan. Relations between the kingdom and the Zionist movement were one of the most important legacies the Yishuv bequeathed to Israeli foreign policy on the Arab-Jewish conflict, and they therefore deserve some exploration.

The Jordanian Option

Was there really a Jordanian option, and if so, how did it emerge? What is the factual basis for analysis, and what is its historical significance? The Kingdom of Transjordan under Emir Abdullah of Hijaz was established in 1921 and funded by the British. It was an artificial political creation, a concept that emerged during World War I and lacked any historical or other roots in the region. Nonetheless, the emir held on to the dream of a greater Arab kingdom for years and therefore remained unsatisfied with his country's existing borders. He persisted in efforts to expand northward and westward. Yet the majority of Arabs in Palestine and Syria opposed his possible rule, while the British, on whom he depended, realized his limitations and—to put it mildly—did not support his efforts. Thus, the Jews remained Abdullah's main hope for the realization of his aspirations regarding Palestine and Syria. The Zionists, for their part, saw Transjordan as a natural and desirable ally. They considered it necessary to reach an understanding with its ruler so as to overcome British reservations about possible Jewish expansion to the east of the Jordan River. Such an understanding was also essential to protect Jewish settlements in the Jordan Valley and elsewhere against Bedouin attacks launched from Transjordan. In time, economic interests also became a factor. These factors formed a basis for rapprochement between the parties, although historians as well as historical participants are divided on the proper term to apply to this relationship. Whatever the terminology, from the Jews' perspective, Abdullah became the favorite neighbor, and he needed them just as much, given both his ambition and his weakness. Therefore, as Yoav Alon concludes, not only did the Jordanian leadership refrain from public expressions of hostility toward the Jews in contrast to other Arab leaders, but it was markedly willing and able to maintain friendly, open relations with the Zionist movement.[29]

What did the Zionist movement have to offer the emir? First and foremost, it could provide crucial support for his continued rule over Transjordan, in light of the domestic and foreign opposition he faced. The emir also hoped that the Jews would support his ambition of ruling over the eastern parts of Palestine. Although the latter issue was somewhat problematic as it entailed territorial concessions, the Jewish Agency consistently provided Abdullah with intelligence on plots against him, primarily by the Husseinis in Palestine. Another very important aspect of the relationship was a financial arrangement that began in late 1921 at the initiative and explicit request of Abdullah. The Zionist reaction, though extremely cautious, laid the foundation for a continuing relationship. The financial payments Abdullah received from the Jews, under various cover stories, were in fact bribes. They become one of the foundational, albeit secret, elements of the relationship that formed between Abdullah and the Jews. The Zionist Archives detail some of the sums transferred, at times through a mediator. From 1932 to 1937, for example, the Jews paid about 10,000 Palestinian pounds (equivalent to roughly $750,000 today). A year later they paid another 3,700 pounds.

The most important give-and-take was at the political and strategic levels. Negotiations on these matters lasted about a decade, beginning in 1936 during the Peel Commission's visit to Palestine. The commission's revolutionary recommendations included the concept of partitioning the land and establishing a Jewish state and an Arab state. Abdullah accepted this proposal because he hoped to gain control of the Arab portion at least. His agreement was conveyed to the Jewish Agency, which also supported the concept of partition, and thus the emir became a potential partner in the agency's strategic plan. Talks between the parties, however, were brief and unproductive, especially after British support for partition waned. Furthermore, the emir realized that residents of his kingdom were not thrilled with the idea, and he eventually dropped it himself. He opted instead to support a plan for the cantonization of Palestine and issued a statement advocating the Arab cause. In a later statement, he also voiced support for the 1939 British White Paper.

After World War II, the political landscape offered another opportunity to renew contact at the strategic level in the form of a "grand deal." The Zionists' open and explicit acceptance of partition provided a basis to explore the possibility of cooperation with Abdullah on the matter. In July 1946 Eliyahu Sasson, head of the Arab Division at the Jewish Agency's Political Department, met with Abdullah. Yoav Gelber, speaking at a conference marking the release of his book on the subject, described this meeting:

> In July 1946, while talks with Abdullah were being renewed, Sasson met with him and reached an unsigned, unwritten agreement. But we know about it because one of the British reports describes Sasson crossing the Allenby

Bridge eastward and being stopped for questioning at the guards' post. Meanwhile they looked in the trunk of his car and saw 5,000 pounds. In the evening when he returned, they stopped him again and took him to the guards' post. They looked in his trunk and saw that the 5,000 pounds were gone. . . . Apparently that was the day they signed, or if they did not sign, at least reached their agreement. Around that time Ben-Gurion wrote an interesting article, which is not referenced much, titled "Judah and Abdullah." He wrote that Mandatory Eretz Israel—that is, both banks of the Jordan River, both sides of the Jordan—has enough space for two states, Judah and Abdullah. The general idea was that Abdullah was interested in population, not territory, so let's give him those parts of Eretz Israel that are heavily populated with Arabs, in exchange for empty land that the Jews can develop, such as the eastern shore of the Dead Sea, the Judean Desert, and the like.[30]

Abdullah agreed to partition in principle, though he postponed discussion of its geographical details to the conference that was supposed to convene in London, where his representative would be instructed to support partition. Shortly afterward, Abdullah even told British high commissioner Cunningham that partition and population exchange were the only practical solution to the question of Palestine. It appeared that the agreement with the emir was working, and at this stage Sharett, for his part, was willing to allocate a significant amount of money to support Abdullah's subversive efforts in Syria. It is unclear, however, whether the Jewish Agency's initial optimism was justified. Soon after this "agreement" had been reached, Abdullah promised the Arabs of Palestine that he would not accept any solution to which they objected. His public declarations and his instructions to representatives at the 1947 London conference, opposing partition, attest that he backed away from the understanding reached with the Jewish Agency. When UNSCOP arrived in Palestine, Abdullah said in a private conversation with the chairman, Justice Sandstrom of Sweden, that partition was the only practical solution, yet publicly he aligned himself with the general Arab policy on UNSCOP. In November 1947 Golda Meir (then Meyerson), Sasson, and Ezra Danin (head of the Arab section of the Haganah's intelligence arm) met with Abdullah in Naharayim, near the border with Transjordan. At this meeting Abdullah proposed a new "partition" with a "Jewish republic" in part of Jewish Palestine, in the framework of a Trans-Jordanian state spanning both banks of the Jordan River.

Once the UN affirmed the partition plan, therefore, the Jewish Agency was uncertain of Abdullah's position, particularly after the Arab League Summit in Cairo resolved to send volunteer forces to assist the Arabs of Palestine. Abdullah tried to ease the agency's concerns, saying that "the League is not a League and its resolutions are not resolutions,"[31] but the agency had information to the contrary. Under British pressure, Arab Legion forces stationed in Palestine did refrain from taking part in the clashes of early 1948, except for a few skirmishes. But volunteers flowed into Palestine through Jordan, including the Arab Salvation Army, led by the Arab nationalist Fawzi al-Qawuqji. The British commander of the Arab Legion, John Glubb, reported to the British War Office that since early 1948 Abdullah had been planning to invade Palestine after May 15 and capture its Arab parts but not enter the Jewish parts. In February of that year, Abdullah also raised the idea of taking over Jerusalem. Nonetheless, and despite the failure of the Palestinian Arabs' war effort, the Arab Legion did not intervene in the fighting in Palestine during the early months of 1948. Palestinian Arab delegations then began approaching Abdullah to seek his intervention, a request backed by Azzam Pasha, secretary-general of the Arab League. Abdullah was initially reluctant, but eventually, in late April, he agreed to invade Palestine as part of an all-Arab military operation. Amman then became the central base for planning the invasion, a fact of which the Jews were aware. In early May, clashes between the Legion and Jewish forces increased, particularly in the region of Gush Etzion. Jewish Agency experts concluded, therefore, that although Abdullah would not completely betray their agreement, he did not intend to adhere to the borders of the partition plan.

This lack of clarity necessitated another meeting—the final one—between Abdullah and Jewish representatives (Meir and Danin). It took place shortly before the invasion. The emir did not deny the earlier understandings and "agreement" but argued that circumstances had changed, saying that "then I was one, and now I am one of five and I cannot [adhere to the agreement]. I have no other option and I cannot act otherwise."[32] As such, he proposed autonomy for the Jews within a single state united under his rule. His proposal was, of course, rejected. In hindsight it is obvious that Abdullah's invasion of Israel on May 15, 1948, was aimed at the annexation of Arab Palestine to his kingdom. As Avraham Sela has suggested, however, it is not clear whether the reason that the Arab Legion did not invade the Jewish parts of the state was in fact loyalty on Abdullah's part to his earlier agreement with the Jews.[33]

Yoav Alon describes this agreement as "of a piece with the negotiations of the 1930s: vague, general, flexible and subjective, and therefore open to different interpretations."[34] Whatever the case—and this is an important historical fact—battles between the Arab Legion and the Israel Defense Forces (IDF) took place only in areas that had been designated as part of an Arab state and where the IDF was present, and in Jerusalem, which was designated to be international. Yet it is apparent, as Gelber has emphasized, that on the eve of the decisive battle for the future of the country and the fate of the Yishuv and Zionist movement, the Yishuv leaders could not base their military and political strategy on any explicit agreement with Abdullah. The emir's renunciation of earlier understandings inevitably meant the loss of regional backing for the Yishuv leadership.

Was there a secret agreement in practice between the parties? According to some historians, particularly Avi Shlaim, the answer is categorically yes. These historians argue that the Zionist leadership collaborated with Abdullah in planning a strategic division of Palestine between the two sides, based on a shared interest in preventing the establishment of a Palestinian state. Others are more doubtful, pointing to glass-half-empty considerations, especially on the Jordanian—but also on the Jewish—side. Gelber, for example, argues that if there was any conspiracy, it was between Abdullah and the British rather than Abdullah and the Jewish Agency.

The historical implications of this story remain complex. But it is hard to argue with two accepted historical certainties that, at the very least, provide a minimal retrospective baseline. First, the contact between the parties established a constructive foundation for ongoing relations and, on occasion, significant understandings. Second, this relationship was not enough for Abdullah to break away publicly from the Arab world's declared and actual hostility. All who have researched this issue share the opinion that although no open and official strategic pact emerged between the parties in 1948, their previous contact and, in particular, their shared interest in preventing the formation of a Palestinian state and in preserving division of the land between themselves created an important and lasting basis for relations between Jordan and Israel. This was evident, for example, during the later stages of war between them, when they joined efforts to prevent the internationalization of Jerusalem. Among other measures, Israel agreed to Jordan's annexation of Arab neighborhoods in southern Jerusalem, and Jordan agreed to transfer the Old City's Jewish Quarter to Israel and to allow Israel access to Mount Scopus.

According to Dan Schueftan's analysis, Abdullah needed four conditions to be met in order to establish his control over the West Bank: Britain's agreement, a weak Palestinian national movement, Arab world validation of his conquest of the territory, and cooperation with the Zionists. Not all of these conditions existed during the Mandate era, but toward mid-1948 they did materialize.[35]

From Jordan's perspective, therefore, the post-Mandate era held greater potential in terms of an "Israeli option." This factor should be weighed against the fatalism and pessimism of the Zionist approach toward reaching an understanding with the Arabs of Palestine. It was only logical that the Yishuv leadership prefer the Jordanian option over a Palestinian option during the Mandate era, for lack of an alternative among other reasons. That preference only grew stronger when Israel emerged as a sovereign state after the War of Independence and the promising new geopolitical facts on the ground along its eastern border. During December 1949 and January 1950, therefore, the two states held clandestine talks. Evidently they found a basis for a peace agreement and even signed a draft five-year nonaggression pact. But the fact of the talks leaked out. In April 1950, the Arab League decided to expel any Arab state that held peace talks with Israel. This threat deterred the king from reaching a peace agreement with Israel, but secret talks between the two states continued. They managed to reach agreements on arms limitations near the border as well as an agreement on preventing cross-border infiltrations, although implementation of the latter was unsuccessful. Nonetheless, Israel's aspiration of achieving a full peace agreement never abated, and neither did the Jordanian interest in maintaining clandestine cooperation. Eventually, in 1994, the aspiration led to fruition, with a peace treaty that is still in place today.

Notes

1. Ernst Rychnovsky, ed., *Masaryk a židovství* [Masaryk and Judaism] (Prague, Mars, 1931), 304.
2. Joseph Heller, *BaMaavak LeMedina* [The struggle for the Jewish state] (Jerusalem Shazar Center, 1996), 174.
3. Ibid.
4. *Moshe Sharett—Rosh HaMemshala HaSheni: Mivhar Te'udot MiPirkei Hayav* [Moshe Sharett—the second prime minister: Selected documents] (Jerusalem, Israel State Archive, 2007), 67.
5. Heller, *BaMaavak LeMedina*, 434–35.
6. Uri Bialer, *Tslav BeMagen David* [Cross on the Star of David] (Jerusalem, Yad Ben Zvi, 2006), 14 [Hebrew].
7. Yaakov Sharett, "Moshe Sharett VeHakhrazat HaMedina" [Moshe Sharett and the declaration of statehood], in *Sokher Shalom: Heibetim U-Mabatim al Moshe Sharett* [A statesman assessed: Views and viewpoints about Moshe Sharett], ed. Yaakov Sharett and Rina Sharett (Tel Aviv, Sharett Heritage Society, 2008), 277–95.
8. Uri Bialer, "Ben-Gurion VeShe'elat HaOrientatsia HaBenle'umit Shel Israel, 1948–1956" [Ben-Gurion and Israel's international orientation, 1948–1956], in *Atsma'ut: 50 HaShanim HaRishonot* [Independence: The first fifty years], ed. Anita Shapira (Jerusalem, Shazar Center, 1998), 217–44. See Ben Guron's letter to Davar, October 30, 1954.
9. Jacob Metzer, *The Divided Economy of Mandatory Palestine* (Cambridge, Cambridge University Press, 1998).
10. https://he.wikiquote.org/wiki/דוד_בן-גוריון.
11. Shmuel Dotan, *HaMaavak al Eretz Israel* [The struggle for Palestine] (Tel Aviv, Ministry for Defence, 1983), 348.
12. Quoted in Amitzur Ilan, "Nevu'at HaMedina HaYehudit VeHitgashmuta, 1941–1949" [The prophecy of the Jewish state and its fulfillment, 1941–1949], *Tsionut* [Zionism] 10 (1985): 294.
13. Letter to Jewish Agency Executive, October 13, 1946, via the Ben-Gurion Archives [in Hebrew].
14. Ilan, "Nevu'at HaMedina HaYehudit VeHitgashmuta."
15. Heller, *BaMaavak LeMedina*, 331.
16. Tuvia Frilling, *Hetz BaArafel: Ben-Gurion, Hanhagat HaYishuv VeNisyonot Hatsalah BaShoah* [Arrows in the dark: David Ben-Gurion, the Yishuv leadership, and rescue attempts during the Holocaust] (Jerusalem, Bialik Institute, 1998), 406.

17. Heller, *BaMaavak LeMedina*, 321.

18. Neil Caplan, *Futile Diplomacy* (London, Frank Cass, 1983).

19. Quoted in Yosef Gorny, *HaShe'ela HaAravit VeHabe'aya HaYehudit: Zramim Medini'im-Ideologi'im BaTsionut BeYahasam el HaYeshut HaAravit BaAretz, 1882–1948* [Zionism and the Arabs, 1882–1948: A study of ideology] (Jerusalem, Shazar Center, 1985), 278.

20. Arthur Ruppin, *Pirkei Hayai* [Chapters of my life], ed. Alex Bein (Tel Aviv, Am Oved, 1968), 3:203.

21. Dalia Karpel, "Interview with Hillel Cohen" [in Hebrew], *Haaretz*, October 24, 2013.

22. Gorny, *HaShe'ela HaAravit*.

23. Heller, *BaMaavak LeMedina*, 498.

24. Yuval Arnon-Ohana, *Mered Aravi BeEretz Israel, 1936–1939* [The Arab Revolt in Palestine, 1936–1939] (, Jerusalem, Ariel, 2013).

25. *Haaretz*, March 30, 2017 [in Hebrew].

26. Heller, *BaMaavak LeMedina*, 491.

27. Yoav Gelber, "Pe'ulot HaMakhlaka HaMedinit shel HaSokhnut BeMitzrayim, 1944–1948" [The activities of the Jewish Agency's Political Department in Egypt, 1944–1948], *Cathedra* 67 (1993): 24–53.

28. Elad Ben-Dror, "The Success of the Zionist Strategy vis-a-vis UNSCOP," *Israel Affairs* 20, no. 1 (2014): 19–39.

29. Yoav Alon, "Friends Indeed or Accomplices in Need? The Jewish Agency, Emir Abdullah, and the Shayks of Trans-Jordan, 1922–1939," in *Israel's Clandestine Diplomacies*, ed. Clive Jones and Tore Peterson (London, Hurst, 2013), 31–48.

30. Conference at Haifa University, June 10, 2004. See also Yoav Gelber, *Israeli-Jordanian Dialogue, 1948–1953: Cooperation, Conspiracy, or Collusion?* (Brighton, Sussex Academic, 2004).

31. Oral reference, Conference at Haifa University, June 10, 2004.

32. David Ben-Gurion, *Yoman Milkhama* [War diary] (Tel Aviv, Ministry for Defence, 1982), 409–10.

33. Avraham Sela, "Transjordan, Israel and the 1948 War: Myth, Historiography and Reality," *Middle Eastern Studies* 28, no. 4 (1992): 623–88.

34. Alon, "Friends Indeed."

35. Dan Schueftan, *Optsiyah Yardenit: HaYishuv HaYehudi U-Medinat Israel El Mul HaMishtar HaHashemi VeHaTenuah HaLeumit HaPalestinit* [A Jordanian option: Israel, Jordan, and the Palestinians] (Tel Aviv, Hakibbutz HaMeuchad, 1986).

3   A State in the Making

Tactical Political Experience: The Bureaucratic Legacy

In his 1959 book, *Three Days: Government Administration in the Jewish State*, Ze'ev Scherf, Israel's first cabinet secretary, argued that the entire construction of Israel's public bureaucracy was completed during the three days preceding official statehood on May 15, 1948. The author attributes this remarkable efficiency to a legacy of active, experienced Jewish governing mechanisms that existed in Mandatory Palestine and created what sociologists Moshe Lissak and Dan Horowitz later described as a "state within a state" throughout this entire period.[1] Thirty years later, Jonathan Fine offered a detailed, documented historical explanation of this phenomenon in a broader chronological context in his book *The Establishment of the Israeli Governmental System, 1947—1951*.[2] It goes without saying, therefore, that understanding how public administration functions in Israel requires familiarity with the historical foundations that preceded statehood. Indeed, during its formative years, some elements of Israel's foreign service apparatus and intelligence agencies were themselves the direct product of those that preceded them.

Throughout the Mandate era, the Zionist movement and Jewish Agency gained more than a little experience in diplomacy, mainly conducted by specifically and officially designated organizations. The most important of these was the Political Department of the agency, founded in 1923. From its inception, it maintained contact with the Mandatory great power governing Palestine. As such, it also had to address matters of internal security, intelligence, and institutional organization. The department personnel formed the core of the emerging intelligence community, which included a department of Arab affairs tasked with monitoring the Arab public and assessing developments. In this context, the agency established SHAI (Hebrew acronym for "information service"), which operated throughout and beyond Palestine under the supervision of the Political Department. In its early days, the department's official staff was very small, comprising only eight personnel in 1925. Until the 1930s, London was the center of diplomatic activity, as the Zionist leadership there was the main institution to maintain contact with the British government. The center gradually shifted to Jerusalem as MAPAI's hegemony within the Zionist movement grew—a hegemony that manifested organizationally and politically at the Eighteenth Zionist

Congress in August 1933. Responsibility for the issue of security also shifted during this time to the Political Department.

Over several years beginning in the 1930s, the department expanded its activities, forming military ties and laying the foundation for a joint struggle with the British against the Arab Revolt. In this context, special night squads were established under the command of Captain Orde Wingate, a "friend" and supporter of Zionism. Another phase in the expansion of the apparatus began after the 1929 Arab riots, mainly within the Department of Arab Affairs. One of its notable activities was the preparation of a "villages file"—a systematic archive of all Arab villages in Mandatory Palestine—which served the Yishuv leadership during the 1940s and provided an important foundation for Israel's domestic and foreign intelligence services after 1948. The Political Department's areas of responsibility further expanded with the Nazi rise to power in Germany, when the Jewish Agency conducted negotiations with German authorities on behalf of Jewish emigration and the salvaging of Jewish properties. Dr. Haim Arlosoroff, head of the department, oversaw these negotiations. His successor, Moshe Sharett, then led the department for the next fifteen years, the decisive period preceding independence. That experience greatly benefited him, as well as the state, when he was appointed Israel's first foreign minister.

The Political Department's areas of responsibility continued to spread during this time, beginning with World War II and the Yishuv's decision to join the British war effort (and form the Jewish Brigade) and, later, to oppose British activity in Palestine politically and physically. As Yoav Gelber explored in his groundbreaking study on the history of Israeli intelligence,[3] the department has maintained operational contact with the US and British intelligence services as well as the Soviet Union, the Vatican, Turkey, Iran, and even India. Among other activities, it cultivated relations with the Jews of occupied Europe in an effort to save them. The Jewish Agency's legation in Istanbul was particularly active in this regard and involved some of its most skilled agents in the area of clandestine diplomacy and intelligence. These included Reuven Zaslanski (Shiloah), Teddy Kollek, Ehud Avriel, Ze'ev Schind, Shaul Meirov, Menachem Bader, and Ze'ev Hadari (Venia Pomerantz), among others. The agency's office in Geneva, led by Chaim Pazner and Samuel Scheps, contributed greatly to this effort, running its operations from neutral Switzerland. After the war, a large-scale effort commenced to locate and monitor Nazi war criminals. A recently published study by Clive Jones on the intelligence ties forged by the Political Department with Britain during World War II found that this relationship "allowed the Jewish Agency to develop and strengthen its transnational links . . . while developing a reservoir of expertise and experience that was to prove invaluable in the struggle for statehood."[4]

In his book *The Roots of the Israeli Intelligence Community*, Asa Lefen provides an in-depth analysis of the department's infrastructure.[5] Yet we still lack precise figures regarding personnel after the 1920s, though we know these numbers were not large. The bureaucratic division of labor in the department was not always clear even to staff members. During the final, critical seven months of the Mandate, for example, the department lacked a formal structure with clear hierarchy and division of responsibilities. The boundaries between it and the agency's other departments or between it and the Haganah (in particular, relations with SHAI) were not clearly delineated at the time. Its headquarters were in Jerusalem, and at the height of its power, it had legations in Washington, New York, Paris, London, and Geneva. The administrative headquarters had only six political staff members. Because the Jewish apparatus that handled diplomacy and intelligence expanded greatly after World War II, as noted, a new network—Yanai (a branch of SHAI)—emerged in late 1947 in Europe, with legations in Italy and Austria. This network focused on building contacts at seaports, given the intensive *Briha* (flight) activities underway, which involved smuggling about 250,000 Jews from Eastern to Western Europe and clandestinely bringing some 90,000 "illegal" refugees to Palestine. The network forged ties with French intelligence and monitored Arab arms deals as well as land-purchasing efforts, with a view to preventing them. SHAI, which also reached the peak of its power during this time, had branches in Tel Aviv and Jerusalem. It gathered military intelligence on the British armed forces in Palestine and political intelligence that involved monitoring the local British bureaucracy. Yanai also gathered information from foreign consulates and conducted surveillance on foreign hotel guests. Toward 1948, as Jewish-Arab military confrontation approached, the number of intelligence agents working on this issue grew to several hundred, according to Gelber (1992).

The political, military, and intelligence activities of the Yishuv's experts naturally entailed successes as well as failures. The most salient example of the latter was a flawed assessment regarding the breakout of Israel's War of Independence in 1948. The staff of the Department of Arab Affairs and leaders of the Haganah expected an armed confrontation with the Arabs after the Arab Revolt and in the aftermath of World War II. Such a confrontation seemed particularly likely given the political clash over the fate of the country. Haganah commanders and experts from the Department of Arab Affairs could envision only one type of clash—a repeat, albeit on a larger scale, of the pattern of the 1930s Arab Revolt. The breakout of what became Israel's War of Independence therefore came as a surprise, according to Gelber, in terms of "timing, warfighting style, the *modus operandi* of the Arab side, and its rapidly worsening pace."[6] Above all, the experts misjudged the possibility of the Arab states' mobilization to fight in Palestine. Israel was therefore unprepared for a massive Arab invasion, which cost the young state dearly during the early stages of the war.

On the other hand, the Zionists achieved a major victory in one aspect—namely, their political campaign against the mufti, which began before World

War II. This extremist Palestinian leader was, according to assessments, a dangerous political enemy, and for years, the Jewish Agency focused on thwarting his efforts. In 1946 it succeeded in enlisting a Jewish American diplomat (Gideon Hadary, discussed below) to convey the mufti's private papers from his stay in Berlin during World War II, which the US military had acquired upon Europe's liberation, to the Haganah's information-service contact in Washington. Beginning in 1946, the Zionists made intensive, public use of this collection. Their aim was to sully the name of the figurehead most likely to be regarded as leader of the Arabs in Mandatory Palestine (although in exile at the time), but in particular they sought to highlight the extremism and militancy of the Palestinians' anti-Zionist stances in the context of international negotiations on the question of Palestine. The papers also provided very valuable operational information about the mufti's important contacts within and beyond the borders of Palestine.

Moreover, the official list of organizations and individuals who formally engaged in foreign relations on behalf of the Yishuv is misleading. These were not the only individuals who contributed to the efforts of the agency's executive in the areas relevant to this book. The agency's political and diplomatic tentacles and operational reach included several dozen, if not more, information sources and other organizational and individual means of operation. The Jewish National Fund's offices in Europe and South America, for example, focused on fundraising and financial donations but occasionally engaged in other activities. The Jewish Agency's Economic Department, which worked on attracting Jewish investors in Palestine, almost certainly engaged in clandestine diplomacy as well. The most important work in this regard—namely, organizing Jewish immigration to Palestine—was the responsibility of the Aliyah Department of the Zionist Organization, seated in London. Its branches, known as the "Eretz-Israeli" ("of the Land of Israel") offices, operated in nearly all European capitals, towns with high Jewish concentrations such as in Poland and Lithuania, and ports of exit to Palestine such as Trieste and Marseilles. The largest of these branches was in Warsaw. After World War II, offices also operated in Geneva, Istanbul, Tehran, Vienna, Munich, and Rome. They coordinated the registration of emigrants, disseminated information about the aliyah movement and the situation in Palestine, and oversaw medical arrangements, among other responsibilities. In the natural course of events, their activities often extended to the political sphere. The branch in Budapest, for example, played a major part in efforts to save Jews during World War II. Toward this end, it reached an agreement with the local interior ministry not to return the refugees who had arrived in Hungary from Slovakia but to allow them to remain in detention camps and grant them priority in immigrating to Palestine. As a result, the numbers of refugees from Poland and Slovakia to Hungary increased, and the local Eretz-Israeli office reached an understanding with the authorities not to turn these refugees over to the Poles or Germans at the border crossings. The office in Turkey was even more active in political matters, as were the offices in North Africa, specifically Tripoli and Morocco, after World War II. During those years, the various Eretz-Israeli offices assisted in organizing clandestine aliyah and Briha efforts, activities that naturally touched on what may be termed "backdoor diplomacy." These offices would also have been providing highly valuable political information. However, beyond that, throughout the Mandate era and especially toward its end, they gathered information that was vitally important to promoting one of Israel's prime postindependence objectives—namely, aliyah—as well as cultivating ties with Jews and fundraising toward this end. Ze'ev Hadari, one of the leaders of HaMossad LeAliyah Bet, thus chose an apt title for his book on this subject: *Refugees Achieve Victory over an Empire.*[7] This victory inevitably entailed the acquisition of highly valuable, multifaceted political and operative experience, which continued to serve the country after independence.

Diplomacy on the Road to Statehood

The Holocaust was a formative event in the history of the Jewish people, the Yishuv, and the latter's foreign policy. The extermination of six million European Jews and physical annihilation of Europe's Jewish communities left a massive void that could not be filled. Zionism emerged from the chaos of World War II and the Holocaust as the strongest ideological and political movement in the Jewish world, which it had not been previously. The reason, as Dan Michman notes, was twofold: First, most of the Jews who supported Zionism's rival movements and parties before the rise of Nazism—Bundists, Unionists, assimilationists of various types, and others—were simply wiped off the face of the earth by the Nazis. Second, after the war the Yishuv was one of the few remaining, vitally important, Jewish population centers.[8] The Holocaust provided monumental ex post facto justification for the historical Zionist call for a refuge. Toward the end of the war, therefore, the Yishuv became the main base for the Zionist call to establish a Jewish state in Palestine that would provide a haven for survivors and protect Jews from another holocaust. For the Jewish Agency's Executive, unsurprisingly, the Holocaust and the fate of Jewish refugees in Europe became entwined with resolution of the question of Palestine. This link manifested itself through diplomacy as well as physical efforts to concentrate the remaining refugees in Western Europe and coordinate their illegal aliyah (giving rise to well-known icons such as "the boys who carry their people on their shoulders") and to use their suffering as a moral and pragmatic argument for statehood. That argument, which later became an inalienable asset of Israeli diplomacy, served Ben-Gurion and his associates well. Years later, however, it also served as a source of harsh moral criticism of Ben-Gurion, as reflected in a poem by Professor Benjamin Harshav (Hrushovski) of Tel Aviv University:

> Peter the Great
> Paved [the land for] St. Petersburg the capital
> In the swamps of the north
> On the bones of farmers.
> David Ben-Gurion paved the way to Jerusalem the capital
> With the bones of the Holocaust's youth. . . .
> Ben-Gurion collected [the] dust
> Of men—to throw in enemy eyes.
> On the bones of the Holocaust's youth
> We paved the circuitous route
> That leads to Jerusalem.[9]

In any event, the Holocaust undeniably played an important part in shaping the perspective of international observers. As Yehoshua Freundlich describes, there emerged "something hard to identify or quantify, a sort of sympathetic embrace and supportive atmosphere, especially at the UN and in public opinion. That supportive political climate formed the connection between the problem of those displaced and the problem of Eretz Israel, [including] their place within the web of issues that emerged after the war and required remedial and supportive care."[10]

There were many who objected to such perspectives. The Arab world as a whole staunchly opposed the establishment of a Jewish state on this basis. Why, it asked, should the people of Palestine pay for the Holocaust committed by the people of Europe? The most significant political opposition to this approach at the time, however, came from Britain. Toward the end of World War II, the high commissioner in Palestine warned his superiors against "sentimentality" over the plight of European Jews, advising them to maintain a "cool head,"[11] and that was indeed how the British Foreign Office operated. The ray of hope for the Zionists in this regard came from the United States, where, toward the end of the war, the Jewish public became highly attuned to the plight of Jewish refugees in Europe. The issue therefore remained on the public agenda, received wide and supportive coverage accompanied by photographs in the media, and became the focus of appeals to government agencies. The refugees' cause made such an impression on US public opinion that even the British ambassador drew the attention of his superiors in London to Jewish public opinion and suggested that Britain allow Jewish refugees to enter Palestine as a onetime gesture. The US government responded swiftly, dispatching Earl Harrison, a special representative of President Truman, to survey the situation in Europe's displaced persons camps in the summer of 1945. Harrison's report, submitted to Truman in late August, advised that one hundred thousand displaced persons be granted immediate entry to

Palestine. Truman's support for this recommendation led to the formation in 1946 of an Anglo-American committee of inquiry and facilitated the decision to allow a limited number of displaced persons to enter Palestine. The change in policy and emphasis on humanitarian aspects were direct outcomes of the approach adopted by Truman himself, who acted in stark opposition to the professional advice he received from the State Department.

Nonetheless, the Anglo-American Committee's conclusions were unsatisfactory from the Zionist leadership's perspective. Although the committee stated, "We know of no country to which the great majority can go in the immediate future other than Palestine. Furthermore that is where almost all of them want to go,"[12] it did not recognize the right of Jews to an independent state. The next committee tasked with addressing the issue, the United Nations Special Committee on Palestine (UNSCOP), established in 1947, produced a report that constitutes one of the greatest diplomatic successes of the Zionist movement. UNSCOP's summary recommendations presented a plan for partition of the land into two states—Jewish and Arab—along borders that the Jewish Agency accepted even though Jerusalem was to have a "separate status" as an international city. Today we know that the Jewish Agency's Political Department contributed to this success. Historical studies have shed light on the conventional means it employed, such as the Yishuv's demonstrably warm and organized reception of UNSCOP members, as well as what may be considered unconventional measures, such as the eavesdropping and surveillance that allowed the Zionists to monitor the committee's closed, internal discussions. They also managed, some months after UNSCOP left Palestine, to tap into an underground cable that connected Jerusalem to Egypt through an international switchboard in Jaffa. Thus, they were able to eavesdrop on thousands of conversations between militia leaders who planned to attack Jews, on policy consultations among politicians in Arab capitals, and on discussions between the Arabs and British. The Political Department had originally developed these surveillance capabilities a decade earlier, when the Peel Commission (which also recommended partition at the time) held its closed meetings at the Palace Hotel in Jerusalem, with Ben-Gurion and Sharett covertly listening to everything.

Moreover, the Political Department's representatives employed highly sophisticated negotiating tactics in its dealings with UNSCOP. They guided the talks in such a way that from the outset it became evident that the Mandate would not work, that a binational state would not emerge, and that only the Jewish side was willing to compromise. The Zionists also held firmly to their stance, adopted in 1946, that the question of statehood was directly linked to the problem of displaced persons in Europe. In addition, they conditioned any agreement regarding partition on the Jewish state having geographical borders that would make its existence viable (in contrast to the Peel Commission recommendations). Notably, UNSCOP was deeply impressed with the Jews' ability to settle the land and recommended granting them 55 percent of Palestine, which was several times more than they had at the time. In this regard, the Arab Palestinians' stance played directly into the Zionists' hands. Although Arab government radio broadcasts called on local leaders to appear before the committee and present their position, the committee concluded its visit without hearing any official Palestinian testimony.

Another victory for Zionist diplomacy was the campaign it ran at the UN in advance of the November 1947 vote on partition. The accepted foreign diplomatic assessments at the time had concluded that UNSCOP's recommendations would not secure the two-thirds majority needed for approval in the General Assembly. For example, Harold Beeley, adviser to the British foreign secretary, told Jewish Agency delegates that "to obtain a positive result, you will need a two-thirds majority in the General Assembly. You will be able to forge such a majority only if the Soviet and American blocs unite and support the partition resolution—such a union between the blocs has not happened up to now, and *it will never happen.*"[13] Shortly after the discussions actually began, however, the pro-Arab British diplomat realized that he had misjudged the situation, making him feel like "a football fan whose group had lost its home-field advantage."[14] It was not only the occasionally raucous Jews seated in the General Assembly who created this atmosphere but also the American media, press editorials, radio broadcasts, and the overall mood.

This was the reality in which the Jewish Agency's Political Department operated, refusing to accept pessimistic assessments at face value and galvanizing itself for what was undoubtedly the greatest diplomatic endeavor in the history of Zionism: "Several groups and individuals invested all of their moral and public influence in this campaign. This was a do-or-die fight, and it involved emotions, opinions, ambitions, and interests," reflected Eliyahu Elath (Epstein), who headed the Jewish Agency's political bureau in Washington, and was later appointed to serve as Israel's first ambassador to the United States. In his revealing memoirs he described how they [would roam] "around the corridors of the hotels where the various delegations are quartered, knock on doors, submit briefs, arrange press conferences and confuse the minds of Gentiles who are willing and able to help us, and who are surprised to receive appeals which sometimes contradict one another."[15] The Political Department's most high-ranking officials oversaw this campaign. Moshe Sharett (Shertok) headed the delegation of fifteen, each one of whom was responsible for a specific group of states based on background, personal contacts, and linguistic skills. Eliyahu Sasson, for example, handled Yemen, Syria, and Iraq, while Moshe Tov was responsible for Colombia, Ecuador, and Mexico, and Eliyahu Elath (Epstein) conducted relations with the Soviet Union. "No corner was left unexplored and no connection unexploited," concludes Freundlich in his authoritative study on the subject.[16]

Tactics varied. Liberia's hesitation, for example, posed a problem. At the time, the Liberians were unsuccessfully seeking a loan from the United States. Their economy depended entirely on rubber exports. As the debate was nearing its end, the Zionists enlisted Harvey Firestone, president of a large tire company, and former secretary of state Edward Stettinius, who had commercial interests in Liberia, to apply direct and ultimately productive pressure on Monrovia.

This difficult, unrelenting struggle required great political sophistication. When the speeches concluded and it came time for states to cast their votes, on November 26, the agency's delegates realized that they were in dire straits and that only by postponing the vote for one or two days could they hope to prevail. They approached two supportive delegates, Enrique Fabregat of Uruguay and Jorge García-Granados of Guatemala, who agreed to filibuster by giving lengthy speeches, as well as Osvaldo Aranha of Brazil, who was serving as president of the General Assembly. Upon conclusion of the two delegates' speeches, Aranha invited additional speakers who carried on long enough for the vote to be postponed until November 29, 1947—the day on which the UN General Assembly decided by a majority of thirty-three against thirteen, with ten abstentions, to establish a Jewish state in Palestine. In hindsight, we know that this success resulted in part from failed Arab efforts and in part, as in the case of the Soviet Union, from a balance of considerations by voting delegates for whom the Zionist diplomatic efforts had no direct bearing. Nor can we doubt that the Jewish Agency's overall strategy of accepting partition, adopted at the highest political level, played its part. Nonetheless, in more than a few cases, on-the-ground Zionist diplomacy was effective and contributed to the ultimate success, albeit with great effort and by a very slim margin. Freundlich identifies this dynamic and concludes that the success of the Zionists' UN campaign stemmed from two fundamental facts: the Zionists' decision to operate within the framework of UN resolutions and to adapt to them and change them as they saw fit and the fact that the question of Palestine was delinked from the interbloc confrontation that paralyzed the UN at the time.[17] Still, the diplomatic situation did not entirely favor the Zionists. The Afro-Asian group of states proved a disappointment. Of the ten, three abstained, and the rest voted against partition—an unflattering outcome for the Yishuv, which saw itself as part of Asia or as a bridge between Asia and Europe. Disappointment along these lines recurred after 1948 in other circumstances as well.

Another achievement on the part of the Jewish Agency's Executive represented not an objective as such but a positive consequence of its efforts and the partition resolution that linked the Holocaust with the founding of Israel: the designation of the Yishuv as the authoritative representative of the Jewish people as a whole. This proved to be a powerful political weapon that served Israeli diplomats for decades to come.

The political experience garnered by the Jewish Agency during the Mandate era and especially in the prelude to statehood, its failures as well as successes, was very valuable strategically, providing important lessons for the future. It served as an intensive training process for adaptation to a new existential reality, the essence of which was the Yishuv's transition from a unipolar diplomatic order centered on Britain to the complex, global, multipolar international order operating within more than fifty states which it has been since 1948. It would therefore be difficult to overstate the tactical importance and strategic impact of this legacy for the State of Israel in matters of foreign relations.

Furthermore, the Jewish bureaucracy in Mandatory Palestine that dealt with intelligence and foreign policy cultivated valuable human and operational resources, as evidenced by the activities of its members after independence. Five of them went on to become government ministers, three became prominent academics, one became the mayor of Jerusalem, and many others had lengthy careers with the Israeli Foreign Service, Military Intelligence, Mossad, or Shin Bet. For example, Ehud Avriel of HaMossad LeAliyah Bet later served abroad for many years as an Israeli diplomat and ambassador. Aba Gefen, who became a senior Foreign Ministry official and Mossad agent after statehood, was a former refugee appointed to lead the Briha operation in Salzburg. Tamar Eshel became Israel's ambassador to the UN, having gained experience as head of SHAI. Gidon Tadmor joined the Foreign Ministry after his service with the Haganah. Reuven Shiloah, who coordinated intelligence operations with Britain during the Yishuv era, became the first director of the Mossad. Chaim Herzog, head of the security division in the Jewish Agency, became director of Military Intelligence. Mordechai Gichon established the first research division within Military Intelligence after having covertly served in Europe during the late 1940s. Haim Pazner, who headed the Eretz-Israeli office in Geneva during World War II, served as economic attaché in South America after independence. In addition, Teddy Kollek, who had led the Jewish Agency's Department for Special Assignments, later became director general of the Prime Minister's Office.

Israel also benefited from the operational experience in foreign and defense policy that members of the political underground accumulated during the Mandate era. These include Yitzhak Shamir, a foreign minister and prime minister in the 1980s, who had acquired various skills as a member of the underground LEHI (Stern Gang) before 1948. After statehood he commanded an operational unit of the Mossad known as HaMifratz (the Gulf), whose mandate included sophisticated warfare in Arab countries. Thus, we see significant continuity at the individual level between the political, diplomatic, and intelligence world of the Yishuv and Israeli foreign and defense policy during the state's formative years. We also see this continuity reflected in the personal history of twenty-five students of the Jewish Agency's Public Service College (known as the "school for diplomats"), founded in 1946 and headed by Walter Eytan, who became the first director general of the Israeli Foreign Ministry.

At the same time, we should conclude this part of the discussion on a note of caution. Throughout the Mandate era, the Yishuv gained its valuable foreign policy experience primarily through interaction with Britain and Europe generally. For various reasons, the Jewish Agency did not operate as intensively in the United States during this period and hardly operated at all in the Soviet Union. Although the internal Arab world of Palestine and Jordan was quite familiar, the same cannot be said for Africa or, in particular, Asia, where there were very few Jews. Regarding these areas, therefore, the leaders of Israel's Foreign Ministry and intelligence services had to undergo a lengthy educational and training process during the state's formative years, with frequent success and, inevitably, failure. They also had to adapt to the declining importance of Europe as a center of global strategic power after 1945 and, especially, to the unyielding stance of the post-1948 Arab Middle East, which shut the door on Israel.

Regional and Global Geopolitics

The geopolitical world into which Israel was born had a great impact on the state's own development and on the constraints within which it has had to operate. These environmental factors created political barriers and often restricted political maneuverability, but they also generated opportunities. To complete the background picture for our analysis of Israeli foreign policy, it is essential that we list some of these factors.

The State of Israel sits in the heart of the Middle East. When Israel achieved its independence, the region had a number of basic characteristics, some of which remained for years to come. The most significant was its extremely rapid political evolution from an imperial province to a turbulent, unstable internal and external political arena. For Israel, another significant characteristic was the refusal of the Arabs and Muslims, who constituted the region's decisive majority, to accept Israel's existence. Yet during the first half of the twentieth century, what had characterized the region was actually a stability that stemmed from the rule of foreign powers, for which the Middle East had important strategic value for several reasons. First, for centuries it had served as a land bridge between Europe and the Far East. Since the late nineteenth century, after the construction of the Suez Canal, it also provided large-scale maritime access to the East. In addition, the Middle East borders Russia's historical (tsarist as well as Soviet) regions of influence, making it a potential launching pad for military invasion or a buffer zone to prevent such invasion. Finally, the discovery of oil in the Middle East at the beginning of the twentieth century and the rapid development of the local oil industry transformed the region into an economic and strategic focal point. In

1930, the Middle East generated only 3 percent of the gross world product. Two decades later, this figure had risen to 17 percent. Compounding all these factors was the religious importance of the Holy Land and the holy sites in Palestine for the Christian and Muslim worlds. This mix of interests gave rise to centripetal great power pressures on the region toward the end of the nineteenth century. At the time, Ottoman rule curtailed the great powers' ability to pursue their interests in the region. Nonetheless, the seeds of what would eventually become Western colonialism were in place even before the end of World War I and the fall of the Ottoman Empire, as the great powers had succeeded through various means in securing political and economic capitulations (extraterritorial rights) and the British had established an economic presence in the Persian oil production industry. After the war there emerged a number of polities under British-French rule (the "Mandate" system), which largely existed on paper rather than in reality. For nearly three decades, therefore, the Middle East came under relatively stable European colonial rule. This stability began to crumble gradually, however, as the imperial powers weakened, and Jordan, Syria, Lebanon, Israel, and Egypt gained political independence. The decolonization process concluded only in the late 1950s, with Qasim's coup in Iraq and the Sinai Campaign of 1956. Notably, however, decolonization removed the source of regional stability but did not lessen superpower interests in the region. Indeed, because of the internal instability, decolonization actually intensified these interests. Although the Middle East did not undergo overt neocolonialism, it endured a strategic superpower rivalry that has not diminished since the 1950s.

Another source of regional instability was internal. The tensions within the Arab Middle East were extremely destabilizing. For example, as responsibility shifted from colonial rules to local elites, the conflicting approaches of the latter came to the fore. Local leaders (especially the Hashemites in Iraq and Jordan) tended to think in terms of regional unity. The Hashemites wanted to change the status quo: rather than a political division of the Middle East into separate states, they sought to unite all under one rule. During the 1920s and 1930s, the struggle over the region's image intensified: Would it be a united monarchy or a group of individual sovereign states? The competing approach (primarily that of the Saudis, Egyptians, and Syrians) sought to support the existing order, which felt threatened by the Hashemites. In addition, since the early twentieth century there has been a constant tension in the Middle East between the transnational, pan-Islamic, and pan-Arab perspective and Western concepts of the nation-state. This tension is still evident today, as recently exemplified by the "Arab Spring."

The historical confrontation between Sunnis and Shiites also created internal schisms within Arab states such as Syria and intensified interstate conflict. Yet another source of instability was the conflict in Palestine. The question of Palestine came to be seen as a yoke around the neck of the Arab world, a material as well as symbolic struggle. Moreover, the struggle between rulers and political elites over regional supremacy and hegemony exploited the question of Palestine, an issue perceived as affecting all the region's population groups. Each side sought to enhance its own prestige and thus outdo its rivals and opponents. The question of Palestine embodied the struggle against foreign presence and colonialism, as well as a religious element in the form of Jerusalem, where Islam's holy places were under threat. This religious element proved a convenient vehicle for enlisting regional support and legitimizing calls to action. Because regional relations were competitive from the outset, characterized by struggles over leadership, prestige, values, and polity, the crosscutting call to support the struggle for Palestine became an inseparable part of the agenda for rulers and society in general. This was a two-way process. It was not only the leaders who were interested in advancing discourse and public debate over the issue; there was also bottom-up interest from society. The cumulative effect was the introduction of another source of instability.

Interstate disputes over the borders delineated during the colonial era and decolonization process further exacerbated the situation. Salient examples are the borders between Syria and Turkey and between Iraq and Turkey. In addition, all the Middle Eastern Arab states had difficulty achieving true independence from the outset because of economic hardship. As developing countries, many of these states were under constant internal pressure in this regard and, despite popular rhetoric, depended in some way on foreign aid. In some Arab states, domestic political pressures had been threatening to boil over since the end of World War II. They therefore sought to maintain stability through authoritarian, antidemocratic, and largely secular regimes. The various implications of this highly complex geopolitical reality are starkly evident in post-1948 Israeli diplomacy.

Finally, one should not lose sight of the material effect that the global scene had on Israel's foreign policy. The State of Israel emerged during one of the first critical junctures of the Cold War, in the same year that the Marshall Plan commenced and only a few months after the Truman Doctrine was announced. The Cold War had far-reaching repercussions for the Yishuv's foreign policy, mainly because the interbloc conflict over the future of the Middle East intensified greatly in the years after World War II. The British and French withdrawal left a new, unfamiliar geostrategic vacuum. The Soviets, extremely concerned that a new form of Western imperialism under US leadership would take hold, demanded full participation in determining superpower policy for the region. The dilemma facing the West was not simple: on the one hand, it still had strategic and economic interests in the region, but on the other, the United States refused to fill the military vacuum left by the British. The Cold War context had a clear impact on UN debates and the resolutions it adopted during this time. The most explicit expression of the Cold

War's regional influence was the surprising Soviet vote of support for UNSCOP's partition plan, but this influence also manifested in Anglo-American strategic planning for the region. In this context the region's states came under intense superpower pressure to choose a side, with neutrality seen as suspicious and unacceptable at least by the United States and its allies. The two major Cold War rivals' concurrence on the establishment of Israel was therefore strikingly exceptional. This was the complex world within which Israel now had to navigate.

Past and Future

On the final day of the British Mandate, Ben-Gurion appeared before the People's Council to present Israel's Declaration of Independence. The document embodies many layers of the historical mound bequeathed by the Zionist movement and the Yishuv, including the major foreign policy developments discussed above:

> Eretz-Israel [the Land of Israel] was the birthplace of the Jewish people. Here their spiritual, religious and political identity was shaped. Here they first attained to statehood, created cultural values of national and universal significance and gave to the world the eternal Book of Books.
>
> After being forcibly exiled from their land, the people kept faith with it throughout their Dispersion and never ceased to pray and hope for their return to it and for the restoration in it of their political freedom.
>
> Impelled by this historic and traditional attachment, Jews strove in every successive generation to re-establish themselves in their ancient homeland. In recent decades they returned in their masses. Pioneers, *ma'pilim* [immigrants coming to Eretz-Israel in defiance of restrictive legislation] and defenders, they made deserts bloom, revived the Hebrew language, built villages and towns, and created a thriving community controlling its own economy and culture, loving peace but knowing how to defend itself, bringing the blessings of progress to all the country's inhabitants, and aspiring towards independent nationhood.
>
> In the year 5657 (1897), at the summons of the spiritual father of the Jewish State, Theodore Herzl, the First Zionist Congress convened and proclaimed the right of the Jewish people to national rebirth in its own country.
>
> This right was recognized in the Balfour Declaration of the 2nd November, 1917, and re-affirmed in the Mandate of the League of Nations which, in particular, gave international sanction to the historic connection between the Jewish people and Eretz-Israel and to the right of the Jewish people to rebuild its National Home.
>
> The catastrophe which recently befell the Jewish people—the massacre of millions of Jews in Europe—was another clear demonstration of the urgency of solving the problem of its homelessness by re-establishing in Eretz-Israel the Jewish State, which would open the gates of the homeland wide to every Jew and confer upon the Jewish people the status of a fully privileged member of the comity of nations.

Survivors of the Nazi holocaust in Europe, as well as Jews from other parts of the world, continued to migrate to Eretz-Israel, undaunted by difficulties, restrictions and dangers, and never ceased to assert their right to a life of dignity, freedom and honest toil in their national homeland.

In the Second World War, the Jewish community of this country contributed its full share to the struggle of the freedom- and peace-loving nations against the forces of Nazi wickedness and, by the blood of its soldiers and its war effort, gained the right to be reckoned among the peoples who founded the United Nations.

On the 29th November, 1947, the United Nations General Assembly passed a resolution calling for the establishment of a Jewish State in Eretz-Israel; the General Assembly required the inhabitants of Eretz-Israel to take such steps as were necessary on their part for the implementation of that resolution. This recognition by the United Nations of the right of the Jewish people to establish their State is irrevocable.

This right is the natural right of the Jewish people to be masters of their own fate, like all other nations, in their own sovereign State.[18]

The second part of the Declaration presented the vision for the future state:

THE STATE OF ISRAEL will be open for Jewish immigration and for the Ingathering of the Exiles; it will foster the development of the country for the benefit of all its inhabitants; it will be based on freedom, justice and peace as envisaged by the prophets of Israel; it will ensure complete equality of social and political rights to all its inhabitants irrespective of religion, race or sex; it will guarantee freedom of religion, conscience, language, education and culture; it will safeguard the Holy Places of all religions; and it will be faithful to the principles of the Charter of the United Nations.

THE STATE OF ISRAEL is prepared to cooperate with the agencies and representatives of the United Nations in implementing the resolution of the General Assembly of the 29th November, 1947, and will take steps to bring about the economic union of the whole of Eretz-Israel.

WE APPEAL to the United Nations to assist the Jewish people in the building-up of its State and to receive the State of Israel into the comity of nations.

WE APPEAL—in the very midst of the onslaught launched against us now for months—to the Arab inhabitants of the State of Israel to preserve peace and participate in the upbuilding of the State on the basis of full and equal citizenship and due representation in all its provisional and permanent institutions.

WE EXTEND our hand to all neighboring states and their peoples in an offer of peace and good neighborliness, and appeal to them to establish bonds of cooperation and mutual help with the sovereign Jewish people settled in its own land. The State of Israel is prepared to do its share in a common effort for the advancement of the entire Middle East.

WE APPEAL to the Jewish people throughout the Diaspora to rally round the Jews of Eretz-Israel in the tasks of immigration and upbuilding and to stand by them in the great struggle for the realization of the age-old dream—the redemption of Israel.[19]

Did Israeli foreign policy help translate these and other expectations into the language of action during the seven decades that have passed since the spring of 1948? If so, how? To address this question, we must first analyze the repercussions of the year and a half that followed Israel's proclamation of independence, when circumstances compelled it to engage in a war that presented existential questions as well as operational objectives and shaped future strategic thinking. This critical period is the subject of the next chapter.

Notes

1. Moshe Lissak and Dan Horowitz, *MeYishuv LeMedina* [From Yishuv to state] (Tel Aviv, Am Oved, 1977).

2. Jonathan Fine, *Kakh Nolda: Hakamat Ma'arekhet HaMimshal BeIsrael, 1947–1951* [The establishment of the Israeli governmental system, 1947–1951] (Jerusalem, Carmel, 2009).

3. Yoav Gelber, *Shorshei HaKhavazelet: HaModiin BaYeshuv 1918–1947* [Growing a Fleur-de-Lis: The intelligence services of the Jewish Yishuv in Palestine 1918–1947 (Tel Aviv, Ministry for Defence, 1992).

4. Clive Jones, "Influence without Power? Britain, the Jewish Agency and Intelligence Collaboration, 1939–45," in *Israel's Clandestine Diplomacies*, ed. Clive Jones and Tore T. Peterson (London, Hurst, 2013): 49–66.

5. Asa Lefen, *SHAI: Kehilat HaModi'in HaIsraelit* [The roots of the Israeli intelligence community] (Tel Aviv, Ministry for Defence, 1997).

6. See Yoav Gelber, "HaModi'in VeHa'arakhato Erev Milkhemet HaAtzma'ut" [Intelligence assessments toward the War of Independence], *Iyunim Bitkumat Israel* 1 (1991): 61–102.

7. Ze'ev Hadari, *Refugees Achieve Victory*.

8. Dan Michman, "MeShoah LeTkuma! MeShoah LeTkuma? Historiographia shel HaKesher HaSimati ben HaShoah LeHakamat Medinat Israel—Ben Mitus LeMetziut" [The causal connection between the Holocaust and the birth of Israel: Historiography between myth and reality], *Iyunim Bitkumat Israel* 10 (2000): 234–57. See also Evyatar Friesel, "On the Myth of the Connection between the Holocaust and the Creation of Israel," *Israel Affairs* 14, no. 3 (2008): 446–66.

9. Unofficial translation. Published under the pen name Gabi Daniel in the anthology *Agra*, vol. 2 (Jerusalem, 1985–1986), 199–200, quoted in Dina Porat, "Ben-Gurion VeShoat Yehudei Eropa" [Ben-Gurion and the Holocaust of European Jews], *HaTzionut* 12 (1987): 293.

10. Yehoshua Freundlich, "HaShoah, Medinot HaOlam VeShe'elat Eretz-Israel" [The Holocaust, the world's countries, and the question of Eretz Israel], *Massuah* 25 (1997): 45.

11. Ibid., 40.

12. Anglo-American Committee of Inquiry, *Report to the United States Government and His Majesty's Government in the United Kingdom* (Lausanne, 1946), http://avalon.law.yale.edu /subject_menus/angtoc.asp.

13. Quoted in Ofer Aderet, "As Palestinians Lobby UN for Statehood, Forget Not the Zionists, 1947 Maneuver," *Haaretz*, September 25, 2011. See also Shlomo Avineri, "Prague 1744—Lake Success 1947: Statecraft without a State," *Jewish Studies at the CEU* 4 (2004–2005): 7–25.

14. Freundlich, "HaShoah."

15. Aderet, "As Palestinians Lobby."

16. Yehoshua Freundlich, *MeHurban LiTkuma* [From destruction to resurrection] (Jerusalem, Academic Publications, 1994), 171.

17. Ibid.

18. The Declaration of the Establishment of the State of Israel, May 14, 1948, official English translation, Israel Knesset, https://www.knesset.gov.il/docs/eng/megilat_eng.htm.

19. Ibid.

4   The War of Independence

The Experience of Battle

The State of Israel emerged from the storm of a war that turned out to be the longest in its history, during which it had to engage in a fierce and bloody struggle while overseeing a complex, turbulent political system. The artillery of the IDF worked in combination with the top hats and tuxedos of Foreign Ministry personnel to help bring about the end of Israel's first military conflict with the Arab states. The confrontation itself began immediately after the General Assembly passed a resolution on November 29, 1947, adopting UNSCOP's recommendations on a partition plan for Palestine. On December 5, 1947, upon conclusion of the three-day strike declared by the Arab Higher Committee in response to this resolution, Eliyahu Sasson, the head of the Arab Division in the Jewish Agency's Political Department, issued a fervent appeal for peace to the secretary-general of the Arab League. The appeal went unanswered, thereby refuting the assumption of many Zionist politicians and diplomats, foremost among them Chaim Weizmann, that the UN resolution would facilitate an agreement with the Arabs. Instead, the Arab states immediately embarked on a path that would lead to war. Although their perspectives varied, until May 1948 they were united in their clear, albeit not always public or explicit, intent of thwarting international discussion regarding the establishment of a Jewish state. After that time, their concerted effort shifted to "killing the infant as it enters the world," in the words of Benny Morris.[1]

Israel's objective was equally clear—to survive and implement the UN resolution, with the declared goal of establishing a sovereign, independent state. The political victory that Israel achieved as a result of its military success was as unequivocal as the Arab defeat was striking. Nor did Israel fail to recognize what it had *not* achieved: Arab acceptance of Israel's existence and the acquiescence of most UN members to the boundaries determined by the war in July 1949. Broadly speaking, the military and political confrontation, its successes as well as its failures, was an experience whose importance for Israel's military-political leadership cannot be overstated. The war was primarily a multidimensional event the likes of which the Yishuv had never known. It was an unprecedented, all-encompassing, existential military confrontation with the Arabs of Palestine and the Arab states. The nineteen months (beginning in December 1947) of war fighting that gripped the entire Yishuv, taking an extremely heavy human and economic toll, would in themselves carve this event into collective memory. Beyond that, the end of the war gave rise to a long list of political, military, and diplomatic questions that inevitably blunted the victory.

This experience and the postwar geopolitical reality were among the most important factors in shaping the state's foreign policy and conduct for decades to come. Only the Six-Day War had a greater impact. This chapter therefore explores the lasting legacy of the War of Independence for Israeli foreign policy.

Our analysis centers on Ben-Gurion. He was essentially the sole decision maker when it came to the conduct and objectives of the war, for three reasons. First, he held seniority in the Zionist leadership, a status he had achieved over the course of decades by solidifying his role as leader in the political sphere, serving first as secretary of the Histadrut and later as chair of the Jewish Agency's Executive. Second, Ben-Gurion actively assumed the post of minister of defense during a very intense period. Third, Ben-Gurion had helped prepare the Haganah for the challenges of the anticipated war, a process that granted him definitive and unequivocal standing as the final authority on matters of security. Eliyahu Golomb, the "uncrowned" leader of the Haganah, had died before the war, making Ben-Gurion the natural choice to fill his shoes. Ben-Gurion further secured his status by expelling individuals and entities that might undermine or challenge his seniority and authority on matters of security. He came to be personally identified with the security portfolio, to the extent that none of the Yishuv's leaders dared dispute his status even when it became evident that he had seized exclusive control. Another factor was that Ben-Gurion's decisions did not deviate significantly from the consensus of the Yishuv. His status was evident, as well, in his relations with military leaders. Although he frequently consulted with IDF leaders, the nature of their relations was clear: Ben-Gurion was the decision maker. The military commanders almost unquestioningly accepted his position as ultimate leader of the war effort, obeying his wishes and orders even when their own opinions differed. Consequently, according to David Tal, the prime minister had nearly exclusive decision-making power over the key aspects of the war: its strategy, its conduct, the timing and locations of renewed fighting, and ultimately, the manner in which the war would conclude.[2] Moreover, few would dispute the claim that the critical influence of the "old man," as he was already known at the time (age sixty-two), continued long after the war.

The war inevitably and predictably had implications for the strategic military sphere. Israel's major defeat of Palestine's Arabs and the Arab states' armed forces taught its leaders that under certain circumstances war could be a very effective means of countering Arab threats. Furthermore, this was the first time the Yishuv faced what it saw as an armed confrontation with the entire Arab world. And it had prevailed. Ben-Gurion gave vivid expression to this viewpoint, referencing biblical events in his speech before the provisional state council in the summer of 1948: "On more than one occasion we have encountered the Egyptians, Ashur [Assyria], Babylon, Aram [Syria], and Tyre and Sidon [Lebanon]. But we never encountered all of them at once. . . . This is the first time all these nations have joined forces to fight us, [such that] our young army had to face all the nations of the Middle East and their armies. Throughout our entire history of 3,500 years, such a thing has never happened." The outcome of this confrontation, according to him, was that "Arab armies no longer doubt the force of the Israeli army . . . which defeated the kings of Lod and Ramle, the kings of [the Arab villages] Nabala and Dir Tarif, the kings of Qula and kings of Sadiq, the kings of Sora'a and Eshtaol, the kings of Artuf and Ein Kerem in the plains, and the kings of Hatta and Hartiya in the south, the kings of Shefar'am and Sepphoris, the kings of Ein Mahal and Kafr Kanna, Nazareth and Nimrin, the kings of Lubya and Hittin in the Galilee."[3]

Consequently, the aversion to such military confrontation, which for moral and operational reasons had dominated toward the end of the Mandate era, undoubtedly declined. Various factors prevented the young state from becoming militaristic (in the sense of warmongering). Yet in light of its overwhelming success, its leaders deemed it necessary to adopt an approach that invariably reduced—but was far from eliminating—the distance between war and peace.

Various factors contributed to this shift. First, the public postwar euphoria did not cloud Ben-Gurion's judgment or his understanding of the unique circumstances that made victory possible. As time passed, he viewed the events of 1948 more critically, for he believed that history does not repeat itself. Even at the height of battlefield success, Ben-Gurion voiced the opinion to senior command officials that victory resulted not from IDF "miracles" but from the Arabs' military disintegration, adding, "Will this weakness necessarily persist?"[4] Moreover, November 1947 to May 1948 was effectively a grace period for the Yishuv, during which the British Mandate was still in force and there was no fear of invasion by Arab states. This allowed the Jewish forces to focus on the local Palestinian-Arab struggle and score significant victories.

The Israeli leadership learned only after the fact that one of the reasons for the Arab defeat was a rift that developed within the Arab coalition and contributed to Jordan's withdrawal during a decisive phase of the war. Although Ben-Gurion viewed this as a singular event, it was dramatic in operational terms: at crucial turning points, in key battles and operations, the Arabs' numerical advantage did not translate into battlefield victory. Israel was able, for example, to concentrate its forces on the Egyptian front and secure important gains, although that was almost the only case of an offensive Jewish victory over regular Arab forces during the war. Thus, although Israel was able to defeat the Palestinian and semiregular forces early and decisively, its confrontation with the enlisted regular Arab forces was more complex, as David Tal has demonstrated.[5]

The IDF successfully thwarted two attempted military invasions (Syria and Iraq) and did not initially respond to a third (Egypt). A fourth army (Jordan) crossed into the territory of Palestine but did not invade the state's boundaries as defined by the UN partition resolution; therefore, Israel did not counter its advances. A fifth state (Lebanon) did not participate in the invasion. These opening events lasted only a few days, after which Israel counterattacked, concentrating its forces on four militaries: Egyptian, Jordanian, Iraqi, and Syrian. All the attacks failed. Ben-Gurion might have been unaware, at the time, of many details that historians uncovered years later, but there can be no doubt that toward the end of the war he became acutely aware of the war's toll and failures. In contrast to his public pronouncements, therefore, behind closed doors he frequently criticized the army's wartime conduct. In July 1956, for example, he reminded Moshe Dayan that despite Israel's great advantage early in the war, "we did not take Fallujah" with its concentration of Egyptian forces that Israel later had to confront.[6] Ben-Gurion himself retrospectively attributed Israel's success less to the IDF's ability than to disintegration among the Arab forces. For this reason, he also feared the rise of any Arab leader who could unite the Arab world against Israel, in particular Nasir and his call for a united pan-Arab front.

Whether or not they accepted Ben-Gurion's view, Israel's leaders were well aware of the war's toll. That strongly dissuaded the prime minister and most of his associates from openly and frequently elaborating on the human toll of this war, which has been poetically portrayed as the "silver plate" on which the state was served to the nation.[7] Four thousand fighters, mostly young men, fell in battle. The total number of casualties, including those moderately or severely injured, reached sixteen thousand—that is, nearly one-third of all the armed forces. Two thousand civilians were killed in the fighting as well. The total number of dead reached 1 percent of the Jewish population at the time. For the sake of comparison, the equivalent would be three million American soldiers today—more than three times the total number of US casualties in World War II. This loss in combination of a strong public consciousness, as reflected in the close sequencing of memorial day commemorations and independence day celebrations, necessarily generated aversion to and fear of a war like that of 1948.

The Hebrew word *damim* (plural of "blood") has a twofold meaning: in ancient rabbinic texts, it referred to money as well. And indeed, the war took a monumental economic toll. By late March 1949, for example, security personnel still numbered 320,000, accounting for no less than 30 percent of the total labor force. A comparative study by Haim Barkai conveys the relative burden of military service and its impact on the Jewish labor force in 1948.[8] If American and British forces during World War II had accounted for the same proportion of their respective populations as Israel's enlisted personnel in late 1948, the United States would have needed 20 million conscripts, and Britain would have had to draft 6 million of its 50 million citizens. But their enlistments peaked at 12.5 million and 2.2 million, respectively. Moreover, the total direct cost of Israel's sixteen-month-long struggle for independence amounted to at least 44 percent of the GNP for 1948—a staggering economic toll. Ben-Gurion voiced deep concern over this situation in November 1948 at a defense ministry meeting, speaking with poetic precision and understatement: "There are no workers to harvest the crops or operate the civil industry."[9]

Nor did this blow to production capacity reflect the total direct cost of the war, which also included foreign arms purchases and the costs of production by Israel's small but already existent arms industry. These are estimated at $75 million, the equivalent of about $500 million in current US dollars. Despite concerns among Israeli leaders, however, the economic toll of the war did not cripple the state. The reasons are beyond the scope of this discussion, but two factors are worth noting: the financial backing of Jews, especially in the United States, who directly financed many purchases, and the double-digit inflation that placed the postwar economic burden on the citizens. In any event, the cumulative cost of this prolonged, all-out war made it imperative, in the view of Ben-Gurion as well as others, to develop an approach aimed at the prevention of such a catastrophic event in the future.

This understanding was an important element of the basic orientation that took shape among Israel's leaders after the war: a concerted focus on building the state and an acceptance of the territorial status quo. That was the stated position, an appropriate one for the new state under the circumstances. As Mordechai Bar-On frames it, the state had just suffered a brutal war resulting in massive casualties, a war "in which it managed to capture a territorial base that greatly exceeded what the UN allocated in its partition resolution. Most of this territory was cleared of its longtime residents and available for settlement by the hundreds of thousands of immigrants whom [the state] sought to absorb." Most importantly, the state had "defeated its enemies and established a military that can now deter its neighbors from dictating events by force."[10] Although, as Zaki Shalom has described, a small group of politicians, military leaders, and oppositionists did entertain the notion of a "second round" launched by Israel, their voices were not decisive during the first half decade of statehood.[11]

The actual decision maker saw things differently. Despite his natural inclination to exploit historical opportunities, the prime minster declared as early as December 1948 that there was "too much drunkenness and victory" and that "aliyah requires armistice."[12] He presented his stance more concretely at a high-ranking consultation in April 1949, where he stated,

> As to the borders—that is an endless issue. The Bible has many different versions of the state's borders, as does our history. . . . No border is absolute. If

the border is a desert, it can also be the other side of the desert. If it is a sea, it can be the other side of the sea. . . . If paths to other planets are built, the earth might never end. . . . Perhaps we could capture the Triangle, the Golan, the entire Galilee, but these conquests would not enhance our security in a way that could improve our capacity for immigrant absorption.[13]

Lessons and Repercussions

Although averse to Israel launching a "second round," Ben-Gurion did not view the postwar situation as permanent. Since long before 1948, he and most of his associates had viewed Arab hostility to Zionism and the State of Israel as practically an existential fact. Arab attempts to annihilate the state while still in its infancy, as well as political events near and shortly after the end of the war, only reinforced this sense of fatalism. The armistice agreement accepted by warring Arab states did not transform into the peace treaty that some Israeli and American leaders had hoped to see. Although its preamble mentions the parties' hope that the agreement would lead to a peace treaty, it soon became evident that signatory Arab states were under mounting pressure by the opposition and radical movements at home to prepare for a second round and refrain from any measures that might imply recognition of the Jewish state. The position that emerged was one of animosity alongside avoidance of war. The animosity took not only a rhetorical or ideological form; it also embodied elements of war. In particular, the Arab states collectively—through the Arab League, which served as a collective forum for policy making regarding Israel—ran a wide-ranging campaign that included economic boycott, a maritime embargo on the State of Israel to the extent possible (Tiran Straits and Aqaba), a prohibition against ships carrying cargo to Israel through the Suez Canal, and assistance for guerilla operations originating in Arab countries. Today we know that the Arab states did not want to be consistently engaged in war with Israel, but what Ben-Gurion saw in his day was continuous Arab support for guerilla activities against Israel. In addition, Arab anti-Israel rhetoric continued and even escalated, despite internal disintegration and the Arabs' inability to relaunch an offensive against Israel.

"Why should the Arabs make peace?" Ben-Gurion asked Nahum Goldmann during a heart-to-heart conversation a few years after independence. He explained,

I don't understand your optimism. Why should the Arabs make peace? If I was an Arab leader I would never make terms with Israel. That is natural: we have taken their country. Sure God promised it to us, but what does that matter to them? Our God is not theirs. We come from Israel, but two thousand years ago, and what is that to them? There has been antisemitism, the Nazis, Hitler, Auschwitz, but was that their fault? They only see one thing: we have come here and stolen their country. Why should they accept that? They may perhaps forget in one or two generations' time, but for the moment there is no chance. So, it's simple: we have to stay strong and maintain a powerful army. Our whole policy is there. Otherwise the Arabs will wipe us out.[14]

The prevailing assumption in Israel was that the Arab world would not accept Israel in the near future and would seek any opportunity for a second chance to annihilate it. In operational terms, this meant that Israel had to formulate a strategy that anticipated and prepared the country for the worst-case scenario— a renewed all-out war launched by all Arab states against Israel, like the war of May 1948. Although as historians well know, the Arab war effort was not all-inclusive and the Arab war front had major internal rifts, realistic operational planning had to take into account the possibility of a renewed all-out war against Israel. "The worst case" therefore became the guiding principle of discussions among cabinet members, Foreign Ministry officials, and the senior military staff. The perception of such a threat had military as well as political repercussions. Ben-Gurion personally was convinced that "even if most or all Arab states made peace and pledged friendship, we would still have to guard against the dangerous illusion that peace guarantees security."[15]

This perspective embodies one of the fundamental precepts of Israel's security doctrine, stemming from its experience of the 1948 war: the Arabs can always hope to end the conflict by destroying Israel, and battlefield losses cannot threaten their existence, whereas for Israel a single defeat could put a permanent halt to the Zionist enterprise in the Land of Israel. "Our downfall," Ben-Gurion later explained to Chief-of-Staff Moshe Dayan in one of their private chats, "is that we cannot lose. They can lose once, twice; we can defeat Egypt ten times—and it means nothing. They defeat us once—and it's over."[16]

These basic precepts developed in 1948 and are still evident among Israeli leaders today. Israel's concept of national security, which took shape toward the end of the War of Independence, embodied two basic and interrelated assumptions. The first was that Israel has no choice but to view the Arab-Israeli conflict as a given fact, regardless of the likelihood of a resolution in the foreseeable future. The second assumption was that under these circumstances Israel must give priority to addressing the narrow security margins it has because of its quantitative demographic disadvantage and lack of territorial depth. The strategy that emerged from these assumptions reflects an approach to security based on the avoidance of risk and the analytical use of worst-case scenarios as a guiding principle. The question for our purposes is, What were the foreign policy implications arising from Israel's security doctrine? First, of course, security considerations had to take priority over all others at all time. Second, for reasons to be explored, Israel had to refrain from launching a war and prevent the state from being dragged into a protracted war that could undermine the state, as happened during the final quarter of 1948. That experience had, at the time, played a key part in the strategic decision to end the war. Defense, on the one hand, and military power, on the other, were thus intertwined with economic and social fortification. One means by which this strategy was to be implemented was by structuring the IDF around the reserves service—that is, maintaining small, effective armed forces that can provide defense until it becomes necessary to call up reserves and take the battle to the enemy. Emerging in the shadow of its War of Independence, accordingly, Israel's security doctrine focused on the principle of defense as a first step, then on taking the fight to enemy ground as the next recourse, and then on bringing the war to a decisive end. This doctrine reflected economic considerations: if the initial threat was not a surprise attack but a threat of force, such as enemy deployment for offensive action along Israel's borders, the state would still have time to mobilize reserve forces, but it would lack the military might of a large, regular force maintained over time at the expense of the labor force. For this reason, among others, in the early 1950s the strategy was revised to offensive-defensive. That is, to defend itself against a clear danger, Israel would immediately attack and take the battle to enemy territory. Ben-Gurion authorized this doctrine, which had far-reaching implications for Israel's foreign and defense policy. After 1948, high-ranking security officials and senior ministers in Israel knew of these doctrines generally, and they were not the only ones. Although the Foreign Ministry tended not to discuss security affairs, most of its diplomats were well aware of what the army intended to do should they fail in their mission and Israel find itself at war.

The new strategy required regular forces that could be mobilized immediately, in addition to reserve forces. The military therefore needed weapons that Israel did not produce, as well as massive investment and diplomatic and other efforts to secure transport. Thus, the evolution of Israeli foreign policy, from the outset of the war and during its aftermath, imposed on its architects an existential mission. By May 1948, they had been put to the test on more than one occasion in this regard. Ben-Gurion personally added a new, revolutionary dimension to their mission. The strategic balance of power between Israel and its neighbors, on the one hand, and the expected price of another all-out war, on the other, compelled Ben-Gurion to pursue another means of protecting Israel's security—deterrence. As soon as the war ended, he sought to further enhance Israel's deterrence capacity by developing a nuclear capability. Despite the many studies devoted to this issue, one is hard-pressed to locate archival records of what Ben-Gurion was actually thinking when he took this formal strategic decision in 1949. He neither spoke of his thoughts nor wrote explicitly about them, and to this day, the topic is a matter of draconian secrecy in Israel.

Nonetheless, bits of information have combined over the years to reinforce arguments such as those presented in detail by Avner Cohen and Shlomo

Aronson.[17] Three factors drove Ben-Gurion to take this revolutionary step. The first was the tragic extermination of most European Jewry, the second was the near tragedy of early to mid-1948 when Israel's fate hung in the balance, and third was the need to counter the vast numerical imbalance, which would persist after the war. Two authoritative, albeit retrospective, statements by Ben-Gurion provide a rare insight into his thoughts on this matter toward the end of the War of Independence. Facing intense US pressure to abort Israel's nuclear program, the "old man" sent a personal letter to John F. Kennedy (his junior by thirty years) in May 1963, explaining,

> I know that it is difficult for civilized people to visualize such a thing—even after they have witnessed what happened to us during the Second World War. I do not assume that it could happen today or tomorrow. I am not so young anymore, and it may not happen in my lifetime. However, I cannot dismiss the possibility that this may occur if the situation in the Middle East remains as it is and the Arab leaders continue to insist on and pursue their policy of belligerency against Israel. . . . As a Jew, I know the history of my people and carry with me the memories of all it has endured . . . and the efforts it has cost to accomplish what has been achieved in this country in recent generations. . . . Mr. President, my people have the right to exist, both in Israel and wherever they may live, and *this existence is in danger.*[18]

A month after the letter was sent and a few days after he retired, Ben-Gurion shared his inner thoughts with staff at RAFAEL (Israel's national R&D defense laboratory at the time), who were involved in the development of nuclear weapons. Apparently, he believed, mistakenly, that his remarks would not become public. Ben-Gurion reiterated a theme from his earlier letter to Kennedy, asserting, "We have major security concerns, unlike those of any other people. I know of no nation in the world whose neighbors have declared that they want to destroy it. Moreover, they not only declare it, but also intend to do it by any means available to them. [Therefore] we [need] all possible means of defense. . . . If we are forced to fight, we will fight." However, added the former prime minister,

> That is not the real aim of our approach to defense. We would relinquish victory if it meant relinquishing war. Our goal is to prevent war. . . . In addition, we can ensure our safety and prevent war only if our enemies know that we have effective weapons, [which] can deter them. . . . I am sure, not only based on what I have heard today, that our science can give us the weapons we need to deter our enemies from war. What I heard today increases my faith in the ability, will, and dedication of our scientists, to provide us with weapons that are in effect weapons of peace.[19]

Ben-Gurion began to pursue his revolutionary and seemingly unrealistic decision even before the Soviets had conducted their first nuclear test. At the time, the state was facing economic hardship and had none of the scientific infrastructure, in human or technological terms, for nuclear R&D. Moreover, the United States, and later the Soviet Union, guarded their nuclear monopoly well, making it difficult to acquire the necessary skills and material abroad. The only plausible explanation for Ben-Gurion's willingness to dive into this issue and invest no small amount in R&D lies in his existential fears. The science corps and its activities are one outcome of those massive investments, which also funded searches for various types of lead in the Negev, overseas education and training in nuclear science and technology, and the establishment of a small core of skilled personnel to advance the issue scientifically, politically, operationally, and economically. As we know, Israel followed a bumpy road in developing its nuclear capability, which came to fruition shortly before the Six-Day War. The topic has been one of the state's best-kept secrets to this day, touching on both diplomacy and security. The whole saga, we must bear in mind, has its origins in the events and lessons of the Holocaust and the War of Independence as Ben-Gurion experienced them.

The prime minister was among the most prominent who drew far-reaching conclusions from this war with respect to immigration. He believed that only by opening the gates of the country to nonselective immigration could the state attain the social, economic, and, above all, military infrastructure needed to fortify itself and to establish a meaningful reserve force. Ben-Gurion expressed this opinion at the start of the fighting, when he recommended the immigration of 1.5 million Jews, arguing that the state would be viable only if its Jewish population reached 2 million within a decade. The war in itself improved the domestic demographic situation. The UN partition plan would have permitted some 450,000 Jews and 300,000 Arabs in Palestine. After the war and conclusion of armistice agreements, however, there were about 600,000 Jews and 100,000 Arabs within the jurisdiction of Israel—a consequence of aliyah and Briha operations as well as the expulsion of Palestinians. Ben-Gurion offered a concise formulation of his approach at the concluding ceremony of an officers' training course on May 15, 1949, when he asserted,

> The main source of security is aliyah. Aliyah represents not only the Jewish commandment to save Jews, that is, *kibbutz galuyot* (the ingathering of exiles). Aliyah is a vital need of the Jews of this Land and a condition for its existence and the security of our state. Without aliyah this state is doomed to become extinct. Seven hundred thousand Jews cannot exist in a sea of Arabs, even though this year these Jews stood up to six Arab militaries. The special circumstances of this year will not necessarily repeat themselves, and in the course of time will be impossible to recreate. The highest priority for Israel's security is mass aliyah, at a rapid pace, on a large and expanding scale. The promotion of aliyah is a war effort that we are commanded [to carry out] in times of peace as well as times of war. Nothing is more urgent or important.[20]

A year later, at a conference in Ein Harod, Ben-Gurion declared that it would not be possible to make the IDF stronger without fulfilling the prime objective of *kibbutz galuyot*. His starting point was that Israel's ability to withstand a ratio of 1:40, as it had in 1948, had been fully exploited, and in the future, the state would not be able to exist without mass aliyah. Therefore, he stressed, "the state is not the goal of Zionism; the [ultimate] goal is continuous Jewish aliyah."[21] It is not surprising to learn that Ben-Gurion regularly opened the weekly Ministry of Defense meetings by citing the latest immigration figures or that upon returning from overseas, government ministers had to report to the Cabinet on aliyah from any country they visited. Above all, we can understand why so much political energy was invested in this issue. The efforts indeed bore fruit, and within the first two years of statehood, more than 520,000 new immigrants arrived in Israel, nearly doubling the population. The repercussions for foreign policy were that the entire foreign policy apparatus was enlisted in a large-scale, continuous effort to promote aliyah for years to come.

Closely linked to the concept of immigration as a central component of security was the view of settlement as its complement. In this case, however, the Israeli leadership refused to internalize the lessons of the War of Independence. It did not realize, for example, that settlement of the land has no security function. Indeed, it turned out that settlements could obstruct the conduct of war, but no conclusions were drawn, and the traditional Zionist concept of spatial defense and construction of settlements along borders continued to prevail. Settlement construction was intended to serve several purposes. First, civilian settlements were expected to defend the territories that the armed forces would presumably be unable to protect. Second, Ben-Gurion was deeply concerned about the large population centers in the country's Central District, which were vulnerable to bombing, and he therefore sought to disperse them. Third, the government considered it important in terms of security and demography to promote the ownership in practice over lands vacated by Arabs and therefore saw it as vital to settle these lands, often on the site of a former Arab village to prevent the return of the original, now refugee, residents.

No less important was the need for Israel to develop independent means of agricultural production, having lost a major portion of its food supply when the Arabs fled. In addition, the government of Israel had to tend to the housing, food, employment, and other basic needs of hundreds of thousands of immigrants. Abandoned Arab properties helped meet this demand by offering a relatively immediate solution in some cases. In any event, this network of frontier settlements inevitably had foreign policy implications, given the international pressure on Israel to withdraw from lands it had occupied beyond the borders of the UN partition plan.

The domestic fortification that Ben-Gurion considered so important required physical as well as human resources. As with aliyah, Israel's borders at the end of the war posed a problem: the state lacked key resources such as oil and water, and securing them depended on the goodwill of Arab and other countries. Moreover, from early 1949, the war and the state's growing economic needs underscored the importance of enlisting international (governmental and Jewish) sources of funding to finance the massive enterprise of constructing a stable economy, absorbing new immigrants, and settling the land. The lessons of the war highlighted the importance of support from world Jewry, especially in the United States. Perhaps more than ever, Ben-Gurion came to view the Jewish Diaspora as the only ally of the fledgling state. We will explore the implications for foreign policy in due course.

In the sphere of international relations, the state's cumulative wartime experience had several ramifications, not all of which pointed in the same direction. The diplomatic success at the UN up to May 1948 generated strong sympathy in Israel for the international organization, manifested explicitly in the Declaration of Independence, which pledges to abide by the UN's spirit and charter. Ben-Gurion expressed these sentiments publicly six years later, writing in the newspaper *Davar*,

> The existence of the Jewish people and the security of the State of Israel, more than the existence of any other people and more than the security of any other State, are dependent upon the rule of law and of justice in international relations. The State of Israel, which embodies the historic will and aspirations of the Jewish people, is therefore duty-bound to do all in its power to enhance the moral and legal authority of the United Nations, and to strengthen its executive capability, so that it can bring law and justice to prevail in international relations and establish a system of international law which would, both in theory and practice, be above the legal systems of the individual states.[22]

Israel had to accept its internationally delineated borders so as to buttress its position and avoid isolation, which it saw as extremely dangerous. The UN resolution had, after all, passed by only a few votes, against the opposition of nearly one-third of the UN member states. Naturally, therefore, acceptance to this international organization was an important operational objective, which Israel achieved only in March 1949 after one failed attempt. As such, it would have been hard for Israel to conduct any foreign policy that clashed directly with the UN. Moreover, the UN had facilitated the conclusion of Israel's armistice agreements with Egypt, Lebanon, Jordan, and Syria, and it continued for many years to oversee their implementation on the ground through various cease-fire committees. Yehoshafat Harkabi, who was responsible for many activities on the Israeli side, wrote, "These committees served for years as the only official meeting place between Israel and its neighbors. In view of the subsequent deterioration in relations between Israel and the Arab states, the conflict resolution processes that took place during committee meetings, the frequent shared meals, and the coexistence, including a joint Egyptian-Israeli unit in Nitzana [that even shared bathrooms], all seem like some incredible, idyllic chapter [of history]."[23]

Moreover, and much more importantly, these meetings reflected a de facto Arab recognition of Israel under UN patronage, which Israel's leaders sought to preserve at all costs despite the frequently dysfunctional nature of these committees. Alienating itself from the UN was therefore inconceivable. Yet during and immediately after the war, Israel privately came to view the UN less as a source of important political support and more as a problem or even a potential threat. As Sharett explained to the Zionist Executive on August 22, 1948,

> Let us not deny the credit due to those thirty-three states that voted for the establishment of a Jewish state in Eretz Israel: they voted in 1947 so that the state could be founded in 1948. However, let us not give the United Nations credit that it does not deserve. It was incapable of implementing [the resolution]. It was incapable of helping. It was incapable of protecting us. It was incapable of protecting itself [and asserting] the authority of its own decision or its moral, legal, and political authority. We were abandoned. We stood alone. Only the fact of our existence in the Land, a few hundred thousand Jews, only the fact of our small force in the Land, only that measure of internal cohesion that we built, the unity of will we discovered, that powerful and wonderful unity of the Jewish people throughout the Diaspora, which enveloped us like a living fortress of encouragement, assistance, and fraternal bond, these [are what] fortified us in times of hardship.[24]

Indeed, from the perspective of Jewish Jerusalem, after adopting its resolution on partition, the UN took no action to enforce it on the Arab side, which strongly opposed the plan. Moreover, the Israeli leadership viewed the UN's mediation efforts, which aimed to bring the warring parties to the negotiating table and secure political agreements, as an attempt to reverse IDF battlefield gains. The assassination of chief UN negotiator Folke Bernadotte in Jerusalem in September 1948 by a Jew was, in the view of Israeli leadership, extremist and unacceptable, but it expressed the prevailing bitterness throughout the country. Eventually Israel succeeded, with great effort, in thwarting the UN's plans. And finally, the UN posed a problem at the end of the war because (thanks to Resolution 194 of December 1948, among other factors) it stood at the head of a camp that demanded that Israel retreat territorially, demographically, and legally from positions it had attained by the start of 1949 to the original plan laid out two years earlier.

Sharett used mathematical terms in speaking before party leaders in mid-1949: "The assumption is that we tried to grasp everything at once. . . . They [the United Nations] know how to do the type of arithmetic that can be summed up by [three] sets of numbers: 1. UNSCOP voted 62:38, 62 for the State of Israel, 38 for the Arab state. 2. The United Nations [Partition] Resolution of 29 November [1947] determined [territorial] proportions of 55 to 45. . . . 3. The present situation stands at approximately 79 [percent of the territory] for the State of Israel and no more than 21 [percent] for the Arab part."[25]

Toward the end of the war, Israel adopted clear policy guidelines regarding the postwar status-quo question. In advance of the Lausanne Conference of April 1949, Israel finalized its official stance on Arab refugees and border arrangements. Its position presupposed that the Arab states were responsible for both the problem and its resolution and, therefore, the answer to these refugees' plight was their resettlement in Arab countries. In recognition of their suffering, Israel agreed to help address the problem, on the condition that any resolution be part of an overall peace agreement with the Arabs. The Israeli position on territorial arrangements took the facts on the ground as its starting point: it proposed that the armistice lines be recognized as Israel's borders but expressed a willingness to discuss redrawing the boundaries in some sectors. This contradicted the UN's stated position. Thus, beginning midwar, a range of issues contributed to continuous confrontation with the UN: international efforts to resolve the Arab-Israeli conflict through Israel's concession of territory captured during the war (the Negev), the right of return for most if not all Arab refugees, reparations for abandoned properties and remaining assets in banks under Israeli rule, and efforts to change Jerusalem's status to that of an international city.

Looking back seven decades later, it is hard to comprehend what this confrontation meant for Israel at the time. Today's observer cannot easily grasp the extent of the country's political and economic weakness—a young state that had barely managed to repel an attack by all its neighboring countries as well as other Arab forces, a state toward which many in the world were less than welcoming. On the other hand, one must not forget that when the General Assembly recommended the establishment of Israel and partition of the land, the UN was only two years old and at the peak of its prestige. The whole world was invariably paying attention to Israel, a brand-new state universally seen as a UN product. In addition, Israel viewed UN engagement in the Korean War as solid evidence of the organization's power and strategic importance. Naturally, therefore, Israel took great care in its dealings with the United Nations during the early years of statehood, as Elad van Gelder explores in his PhD dissertation:

> Initially it seemed that all the parties—from the cabinet to the Foreign Ministry and UN delegation—wanted to formulate and implement a policy regarding the UN in a systematic and orderly manner. Even before Israel was admitted to the UN, ministers were receiving near-daily updates on the General Assembly's activities, and after it was admitted in May 1949, they continued holding lengthy discussions. . . . Immediately after Israel was accepted as a UN member state, the full cabinet met to discuss the basic guidelines of

Israeli policy towards the organization. In later meetings, it addressed a series of formal issues related to the UN, such as Israel's participation in the UN budget, accession to various treaties, and membership in various international bodies operating under UN auspices. Before the fourth session of the General Assembly (which began in September 1949, the first full session in which Israel participated), the cabinet held a number of wide-ranging discussions on the delegation's directives regarding subjects related to Israel as well as general issues. The process included the presentation of a proposed position, review of the draft instructions by ministers, and further discussion to incorporate the ministers' comments and formulate the final instructions for the session.[26]

Israel's nearly continuous clash with the UN inevitably generated a negative predisposition among successive administrations, although it could never cause Israel to withdraw from the organization. On the contrary, it demanded decades of Israeli political activity and effort within the UN framework itself.

Early in the summer of 1949, the roar of artillery ceased. Israel could now focus on its vital interests around the world without the immediate and constant threat of war. What were its operational goals now? How did it proceed, and why? Where did it succeed, and where did it fail? I address these and other questions in the next chapters.

Notes

1. Benny Morris, *1948: Toldot HaMilkhama HaAravit-Israelit HaRishona* [1948: A history of the first Arab-Israeli war] (Tel Aviv, Am Oved, 2010), 427.

2. David Tal, "Milkhemet Tashakh—Milkhamto shel David Ben-Gurion" [Israel's War of Independence—David Ben-Gurion's war], *Iyunim Bitkumat Israel* 13 (2003): 115–38.

3. Matia Kam, "David Ben-Gurion al Tsava U-Milkhama BaMikra U-Ve-Israel" [David Ben-Gurion on the army and war in the Bible and in Israel], *Mikranet* (2012), http://mikranet .cet.ac.il/pages/item.asp?item=23373. See also Anita Shapira, "Ben-Gurion and the Bible: The Forging of an Historical Narrative?," *Middle Eastern Studies* 33, no. 4 (1997): 645–674.

4. David Ben-Gurion, *Yoman Milkhama* [War diary], November 27, 1948 (Tel Aviv, Ministry for Defence, 1982).

5. David Tal, "Ha'im Israel Nitzkha BeMilkhemet 1948 Ve'im Lo Modu'a Ken?" [Did Israel win the 1948 Palestine War?] *Zmanim* 80 (2002): 42–54.

6. Moshe Dayan, *Avnei Derech* [Milestones] (Tel Aviv, Idanim & Dvir, 1976), 213.

7. *Davar*, December 19, 1947.

8. Haim Barkai, "HaAlut HaRealit shel Milkhemet HaAtzma'ut" [The real cost of the War of Independence], in *Milkhemet HaAtzma'ut: Tashakh-Tashat* [The War of Independence: 1948–1949], ed. Alon Kadish (Tel Aviv, Ministry for Defence, 2005), 759–63.

9. Yitzhak Greenberg, "Hashpa'at HaIlutz HaKalkali Al Mivtsa'ei HaHakhra'a BeMilkhemet Ha'Atzma'ut" [The effect of economic constraints on decisive operations in the War of Independence], in *Milkhemet HaAtzma'ut: Tashakh-Tashat* [The War of Independence: 1948–1949], ed. Alon Kadish (Tel Aviv, Ministry for Defence, 2005), 797.

10. Mordechai Bar-On, "Status Quo Lifnei—O Akharei? He'arot Parshanut LeMediniyut HaBitakhon Shel Israel, 1949–1958" [Status quo before—or after? Commentary on Israel's defense policy, 1949–1958], *Iyunim Bitkumat Israel* 5 (1995): 65–111.

11. Zaki Shalom, "Emdot BeHanhagat HaMedina BeSugiyat HaStatus Quo HaTeritoriali BaShanim HaRishonot Shele'akhar Miklhemet HaAtzma'ut—Bekhina Mekhudeshet" [Positions of Israeli leaders regarding the territorial status quo—a new perspective], *Iyunim Bitkumat Israel* 8 (1998): 110–49.

12. Bar-On, "Status Quo."

13. Foreign Ministry Consultation, April 12, 1949, Foreign Ministry Documents, via Israel State Archives (hereinafter "ISA"), file 3/2447 [Hebrew].

14. As quoted in *The Jewish Paradox: A Personal Memoir* by Nahum Goldmann (London, Weidenfeld and Nicolson, 1978), 99.

15. Yemima Rosenthal and Eli Shaltiel, eds., *David Ben-Gurion: Rosh HaMemshala HaRishon* [David Ben-Gurion: The first prime minister] (Jerusalem, Israel State Archive, 1996), 85.

16. Dayan, *Avnei Derech*, 213.

17. Avner Cohen, *Israel VeHaptsatsa* [Israel and the bomb] (Tel Aviv, Shoken, 2000); Shlomo Aronson, *Neshek Gar'ini BaMizrakh Hatikhon, 1948–2013* [Nuclear weapons in the Middle East, 1948–2013] (Jerusalem, Academon, 2014).

18. Avner Cohen, *Israel and the Bomb* (New York, Columbia University Press, 1998), 14.

19. Meir Mardor, *RAFAEL—BeNetivei HaMekhkar VeHaPituakh LeBitakhon Israel* [RAFAEL—on the path of research and development for the security of Israel] (Tel Aviv, Maarachot, 1981), 352–53.

20. Rosenthal and Shaltiel, *David Ben-Gurion*, 86.

21. David Ben-Gurion, *Khazon VeDerekh* [Vision and path] (Tel Aviv, Am Oved, 1951), 3:18; Gideon Shimoni, "HaDiyun HaIdeologi BeTsionut BeIkvot Kinun HaMedina" [The ideological debate over Zionism following the founding of the state], in *Etgar HaRibonut: Yetsira VeHagut Ba'Asur HaRishon LaMedina* [The challenge of independence: Ideological and cultural aspects of Israel's first decade], ed. Mordechai Bar-On (Jerusalem, Yad Ben Zvi, 1999), https://lib.cet.ac.il/pages/item.asp?item=21256&source=2389; Lissak Moshe (ed.), *Toldot Hayeshuv Hayehudi Beretz Israel Meaz Haaliya Harhishona—Medinat Israel—Haasor Harhison* [History of the Jewish community in Eretz Israel since the First Aliya—the State of Israel—the first decade] (Jerusalem, The Bialik Institute, 2009).

22. Ben-Gurion, "HaUmot HaMeuhadot VeBitchonenu" [The United Nations and our security], *Davar*, March 26, 1954.

23. Yehoshafat Harkabi, "Heskemei Shvitat HaNeshek—Mabat LeAkhor" [The Armistice Agreements—a retrospective view], *Maarachot* (July 1984): 5–24. See also Aryeh Shalev, *Co-operation under the Shadow of Conflict: The Israeli-Syrian Armistice Regime, 1949—1955* (Tel Aviv, Ministry for Defence, 1989); Raphael Israeli, *Jerusalem Divided: The Armistice Regime (1947–1967)* (London, Routledge, 2002).

24. Moshe Sharett, remarks at the Zionist Executive Meeting, Jerusalem, August 22, 1948, http://www.sharett.org.il/cgi-webaxy/sal/sal.pl?ID=880900_sharett_new&dbid=bookfiles&act=show&dataid=3290.

25. Uri Bialer, "Top Hat, Tuxedo and Cannons: Israeli Foreign Policy from 1948 to 1956 as a Field of Study," *Israel Studies* 7, no. 1 (2002): 1–80.

26. See the article by Elad van Gelder (based on his PhD dissertation), "Iltur U-Mediniyut Khutz: Sipura shel Mishlakhat LaUm, 1948–1956" [Improvisation and foreign

policy: The story of the Israeli mission to the UN, 1948–1956], in *Perspectivot Khadashot Al HaHistoria Shel HaYakhasim HaBenleumi'im* [New perspectives on the history of international relations], ed. Gadi Heimann (Jerusalem The Davis Institute, 2012). On the general international perspective of the subject, see Mikulas Fabry, *Recognizing States: International Society and the Establishment of New States since 1776* (Oxford, Oxford University Press, 2010).

PART II

THE GOALS AND THE
TEST OF REALITY

THIS SECTION WARRANTS a few prefatory remarks. One of the most important reasons for the success of the Zionist movement before 1948 was its adherence to a pragmatic worldview centered mainly on material needs as strategic objectives and on the need to compromise at the tactical level in order to attain them. No doubt this dynamic has continued to dominate Israeli foreign policy since that year. Moshe Sharett expressed it vividly when, in early September 1952, he responded in a detailed letter to Zvi Givon of the Foreign Ministry's Asia Department, who had criticized what he called the neglect of the Asian continent. In none of my archival wanderings have I come across any document that is comparable in its detail, quality, clarity, and piercing insights regarding the pyramidal relation among Israel's foreign policy objectives during its early days. The text therefore deserves to be cited in full.

"Mr. Givon is making a mistake," wrote Sharett,

> when he attributes the deliberate preference we supposedly had for Europe and America over Asia to the Jewish factor. It is true that a fundamental, and sometimes decisive, factor in our foreign policy considerations is the vital interest Israel has in maintaining a relationship that is as close and bold as possible with Jewish communities worldwide. It is also true that the vast continent of Asia is "clear" of Jews. . . . And it is also true, though often not taken into account, that most Asian countries lack the basic elements necessary to know the Jewish People, to assess its role in world history, and to understand its problems and aspirations, given that they do not share the heritage of the Hebrew Bible as the established foundation of human moral doctrine, and given that the biblical view of global history is completely alien to them.
>
> But it is completely untrue that the concentration of the Jewish Diaspora in Europe and America is what led us to turn first to these two Western continents, while the absence of Jewish communities across Asia led us to turn our backs to the vast Eastern continent. The truth is that during the early years of statehood we focused on strengthening our ties with the great Western powers and several other states in Europe and America because of factors and considerations that have nothing in common with the distribution of Jewish communities around the world. A striking example of this is the story of our relations with England. . . . Although England has an important and valuable

concentration of Jews, our relations [with it] are determined at a completely different level. Educate yourself: Most of Israel's citrus fruit exports are sold in England. . . . We purchase large quantities of fuel from British companies. . . . When the state was founded, tens of millions of British pounds sterling were frozen [there]. . . . Thus, we found ourselves bound, conjoined, with messy open accounts with the British government. All these decisive ties are reflected in the development and shaping of relations between Israel and England . . . unrelated to the Jewish factor.

The same applies, and even more so, to our relations with the United States. There is no doubt that the presence in the United States of five and a half million Jews—more than half of the global Jewish Diaspora and nearly two-thirds of the Jews of the "free world"—a Jewry with equal rights that is politically active, wealthy, and educated, and which has made its special mark on the fabric of our relationship with that superpower. But it would be a mistake to conclude that had it not been for the Jewish factor, our relationship with United States, for all its risks and constructive opportunities, would have been fundamentally different. The political, economic, and military power of the United States in the world generally and the Middle East specifically would be the same as far as we are concerned. The pressing needs of our economy and construction enterprise, our status as a young nation knocking on the door of the United Nations and carving out its first path in this arena, the lack of peace between us and the Arab countries, and our constant dependence on public understanding, international aid, defensive support, and the creation of direct influence favorable to us—all these and many other considerations would in any event oblige us to cultivate the closest possible ties with the United States, whether or not Jews lived there and whether or not these Jews had any influence.

Sharett concluded,

I could continue in the same vein to analyze our relations with France, with Italy, with the Benelux states, with the Scandinavian states, but that would take time. One more example will suffice. At face value, what and whom do we have in Argentina, besides a Jewish population of 400,000 with a consolidated national character and solid, rooted identity? But here too, the fact that Argentina is our main, if not only, source of meat—a fact unrelated to the Jewish presence there—is of utmost importance, and accordingly, for now, there is no competition between Argentina and any Asia country from our perspective. Thus, we have indeed focused, first, on cultivating relations with Europe and America. We followed the dictates of our existence as a state—and not just any state but a special one in terms of its population size, economic structure, and isolation from its neighbors—a state that, above all else, needs food, fuel, raw materials, capital investment, defensive arms, economic, scientific, technological, and military training, and political understanding.[1]

Sharett's analysis is interesting and even illuminating not only in what it contains but also in what he chose to ignore, perhaps for understandable reasons.

Israel's political relations with the Soviet Union and Eastern Europe were actually, as we shall later see, intimately tied up with the issue of Jewish immigration and the Jewish factor. In any event, there is no doubt that Israel's foreign policy objectives reflected, more than anything else, material and pragmatic perspectives. Three of these aims—international recognition, Jewish immigration, and fuel supplies—are explored in detail in this part of the book. Several others are examined in part III.

Note

1. Moshe Sharett to Walter Eytan, September 3, 1952, in *Documents on the Foreign Policy of Israel*, ed. Yehoshua Freundlich (Jerusalem, Israel State Archive, 1992), 7:485–88. See also Israel State Archives (hereinafter "ISA"), file 2415/31.

5 "Our Raison d'Être"

Among Zionist and Israeli political leaders, Ben-Gurion was the most prominent representative of the view that establishing facts on the ground was the greatest need of the Yishuv and the Jewish state, sometimes without considering external constraints. The 1948 War was, in his view, definitive proof of the validity of this perspective, which he took pains to explain at the first conference of Israeli ambassadors, in Tel Aviv in late July 1950. He described foreign policy and security policy in the following terms:

> They are an art, not a science, and they are not subject to absolute rules. They both serve one purpose, not only because they carry out the mission of one body, but because their methods of operation are identical: persuading the other side to accept the opinion of our side. . . . Our independent existence—when it is real—can only be explained to others as a fact. On the face of it, there are two events that contradict this assumption: the Balfour Declaration and the UN resolution. The declaration was the product of the circumstances and requirements of the war, [but] without our constant pressure, it would have been forgotten. The declaration had no means of implementation, and the state was founded by the force of our war and in defiance of the borders delineated by the UN. When the state was founded, it faced three problems: borders, refugees, and Jerusalem. None of these was resolved, or will be resolved, through the power of public relations, but rather by the power of facts. . . . It is not that things should be set in stone, but it should be assumed that establishing facts on the ground in seeking to resolve these problems precedes public relations, and you should not shy away from action because it will generate an unsympathetic or angry reaction towards us. That does not matter. Of course, there are limits to such indifference—we depend on the world at large, as does every state, even more than any other state. However, changing the balance of power in practice precedes the formation of friendly relations. True, there is no absolute means of [implementing] policy: everything is relative, including both power and public relations. But we are in the process of constructing our state, which supersedes all else, and therefore establishing facts on the ground entails public relations but is not subordinate to public relations or its outcomes. Thus foreign policy is no more than a tool of the second order for us, in contrast to [any actual] state of affairs.[1]

Yet the prime minister was also aware of the great risks, as he labeled them, that stem from dependence on the external world. Israel lacked vital resources such as oil and water, which it could not access because of its conflict with the

Arab world. It needed arms from foreign suppliers that, for various reasons, were reluctant to provide them. At times, it desperately needed funding that was available only beyond its borders and was preconditioned on its international legal status. Moreover, in order to realize the vision of Jewish immigration, Israel needed to establish cooperation with several states that prohibited emigration. Finally, the need for strategic allies not only persisted after independence but actually increased for a variety of reasons stemming from Israel's weakness and the threats it faced. Diplomatic recognition was therefore a precondition for the realization of these material and operational aims and not merely a matter of morality, legality, or principle. It was intended, above all else, to advance Israel's primary practical objective: construction of the state. In an interview with *Haaretz* on October 2, 1959, Ben-Gurion said, "Anyone who believes that it is possible these days to resolve historical issues between nations through military force alone does not understand the world in which we live." According to him, "today every local question becomes an international one, and therefore our relations with the nations of the world are no less important than our military might, which we must continue to cultivate in order to deter attacks and to emerge victorious if we are forced to fight."

It is no coincidence, therefore, that Sharett described diplomatic recognition, based on favorable public opinion toward Israel, as "a necessary condition for the maintenance of the state's security."[2] Nor is it surprising that, except for three unusual instances (China, Spain, and the Federal Republic of Germany), Israel did not decline any offer to establish diplomatic relations during its early years of statehood.

Achieving diplomatic recognition was far from a simple matter for the architects of Israel's foreign policy because for many years a large portion of the international community refused to recognize the state. The data are consistent and unequivocal: when Israel joined the UN in 1949, 42 of the organization's 89 members (47 percent) refused to recognize it; a decade later the figure dropped to 33 (35 percent of UN members); on the eve of the Yom Kippur War, the number had risen to 57 (38 percent); and in 1992, around the time of the Oslo Accords, the figure stood at 78 (41 percent). There were also states that severed diplomatic ties with Israel. In 1984, for example, 115 UN member states recognized Israel, 41 did not, and 33 decided to revoke their recognition. Moreover, for many UN member states, diplomatic recognition of Israel did not necessarily mean recognition of its borders or of the displacement of Palestinian refugees during the 1948 War. Even a sizable portion of Israel's important supporters in the international arena regarded the borders and the refugee situation as unacceptable. For years, a front comprising between one-third and nearly half of all UN members consistently opposed Israel's existence as a political entity. Suffice it to say that as of 2017, not a single foreign embassy was located in the capital city of Jerusalem. Two years later only two of them (USA and Guatemala) moved to the city. Furthermore, the above figures do not reflect the many repercussions of this situation for the Israeli government, some of which were quite problematic. The government therefore invested a good deal of effort in changing the situation. The continuing difficulties Israel faced in this regard were complex and multidimensional. The most salient and important of these was the challenge posed by the hostility of Arab Middle Eastern countries.

Arab Recognition of Israel

The cease-fire arrangements and armistice agreements signed with Jordan, Egypt, Syria, and Lebanon in mid-1949 gave Israel significant advantages, the most important of which was the cessation of hostilities. The practical, implicit, and inevitably temporary Arab recognition of Israel's borders was also highly significant, despite strong differences of opinion regarding the interpretation of many clauses in these agreements and despite the many problems that remained unresolved. From Israel's perspective, this recognition constituted an important seal of approval for its existence. At the same time, there were those in Israel who expected that during negotiations on these agreements and in their aftermath, it would be possible to reach peace agreements that could be much more advantageous for Israel. Their expectations sustained Israel's participation in meetings that began in the latter half of 1948 and continued for about eight years but ended in failure. Consequently, in the decades that followed, the cease-fire arrangements continued to serve as the only basis of official agreement between Israel and the Arab states.

The failure of the above efforts has been the subject of several recent studies. These studies make it plainly evident that at the time they signed the armistice agreements, the parties did not view them as heralding the end of any contact. Declassified archival records (primarily but not only in Israel) document intensive diplomatic activity beginning at the official end of the war and lasting about three years, then continuing less intensively. The point of this activity, for Israel, was to reach a peace agreement with the Arab states. The talks were bilateral and multilateral. The first series took place under UN auspices, with the most notable sessions in Lausanne in the spring and summer of 1949 and in Paris in the autumn of 1951. Israel held a second set of bilateral meetings with Jordan, with Egypt, and with Syria in 1949–1952 and with Egypt for about three years thereafter. The points of contention were apparent from the beginning. The Arab side demanded significant concessions from Israel vis-à-vis the understandings its leaders had reached in the armistice agreements. During the meandering negotiations on the return of Palestinian refugees to their homes, for example, King Abdullah of Jordan demanded territorial concessions, including the return of Lod and Ramle and the formation of a corridor under Jordan's sovereignty that would connect the West Bank to the Mediterranean Sea near Gaza. Egypt demanded territorial concessions from Israel in parts of the Negev, and Syria sought concessions along the Jordan River. Other demands surfaced during discussions in Lausanne, including a concrete demand that Israel declare its willingness to absorb hundreds of thousands of Palestinian refugees as a precondition for proceeding toward peace agreements. Israel rejected all of these demands (except a qualified willingness to accept about one hundred thousand refugees) and, in one instance (during negotiations with Syria), even declined an offer to meet at a higher political level. Only in one instance (during negotiations with Jordan) did the parties reach a strategic agreement, in the form of a five-year nonaggression pact. They initialed but never implemented the pact because Abdullah retreated politically and later, in 1950, was assassinated. The cumulative talks ultimately ended in failure. Moreover, as Laura Eisenberg and Neil Caplan demonstrate in their comprehensive study on all the meetings held since the 1948 War, the parties never progressed beyond political maneuvering aimed at avoiding concessions.[3] Thus, the talks ended at a preliminary stage, before the start of substantive negotiations.

Alongside these basic facts, there emerged new, inconsistent historiographical interpretations regarding the responsibility of those involved for the failure of the talks. Some of these interpretations ascribed the failure largely to the Israeli side, while others argued that given their incompatible and irreconcilable interests, both sides share the blame. Another interpretation places the responsibility directly and indirectly on the Arab side. The common denominator in all these approaches is their strong reliance on Israeli (as well as British and American) political and military documentation, which is abundant and substantive, and the nearly complete absence of comparable material from the Arab side, which would have offered genuine insights into the latter's policy-making processes, providing a solid foundation for comprehensive historical analysis. Bias is inevitable in all the existing studies, which seek to draw conclusions about the parties' reciprocal relations yet rely on material from only one side, and readers should take note of the imbalance. This is one of the reasons the present study does not aim to pass judgment on the matter. Another factor is the author's fundamental outlook, which holds that the historian's role is to explain rather than judge and which limits itself, particularly in this case, to trying to shed light on the perspective of at least one side.

That perspective is also evident in the historiographical polemics that followed publication of the various studies. Interestingly, alongside lack of consensus among historians regarding overall responsibility for the negotiations' failure, there is a high degree of agreement on another matter. Nearly all of them identify a number of basic approaches in Israeli foreign policy to resolution of the Arab-Israeli conflict, which developed during this formative period. These approaches lasted for many years and proved critical to the question of recognition. Studies on Israel's national security also highlight the consensus behind these approaches. Declassified Israeli documents reveal that after the 1948 War, the leadership of the young state, under Ben-Gurion and through a series of decisions that enjoyed widespread internal support, adopted a political strategy that explicitly subordinated Israeli foreign policy on peace and many other issues to security considerations. The strategy rested on two fundamental premises. The first identified a decisively hostile perspective on the part of the entire Arab world and its tens of millions of residents in the Middle East and North Africa. That perspective, which Israel assumed would not change in the foreseeable future, aimed for Israel's annihilation. Ben-Gurion spelled it out starkly before cabinet members a few months after the assassination of King Abdullah:

> In this deplorable situation, we must face the real danger, the real problems, and not look for illusory or trivial [solutions]. . . . Our main problem is that there are twelve Arab countries. . . . For every Jew in Israel there are forty-four Arabs; their land mass is fifty-seven times [the size of ours]. . . . Those who aim their words at the Arabs imagine that their whole bloc will be a united empire. I too would like to believe so, [though they themselves] do not know when this will happen, but it will and they [the Arabs] have the time to wait. They know something about history; they know that once upon a time there was a Christian state in Eretz Israel that lasted two hundred years; [and was then] destroyed by them. [The Arabs] have time [on their side]. . . . It is in their interest to erase all trace of the Jews from Eretz Israel, not only to bring about the end of the State of Israel, [but because] they know that [these people] will never surrender. . . . [Therefore] they realize that they must destroy this [the Jewish] population. . . . This is [our] terrifying problem. . . . Today the formulators of Arab policy are willing to make peace with us, [only] if we transfer to Madagascar or elsewhere and forfeit the land. This is the inescapable problem.[4]

Trust in the sincerity of Arab desire to reach a genuine peace agreement was therefore negligible. This assumption had two implications: on the one hand, that Israel had no choice but to treat the conflict with the Arabs as a given, and on the other, that under these circumstances, given its demographic inferiority and lack of geographical depth, Israel must give priority to considerations arising from its narrow security margins. The practical conclusion was to adopt a political security strategy based on avoidance of risk and analysis of "worst-case" scenarios when formulating foreign policy.

All foreign policy matters were subject, and secondary, to considerations of national security and to the axiomatic assumption that the Arab world was intent on destroying the Jewish state. In Israel's struggle to thwart such efforts, advancing the official goal of peace with Arab countries was not a priority. The logic behind this approach was distinctly unambiguous: the prospect of peace, even if significant, was always in doubt, whereas the destruction of Israel in the event of its defeat was a certainty.

Open Arab hostility persisted even after the signing of armistice agreements, as evident in UN General Assembly debates. "It is hard to imagine the humiliation," lamented Israel's UN representative to his superiors, "of sitting through a lengthy meeting in the midst of delegates from Iraq and Lebanon who speak to one another as if I do not exist."[5] Arab enmity had far more resounding repercussions, including the closure of borders and blockade of maritime passageways in the Straits of Tiran and the Suez Canal, economic embargoes, the boycott of Israel's representatives around the world, open opposition to the 1952 UN resolution calling on Israel and the Arab states to negotiate directly on resolution of the conflict, the unequivocal Arab position that the armistice agreements had not in fact ended the war, and the constant Arab call for a "second round." This incessant open hostility reinforced Israel's perception that only in the distant future might it be possible to reach a peace agreement. As Sharett explained to his subordinates in late 1952, "If the Jewish People could patiently wait two thousand years for the founding of the state, we can wait twenty years until Israel is integrated into and accepted among the states that surround it."[6] The main way to achieve this goal in the long term was through a focused and sustained effort by the nation to strengthen itself demographically and economically and, in particular, through military buildup and deterrence, which would, sometime in the future, make the Arab world realize that it had no chance of success in a "second round" and might as well come to terms with Israel's existence. Israel therefore attributed critical strategic significance, as a requisite for security under conditions of constant conflict, not only to military power but also to ensuring other vital resources such as population, water, capital, and oil.

This approach also explains the second pillar underpinning Israel's political strategy, which was its absolute refusal to relinquish even a sliver of the territorial and demographic fruits of its military victory of 1948–1949 unless and until that distant and longed-for future becomes a reality. Because the approach to negotiations with each of the Arab states was collective from the outset, Israel viewed any partial concession in the bilateral negotiations it conducted in 1949–1951 and the early 1950s as jeopardizing the entirety of its achievements by opening the door to further concessions. This would, in Israel's view, shrink the country to the borders recommended by the UN in 1947 and grant the Arab side a better strategic opening for its inevitable attempt to annihilate Israel. Alongside these basic premises, after 1948 two additional factors made peace negotiations with the Arab world a marginal issue for Israel in practical terms. The first was Israel's awareness, in 1949–1954, that in light of its decisive defeat of the Arabs in the 1948 War, the latter's inability to rebound strategically in the near term, coupled with the armistice agreements, reduced the immediate military threat. The second factor was the massive effort needed to address difficult and pressing internal problems, foremost among which were immigrant absorption and the economy. Under these circumstances, national attention naturally shifted from foreign to domestic affairs. One logical manifestation of this new orientation was a drastic reduction in the defense budget during the early 1950s. Another was the marginalization of the issue of peace with the Arab world. This analysis was plainly and openly a motive for Ben-Gurion to take action domestically and to refrain from action internationally. The policy makers in Jerusalem feared that frequent assertions of Israel's desire for peace would be seen as weakness on its part; they therefore adopted a policy of refraining from any declaration that peace was urgent.

This basic diagnosis enjoyed complete consensus within the Israeli establishment, which was, however, divided on the question of prognosis. On one side were "activist" security officials, led by Ben-Gurion and Chief of Staff Moshe Dayan, who believed in exerting power and conducting military action against Arab targets, including as an effective means of deterrence that would eventually lead the Arab world to accept Israel's existence. Such action seemed essential in the immediate term, as Israel had, since independence, faced a difficult "current security" problem that required defending its borders and citizens from entry by Arab "infiltrators," as termed at the time.

Israel perceived the infiltration by tens of thousands of Arabs between the 1948 War and the 1956 Sinai Campaign as a direct threat to its recently acquired territorial sovereignty, although many of these infiltrators had no links to military operations and posed no threat to life. More than two-thirds of the infiltrations between May 1949 and January 1953, for example, were for the purpose of theft. Others, however, were aimed at committing acts of murder, sabotage, or violence, and by the mid-1950s, their numbers had grown significantly. The challenge posed by infiltration was therefore a strategic military one: Israel perceived the loss of life (between 1951 and 1955, 967 Israeli citizens were killed by infiltrators), damage to property and essential services, and threat to the security of settlements near the border and to the status of security forces in general as undermining the fundamental principles of its sovereignty. The problem, in operational terms, was how to prevent infiltration, and the solution relied primarily on reprisals against targets in Arab states, with the aim of pressuring them to seal their borders with Israel hermetically. Former chief of staff and then minister of agriculture Moshe Dayan offered the following retrospective explanation:

> We had no way of safeguarding every water pipeline from explosion or every tree from being uprooted. We had no means of preventing the slaughter of workers in the fields or families in their sleep. However, we had the means of exacting a steep price for our [spilled] blood, a price too steep for the Arab world, Arab militaries, and Arab governments. Reprisals are an indication that Israel views infiltration as an intolerable act of hostility and will deploy

its forces across the borders to strike at Arab countries. This was not an act of revenge. It was an act of punishment and a way of notifying a government that if it did not control its residents and prevent them from striking against Israel, then Israeli forces would wreak havoc in its land.[7]

At a certain point, these actions began to serve more far-reaching aims as well. Today we know that during the early to mid-1950s, the Israeli military establishment sought, through such actions, to foment war against Egypt not only to resolve some of Israel's current security problems but also to gain strategic territory and reinforce its deterrence capability. At the same time, general acceptance of the strategic reality established by the armistice agreements was not only stated policy but also the basis for action at least until early 1955.

In contrast to this militant approach, moderates led by Sharett sought to reduce violence and friction to the extent possible to prevent or contain the overall conflict. They therefore tried to limit transborder military action. The debate spilled over to organizational matters, including the internal struggle between the Foreign Ministry and the army regarding organizational supervision over the armistice commissions. Simultaneously, the Israeli establishment was engaged in another internal conflict over the question of national responsibility for Israel's intelligence and clandestine diplomacy, particularly in the Middle Eastern context. Initially the conflict was between two branches of the Foreign Ministry—the Middle East Department and the Political Department—each of which demanded primacy. Eventually the Political Department prevailed, thereby contributing to the weakening and ultimate dissolution of its organizational rival. The second and more significant struggle took place between the Political Department, on the one hand, and Military Intelligence and the General Security Service (Shin Bet), on the other. Each claimed authority over this critical sphere of influence in the shaping of national strategy. It is important to note, however, that both the militants and the moderates were united in refusing to pay for peace through territorial and demographic concessions, and both were therefore pessimistic about Israel's ability to resolve the conflict with the Arab world in the near future.

These internal debates over foreign and security policy making were resolved in the early 1950s, with the militants emerging victorious. In early 1951, strict guidelines were established regarding responsibility over national intelligence. Within Israel, Military Intelligence, the General Security Service, and the police would oversee intelligence activities, while the Mossad LeTeum (later known as the Mossad) in the Prime Minister's Office would be responsible for activity outside Israel. As a result, from 1952 the Foreign Ministry lacked a crucial means of shaping relations with Arab countries. Military Intelligence and the Mossad filled the void in the sphere of relations with the Arab world.

One of the best-known examples of the Israeli defense establishment's hawkish orientation during this period was its 1954 decision to operate a Jewish spy network in Egypt. The purpose of the network was to carry out acts of sabotage aimed at fomenting strife between Egypt and Western powers in the aftermath of the British decision to evacuate its military bases in that country. These activities later earned the label "HaParasha" ("the Affair"). Simultaneously the IDF also took over the armistice commissions, which were an important channel of communication with Arab states. This historical development, which Ben-Gurion fully supported, both reflected and reinforced hawkish orientations in Israeli foreign policy regarding the Arab-Israeli conflict, and it entrenched opposing views within the Foreign Ministry. The hawkish approach came to dominate fully only after Sharett resigned as foreign minister in mid-1956, marking the end of this debate at the strategic level. The militants thus faced no internal opposition when, in 1956, Israel joined the war initiative against Egypt known as the Sinai Campaign. The historiographical implications of these developments are also apparent. Given that the lion's share of Israel's clandestine contact with the Arab world came under the purview of the army and the Mossad and that these organizations (especially the latter) do not declassify their documents even after half a century, historians are severely curtailed in their ability to paint a comprehensive picture of the situation and its impact on Israeli policy regarding war and peace during the 1950s and ever since.

Nonetheless, the documents that have been declassified reveal that even after the assassination of King Abdullah, Israel's Foreign Ministry sought to maintain communication, to the extent possible, with the few contacts in the Arab world who were willing to do so. Its activities were aimed at gathering vital information about relevant developments and at providing an indication of the likelihood of reaching political agreements and understandings (particularly with Egypt after the Free Officers Revolt of 1952) on Israel's terms—that is, without conceding any of its gains from the 1948 War. These activities took place during the late 1940s and early 1950s, in the course of the Foreign Ministry's aforementioned efforts to maintain the primacy that the Jewish Agency's Political Department had in this sphere during the Mandate era. A special branch of the Israeli Foreign Ministry based in Paris maintained frequent but fragmented contact with Arab representatives until mid-1956, both directly and through mediators primarily but not exclusively from outside the Middle East. These activities, detailed in dozens of files in the State Archives and several books and articles, validate the claim that even after King Abdullah's assassination, Israel conducted a diplomatic dialogue of sorts with the Arab side. The outcome in practical terms, however, was negligible. The parties to the Arab-Israeli conflict needed another two decades and three wars to reach their first peace agreement. Among the factors contributing to this development was Israel's control, after the Six-Day War, over Judea and Samaria,

Sinai, and the Golan Heights, which provided grounds for dialogue with its Arab neighbors on matters other than the 1949 armistice lines and for introduction of the formula "land for peace" into the negotiations. The final chapter of this book further explores these issues.

International Recognition and the Arab-Israeli Conflict

Throughout its history, Israel has faced additional political challenges that stemmed from the Arab-Israeli conflict and threatened to isolate the state. In the eyes of Israel's leaders, global alienation posed tangible threats for several reasons. First, it bolstered Arab demands for pressure on Israel, especially within the UN arena, to relinquish the assets it had acquired in the 1948 War. During the early years of statehood in particular, Israel's leaders saw this pressure as a genuine threat to the young state—a state recently founded on the basis of a UN resolution and, sixteen months later, accepted as a member and granted vital legitimacy by that organization. Second, international nonrecognition could have practical repercussions such as the inability to secure economic aid, which would have devastated Israel in the 1950s. The strategic implications of political isolation could have been much more severe in view of the persistent condemnations of Israeli reprisals and frequent calls for their cessation. Under these circumstances, Israel's political efforts to defend and explain its actions, and in particular to prevent a detrimental international response, were of utmost importance. Such a response could, in the event of Israel's acquiescence, severely constrain it militarily or, in the event of its refusal, subject it to political and economic sanctions that would prevent the state from acquiring arms, among other essentials, and thus undermine its security.

It comes as no surprise, therefore, that minimizing Israel's international isolation beyond the Middle East and securing the recognition that would legitimate its borders and demographic integrity—which Israel views as elements of its right of self-defense—have constituted its prime diplomatic objectives. Efforts to realize these goals have centered on activity within the UN framework aimed at thwarting resolutions that call for any change to the status quo of July 1949.

Activities toward this end entailed nearly continuous contact with the international community in the UN corridors and elsewhere, with the aim of preventing discussions on "the question of Palestine" and ensuring that resolutions on this agenda item would be superficial. This was not an easy mission, given the resolution that the UN General Assembly had passed on December 11, 1948. This resolution called for the establishment of a reconciliation commission to assist the parties in bringing their war to an end; reaffirmed the UN's resolution on the internationalization of Jerusalem, to be implemented through the reconciliation commission; and called on Israel to allow the return of Arab refugees who wanted to return and to compensate those who opted to remain in exile. Israel's main rivals in this struggle were, naturally, the Arab states, which adopted a position diametrically opposed to Israel's. The Arab states drew the support, at least in principle, of many UN member states. This dynamic reinforced an interesting conceptual reversal among Israeli leaders with respect to the UN, marking a shift in attitude that began during the 1948 War and long continued to shape Israeli foreign policy. Israel's initial contact with the organization in the late 1940s was extremely positive. The UN provided Israel with a platform for fruitful diplomatic activity, which greatly assisted it in securing the majority needed to ensure international backing for the creation of a Jewish state. Those circumstances generated what one historian, perhaps exaggeratedly, termed "a symbiotic relationship of sorts between the Zionists and the UN."[8] Yet the traumatic war Israel then had to fight underscored the absolute powerlessness of the UN in implementing its resolutions and exposed its limitations in the eyes of many. After the war, this perspective gained ground, as the UN became the main arena for the Arab struggle to reestablish the Palestine of yesteryear. The many confrontations that resulted from Israel's unceasing efforts to prevent this action contributed, in large part, to the image of the UN that took hold in Jerusalem—as a hostile entity.

The United Nations has always reflected the political forces that compose it. For Israel, the three great powers were the focus of its attention. In all matters related to the process that would bring the Jews and Arabs to resolution of their conflict, the US position posed less of a challenge than did the British one. On questions of procedure, Israel consistently held that the conflict could be resolved only through direct negotiations between the parties without preconditions, a stance the US State Department could accept in principle. Until late 1954, Washington opted to leave resolution of their problems to the two sides and therefore rejected a policy of coercive diplomacy. The Soviet approach was similar. The British, however, took a more active stance: they were prepared to apply pressure and rejected the Israeli view on procedural matters. As such, Britain's position was the most troubling for the Israelis. The divergence among the superpowers and complexity of the conflict resulted in most of their activity vis-à-vis the Arab-Israeli conflict being relegated to the sphere of conflict management (preventing escalation and reducing tension) rather than conflict resolution. Only in 1955, after the United States and Britain reached an agreement to try to impose a settlement on the parties through Project Alpha (which included pressure to transfer parts of the Negev to Egypt), would Israel have to face pressure from two superpowers in the form of a threat to its territorial integrity, although that project failed. Despite their differences of opinion, the British and the Americans had always seen eye to eye on the importance of UN-based efforts to resolve the Arab-Israeli conflict. That concurrence, in combination with the interests of other states outside the Arab world, led to intensive activity on the part of the

UN between 1949 and 1952 and, consequently, significant challenges for Israel. In particular, Israel faced the possibility that the international community would translate nonrecognition of its borders into political and practical terms.

Israel's diplomatic efforts within and outside the UN forum on the matter of recognition centered on four issues: borders, Jerusalem, refugees, and reprisals. A salient political consideration for Israel was the lack of recognition by any entity in the international system of the finality of the armistice lines. The recognized boundaries were either those of British Mandate or those of the November 1947 partition plan between the Jewish state and the Arab state that would have emerged. This bolstered the Arab position of conditioning any negotiations with Israel on the latter's willingness to make territorial concessions. Even more significant were the demands of major players in the international arena, and foremost the United States and Britain, that Israel relinquish territories such as the Western Galilee and parts of the Negev in order to advance peace in the region, resettle Arab refugees, provide Jordan with overland access to the Mediterranean Sea, and create territorial contiguity between Egypt and the Arab world east of Israel. Israel's unwavering position was that any discussion of its permanent borders had to be based on the armistice lines. The only alterations to its borders that it was willing to consider were minor and reciprocal ones.

A notable example of the above territorial disputes, which has received renewed historiographic coverage, is the struggle over the Negev. This region was one of the focal points of international efforts to redefine Israel's borders during its early years. The British, who led these efforts, had a longstanding interest in controlling a land corridor from Egypt to Jordan and Iraq, thus establishing a territorial contiguity that would stretch across Israel. From November 1947 until the signing of the armistice agreements in mid-1949, the British tried to change the partition plan for the Negev. Even after their efforts failed, they maintained the same approach. The Americans, for their part, vacillated but generally took the British approach. Accordingly, at the Lausanne conference, the State Department demanded that Israel be flexible regarding the Negev, as the key to resolving the conflict, and even threatened severe measures. At the same time, however, considerations related to elections in the United States limited the government's ability to implement a firm, consistent policy toward Israel in this area. In practical terms, the British, too, found it very difficult to apply effective political pressure on Israel, which rebuffed any effort to undermine its sovereignty over the southern part of the state. Nor did the steadfast support Israel received from the Soviet Union in this regard make matters easy for London. However, the situation changed in late 1954 with the Alpha Project. For the first time since November 1947, the British succeeded in securing US approval for an Israeli-Egyptian peace plan, a basic condition of which was that part of the Negev would be severed from

Israel and transferred to Egypt. Israel, which had not been party to the conspiracy that hatched this plan, thus found itself facing a formidable international front in 1955. Still, Israel's prime minister refused to make even the smallest concession. Given that Nasser's primary precondition for peace negotiations was sovereignty over a large portion of the Negev, the proposed plan faded away that year.

Another source of confrontation between Israel and the Arab states was the problem of demilitarized zones, for which the armistice agreements did not assign sovereignty. When Israel claimed these areas, the Arabs objected, and the ensuing political conflict often sparked military clashes, especially on the Syrian front. Israel thus faced political pressure from states outside the region, particularly the United States, whose approach to the dispute was based on strict adherence to the armistice agreements and absolute reliance on the reports of UN observers. Many of these reports (as well as subsequent historical studies) identified Israel as the military aggressor and initiator of the clashes. That perspective was a source of constant friction between Israel and the United States as well as other states. Israeli diplomats tried unceasingly to explain Jerusalem's approach to the question of sovereignty over these areas and to present Israel's official version regarding the source of the various military skirmishes, in an effort to rebut the persistent (and not always historically accurate) Arab version. Israel devoted a significant portion of its diplomatic energy to this issue.

Jerusalem's approach to the refugee problem assigned the blame and the responsibility for resolution to the Arab states. It held that the guiding principle in addressing the plight of the refugees should be their resettlement in Arab countries. At the same time, it agreed "for humanitarian reasons" to assist in resolving the problem but conditioned such assistance on the resolution forming part of a comprehensive agreement with the Arabs. Here, too, Israel faced international pressure. The Americans, for example, tried in 1949 to promote a solution that would entail the resettlement of about 250,000 refugees in Israel and deliberately gave the impression that failure to comply would result in US opposition to Israel's UN membership.

The political fate of Jerusalem was a particularly difficult challenge for Israel because, contrary to expectations, in 1949 the reconciliation commission adopted a plan for an international regime in the city, and in early December, the UN, with the support of most member states, affirmed the principle of Jerusalem's internationalization. International pressure on Israel to change the status quo in the city was therefore immense. No less intense, perhaps, was the collective and bilateral pressure on Israel in the UN arena following reprisals, some of which directly and deliberately violated Arab sovereignty (although at times Israel falsely claimed that these were civilian acts of revenge). The violation of Arab sovereignty, coupled with the risk of escalation and renewed warfare, underpinned international efforts during the early to mid-1950s to restrain Israel generally and constrain it militarily.

How did Israel employ its foreign policy in the face of this multifaceted pressure? What tools did it have at its disposal? And how did it prevent the loss of its gains from the 1948 War? Jerusalem had several cards up its sleeve, which it used quite effectively. First, the facts on the ground gave it the physical ability to veto any practical proposal of the international community. Territorial change or the return of refugees in the face of determined Israeli opposition would be possible only through military coercion or extremely harsh sanctions and credible collective threats. Although Israel's foreign minister at the time lost sleep over these possibilities, in hindsight none was realistic in the international climate of the time. One reason was the differences of opinion among the superpowers, each of which held various and conflicting views at various times regarding the solution and especially the path to it. In addition, on certain key issues, the superpower positions were not too far from Israel's in practical terms. US ambivalence on the refugee issue, for example, was very advantageous for Israel. Moreover, when Israel sought to preserve and secure international recognition for the physical division of Jerusalem, it received significant practical support (albeit indirect and undeclared) toward this goal from the United States. The unstated American policy at the time was to promote an agreement among Jordan, Israel, and the Vatican that would satisfy those closest to the question of Jerusalem and to oppose plans for its internationalization that went against their will. An American historian who wrote about Washington's decision-making processes in this area described the US policy as one of "alignment by coincidence" with Israel.[9]

Britain, which firmly supported Jordanian control of Jerusalem, had a clear interest in preventing the implementation of UN resolutions making Jerusalem an international city. This gave considerable backing for those countries that did not want the United Nations to take coercive measures that would effectively advance its resolutions of November 1947 and December 1949 in this area.

A second factor that made the punitive strategy unacceptable to the major powers and to most UN members was the natural hope that an organization such as the United Nations could in time lead the parties to compromise using less severe measures. The Arabs' rejection of such proposed compromises made it easier for Israel to point out the futility of imposing an international arrangement on one party to the conflict. Furthermore, on several international topics, and Jerusalem foremost, Jordan and Israel in effect posed a united front against the international community because of their common interests surrounding Jerusalem. Both sought to prevent any major changes to the state of affairs in Jerusalem that had emerged from the 1948 War, as both benefited from it. Specifically, both the Jordanian ruler and the Israeli leadership wanted to keep the city divided and therefore created a very effective coalition against the principle of internationalization. Under these circumstances, the UN was unable during those years to formulate, implement, or oversee any plan in this area.

Israel also made effective use of proposals for concessions to neutralize international, and especially American, pressure. In 1949, for example, it expressed a willingness to consider resettling one hundred thousand refugees and reaching an agreement for territorial exchange with Egypt, in which Egypt would receive parts of the desert along the border in return for Israeli annexation of the Gaza Strip. The Arabs rejected these proposals. Israel then agreed to cooperate with representatives of an international survey commission that was intended, but eventually failed, to propose mutually acceptable economic solutions to the refugee problem. In 1950, as US pressure on Israel decreased in scope and intensity, Israel retreated from its offer to resettle Arab refugees but expressed willingness to establish a "rehabilitation fund" to which it would contribute in support of refugee resettlement in Arab countries. A year later, in another gesture, it announced its willingness to enter into negotiations with an authorized UN body or a reconciliation commission to discuss compensation payments for abandoned Arab lands, on a few conditions: the negotiations would be based on voluntary agreement; the contributions demanded of Israel would be reasonable and take into consideration its economic situation; Israel would receive international assistance in providing the required funding; no additional demands would be made of Israel; Israel's obligations would be to the UN, not Arab states or landowners; a portion would be deducted from Israel's payment in the amount due for the seizure of Iraqi Jewish property; and above all, it would be understood that by meeting its obligations under the agreement, Israel had fulfilled its commitment toward resolution of the refugee problem, and no future demands for their resettlement would be made of Israel. And perhaps more significantly, Israel greatly benefited from the Palestinians' circumstances in the early 1950s, when refugees had no means of forming a leadership capable of effectively promoting their interests in the inter-Arab arena, not to mention the international forum.

The issue, however, remained on the UN agenda, and the resolutions adopted in December 1948 continued to concern Israel, although the international diplomatic energy devoted to the matter decreased substantially during the early to mid-1950s. Unilateral Israeli activity was not the only reason for this decline, but it is still safe to conclude that the combination of Israel's refusal to succumb to international pressure and its sometimes tactical, sometimes disingenuous willingness to respond with independent proposals proved very effective in the matters of borders and refugees.

At one point, it had not seemed so for Jerusalem. In 1949 Israel tried to link rejection of the reconciliation commission's plans for an international regime in Jerusalem with a declaration of its willingness to reach an agreement with the UN on the oversight and defense of holy sites in the city. However, the negotiations took an unexpected turn, and in December, the General Assembly approved the full internationalization plan. Israel saw the plan as a strategic threat requiring an extraordinary response, an unusual one in the state's brief history. Israel's greatest concern was that the powerful majority support for the plan (which included the United States, the Soviet Union, and France) and its implicit approval for the 1947 plan meant that unless the young state responded firmly, not only might it lose Jerusalem, but its territorial and demographic status quo might be permanently changed. This concern led Ben-Gurion to open defiance of the UN resolutions, and in early December 1949, against his foreign minister's opinion, he declared Jerusalem the capital of Israel.

In reaching this decision, Ben-Gurion had correctly assessed the international organization's inability and the American unwillingness to confront Israel directly, especially given the impracticality of implementing any internationalization plan and the resistance of Jordan and Israel, the two states that controlled the city. Israel did, however, temper its unilateral decision of 1949 with proposals to resolve the question of Jerusalem through vague framework agreements for UN oversight in holy places. Sharett and Ben-Gurion knew that this would be very problematic as most of the holy sites were in Jordan, which categorically opposed any threat to its sovereignty over East Jerusalem, and because the Vatican, which was emphatic in its demand for internationalization, had no room for compromise in what was essentially an empty demand. British and, from 1950, Soviet opposition, in combination with the ambivalence of the United States and several non-Catholic states, ensured that by 1954 the call for Jerusalem's internationalization had dissipated, and with it one of Israel's greatest perceived threats in the UN arena. Indeed, the issue had steadily been losing salience, as indicated by the initial lukewarm reactions to Israel's declaration of Jerusalem as its capital and the official transfer of its foreign ministry to the city in 1952.

Still, these unilateral moves did not meet with universal approval. In a recent study of Brazil's attitude toward this subject, Jonathan Grossman demonstrated that in the early 1960s, notwithstanding Israeli pressure and the Brazilian president's authorization for the transfer of its embassy from Tel Aviv to Jerusalem, Brazil's foreign ministry eventually denied approval because such a transfer would conflict with Brazil's traditional position of maintaining equidistance vis-à-vis the Arab-Israeli conflict while also "failing to serve in any substantial way the Brazilian national interest of social and economic development."[10] Generally speaking, therefore, Israel's strategy was not successful in translating the international community's qualified acceptance of reality into judicial recognition. Most of the world's states refused to recognize Jerusalem as Israel's capital from the 1950s and did not station their embassies in the city. The political struggle over Jerusalem therefore remained unresolved. To this day, it serves as a vivid reminder that a portion of the international community does not accept the post-1948 state of affairs in Jerusalem.

Israel also failed in its efforts toward repeal of the UN resolutions on refugees, which continue to serve as an internal and legal foundation for attacks on Israel. Moreover, it was only partially successful against international condemnation of its reprisals following infiltration. The attacks on Israel stemmed in large part from assessments by many capitals outside the Middle East, especially Washington, London, and Paris, that besides violating the armistice agreements, Israel's actions posed the threat of military escalation.

It should be noted that the Israeli response to these attacks was influenced in no small measure by Ben-Gurion's evidently correct assessment (which was not generally accepted within the Foreign Ministry) that international pressure would not be backed by effective means of coercion. At the same time, the campaign against Israel, which peaked in October 1953 after the Qibya operation, did lead to an IDF policy of using force only against military targets and strictly avoiding harm to civilians. Although the Israeli Foreign Ministry assessment at the time was that international hostility toward Israel threatened its status in the global arena, in retrospect it seems that the Western powers accepted Israel's self-defense arguments, at least partially.

The Americans issued threats against Israel on several occasions, especially in the area of procurement, as well as hints of a possible strategic alliance, but Ben-Gurion was determined to give absolute priority to matters of security. He lectured Sharett on his "legal doctrine": "Although a pact with the United States was of utmost importance, security is no less important, even if it means conflict is unavoidable."[11]

It is therefore not surprising that this international pressure did not lead to a fundamental change in Israeli strategy. Nor, for various reasons, did it destroy Israel's diplomatic relations with the great powers. Moreover, the military initiative and capability Israel demonstrated in its reprisals probably helped convince the French military establishment of its strategic value, paving the way to their Sinai Campaign alliance. At the same time, it is hard not to accept the current and retrospective argument that Israeli reprisals could only contribute to the Arab world's hostility toward Israel, and therefore they had a negative impact on the likelihood of an Arab-Israeli settlement, at least in the immediate future.

From a public relations perspective, Israel's 1967 conquests initially seemed an ideal benefit. On June 14 of that year, Foreign Minister Abba Eban told a cabinet meeting, "There has never been such a public relations coup as the one Israel had this month, when it spread its reach so far and the world applauded."[12] Nevertheless, as we know, the capture of these territories soon became the pivotal issue in an ever-intensifying political struggle against Israel within and outside the UN. It led to a long series of African and Soviet Bloc states severing diplomatic ties with Israel and remains a basis for attacks on Israel to this day. The massive decolonization that took place around this time, as African and Asian states largely hostile toward Israel shed the yoke of imperialism, only contributed to its isolation. The most painful expression of these developments for Israel was the UN resolution of November 10, 1975, asserting that "Zionism is a form of racism and racial discrimination." Although several Israeli diplomats and politicians regarded it as ridiculous, the resolution unmistakably spotlighted the state's growing isolation. It surely explains why some academic articles of the time grouped Israel with other "pariah" states around the world. In 1981, for example, Robert Harkavy stated in the most prominent international relations journal, *International Organization*, "In recent years, a new international actor—the pariah state—has mounted the global stage. Although rough historical precedents may be discerned, the present international system appears to have produced a novel phenomenon, whereby some isolated small states, lacking assured and credible outside security support, find themselves unable to take advantage of traditional balance-of-power mechanisms. Taiwan, South Africa, and Israel fit this description best, South Korea less so; Pakistan and Chile are also candidates."[13]

In any case, Israel waged most of its efforts against this trend at the UN itself, which devoted an extraordinary amount of the organization's attention to the Arab-Israeli conflict. Sharett began to see this as early as 1948, when he reported to senior members of his party, MAPAI, on May 11 that one of the biggest surprises for him was "the vast amount of time this global organization has paid to date—and apparently will continue to pay—to the matter of Eretz Israel."[14] Indeed, between January 1946 and December 1974, 420 of the 1869 official Security Council meetings focused on the Israeli-Arab conflict. Of the 2444 General Assembly meetings during that time, 243 were devoted to this subject. This preoccupation placed a heavy burden on Israeli diplomacy. As Shabtai Rosenne concluded in his authoritative review of the subject, "It would be safe to say *that the primary task* of the Israel Foreign Service is to explain Israel's position in the debates in United Nations organs (including the specialized agencies) and to urge other countries to support it, or at all events, to adopt a balanced stand and not give blind support to Arab propositions."[15] Cabinet members often had a glimpse of this diplomatic struggle, when called on to participate in the efforts. However, events at the UN arena demanded their presence at no fewer than 187 General Assembly meetings between Israel's declaration of independence and January 1957. Israel's efforts, which deserve analysis beyond the scope of this book, also took place on several fronts other than the UN but were never fully successful.

In the midst of this atmosphere of hostility, Israeli diplomats had a few "sources of strength and assistance," in the words of Shamai Kahane (who devoted many of his Foreign Ministry years to the UN).[16] Among these sources he numbers the "sense of an international debt to Jews as victims of Nazism," the "political support of Jews as individuals and organizations," the "sympathy and [political] support of governments, publics, and public figures" stemming from cultural, historical, and even religious reasons, and the fact that for its first three decades, "when social-democratic parties controlled Israel, the state benefitted from the proactive solidarity of governments and parties with a similar ideological and international orientation."

Yet it is also worth recalling Aaron Klieman's observation in his comprehensive and favorable survey of Israel's foreign policy during its first forty years of independence: significant entities in the international community continue to question the existence of the Jewish state.[17] At present, thirty-one UN member states do not recognize the State of Israel. Likewise, the actions of many other nations also demonstrate nonrecognition. For example, US president Trump's December 6, 2017, public recognition of Jerusalem as Israel's capital was rejected by a majority of the world's states, and the United Nations Security Council held an emergency meeting on December 7, at which fourteen of its fifteen members condemned the presidential decision. Moreover, three weeks later a majority of the world's nations delivered a rebuke to the United States, denouncing its decision on Jerusalem and ignoring President Trump's threats to retaliate by cutting aid to countries voting against it. In a collective act of defiance toward Washington, the United Nations General Assembly voted 128 to 9, with 35 abstentions, in support of a resolution demanding that the United States rescind its declaration on Jerusalem, the contested holy city. No less significant is the fact that the UN resolution unequivocally illustrated Israel's diplomatic isolation with regard to a central pillar of its foreign policy. Moreover, the recent Europa's refusal to allow the Eurovision Song Contest, which draws 200 million viewers from 42 countries, to be held in Jerusalem, in contravention of Eurovision's own rules, has constituted a clear victory for the BDS movement. The widely felt sense of isolation certainly explains the recently launched public diplomacy campaign "Presenting Israel," which, as Rebecca Adler-Nissen and Alexei Tsinovoi demonstrated,[18] mobilized ordinary Israeli citizens through parody video clips to engage in peer-to-peer public diplomacy when traveling abroad.

Missed Opportunities? China, Spain, and Germany

Achieving international recognition was a prime objective of Israeli foreign policy, and accordingly, the Foreign Ministry devoted great effort to the cause. It sought recognition from nearly every state with which it had contact. Its failures could usually be traced to the position of other countries regarding the Arab-Israeli conflict, with three interesting exceptions. Israel's failure to establish diplomatic relations with the People's Republic of China, Spain, and the Federal Republic of Germany resulted primarily from Israel's own reluctance and subsequent rejection of those states' offers. The phenomenon requires an explanation.

China initially viewed relations with Israel as an opportunity to strike another blow against the international US-led embargo against it. China's political elite knew little about the Jewish people, and ideologically it viewed Zionism as an aggressive movement linked with imperialism. Still, because Israel had a socialist orientation and was one of the few states to recognize China, until the mid-1950s the latter made efforts to cultivate reciprocal relations. For its part, Israel's position on the recognition of China had to consider the Cold War context first, necessitating a very cautious approach that was often ambiguous or unclear. On January 9, 1950, after a few months of uncertainty, Israel granted diplomatic recognition to the People's Republic. Its vacillations reflected internal disputes in the Foreign Ministry between those who handled relations with the United States, led by Abba Eban and Eliyahu Elath, and experts on Asian affairs, foremost among whom was Yaakov Shimoni. The former feared a negative impact on relations with the United States, which supported Taiwan over China, while the latter called on Israel to establish diplomatic relations throughout Asia. Foreign Minister Sharett eventually opted for a policy of recognition without diplomatic representation. Israel would handle relations with China through its embassy in Moscow and would not recognize Taiwan or meet with its representatives.

In mid-1950, a different political outlook began to take shape in Jerusalem, one that ignored the concerns of the ministry's "American Desk" and resulted in Israel deciding, during the final week of June, to establish full diplomatic relations with China. The Korean War, however, erupted a few days later, instantly reversing this decision. The superpower shift from cold war to military conflict caused Israel to retreat. It subsequently refrained from declaring an interest in establishing formal ties with China but continued trying to maintain a balance of sorts in its position. After China entered the Korean War directly, for example, Israel voted against it at the UN and in support of an arms embargo. However, it also voted in favor of China's UN membership in July of the same year. Jerusalem sought to establish an economic relationship with China but, for reasons related to international commerce, was generally unsuccessful. In September 1954, Prime Minister Zhou Enlai announced before the National People's Congress that China was holding talks on normalization with Israel, which did nothing to diminish fears of a US reaction among several ministers, including Pinhas Lavon and Zalman Aran. Neither did the Foreign Ministry's conclusion, backed by Abba Eban, Reuven Shiloah, and Walter Eytan, that at this stage it would not harm relations with Washington.

The conference of nonaligned states in Bandung a year later marked the start of closer ties between China and Egypt and the suspension of ties between China and Israel until the late 1970s. From then until 1992, the two countries maintained clandestine relations, mainly in Hong Kong, as well as partial diplomatic relations. Israel's realpolitik considerations during its early years were not the only factor that determined its position on China. Others were ideological, political, or domestic. In early August 1954, for example, Sharett wrote to Israel's delegate in Prague,

> Although we claim that China is . . . an Asian Power, which is the major posi-tive reason for our contacts with her, we should never forget that she is also a Communist Power, and [that] her penetration into Israel means the solidifica-tion of the Communist front in our country with which we are in a state of total war. . . . It is not simple for us to be the first state in the Middle East to open its gates to the representatives of the same militant Asian Communism, which threatens to swallow the entire continent. . . . We cannot ignore the consequences of such a Chinese appearance, which will plant a deadly Com-munist dagger in the heart of our state in the Middle East.[19]

Whatever Israel's considerations, the question today is whether it missed a histor-ical opportunity to establish official ties with China, as many experts claim. The question remained long unanswered, until documents recently released by the Chinese Foreign Ministry revealed that as early as November 1953, Beijing had decided to suspend preparations for diplomatic relations with Israel. Although China would have benefited from friendly relations with Israel, the growing pol-itical power of Asian and African countries was decisive. In November of that year, the Chinese Foreign Ministry sent a telegram to its overseas emissaries say-ing that "although in January 1950 China and Israel recognized each other, dur-ing the early phase [of the relationship], the other side [Israel] hesitated about normalizing the relations. . . . Our interest then shifted to establishing relations with Egypt, and we decided to suspend contact with Israel. . . . Establishing rela-tions with Israel in the economic and political spheres is not an urgent need, but relations with Arab states—in every sphere—is something we want to con-sider as part of our participation in the international struggle."[20] Abba Eban was therefore largely justified when he later said that Israel had deliberated in vain, as any benefits China could derive from their mutual relations were ultimately marginal in its overall balance of considerations.[21] Nonetheless, Israel's support for the US-led stance at the UN on the Korean crisis undoubtedly solidified Chi-na's negative view on relations with Israel. Notably, China did not inform Israel of its change of heart, and it maintained low-level contact, thus contributing to perceptions of a missed opportunity in Jerusalem, until the two established full diplomatic relations in 1992.

The relations between Israel and Spain followed a comparable pattern. In November 1947, when the UN General Assembly adopted its partition plan, Spanish diplomats approached Zionist delegates and offered to establish diplo-matic ties immediately, on the condition that they proceed as soon as possible. Spain's interest was obvious: it wanted to counter its post–World War II isolation.

Yet the two only forged formal ties thirty-eight years later, in large part because of the Israeli position, at least initially. Notably, Spain was not among the countries Israel approached in May 1948 to seek recognition. The trauma of the Holocaust and Spain's support for the Nazis under General Franco—who still ruled—were too fresh in Israel's memory. In addition to Jerusalem's firm stance, in 1949 Israel supported a proposed UN resolution to maintain international sanctions against Spain. It also opposed Spain's UN membership. Sharett explained Israel's perspective at the time:

> The compelling consideration in Spain's case is that the Franco regime was a loyal ally of Nazism and fascism, that is to say, it yearned for their victory and saw its future in a world regime built on, among other things, the graves of the Jewish nation, and soaked with [that nation's] blood. The comparisons with Italy, Austria, and Japan, and even Germany, are not appropriate here, since in all those countries new regimes have arisen which have renounced, at least in word, and most in deed, the bitter tradition of [the] former regime. Not so with Spain, where the same regime has remained intact without any change in nature or habits within the country.[22]

At the time Sharett did not voice all the reasons for his opposition or explain the outlook shared by many in the ruling party. We find an explanation in a 1951 letter from Gershon Avner, a senior Foreign Ministry official, to Michael Amir, Israel's ambassador in Brussels:

> One has to take into account another internal consideration. . . . The central psychological complex stems from the fact that all our leaders are members of MAPAI who from very early on personally denunciated Franco. In 1936 they collected money to help the Republicans. . . . Moreover for people of my generation those years fueled a trauma. The Spanish Civil War shocked us. . . . The prospect of the rise of yet another Fascist state in Europe had been perceived as a terrible thing. . . . Franco has remained for us as a monster, the darkest thing one could imagine. . . . He has now become a symbol for what has been left of Hitler.[23]

This attitude remained for years and in fact dominated the Israeli MAPAI government until Franco's death in 1975. During those years, Madrid developed a pro-Arab perspective that further delayed the formation of open, official Israeli-Spanish relations for another decade.

The political reality behind the scenes was somewhat different. In a recent study based on newly released Israeli and Spanish documentation, Guy Setton and Raanan Rein found that Spanish-Israeli relations did expand across several fields throughout the 1960s when the two states engaged in commercial relations.[24] As an outcome of these contacts, Israel's Ministry of Foreign Affairs had an informal legation in Madrid during the second half of the 1960s, including at least three semiofficial representatives operating with the full knowledge of

Madrid. The first handled trade between the two sides; the second oversaw the development of relations with academic, diplomatic, media, and cultural circles in Spain; and the third strove to advance tourism between the two countries. According to Setton and Rein, "In essence, the three functioned as an unofficial Israeli legation in the Spanish capital." Clandestinely, there was also a Mossad station in Madrid in liaison with the local intelligence services.

However, this entire framework, claim Setton and Rein, was never referred to as a single cohesive unit, nor was collaboration consistent. It is interesting to note that Israeli-Spanish relations at that time were not unique. Several Eastern European governments did not have diplomatic relations with Spain at this time because of the anti-Communist nature of Francisco Franco's regime, but they still maintained trade relations with Spain and conducted their dealings with the Spanish through another friendly resident embassy. In any case, it was only Spain's entry into the European Economic Community years later that led Madrid in January 1986 to establish formal bilateral relations with Israel. Viewed from Jerusalem the story could therefore be labeled a missed opportunity.

This label also seems appropriate in describing the temporary absence of full diplomatic relations between Israel and the Federal Republic of Germany. Jerusalem's contact with Bonn on this issue began in the early 1950s, with talks on a reparations agreement. Despite appeals from Germany, however, Israel refused to formalize their ties until 1955. Besides the memory of the Holocaust, domestic reactions to the agreement and the leadership's concerns about opening the door to Germany too soon after World War II contributed to this delay. Nonetheless, as Roni Stauber discovered, in late 1955 Ben-Gurion and Sharett reached the conclusion that Israel's security concerns, in light of that year's Egyptian-Czech arms deal, justified diving into these deep waters.[25] As it turned out, though, Germany had withdrawn its offer and was no longer interested in full diplomatic ties with Israel, a position it maintained until 1965.

Limited Success in the Peripheries: Iran and the Vatican

Israel's greatest singular achievement in terms of diplomatic recognition came in 1979 when it signed a peace treaty with Egypt, followed some years later by an agreement with Jordan. Two additional achievements in Israel's foreign relations history stand out against its not infrequent failings at the systemic level. The first was recognition of Israel by Persia (Iran) in 1950, and the second came forty-three years later with recognition by the Vatican. The dynamics of these two cases provide important insights into this aspect of Israel's foreign relations.

Iran

In March 1950, Iran (then Persia) became the second country in the Middle East, after Turkey, to recognize Israel, marking the start of twenty-eight years of a complex and sometimes convoluted relationship with many vicissitudes. Israel's main initial objective was not strategic or aimed at intelligence gathering, nor was it even economic. Rather, Israel sought to use its relationship with Iran to form a logistical and operational base for the illegal immigration of Iraqi Jews. In mid-1949, the Mossad LeAliyah Bet set the aliyah of Iraq's Jewry as a prime objective. Vast numbers of Jews would have to be smuggled through Turkey, Syria, and Jordan, a practically impossible mission that posed many challenges to Mossad LeAliya personnel. The only viable land transit at the time was the service route through Iran, while Iran's flight routes offered a convenient option. This situation remained until Jews were granted the right to leave Iraq; later, in 1951, direct flights began to bring Jews from Iraq to Israel. Mossad agents had operated clandestinely in Iran since long before 1948, but the spread and presence of their network were relatively unproblematic. Contributing factors included the long border between Iran and Iraq, which was hard to seal, and the effectiveness of personal bribes ("greasing the wheels of aliyah," as the agents described it). The massive bribes required for border guards gave the agency's treasurer the idea of using the same means in a different way to secure the Iranian government's permission for the transit of Iraqi Jews through its territory and ultimately saving vast sums of money—that is, through diplomatic recognition of Israel by the government of Iran.

This recognition was problematic for several reasons. First, both before and after May 1948, Iran's official stance on the question of Palestine was fully aligned with the Arab position. Iran therefore declined to recognize Israel, and as a result, Zion Cohen, an Iranian-born Mossad LeAliyah agent stationed in Tehran at the time, had to return to the country with an Iranian passport (pretending to be an expert in Eastern music) and to hide his fair-haired wife at home.[26]

Second, the Jewish Agency's representative in Tehran could not make contact with senior Iranian officials at the level needed to "grease the wheels of government." Third, it was unclear what sums would be required and whether the Israeli government would agree to provide them. However, in the end, these problems did not prevent the idea's implementation, for several reasons. First, Iran's public hostility to Zionism and Israel was largely only rhetorical. Tehran's sole contribution to the war in 1948 had been to send ambulances for Arab wounded. Its alienation from the Arab world and distance from Palestine evidently allowed Iran to deviate from the uncompromising Arab position. During those years, moreover, Tehran hoped to secure large-scale financial and military assistance from the United States, and its belief in the Jews' ability to influence the US government provided the Iranians with a positive incentive from Israel's perspective. Another positive factor in Israel's eyes was the hostility between Iran and Iraq. A factor that eased implementation for Israel was the smuggling and use of Iraqi Jewish capital as loans to help ease the process.

Finally, Israel had very important personal leverage in Tehran in the form of Dr. Gideon Hadary, publicly the US attaché for agricultural affairs and covertly an intelligence officer. Hadary, who was educated in Mandatory Palestine as a youth before immigrating to the United States, provided an important link between the Jewish Agency and US intelligence in Cairo during World War II. Upon arriving in Tehran in 1949, he made the acquaintance of a business partner of the Persian prime minister, and through the former he established contact with the latter. After lengthy negotiations, the prime minister agreed to a very large bribe (thirteen million rials, today's equivalent of roughly half a million dollars), to be paid in gold coins and transferred in the diplomatic bag of the Joint Distribution Committee, a Jewish but non-Zionist American aid organization with an office in Tehran. In exchange he agreed to have the government approve the de jure recognition of Israel and to allow Iraqi Jewish refugees passage through his country. Nevertheless, Persia only partially fulfilled the terms of the agreement. On the one hand, in early March 1950, Iran announced that its border would be open—a message that apparently persuaded Iraqi authorities to allow Jewish emigration to Israel. This greatly facilitated immigration from the end of 1950 to 1952. On the other hand, Iran refused to grant Israel de jure recognition, opting instead for a declaration of de facto recognition, which did provide the Jewish Agency representative with some freedom of action. Israel made concerted efforts to persuade the Iranians to keep their word, including allowing Iranians who had fled Palestine in 1948 to return. Despite a bribe for a local politician, funded by the Jewish community in Tehran, Israel was not successful. Iran made its positions abundantly clear in July 1951 when it closed its consulate in Jerusalem but simultaneously decided not to retract its de facto recognition. From the late 1950s, Israeli-Iranian relations developed and expanded, greatly benefiting both states strategically (chapter 6 addresses the issue of oil). Nonetheless, Iran's uncompromising stance on the question of recognition and covert contact continued to define their relations until the fall of the shah in 1979. That year Iran not only severed ties with Israel but also adopted and has maintained a policy of extreme hostility toward the very existence of Israel, as vividly conveyed by its Islamic leadership. The Vatican political arena was also problematic for the Israelis.

The Vatican

From the moment of statehood in May 1948, or indeed a year earlier, when the question of Palestine first appeared on the UN agenda, Israel found itself facing a complex of problems vis-à-vis the Christian world, particularly the Catholic Church. First, Israel sought to reach an agreement with the Vatican to ensure it did not adopt an anti-Zionist position. Many countries were likely to be swayed by the Vatican in determining their stance on the question of a Jewish state. Second,

Israel had to devote considerable effort to reducing the damage from a Catholic policy that effectively denied the legitimacy of Israel's 1948 War gains. Third, it had to address the many complexities arising from the presence of Christian holy sites and a Christian minority in the lands it now held.

The key problem for Israel was the church's fundamentally hostile policy toward the Zionist movement from the outset. Zionist leaders and Israel's diplomatic architects were familiar with the theological underpinnings of the Vatican's attitude. When Herzl met with Pope Pius X in Rome in 1904 to seek his support for Zionism, the pope famously responded that Jerusalem is sacred ground, "sanctified by the blood of Jesus Christ." As the head of the church, the pope said, he could only comment that "the Jews did not recognize our Lord, and therefore we cannot recognize the Jewish People. If you come to Palestine and if the Jewish People settle there, we and our churches and priests are willing to baptize all of you."[27] This statement made two facts abundantly clear: First, the Catholic Church recognized neither Jewish claims to Israel as a homeland nor Jewish rights to territorial and national assembly in the Christian "Holy Land." Second, Christianity's claims to the land were still very much in force.

The church's response reflected its view that the Jewish people's political governance of ancient times could not be resurrected. The church, as it conveyed to early Zionist leaders, viewed the destruction of Jewish political sovereignty as irreversible—resulting from the wrath of God, who then created Christianity as the universal alternative, replacing not only the people but the temple as well. Nearly half a century later, Moshe Sharett described the Vatican's stance toward the Jewish people and Zionism as "a search for vengeance over an ancient sin and a nineteen-centuries-old grudge."[28]

Yishuv leaders had had a particularly painful reminder of this stance earlier, when they failed to enlist the Vatican in saving Jews during World War II. The Vatican had many excuses, but the real reason, seldom voiced openly and honestly though well known among Zionists, was that the growing presence of Jewish refugees in Palestine would substantially weaken the standing of the church in the Holy Land. For these reasons, the pope strongly opposed the British plan to withdraw from Palestine and leave the UN to decide its fate. Jewish Agency representatives received further proof of the Vatican's categorical rejection of Zionist aims during their political struggle at the UN in 1947, when the pope categorically refused to openly use the church's influence among South American states in support of the Zionist cause. Finally, the day before Israel's independence, the *Observatore Romano* published the Vatican's position, stating, "Modern Zionism is not the true heir of biblical Israel. . . . Therefore the Holy Land and its holy places belong to Christianity, which is the true Israel."[29]

Although the papal approach to Zionism did not change after World War II, Yishuv leaders were able to identify tactical opportunities that did not conflict with the Vatican's stance yet still served their own needs. The Zionists gradually realized that the Vatican would not oppose plans for partition, particularly given the provision on Jerusalem's internationalization. However, one of the outcomes of the 1948 War was the failure of this plan and the actual division of the Holy City between two non-Christian states—Jordan and Israel. This situation was anathema to the pope, whose emissary to the region, McMahon, described the Vatican's reaction to alternative Israeli policy proposals in late 1953 as "a person looking through the window of his house and seeing a burglar who tells him that he can receive any compensation other than the right of ownership [of the house]." The pope's representative therefore proclaimed, "We will fight!!!"[30]

Moreover, more than half a million Palestinians, many of them Christian, were uprooted from the lands acquired by State of Israel. Entire Christian communities disappeared, and many churches and priests were left without a purpose. The pope's fear of unwanted consequences for Christians throughout the Arab Middle East was presumably another important factor in his refusal to recognize Israel.

For these reasons, which added weighty political considerations to its ideological stand, the Vatican categorically refused to accept the outcome of the 1948 War. Jerusalem naturally sought to forge ties with Rome to minimize the expected political fallout resulting from this stance and from the inevitable difficulties that Christian communities in Israel would face after mid-1948. The simplest approach was to explore the possibility of papal recognition of Israel, but that seemed unrealistic at the time. The Vatican was not among those Israel had approached in seeking de jure recognition immediately after declaring independence, for it had chosen to focus on states that were likely to be supportive. In Herzog's words, "at the time, the newborn [state] was happy that the Vatican would make do with non-recognition and not seek to make matters worse."[31]

The option of seeking de facto recognition from the Vatican through local contacts was also unrealistic, as Israel faced hostility from all the local Catholic leadership bodies. At the time, the Latin Patriarchate, established in 1099 by the first Crusaders, oversaw the administration of Catholic affairs in the land. A second body was the Custodia de Terra Santa, founded in 1217 and granted extensive powers as a special branch of the Order of the Franciscans. Its mandate was to protect and preserve the holy places that came under Muslim control after the fall of the Crusaders. The Catholic Church administration in Israel was subordinate to the Congregation of Eastern Churches, but the Vatican also had a permanent observer in the region, the delegate apostolico, a papal representative without diplomatic authority. His role was to observe the local Catholic Church closely and report on its condition. His area of jurisdiction corresponded with that of the Latin Patriarchate: he too was based in the Old City and accountable to the Congregation of Eastern Churches. Thus, the Catholic clergy in Israel depended on a patriarch who resided in an Arab country and was known for his negative attitude toward Israel. Likewise, the "Guardians of the Holy Land"—based in the Old City with nineteen monasteries and more than fifty monks throughout Israel—had a distinctly hostile attitude toward Israel in light of its historical role as protector of Christianity's holy sites in the Holy Land. When Israel was founded, the head of Terra Santa, Father Kohn, became the "lead instigator," in the words of Herzog.[32] The delegate apostolico adopted an equally hostile attitude. Gustavo Testa, who served in this role until the late 1950s, was particularly hostile toward Israel. Among other factors, Israel had seized his properties and archives during the 1948 War. His residence in the Old City aided him in evading accusations of hostility, given the nearly complete severance of ties. Behind all of the above lay a demographic reality that inevitably fostered a fundamentally pro-Arab stance among the Catholic clergy of Palestine.

The Vatican played a very active anti-Israel role in securing approval in December 1949 for UNSCOP's recommendations on the internationalization of Jerusalem, allowing Sharett and Ben-Gurion to witness the pope's tremendous political power. The realization filled both, each in his own way, with fear and gave rise to a trilateral threat perception, with the UN and international community at the base and the pope at the peak. Until December 1949 Israel might have been able to minimize the significance of the Catholic anti-Israel stance and view it as primarily relating to Jerusalem, but henceforth it would be a permanent matter of concern. From that moment, the pope appeared to pose the most dangerous challenge to Israel's rule over West Jerusalem and, indirectly, all its gains from the 1948 War. Israeli policy toward the Catholic Church accordingly became largely intertwined with Israel's struggle for the repeal of UN resolutions on Jerusalem's internationalization.

The Catholic Church maintained its policy of nonrecognition for decades. Israeli state documents reveal that during the first ten years after independence, not only did the state's architects come to terms with this situation but, despite the significant political damage, they also saw positive sides to the church's stance. The recently opened archives in Jerusalem unequivocally indicate a reluctance on the part of Israel's leadership, from mid-1949 and for a long time thereafter, to adopt a strategic political initiative involving direct negotiations with the pope. The main factors were the axiomatic assumptions that Israel would not concede its position and that, given Israel's negligible chances of overcoming the "brick wall" posed by the Vatican, any agreement would require concessions. Sharett presented this position to his senior personnel in the first week of 1950, noting that "the question is not how to find a path to the Vatican, but what to bring. The paths exist, but the question is whether we have the elements for an agreement. The Vatican has just achieved a great victory, perhaps its greatest parliamentary victory ever [UN General Assembly approval for Jerusalem's internationalization]. It sees itself as having great bargaining power."[33] In any event, as he described to the cabinet a few weeks later, the pope "would never agree to have the Holy City at the mercy of the people who killed Jesus, and this has been his stance to date." One of the Foreign Ministry directors called for even greater caution when he wrote, "During this period of 'sitting and doing nothing,' it is best to refrain from contact in other matters as well, so as not to give [the Vatican] the impression that we are sneaking up." Such "sneaking up" would have negative repercussions, as Herzog later explained to an Israeli diplomat in London: "It is clear to us that efforts to hold talks with the Vatican under the current circumstances would be seen as Israeli weakness and nervousness. They also provide fuel for it to pressure those Catholic states that do not support the two clauses on Jerusalem." The diplomat responded that negotiations with the Vatican would "inspire the Americans to propose a compromise between the parties [and create] complications . . . in our relations with various Protestant organizations, with the Greeks, with the Jordanians, and even with the Russians and English."[34] Moreover, the pope's tough stance as seen in Jerusalem did not preclude the possibility of reaching a compromise outside the framework of bilateral negotiations. Israel's foreign minister explained this to the Knesset Foreign Affairs and Defense Committee in early July 1950:

> They [the Catholic Church] achieved a ruling in their favor at the last General Assembly. They will not willingly make concessions or initiate compromise in this matter. [On the other hand] they now have obligations towards the UN. If the UN changes the current state of affairs, then they will be morally free to reach agreements with the local authorities, but they cannot take this measure unless the UN retreats from its position. They would not [want to bear] the responsibility, historically or towards Christianity, for having lost this treasure. If the question depends on the UN then we will need to work it out with the UN, and if the arrangement with the UN depends on the Vatican, then we will have to make the UN decide in our favor and against the Vatican. Because the Vatican is not prepared to make any other settlements before it reaches an arrangement with the UN, we have no reason to shift the issue from the UN to the sphere of religion, where we would have to pay a higher price, when it might be possible to reach a settlement with the UN at a more-or-less reasonable rate.[35]

At the first postindependence conference of Israeli ambassadors, Sharett voiced this view more poetically: "The Vatican has no reason to negotiate with us unless the General Assembly has changed its position," he said. "Then if it does so, the Pope can explain to the Creator that he had no other option." Israeli representatives in Rome during that time also tested the waters, quietly exploring options. Their conclusions supported the view in Israel regarding the pope's basic approach and reinforced Israeli policy on the matter. Furthermore, this policy was largely grounded in an understanding of the different historical significance of the time for Israel versus that for the Vatican. As an Israeli diplomat in Rome put it,

> Something has happened that is unsettling [for the leaders of the Catholic Church]. For the first time in the Vatican's history, a new element has appeared that voids the principle "the Vatican can wait." In the dispute with Israel, the Vatican cannot wait. If it waits even one generation and Israel's position does not change, the Christian community in Israel will naturally die out, and then [the Vatican] could no longer speak in the name of and on behalf of the Christian community in Israel. What would then be [the Catholic Church's] status in Israel? As a guardian only of holy places and stones?[36]

Israel's position changed somewhat in the mid-1950s, but the Vatican systematically rejected all of its diplomatic initiatives. Additionally, the *Decree on the Jews* contained in the *Nostra aetate* adopted by the Second Vatican Council in 1965, absolving Jews of the responsibility for Jesus's death, did nothing to facilitate diplomatic relations. Nor did Israel's control over all the Christian holy sites after the Six-Day War alter the situation significantly. Only in 1993, with the Oslo Accords, was there a crack in the wall of official nonrecognition dividing the two, mainly because from the church's viewpoint, the agreement between Israel and the Palestinians removed a key obstacle to recognition. Notably, however, after more than two decades of negotiations, the Fundamental Agreement of 1993 on mutual recognition still awaits ratification by both the Vatican and Israel. The official disagreements of the past twenty-five years between Israel and the Vatican on technical, economic, and legal matters obscures a theological and political dispute with very deep historical, religious, and emotional roots, which is still far from resolution.[37] It is hardly surprising, therefore, to read a recent article on the image of Christianity and Christians as expressed in the narratives used to guide Israeli pupils at Christian sites in Jerusalem, which suggest that "despite the power of Jews in the Israeli state, there is a growing sense of victimhood in Israeli society, one that leads to the introduction of Jewish-Christian polemics into the Zionist narrative, and to the transformation of tours—ostensibly designed to expose students to cultural/religious pluralism—into a means of perpetuating the notion of hostile 'others.'"[38]

Later chapters—addressing Israel's relations with France, the United States, sub-Saharan Africa, and Egypt—provide additional insights into Israel's efforts on behalf of recognition, a matter of utmost salience for Israel's diplomatic architects before independence and still at the time of this writing. Another matter of utmost importance, which the next chapter explores, was the quest to ensure energy supplies.

Notes

1. Diary of Ben-Gurion, July 22, 1950, via Ben-Gurion Archives (hereinafter "BGA") [in Hebrew].

2. Moshe Yegar, "Misrad HaKhutz: Mivneh, Darkei Avoda VeLekakhim (Mitokh Yomanei Sharett)" [Foreign Ministry: Structure, work methods, and lessons (from Sharett's diaries], in *Ministry of Foreign Affairs*, Yega et al., Ministry for Foreign Affairs (Jerusalem, Keter, 2002), 50.

3. Laura Eisenberg and Neil Caplan, *Negotiating Arab-Israeli Peace: Patterns, Problems, Possibilities* (Bloomington, Indiana University Press, 2010).

4. January 20, 1952, ISA [in Hebrew].

5. Leo Kohn's words quoted in Comay's dispatch to Elath, January 23, 1951, ISA file 2592/22 [in Hebrew].

6. Shimon Golan, *Gvul Kham, Miklhama Kara: Hitgabshut Mediniyut HaBitakhon Shel Israel, 1949-1953* [Hot border, cold war: The foundations of Israel's security policy, 1949–1953] (Tel Aviv, Ministry for Defence, 2000), 90.

7. Micha Bar, *Kavim Adumim BeEstrategiyat HaHarta'ah HaIsraelit* [Red lines in Israel's deterrence strategy] (Tel Aviv, Ministry for Defence, 1990), 92.

8. Yehoshua Freundlich, *MeKhurban LiTkuma* [From destruction to resurrection] (Jerusalem, Universities Workshops, 1994), 260.

9. Peter L. Hahn, "Alignment by Coincidence: Israel, the United States, and the Partition of Jerusalem, 1949–1953," *International History Review* 21, no. 3 (1999): 665–89. See also Gadi Heimann, "Divide and Rule: Israel's Tactics Regarding the Jerusalem Question and America's Response, 1949–1950," *Cold War History* 17, no. 1 (2017): 21–38; Gadi Heimann, "The Struggle between the United States and Israel over Recognition for Jerusalem as Israel's Capital, 1952–67," *International History Review* 37, no. 4 (2015): 790–808. For a later period, see Lior Lehrs, "Jerusalem on the Negotiating Table: Analyzing the Israeli-Palestinian Peace Talks on Jerusalem (1993–2015)," *Israel Studies* 21, no. 3 (2016): 179–205. For the broader context of this topic, see Michael Fischbach, *Jewish Property Claims against Arab Countries* (New York, Columbia University Press, 2008); Itamar Levin, *Locked Doors: The Seizure of Jewish Property in Arab Countries* (Westport, CT, Praeger, 2001).

10. Jonathan Grossman, "Impartiality as a Lack of Interest: Israel, Brazil, the Jewish Diaspora, and the Question of Jerusalem," *Israel Studies* 23, no. 1 (2018): 152–76.

11. Uri Bialer, "Ben-Gurion VeShe'elat HaOrientatsia HaBeinleumit Shel Israel, 1948–1956" [Ben-Gurion and the question of the international orientation of Israel, 1948–1956], *Cathedra* 43 (1987): 170.

12. Ofer Aderet, "BeMukdam O BeMeukhar Ish'alu Ma Ankhnu Oshim Im HaAravim" [Sooner or later they will ask what we are doing with the Arabs], *Haaretz*, May 18, 2017. See also Giora Goodman, "Explaining the Occupation: Israeli Hasbara and the Occupied Territories in the Aftermath of the June 1967 War," *Journal of Israeli History* 36, no. 1 (2017): 71–94; Jonathan Cummings, *'Muddling through' Hasbara: Israeli Government Communications Policy, 1966–1975*. (PhD diss., The London School of Economics and Political Science, 2012).

13. Robert Harkavy, "Pariah States and Nuclear Proliferation," *International Organization* 35, no. 1 (1981): 135–63.

14. Yaakov Sharett, *Davar Davur, 1948* (Tel Aviv, Moshe Sharett Heritage Society, 2013), 2.

15. Shabtai Rosenne, "Israel and the United Nations: Changed Perspectives (1945–1976)," *American Jewish Year Book* 78 (1978): 3–59. See also Avi Beker, *The United Nations and Israel—from Recognition to Reprehension* (Lexington, Free Press, 1988).

16. Shamai Kahane, "Israel BeZirat HaUmot HaMeukhadot" [Israel at the United Nations], in *Ministry of Foreign Affairs*, ed. Yegar et al., 789–823.

17. Aaron S. Klieman, *Israel and the World Order after 40 Years* (New York, Pergamon, 1990).

18. Rebecca Adler-Nissen and Alexei Tsinovoi, "International Misrecognition: The Politics of Humour and National Identity in Israel's Public Diplomacy," *European Journal of International Relations* (2018): 3–29.

19. Uri Bialer, *Between East and West: Israel's Foreign Policy Orientation, 1948–1956* (Cambridge, 1990), 278. On the issue of "orientation" in Israel's foreign policy, see Zach Levey, *Israel and the Western Powers, 1952–1960* (Chapel Hill, University of North Carolina Press, 1997).

20. Yoram Evron, "Yakhasei Israel-Sin BeMabat LeAkhor: Mikhsholim, Hatslakhot, VeKivunim Efshari'im" [Perspectives on Israel-China relations: Obstacles, successes, and possible directions], *Iyunim Bitkumat Israel* 18 (2008): 237–64; Schichor Yitzhak, "Striking When the Iron Is Cold: Moshe Sharett and Sino-Israeli Relations," *Israel Studies* 20, no. 3 (2015): 102–30.

21. Evron ibid.

22. Raanan Rein, *In the Shadow of the Holocaust and the Inquisition: Israel's Relations with Francoist Spain* (London, Routledge, 1997), 145.

23. Rein, *In the Shadow*, 21–61.

24. Guy Setton and Raanan Rein, "Is an Embassy Really Necessary? Israeli-Spanish Relations in the 1960s," *Diplomacy and Statecraft* 26, no. 4 (2015): 678–95. This is the source for the analysis and excerpts that follow.

25. Roni Stauber, "Israel's Quest for Diplomatic Relations: The German-Israeli Controversy, 1955–1956," *Tel Aviver Jahrbuch für deutsche Geschichte* 41 (2013): 215–28. See also David Witzthum, *The Beginning of a Wonderful Friendship* (Tel Aviv, Shoken, 2019) [Hebrew].

26. Personal interview with Tzion Cohen, December 14, 1983; Uri Bialer, "The Iranian Connection in Israel's Foreign Policy, 1948–1951," *Middle East Journal* 19, no. 2 (1985): 292–315; Tzion Cohen, *From Tehran and Back* (Tel Aviv, Ministry for Defence, 1995) [Hebrew].

27. Uri Bialer, *Cross on the Star of David: The Christian World in Israel's Foreign Policy, 1948–1967* (Bloomington, Indiana University Press, 2005).

28. Ibid., 29.

29. Ibid., 6.

30. Ibid., 29.

31. Ibid., 30.

32. Ibid., 33.

33. Ibid., 31.

34. Ibid., 30–31.

35. Ibid., 31.

36. Ibid., 31.

37. Raymond Cohen, "Israel and the Holy See Negotiate: A Case Study in Diplomacy across Religions," *Hague Journal of Diplomacy* 5 (2010): 213–34.

38. Orit Ramon, Ines Gabel, and Varda Wasserman, "'We Were Here First': Guiding Jewish Israeli Pupils at Christian Sites," *Israel Studies* 22, no. 3 (2017): 77. See also Amber Taylor, *Contest and Controversy in the Creation of the Brigham Young University Jerusalem Center* (PhD diss., Brandeis University, 2019).

6 A Land of Milk and Honey but No Oil

A FEW PRELIMINARY remarks regarding the style of this chapter are in order. For various reasons related to secrecy and lack of expertise, the Israeli Foreign Ministry and Cabinet were not systematically involved in the issue. Pinhas Sapir, the finance minister, and Levi Eshkol, also finance minister and later prime minister, focused more on investment, agriculture, and water than on energy and tended to measure oil pipelines in Zolls, a German term they used for water pipelines. The main players, therefore, were not diplomats and politicians, and writing did not come naturally for them. As such, the analysis that follows relies primarily on exceedingly dry financial reports prepared by Israeli officials whose duties were to buy and sell this "black gold" and whose expertise lay in the fields of economics and fuel. Literary writing was not their strong suit, and their written records provide rather dull raw material. In combination with more illuminating British and American documentation, however, an important, interesting, and previously unknown story emerges, filling a major gap in the field of Israel's economic diplomacy. This story deserves to be told not only because it highlights Israel's ability to secure fuel in a particularly dangerous environment but also because it demonstrates Israel's steadfastness in facing the Arab boycott, an ongoing threat since the founding of the state.

In the Shadow of the British Mandate

A few background comments on geo-economics are also necessary. The discovery of oil in Iraq in 1927 had a decisively positive effect on the British economy. However, before Britain could reap the rewards of its investment as a Mandatory power in Iraq, it was necessary to construct a pipeline to transport this new oil from northern Iraq to the Mediterranean. Yet the route of the Iraq Petroleum Company (IPC) pipeline—finally completed in 1934—proved to be a thorny matter. The British government (through the Anglo-Persian Oil Company, a major partner of the IPC, and prompted by the Admiralty and the Colonial Office), for a variety of strategic and economic reasons, pushed for the pipeline to pass through the British mandates of Transjordan and Palestine before terminating at Haifa. The French partners of the IPC (through the Compagnie Française des Pétroles), by contrast, preferred that the northern route transit their mandates in Syria and Lebanon, with a terminus at Tripoli. Each side wanted its particular mandates to enjoy the economic benefits of hosting the pipeline (employment for local workers and transit revenues). In addition, the British Admiralty expected to use Haifa as an alternative source of fuel in the Eastern Mediterranean, assuming the IPC went ahead with its plans to build a refinery there, even though the Tripoli line was shorter than the Haifa route (529 miles versus 640 miles).

It is interesting to note that British plans at that time involved reaping the benefits of not only bringing Iraqi oil production online but also expanding production in Persia with a pipeline connecting the Abadan refinery (built in 1912 by the Anglo-Persian Oil Company, later British Petroleum) near the coast of the Persian Gulf to the IPC line to Haifa. This connection would reduce the distance Persian oil needed to travel by sea to reach Europe by 6,400 miles (round-trip) and greatly reduce the expenditures on Suez Canal tolls. According to British sources, the Jews who supported them initially hoped that a pipeline to and refinery in Haifa would convince Britain to "retain indefinitely the mandate for Palestine, without which Zionism must perish."[1] This position changed significantly during the late 1940s.

One of the harshest consequences of the 1948 War for Israel was being cut off from its natural energy sources. Mandatory Palestine and later the State of Israel were entirely dependent on imports for oil, as the first discovery on Israeli territory took place only toward the end of 1955 (a limited supply that briefly met 6 percent of local needs), and coal consumption had been almost entirely phased out by the late 1930s. Until Britain withdrew in 1948, oil was imported at steep rates for the local population because the British government in effect granted a monopoly for only four fuel companies to operate in Palestine, the smaller two of which were American (Socony Vacuum and Esso). The British terms prevented other companies from entering the local market, thus effectively granting fully or largely British-owned companies (Shell and Anglo-Iranian) the exclusive right to set local rates. The prices were indeed steep, as they were based on the cost of fuel imported from the Gulf of Mexico even though the oil actually came from the Middle East. Local consumers had no alternative to these exorbitant prices, despite the presence since 1944 of operational British-built and -owned refineries in Haifa and the pipeline that supplied them directly with crude oil from Kirkuk, Iraq.

At the same time, however, as long as the British controlled Palestine, there was no problem securing fuel. This state of affairs changed in 1948. As the Mandate era ended, the British gradually reached the conclusion that they should shut down and decommission the refineries. Their main concern was that the warring parties, specifically the Arabs, would strike the facilities. When Iraq stopped transferring oil to Haifa through the pipeline and the war broke out, weighty political considerations also came into play. The British did not want to appear to be helping the Jews, whose control over Haifa was secured by late April 1948, and they therefore imposed an embargo on fuel shipments to Israel, a measure that threatened to paralyze the country during the early months of the war. Israel's tactics—a combination of limited fuel imports and the maintenance of reserve supplies—and threats of nationalizing the refineries eventually persuaded the British to provide limited fuel supplies for a specified period. However, efforts on the international scene to ensure operation of the pipeline and refineries, using Iraqi or Persian oil shipped through the Suez Canal, failed: the Arabs, officially committed to boycotting Israel, would not concede; the British preferred not to exert pressure on Iraq and Egypt; and the Americans had their own reasons for not challenging Britain. Israel, for its part, opposed any demands, such as Iraq's and Egypt's preconditions for compromise, that threatened its sovereignty over Haifa. The cumulative outcome was a British decision in early 1950 to close the refineries in Haifa.

Israel's credible threat of nationalizing the facilities was effective in preventing Britain from implementing its decision for two reasons. First, there was a trend among states in the region as a whole at the time, and particularly in Iraq, to distance themselves from British oil companies. The trend peaked a year later, when Iran nationalized its fuel industry. Britain feared that Israel would establish a precedent that other Middle Eastern states might emulate. The second reason, and the fortuitous fact that ultimately prevented closure of the refineries, was the demonstrable capability of using the Suez Canal as part of Israel's fuel supply network. The concept behind this operation, code-named Operation Vasco de Gama, was to bring fuel from the Persian Gulf to Israel through the Cape of Good Hope and return the empty tankers through the canal. As it turned out, the Egyptians either were unaware of this undertaking or chose to ignore it. In any event, the operation allowed the oil refineries to operate using fuel whose price justified the arrangement. This fact was important in determining whether to operate the refineries, especially in light of the British oil companies' argument that the price of oil and its shipment from Venezuela (the only viable option for crude oil in the Middle East) made the refineries in Haifa unnecessary and impractical. The agreements eventually reached between May and July 1950 stipulated that the refineries would operate for local needs only, not for export as originally intended (which would have required the British to organize a large-scale operation to bring Middle Eastern fuel to Haifa, an idea they rejected categorically for political reasons). Because of these events, during eight critical years, Israel was effectively under the umbrella of fully or partially British-owned oil companies that controlled two-thirds of the market.

The British decision also stemmed from considerations of certain perceived benefits. The refineries did not yield large profits, but the import and sale of crude oil paid off. Moreover, there was some hope, however slight, that after political resolution of the Arab-Israeli conflict, the refineries would return to pre-1948 production levels, making it possible to resume exports. Israel, for its part, sought to avoid sole strategic responsibility for ensuring its fuel imports. That goal, in combination with Jerusalem's strong interest in maintaining ties with international fuel companies, further contributed to the overall dynamic. Given that the reverse phenomenon was the prevailing trend throughout the Middle East—that is, national movements viewed control by foreign companies as a blatant manifestation of Western imperialism, against which they must fight to the end—the Israeli case requires an explanation.

Israel categorically rejected the option of acting immediately to establish full control over its energy economy during the first decade of statehood, for several reasons. First, nationalization of the refineries would have led to direct confrontation between Israel and the oil companies in the areas of import, refinery, and trade, as all the companies were engaged in each of these processes. Such confrontation would have been dangerous because Israel's claim to the Mandatory-era contracts was legally weak. Even were it able to prevail in an international legal proceeding, it would almost certainly have to pay costly damages, which it did not have during those years of hardship. Moreover, nationalization of the energy industry could sabotage foreign investment—existing or potential—in Israel, including investments in energy and oil exploration.

In Jerusalem, it should be noted, hope persisted that despite minimal success to date, these efforts would one day yield results. The despair Eshkol voiced during a debate on a May 11, 1958, exemplified this, when he commented that "the earth's geologists say there is oil, [but] we no longer have any geologists who know what lies deep in the earth," and again six years later, when he described Israel's activities in this area as "treasure hunting while burying money in the ground."[2] Moreover, driving out the foreign companies would have triggered a harsh reaction that could have hurt Israel. Israel stood little chance of being able to purchase fuel within the international cartel system if it expelled the major oil companies. It was also unlikely that Jerusalem would be able to ensure fuel transportation, given that the major companies controlled the worldwide tanker market as well.

At the same time, closure of the refineries was unacceptable to Israel, as this would mean a missed opportunity to develop a petrochemical industry and would necessitate the import of expensive distillates. Funding was also a serious concern. Were Israel to nationalize the refineries, there was no doubt Britain would prevent or impede Israel from accessing its British pound sterling reserves in London. Conversely, by maintaining contact with the British companies, Israel could use its reserves to purchase fuel, a complex issue given the state's precarious standing with respect to foreign exchange reserves. Pushing out Socony Vacuum, the American company operating in Israel, would presumably have quashed any possibility of receiving financial support from the US government.

Above all, the young state lacked any experience operating a fuel supply system. Most of its economic endeavors during the Mandate era focused on agriculture, a few on industry, and none on the energy sector. The reason is evident: Britain had unlimited control over this economic activity, and there was no point in cultivating capabilities that could never be implemented. Even had Israel wanted to develop energy independence in May 1948, it lacked the ability to do so in the immediate term. Israeli diplomacy in this area during the 1948 War confirms two premises that became axiomatic for Jerusalem many years later. First, the state would not be able to challenge the oil companies on its own; and second, even if it did somehow succeed in doing so during peacetime, in times of war its energy sector would be completely vulnerable, unable to secure vital fuel supplies from the major oil companies. The inevitable conclusion was that Israel should do all it could to ensure that the British oil companies continued operating in the country. In this context, the presence of two American companies, Socony and Esso, had two important implications. First, they prevented a British monopoly and allowed Israel some maneuverability. Second, they served as a concrete representation of Israel's relationship with the United States, to which the state attributed great importance.

The possibility of financing fuel purchases through the release of British sterling accumulated by the Yishuv in English banks (mainly during World War II), as well as US aid, was a decisive factor in shaping Israeli policy in 1950. This policy, essentially an extension of the Mandate-era pattern of foreign control, was further reinforced two years later when an additional financial dimension emerged: After depleting its sterling accounts in 1951, Israel could no longer fund fuel purchases. The British companies then decided to stop selling to Israel—a move that would have paralyzed the latter's economy had it not been for the reparations agreements with Germany. Under these agreements, the German government committed itself to funding Israeli fuel purchases from British companies, in British pounds sterling, for about five years. Although the arrangement substantially eased the challenge of ensuring energy sources for Israel, it also reduced the state's ability and willingness to disengage from the British fuel companies.

Other factors, however, reinforced the reverse trend. The view in Jerusalem, naturally, was that absolute and lasting foreign control in such a strategically important sphere was unacceptable. Although the situation did not allow for immediate, unilateral disengagement from the British, a series of decisions made in 1949 set it as a national objective for Israel to break into this arena—slowly, steadily, and prudently. Accordingly, a national fuel company was established, with the aim of entering the market and gradually gaining acceptance among the foreign companies. Such recognition by the foreign companies seemed within the realm of possibility given Israel's newly gained independence. Israel's great need for fuel during its first decade also ensured that all the foreign companies could increase activity and revenue without sabotaging one another's interests. These were the factors behind the founding of Delek, Israel's national fuel company, which began operating in mid-1952 as an independent importer for the state and a participant in the international fuel market.

The final element of Israel's fuel economy during early statehood, which is also essential to understanding the massive change this economy underwent in late 1954, was the legal framework that shaped it. The foreign companies and Israel had clear, albeit opposing, interests in reaching new legal arrangements. However, when the companies ultimately ceased operations in Israel in 1957–1958, no contract bound them to the government of Israel. The reasons for this strange state of affairs are complex. Suffice it to note that Israel was politically averse to public disclosure of its dependence on foreign companies, while the latter were opposed to any official recognition of the advantages Israel derived from sovereignty over the land. Their explicit agreements did not reflect this, of course, focusing instead on dozens of technical points of dispute. Consequently, draft agreements reached in 1951 and 1953 were never ratified, but practical arrangements based on mutual ad hoc understandings proceeded as though they had received approval. The outcome was that despite the presence of an independent Israeli fuel company, for nearly a decade the fuel economy in Israel was actually under British control, which in turn largely determined Israel's options. One of these, effectively vetoed until early 1955, was the importation of fuel from Iran.

Independence under Foreign Rule

From its inception, and particularly after Delek was founded, Israel set itself the goal of renewing fuel supplies from Middle Eastern sources. This fuel had two important advantages: Its FOB (free on board) price was usually below that of the other realistic alternatives, which would involve importing fuel from the American continent. Moreover, the costs of transport through the Iraqi pipeline or Suez Canal were lower than those of transporting fuel from Venezuela or Mexico. In all, the CIF (cost, insurance, and freight) price of Middle Eastern fuel in Haifa during the early 1950s was 30 percent below the price of fuel from Central America. Additionally, Haifa's oil refineries had from the outset been built to process Middle Eastern (Persian) oil, which was lighter than other types. Distillation of other types of oil was expensive and generated more wear and tear. Nor did it yield the composition of distillates that Israel's fuel economy needed or the by-products essential for creating a petrochemicals industry. For the same reasons, until 1948 British companies had also preferred to import oil from the Persian Gulf and had drawn their fuel supplies mainly from this source, alongside crude oil from Iraq. It is not surprising, therefore, that shortly after the Haifa refineries resumed operation, Anglo-Iranian made an overt attempt to revive this source of supply, even without using the Iraqi pipeline. Given the economic environment of early 1953, it had a clear interest in turning Kuwait into Israel's main source of fuel: the massive development of oil fields then underway in the area offered options for channeling fuel into the developing Israeli market without violating the global quota allocation system agreed upon by the fuel companies after World War II. Indeed, agreements specifying that Delek would purchase Kuwaiti oil through British sources reflected the mutual interests of Delek and Anglo-Iranian. For about two years, therefore, Israel acquired Kuwaiti oil through this channel. The arrangement ended in early 1953, however, after intervention by the Foreign Office, which was concerned about the impact for Britain if the Arab world discovered that British sources were providing Israel with Arab fuel supplies. By 1954, therefore, all the companies were compelled to resume imports of expensive fuel from Venezuela.

At the time, Anglo-Iranian and Shell could not rely on Iranian fuel imports because of a severe crisis that erupted in 1951, after the nationalization of the country's oil industry. The crisis thwarted the companies' plans, freezing them until early 1955. Delek sought, despite opposition by the British companies, to compensate for the situation by exploiting the sizable increase in Soviet fuel exports then underway so as to secure a substantial reduction in the purchase price of crude oil, especially fuel oil (which is essential for industrial needs and electricity production). The Soviets were offering fuel at attractive prices without political conditions, and the timing was perfect for Israel. The result was that from late 1955 until late 1956, when imports from the Soviet Union ceased after the Sinai Campaign, this channel provided up to one-third of the total consumption.

However, Israel did not fully appreciate the cheap and convenient option of Russian fuel as a long-term strategic solution to its fuel needs. The sole solution it envisioned was importation from Iran, even before that became a viable option. One reason was that Iranian oil was generally of higher quality than what the Russians had to offer, and it could generate the by-products needed for a commercial-scale petrochemical industry. Moreover, although the British fuel companies agreed to refine Russian crude oil imported by Delek, they did so reluctantly. Their strong preference was for Iranian fuel, and they refused to import from the Soviet Union for their own fuel needs. Because they controlled about 75 percent of the local market, they hoped to transform Haifa's refineries into a base for the export of Iranian fuel that they would import. In addition, fuel supply agreements with Iran had different political ramifications from agreements with the Soviet Union. Economic engagement with the Iranians would serve political aims that Israel was interested in pursuing, whereas it wanted to avoid ascribing any political significance to fuel sale agreements with the Russians because, from the early 1950s, a prime objective of Israeli foreign policy was the formation of political and strategic ties with the West.

Israel's reluctance manifested in several forms, such as refusing to conduct negotiations at a ministerial or even ambassadorial level, not offering the Russians any strategic goods (whose export to the East the United States prohibited) as an incentive for more favorable sale terms, rejecting the Soviet offer to help the state build an oil plant (in the absence of any other foreign aid), and not ordering tankers based in Russian shipyards. Furthermore, the Russian fuel supply was of limited capacity and subject to extreme fluctuations, making it unreliable for long periods. The Soviet Union's own need for fuel sources left relatively little for export, and slight fluctuations in domestic demand could diminish or deplete this supply, whereas the Iranian supply remained relatively untouched by domestic demand. Finally, the agreements provided that some of the Soviet oil be purchased on the basis of barter, but Israeli products (such as oranges) were classified as luxury items in Russia. Thus, their quantity was circumscribed, and it was always possible that Russia would refuse to accept them. For these reasons Israel decided around 1954–1955 to limit the import of Russian oil to approximately one-quarter of all imports. In particular, it wanted to ensure diversification of supply sources, maintain some bargaining chips for negotiations with the British companies, and reduce the cost of imports. The balance—roughly three-quarters of Israel's oil imports—was expected to come from Iran.

Gateway to Tehran

The path toward this objective was complex and thorny. The gates had seemingly opened for Israel in August 1954 when Iran and Britain reached an agreement, finally settling the dispute that began in late 1951. Their agreement established an international consortium, with a relatively large number of members, to manage Iran's fuel economy, thus depriving Britain of its monopolistic status in the Iranian fuel economy. It further established the National Iranian Oil Company (NIOC), which was granted a production quota of 12.5 percent of the consortium's total, as well as the option of processing and selling the fuel or receiving financial compensation for it. Thus, Israel had two potential courses of action for ensuring Iranian fuel supplies. One relied on contacts with international companies (mainly the smaller ones—the IRICON group that had no business in the Arab world), while the other, the immediate one, involved forming ties with NIOC, which was keen to exercise its rights and become an independent national alternative to the foreign companies that still held sway in Iran.

The problems facing Israel, however, were complex. The first was reluctance among the consortium's British partners to supply Iranian fuel to Israel, for fear of Arab reaction. Their reservations were strong, even though they recognized that the ideal solution, for themselves as well as Israel, was indeed to import oil from Iran. A parallel concern among smaller companies in the consortium posed another problem, and a third was NIOC's reluctance to enter into an agreement with Israel, for the same reasons the others hesitated. In late 1954, therefore, Israel focused its efforts on trying to break this vicious cycle using a three-pronged approach. First, it aimed at signing at least one agreement for the supply of Iranian fuel, thereby setting an important precedent with respect to the British companies, IRICON, and NIOC. Fortunately for Israel, SUPOR, an Italian company whose interests in Iran were threatened by the consortium, was willing to take the risk of selling Iranian fuel to Delek, and in November 1954 it signed a deal to do so. This agreement (to be implemented at the start of 1955) was an important contributing factor toward the second approach—negotiations that began that month between Israel and the British-controlled companies. Israel's greatest achievement during those talks was obtaining Shell's consent to an experimental shipment of Iranian fuel, with further supplies conditional on regional reactions. British Petroleum (BP), which was more dependent on the Arab world, declined to participate in this trial. Given the uncertainty surrounding its agreements with Shell and SUPOR, it is no wonder that Israel sought to cultivate direct ties with NIOC as the third element of its strategy. Its efforts were successful, and in June 1955, it sealed a deal for the purchase of seventy-five thousand tons of Iranian crude oil. Under the terms of the agreement, the transaction would take place from October 1955 through September 1956, with the fuel sold to an Israeli-owned straw company based in Geneva. The Iranians did not intervene in matters of transport, which was to be carried out along the route of Operation Vasco da Gama. One of the major repercussions of this development was that the foreign companies operating in Israel, having overcome their reluctance, were now importing Iranian fuel into Israel.

The new fuel-supply map that emerged for Israel in mid-1955 lasted until the close of 1956. It teaches us, in contrast to what is perhaps widely believed, that in 1955 Iran became Israel's main source of crude oil, and this situation remained unchanged in 1956 even when American companies decided to cease operations in Israel. Shell, too, continued to supply fuel from Iran in 1956, under the same conditions as at the beginning of 1955. Foreign companies maintained control over two-thirds of the Israeli fuel market, the vast majority of which was supplied by Iran. During this period, Delek was expected to meet slightly more than a third of the local demand, mainly importing crude oil and fuel oil from the Soviet Union using several small tankers. Some of these tankers, financed by the reparations funds, belonged to Israel, while others were leased.

The Sinai Campaign thoroughly redrew Israel's fuel-supply map, prompting a Soviet decision to halt oil supplies and hastening the departure of foreign companies from Israel during the following year. Consequently, Israel's dependence on the foreign companies ended. Israel purchased the refineries in Haifa and established a new national fuel company, Paz, as an alternative to the existing system. Interestingly, it was actually a British Jew with very poor spoken Hebrew, Isaac Wolfson, who coined this one-syllable Hebrew name, somewhat reminiscent of the name of a major global fuel company—Shell—that had been proposed in the 1870s by another Jew, Marcus Samuel. Samuel had chosen the name to honor his father's business, selling seashell-crafted souvenirs in the Whitechapel market of London. Israel's other alternative was the Iranian oil market, which in 1957 became the main supplier of oil for Israel.

Israel's political interest in Iran was, at the time, primarily economic. Oil was the objective, and the intelligence and military cooperation that developed, mainly from 1958 onward, was originally intended to ensure continuing supplies from this all-important and nearly exclusive source. Nonetheless, during the two decades that followed, until the fall of the shah in 1979, Israel had to invest a good deal of diplomatic effort into the preservation of this source of fuel.

The Small Pipeline

One important means toward this end was a pipeline from Eilat to Ashkelon, a joint project with the Iranians. The concept of a pipeline from Eilat to the Mediterranean, which could meet acute political and economic fuel needs, first emerged in Israel toward the end of the 1948 War but crystallized only in the mid-1950s. Contributing factors included the international fuel companies' decision to sever contact with Israel, a similar decision by Moscow, the acquisition of the Haifa refineries by Israel, and the emerging possibility of finding, through independent and indirect activity in Iran, a strategic solution to the country's fuel-supply problems. These factors transformed the idea of the Eilat pipeline into a concept worth considering as a pragmatic option.

An important fact, not widely known, is that internal debate on the subject actually began immediately after Egypt nationalized the Suez Canal in July 1956, thereby posing a blatant strategic threat to a major route of fuel supplies to Europe. The Foreign Ministry in Jerusalem saw this as a good opportunity to renew its pipeline proposal, which Foreign Minister Eban conveyed during a meeting at the US State Department on the thirtieth of that month. Five days later, Ben-Gurion had occasion to note in his diary that it was necessary to prepare a budget estimate to address this matter, and subsequently the Foreign Ministry engaged in the issue for several months.[3]

According to Foreign Ministry assessments, Western powers stood to benefit from the project. First, it could circumvent the bottleneck problem of transporting oil through the canal at a time of growing demand. Eilat could serve as a convenient port for large tankers of nearly two hundred thousand tons that were unable to transit the Suez. Second, having an alternative of this sort could, in light of its potential use by Persian Gulf states, reducing the Arabs' ability to practice economic and political extortion. Third, because of its depth, the gulf of Eilat was less vulnerable than the Suez Canal to attempts to block it. Fourth, and most importantly, a pipeline to Eilat could teach the Egyptians that nationalization did not pay Jerusalem was well aware of the various obstacles to implementing this plan, and the situation following Egypt's nationalization did not pose an immediate threat to Israel's fuel supplies. Israel's objectives were primarily political: to apply pressure to allow Israeli transit through the canal, to ensure passage through the Straits of Tiran, and to thwart what was perceived as unilateral aggression by an Arab state. These goals did not seem unrealistic. However, the practical difficulties associated with construction of the pipeline seemed much greater. The entire project, using a thirty-two-inch pipe, was expected to cost $65 million, far beyond Israel's capacity at the time. Moreover, Israel lacked the capability to produce such pipelines, and naturally, it feared that without strong political support, none of the oil companies would join the endeavor. The projected timeline of the venture was quite long (two years), which detracted from its appeal. Above all, there was great uncertainty surrounding Iran's willingness to supply fuel.

It soon became clear to Israel that its fears were founded. The British Foreign Office termed the plan a "pipedream" and "white elephant" given that Egypt could quite easily block transit to Eilat (219). The expected opposition of the Arab world precluded any receptivity to the plan among the British and other oil companies. The US stance was similar to that of the British, though less overt. Both countries apparently preferred to construct a pipeline from Iran to Turkey as a partial and more realistic alternative to the Suez Canal, and American oil companies shared these views. One US expert, to whom Israel turned for advice, described the plan as "excellent . . . but totally unrealistic" (ibid.). A British specialist, however, took a different view, stating that it would be "either unnecessary (in a rational world of peace) or not applicable (in a world where there is no power struggle between Israel and the Arabs)" not only because of Arab opposition but also because members of Iran's oil consortium were expected to be averse (ibid.). The only positive responses came from a few French businesspersons and government officials who wanted "not to put all their eggs in one basket" and were prepared "to stab Nasser in the back." They were also willing to assist in financing the preparation of a construction plan, which the French company Trapil then implemented. Israel continued, in addition, to pursue the possibility of US participation, as the US companies had special weight in the Iranian consortium. The state followed this three-pronged approach for three months, until war broke out. However, its efforts became operationally significant and yielded practical results for the first time only in the war's aftermath.

The main factor was the Soviets' termination of fuel supply agreements that would have met more than a third of Israel's needs. Another was the unavailability, once fighting broke out, of two Middle Eastern fuel supply routes: in early November, a section of the Iraqi pipeline in Syria was destroyed, and the Egyptians blockaded the canal. Moreover, because of this blockade, oil tankers transiting from Iran to Haifa through the Cape of Good Hope could not make the return journey, as in the past, through the Suez Canal, and the situation compelled Israel to seek significantly more expensive fuel from Venezuela. Israeli control over Sinai, and the hope that it would be possible to guarantee freedom of navigation in the Straits of Tiran, thus gave the pipeline project immediate operational significance. Unsurprisingly, a few days after the outbreak of hostilities, Ben-Gurion voiced the opinion to IDF commanders that freedom of transit for fuel transport through the Straits of Tiran was a matter of "life and death" for Israel. He also expressed the view that "if we can exploit the oil [in Sinai] and bring it from there to Haifa . . . by ship . . . then we are free of foreign [dependence]. We have oil" (34).[4] Shortly thereafter, Israeli officials concluded that a small oil pipeline from Eilat was a realistic way of covering some of Israel's needs while simultaneously pursuing the "grand plan." These efforts, however, did not yield any results despite interest on the part of a French company, Lazard Frères. The British held to their previous position, and Paris eventually conceded to American pressure and dropped the issue.

Under these circumstances, considering the relatively cheap cost of laying an eight-inch pipe from Eilat to Be'er Sheva and a sixteen-inch pipe from there to Ashkelon, within a projected time frame of a few months, Israel decided to give the operation a green light. To expedite matters, the state claimed the right to confiscate equipment such as pipes (totaling nearly two hundred kilometers in length), pumps, shipping containers, and tanks belonging to the Italian oil company ENI, which was working with a Belgian company at the preoperational Blaim oil field south of Ras Sudar in the Sinai. Israel began taking practical measures in the first week of December 1956. Some of the policy makers in Jerusalem were skeptical, calling the plan a "gamble." Israel Kosloff, a leading oil expert at the time, termed it a "guinea pig" in a private letter. One of the crucial variables was Iran. The possibility of making a profit if this channel could be guaranteed was indisputable. A ton of Iranian crude oil, for example, cost about twenty-one dollars in Eilat, twenty-eight dollars in Haifa, and thirty-one dollars if imported from Venezuela. In addition, despite the skepticism in Jerusalem regarding the stance among the large oil companies in the Iranian consortium on the issue of supply through Eilat, IRICON and NIOC had the right to exploit about 18 percent of the total output. They could also buy fuel from the major companies and market it as they wished. Assessments in Jerusalem therefore concluded that Israel could potentially acquire five million tons of crude oil per year—well beyond its own needs—at least two million tons of which could have been distilled in Haifa.

These optimistic forecasts, however, were unable to clarify NIOC's true stance, which became evident only in early 1957. That, alongside the "green light" granted to independent Israeli imports after Shell's departure around the same time, marked the start of a new era. Iranian oil flowed into Eilat unhindered, while the deal itself remained highly secret and, publicly, Tehran vigorously denied any involvement. Meanwhile, construction soon began in Israel to produce a sixteen-inch pipe that would replace the existing one. By 1958, most of the fuel for local consumption was reaching Israel through the pipe. Two years later, two Israeli tankers began conveying oil from Iran, allowing Israel to engage in small-scale export. The refineries in Haifa increased operations substantially over the years, and by 1966 they were processing some 3.5 million tons of fuel, with 200,000 tons of it designated for export. Moreover, Israel succeeded in enlisting Iran's participation in the financing and operation of the "midsized" pipeline after Baron Edmond de Rothschild agreed to underwrite a large portion and head the managing company, Tri-Continental. It was actually the Iranians who insisted that the company not be owned by the Israeli government, in order to reduce political obstacles to the steady supply of oil from sources east of the Suez.

The move also reflected Israel's policy of pursuing large international investors. Iran's acquiescence to the partnership apparently took shape after the concept of building a pipeline through Turkey and Iraq fell through in 1958. Other contributing factors included Israel's promises of a worthwhile return on their investment and above all Iran's strong interest in gaining experience in the international marketing of oil, which it was producing for the first time. Under the terms of the agreement, Iran would receive 10 percent of the shares. In order to conceal the partnership, the Iranians insisted on the creation of a straw company. Subsequently such an entity, named Fimarco, was registered in Liechtenstein, and the agreement entered into force on July 17, 1959. Besides resolving Israel's fuel problem, the arrangement was also an important strategic and political achievement.

The Big Pipeline

Israel's success in achieving the uninterrupted flow of Iranian oil into the country from the mid-1950s begs the question: Why did the ambitious plan for a large pipeline from Eilat remain on the national agenda? There were two main reasons: The first—the logical, expected, and public reason—was that such a project would transform Israel into a serious contender in the global oil market, the political importance of which could not be dismissed. The second, usually hidden, reason was Israel's near-absolute dependence on Iranian oil supplies (50 percent from NIOC and roughly 50 percent from consortium members). Foreign and domestic pressure by opponents of any ties with Israel made this an uncertain source. Furthermore, Israel's dependence allowed the Iranians to demand and receive prices that far exceeded market rates for more than a decade. Despite the absence of official diplomatic ties, the relations that existed between Iran and Israel were, in the words of an internal Foreign Ministry document at the time, "unique" and formed "an unwritten secret alliance." Israel fully appreciated that the best economic incentive it could offer the Iranians to ensure continuing supplies would be the establishment of a joint company "to carry out all operations, from transit to the sale of distillates abroad." The large pipeline remained a clear objective, but there was no point in proposing it as long as NIOC lacked the independent sources needed to enter into such a partnership. The relative stability of European demands for fuel and Iran's ability to meet them while maintaining current prices diminished the incentives for Iran to renew activities in this area. That changed, however, in the mid-1960s.

It was evident to Israel's policy makers that in a few years' time, the demand for transit through the Suez Canal by tankers would exceed capacity. The projected demand for 1970 was more than 250 million tons, but technical constraints limited the canal's capacity to 230 million tons. Israeli decision makers regarded the growing demand for oil from the Persian Gulf as a key factor in this context. In 1964, for example, 145 million tons transited through the canal, twice the amount conveyed during the year preceding the Suez crisis of 1956, and the forecast for 1970 predicted a 70 percent increase. Regarding the transit of Iranian fuel, the data in Israel's hands indicated an increase from 5 million tons in 1955 to 33 million in 1964 and a projected 60 million in 1970. This could have served as incentive to build giant tankers, which would have had to transit the Cape of Good Hope because the canal was too narrow and shallow, but many of Europe's ports were unable to accommodate vessels of this size. Moreover, transit through the cape was economically attractive for Israel only if the tankers could, after unloading, return to the Persian Gulf through the canal, but the forecast in Jerusalem was that the canal would not be able to meet the corresponding demand for transit. The estimated cost of installing a forty-inch pipeline in Eilat capable of pumping 45 million tons of oil a year was roughly $150 million, only half the cost of increasing the capacity of tankers destined for European ports via the cape. Construction of the pipeline could attract a good deal of traffic by giant tankers in the deep waters of Eilat's port, as well as the transport of oil from Ashkelon to Europe by small tankers capable of unloading at various European ports. Above all, for the first time NIOC had the independent capacity, to a certain degree, to feed some of the supply needed into the pipeline in a way that was economically viable. At the time, Israel was considering a gradual increase, beginning with 10 million tons of crude oil upon completion of the pipeline, within two to three years. This amount would, of course, cover Israel's annual consumption needs of close to 3 million tons, and the rest would be for export to Europe.

The concept was raised during a closed-door meeting between Israel's foreign minister and the Persian shah in July 1965. Subsequently, Israel prepared a detailed memorandum for the Iranian leader, which it also conveyed orally at a meeting in Tehran on August 15 between Fatollah Nafici (one of the heads of NIOC and the official in charge of contact with Israel) and Israel's director of water planning.

The signals coming from Iran at the time were encouraging: Israel heard that the shah "continue[d] to display great interest in the plan" and sought further technical details.[5] Evidently, Iran's leader wanted to see a specific work plan delineating Israel's initial steps, particularly with regard to funding. The project's complexity and secrecy necessitated a high-level sub-rosa meeting, and toward this end, Israel dispatched Zvi Dinstein (then senior aide to the prime minister at the Defense Ministry) to Tehran in the first week of January 1966. After Dinstein met with the shah, the chair of NIOC, and authorized directors, the Foreign Ministry in Israel received notice that "the pipeline had been reapproved [and] willingness to implement it . . . now seem[ed] more likely than what we previously thought." Apparently, Israel's promise of securing funding sources in Germany and elsewhere at an interest rate of 4 percent swayed those Iranians who were reluctant.

It should be noted that responsibility for the resolution of the project's financial problems fell to Israel. Nor did Iran commit itself regarding an equally weighty issue and a precondition for the pipeline's economic viability—namely, the volume of fuel from Iran to be delivered through the pipeline (the throughput), which remained a matter for later discussion. During the first weekend in February, Shinar and Nafici met in Geneva with Hermann Abs, the chair of Deutsche Bank, to explore options for financing.

Not until mid-March did the bank send its official reply, which was affirmative in principle but, regarding the crucial matter of terms, did not provide concrete figures. Rather, it noted in an appendix that the current rate was 8.5 percent, but it promised to try to improve on these terms in the global, including German, financial market. The letter also noted the need for Iranian guarantees. Iran's reaction was predictably negative, both because of the interest rate and, in particular, because of the pledges the bank required from both parties. These created a situation in which "the deal could not go through without being publicized; however, the principle of secrecy was and remained the *sine qua non* in all aspects of the transaction until sometime in the unforeseeable future when both sides decide explicitly to publicize the deal."

As expected, Tehran's reaction was to abort the process, at least temporarily, and deflect Israeli pressure to convene a meeting. Israel's emissaries to Tehran described such pressure as "counter to the Persian temperament and workstyle, and liable to aggravate them and make them suspect us of special interests that trump their own." Under these circumstances, Israel's emissaries believed, "the Iranians would conclude that Israel is passionately and keenly interested in [building the pipeline], when we should be acting as though the two sides have an equal interest. Otherwise [they] might be deterred or conclude that they can place the entire burden on us." Nafici's answer to the proposed interest rate left little room for optimism as it ran counter to "the Shah's credit policy and was liable to sabotage other business deals for them." The shah, accordingly, regarded the bank's reply as "a polite close to the first phase of examining the possibilities," leaving the responsibility to Israel to identify "more agreeable" sources of financing such as the United States, among others. He also noted that "for political reasons . . . it is best if the Israelis start establishing contact with international companies [with the understanding that] this is an Israeli initiative that has explicit Iranian approval, and that the Iranians will become more actively involved at a later stage as need and circumstances dictate." Thus, the ball was once again in Israel's court. Consequently it probably had no choice but to accept the shah's recommendation: Israel would submit what appeared to be an independent request to BP, which seemed the most positively inclined to supply oil to the pipeline. Israel and Iran also agreed that if BP refused for political reasons to use its fleet of tankers, NIOC would assume the responsibility.

On October 11, William Frazer of the BP directorate delivered the official reply: BP's calculations showed that at best the pipeline was not profitable and at worst it would incur losses and reduce the company's flexibility in the market; therefore, he could not respond in the affirmative. The reply effectively thwarted chances of advancing the issue. The shah, for his part, insisted that at least one member of the consortium commit to using the pipeline to ensure its profitability, and he still believed that "this task falls on [Israel]." Understandably, Israel drew the conclusion that "the Shah has developed misgivings over a partnership with us in the plan. He apparently feels [that] the use of supertankers keeps the Egyptians from interfering in the transit of Iranian oil, [that] partnership with Israel in the plan advances nothing in terms of Iran's national interests, [but] on the other hand [could] interfere with the Shah's regional political plans of forming an anti-Nasser front, drawing closer to Iraq, and separating [Iraq] from the Arab nationalist camp." Whether or not these were actually the shah's considerations, Israel and Iran resumed negotiations on the pipeline only after the Six-Day War.

The Project Springs to Life

The 1967 War was a formative event in Israeli-Iranian oil relations. Initially it did not seem so to Israel's delegates in Tehran, who had issued warnings shortly before the war that NIOC might cancel its transactions with Israel and sell the oil to other states, Japan in particular. At the same time, the Suez Canal's closure gave new impetus to Israel's envoys. From unofficial talks with Nafici, they concluded that he believed it was "now or never." They understood that the blockage of the canal justified operating the existing pipeline at full capacity for the sale or transport of crude oil to Europe, thus reinforcing the concept of oil conveyance through Israel, which "could serve [them] well in negotiations over the big plan." In a matter of days, the green light came from the shah, who was expecting a visit from an Israeli delegation to discuss the issue. During initial talks, Nafici responded very positively to the idea that Israel grant NIOC a concession for an exterritorial strip of land while outwardly remaining the owner of the pipeline, thus making it easier for the company to secure the required throughput from the consortium. Israel also received encouraging news from London and New York.

Given the earlier Iranian position on the need for the consortium members' support of the plan, and despite (or perhaps because of) the failure to enlist BP's backing, the finance minister instructed Israel's ambassador in London, with the help of a supportive intermediary, to approach Prime Minister Harold Wilson in order to understand his position and solicit his advice on the most effective way to continue inquiries regarding an oil supply to the pipeline. Wilson, who was known for his friendly attitude toward Israel, displayed "great interest" in the matter and recommended sidestepping the Foreign Office and BP by delivering a letter through Marcus Sieff, a leading member of Britain's Jewish community. Thus, under instructions from Wilson, Sieff met with Chancellor of the Exchequer James Callaghan on July 12 and handed him financial information on the pipeline.

At the same time, Israel focused on renewing the Iranian track. Zvi Doriel, Israel's semiofficial delegate in Tehran, received the official reply in mid-July: the shah dismissed the idea of NIOC as the official owner of the pipeline because, in the absence of formal relations, he did not see how Iran could publicly admit to owning a concession in Israeli territory. Iran also rejected Israel's earlier proposed solution to the problem of guarantees and ensuring oil flow, as it was unable to commit itself to the necessary throughput. Likewise, Nafici dismissed the idea of approaching the oil companies a second time. Instead, he recommended seeking clarifications with the British and US governments, as "the American presidential elections are not far off, the Jewish vote pulls a great deal of weight there, and in England public opinion towards Israel is favorable." In any event, Israelis engaged in the issue concluded that Iran was in no rush to finalize the oil deal.

That impression was reinforced in late July, when Israel learned that Iran had simultaneously tried to promote the failed concept of a pipeline to Turkey as an alternative to the canal and had hidden its efforts from the Israeli envoys in Tehran. The clarifications with Callaghan also came to naught after his experts and the cabinet's Committee on Foreign and Economic Affairs concluded that the project was economically unviable and "politically volatile." Thus, the notion of circumventing the British Foreign Office and oil companies was effectively thwarted.

These disappointments explain the pressure that Israel exerted in seeking the shah's agreement to invite Israeli finance minister Sapir to Tehran. Israel was now willing to concede on its demand that project costs be divided equally. Sapir, with Prime Minister Eshkol's authorization, proposed starting construction on the pipeline even if Iran agreed to foot only 20–25 percent of the investment. The information currently available does not tell us whether Israel had an alternative source of financing, but it seems reasonable to assume that this proposal was intended primarily to persuade the shah to reengage. The director of NIOC expressed "his supreme joy over the proposal," and the shah confirmed that he was anticipating a visit from Sapir. At their meeting, on September 12, Sapir proposed that, without the previous guarantee of throughput, Israel no longer insisted on a fifty-fifty partnership but would be satisfied with an Iranian partnership of 20–30 percent in which each side was committed to fulfilling its part. Presumably Israel was relying on the potential of exploiting the Sinai's oil fields (which it had seized during the war and whose output exceeded Israel's needs) to ensure the projected oil flow through the pipeline. Sapir informed the Iranian leader that several German and other companies were prepared to purchase oil from the pipeline at a yearly rate of five million tons if it operated at an annual flow capacity of ten million tons. The loans, it was expected, would be repaid relatively quickly from the pipeline's income. Israeli journalists Yuval Elizur and Eliyahu Salpeter quoted Sapir as telling the shah that "a person doesn't take out an insurance policy because he fears dying, but in the hope of making a profit. Iran can overcome the Western oil companies and—with help from Israeli and its allies—become an oil superpower on a global scale."[6] The protocol reveals nothing of the shah's specific commitment, but all of his comments seemed supportive. Sapir evidently drew his own conclusions and, before leaving Tehran, issued instructions to begin purchasing the equipment necessary for the pipeline. The information that arrived from NIOC's director two days later indicated that the shah "[was] determined and very serious" about the matter, which he personally "regard[ed] as concluded."

The message seemed credible. A week later, the shah's official reply arrived, approving the general contours of the plan. He requested that the project be announced as a purely Israeli affair "without any mention whatsoever of Iranian partnership until the time is right." Sapir was told that "in Iran and within NIOC the matter remains one of top secrecy, and no living soul other than Nafici and Manuchehr Eqbal [the company manger] should know about it." The company's shares would be registered in Zurich under the name of an Israeli proxy, and after registration, the proxy would sell half its shares to an Iranian company. The shah seemed to have rejected the Israeli proposal for an asymmetrical partnership, despite the larger financial investment therefore required on Iran's part. Sapir understood that Iran had fully approved the deal, and he set off for Europe and South America during the latter half of September to seek investors. As with the midsized pipeline project, Israel needed investors willing to purchase the majority of its own portion of the shares.

Sapir failed, however, to enlist support from Baron Edmond de Rothschild, who judged the venture unprofitable and doomed to failure. The baron had never (since well before the agreement with Iran began to take shape) tried to conceal his opinion from government representatives. In order not to compromise the deal, therefore, Israel kept him in the dark regarding its progress. Only when agreement seemed near did Israel inform the baron of the negotiations and request his support. He replied that in his view, still, "there was no economic justification for laying a huge pipeline absent any guarantee from a party with independent oil sources to use it," although he "[could] understand the government's political reasons and consideration for allocating the necessary funds for the project." His decision also disappointed the Iranians, who continued to pressure Israel, in vain, to find a way to satisfy the Jewish banker. They believed that Rothschild was deeply offended by Israel's having "hidden the entire plan from him for two years."

A parallel attempt to interest the American millionaire David Rockefeller in a partnership also failed. Rockefeller informed the Israeli representatives that the project was economically unsound "because of the reality that had been created with the closure of the Canal and the decision to build supertankers as an alternative." However, he expressed willingness to help with respect to the loan. Israel's fervid activity also included clandestine contacts with Shell regarding the leasing of their tankers. On October 3, Sapir and Nafici met in London and agreed that the pipeline company be divided equally among the partners; each side would purchase $8 million worth of shares and provide guarantees for a loan of 50 percent of the outstanding amount. They also agreed that joint companies be set up in a third country to disguise the arrangement (as with the small pipeline) and a joint committee be established to implement the project. The bilateral agreement contained Israel's promise to help NIOC obtain the necessary loan to finance its part of the pipeline, which amounted to $22 million. The question of the pipeline's throughput was conspicuously absent. Israel's decision to yield on this point was conveyed directly to the shah.

Despite all the efforts at keeping it secret, such intense, behind-the-scenes activity was bound to be discovered. Given the leaks, and to minimize damage, on October 20, 1967, Israel announced its decision "to replace the existing oil line between Eilat and Ashkelon with a new 42-inch-diameter pipe. This operation will enable a significant expansion in oil passage from the Port of Eilat to the Mediterranean." The publicity was apparently also meant to signal that Israel was committed to implementing the project. Two days later the cabinet Committee on Economic Affairs barred any further publicity on the subject. Iran also had to expand the circle privy to the matter in order to advance the deal and obtain official and domestic approval, according to reports that reached Jerusalem. Not all Iranian cabinet ministers approved of the proposed pipeline. Thus, during a critical meeting in Tehran, the finance minister, Dr. Jamshid Amuzegar, displayed discomfort with the project and posed "vexing questions" despite opening remarks by NIOC's director stressing that the shah had already sanctioned the plan. The minister of economy was also unfavorably disposed toward sharing the burden of investment equally. Nafici therefore sought the indirect assistance of Israeli delegates in Tehran in averting a "scene" before the shah that "would put a bee in his bonnet." He also asked them to ensure that the shah not form the wrong impression about Egypt's military ability to derail the project, given Egypt's recent missile assault and sinking of the Israeli naval destroyer *Eilat*.

It is hard to say how much this activity actually contributed, but any economic value was not immediately apparent. While the Iranian minister of economy apparently changed his position, the finance minister stuck to his rejectionist view of the project even at a crucial cabinet meeting on November 13 (attended by the shah and a small number of ministers). Israel's representatives later learned that Amuzegar's reservations revolved around two main issues: the position of the companies and the need to consult with them before deciding on the construction of the pipeline, and the position of the Arabs who undoubtedly knew about Iran's involvement in the project. The shah responded unequivocally that a partnership in the construction of the pipeline was a done deal, "regardless of any reservations, whether justified or not." He told the forum, "Even if the pipeline lies empty . . . and Iran loses several million dollars this year, the project will still have been productive . . . since this is the most important political step that Iran has taken in protecting its national interests." According to Iranian sources, when the shah finished speaking, "everyone remained silent, and this was the signal to take action."

This was not, however, full strategic acquiescence by Iran but rather the start of difficult legal, economic, financial, and technical discussions on the practical aspects of the bilateral understandings. During three months of talks, the possibility of reaching agreement often seemed highly unlikely. Understandably, Israel pressed for a meeting at the highest level of government to ensure a settlement.

In late January 1968, Eban arrived in Tehran for a closed-door meeting with the shah, the importance of which cannot be overstated. Framing the pipeline as the primary issue in Israeli-Iranian relations, Eban stressed that "we must not pull out of the project . . . which is of such tremendous political and strategic importance and economic advantage." The shah replied, "Regarding the nineteen million [tons of Iranian oil that would pass through the pipeline], I am convinced of the project's potential and I see no difficulties. Let us implement the first stage. As for what will happen later, the question is who will take the risk of buying from the pipeline? You, we, and Romania are not enough." Despite the positive exchange of words, the following weeks demonstrated that there remained seemingly inextricable obstacles that required major efforts on Israel's part.

One of these difficulties was the critical question of German financing. The issue was resolved only on the very eve of the pipeline agreement's day of signature. The bank had to receive government approval to grant credit for the project, which was a delicate political issue. Moreover, the timing was most inconvenient because in early 1968 the government was fully engaged in efforts to renew relations with the Arab world, which had soured after it established full diplomatic ties with Israel in 1965. Ten Arab states had suspended ties with Bonn, and three had closed their embassies. German support for the Israeli project was liable to sabotage these reconciliation efforts. Initially the government therefore asked the bank to withdraw its proposal, a step that would have aborted the entire project. Eventually, though, it decided to honor its promises. Only a final effort by Dinstein, which required a visit to Tehran in his capacity as deputy finance minister, succeeded in removing other critical obstacles. One week before signing the deal, Iran sent a draft detailing the financial matters, which they posed as an ultimatum: Israel had to sign the agreement or view it as "null and void, and return to square one." Lacking any alternative, Israel accepted the draft in its entirety.

The final agreement, the details of which for some reason still remain classified at the Israel State Archives, was signed in Tehran on February 29, 1968, by Eqbal, the president of NIOC, and Sapir, who officially inaugurated the jointly owned Trans-Asiatic Company. It was licensed to operate for forty-nine years under the contract, which also stipulated that alongside an Israeli general manager, there had to be an Iranian company chair. Considerations stemming from its obsessive secrecy, however, led Iran to concede eventually to an Israeli (Ben Dror) as company chair. When disagreement arose over the price that Israel would have to pay for Iranian oil, Sapir was adamant that in light of the great risk Israel was taking, there was no room for Iran's traditional insistence on prices above current market rates. It was only with the shah's intervention that Iran ultimately consented, evidently just this once, to Israel's demand. Under the arrangement, the pipeline's capacity would be limited to nine million tons per year during the first stage. Israel estimated that within two years this would reach sixteen million, of which six million would serve consumption needs and be used to generate by-products for export, and ten million would comprise oil in transit to other markets.

The pipe laying began in June 1968 and was completed within a year. The first batch of oil began flowing through the Eilat-Ashkelon line in early December 1969. By 1970, the Eilat port was receiving 162 tanker shipments of oil totaling nearly ten million tons a year for the pipeline, 92 from Iran and 70 from Sinai. At a secret meeting with Eban near the end of the year, the "landlord"—as the shah was occasionally termed in Israeli internal correspondence—expressed his pleasure "with the developments respecting the pipeline." When Eban pointed out that there was no lack of demand, the shah replied, "If there's a supply, there will be a demand."

In August 1971, Israel and Iran agreed to allocate additional investments in order to increase production in 1973 to forty million tons per year. German financial credit totaled 30 million marks. Later, the project received an additional credit line of $6.75 million. A large portion of both the actual and projected growth was influenced by the steep rise in NIOC's independent output of crude oil, which started at seven million tons in 1969 and was expected to reach twenty-nine million within six years. NIOC undoubtedly influenced foreign firms in Iran with franchises to search for and produce oil, persuading them to convey it through the pipeline. Documentation on the identity of non-Israeli oil buyers and their portions of the purchases is unavailable, but it is known that Romania was one of the biggest importers of Iranian oil being conveyed through the pipeline. The British ambassador to Israel claimed that the reason the Arabs refrained from protesting the profitable Israeli-Iranian cooperation was that this destination, Romania, was an ally of the Arabs. It should be noted that for Nicolae Ceaușescu, the ambitious Romanian leader, achieving development targets depended on Romania's ability to quench its growing thirst for oil. The biggest impediment was that Romania had already reached peak crude production and had repeatedly failed to meet industrial demand. Iranian oil imports allowed the Romanians to intensify industrialization while preserving their own energy resources. However, as Roham Alvandi and Eliza Gheorghe recently demonstrated, there was more to this story.[7] Romania actually had significant oil reserves, but it preferred to import lower-quality crude oil from Iran for its own consumption, while exporting gasoline and other refined products derived from the more profitable and better-quality Romanian oil. Israel and Iran both benefited from these circumstances, which facilitated the passage of large quantities of this oil thorough the Eilat-Ashkelon pipeline.

One manifestation of Israel's high expectations at the time was its decision in 1969 to build another oil refinery, in Ashdod. One of the underlying rationales was the need to provide employment in Israel's development towns and developing regions for security and strategic considerations. In August 1971, the parties agreed to increase output to fifty million tons. Operations peaked in the immediate aftermath of the 1973 War, with profits that reached $20 million. The decline began shortly afterward, even before the opening of the Suez Canal in 1975, creating genuine competition between the possible routes of transit for Iranian oil. The entire project shut down after the shah's fall in 1978 and the decision of the revolutionary Islamic government to sever all ties with Israel. To this day, Israel and Iran are engaged in a legal battle over the financial repercussions of the project's termination.

Interestingly, closure of the canal and the concomitant loss of income ($300 million a year), on the one hand, and the public announcement of the Eilat-Ashkelon pipeline, on the other, led Cairo to decide in February 1968 to build a forty-two-inch pipeline in Egypt to convey oil from the Gulf of Suez to the Mediterranean. Three years later, it signed an agreement toward this end. For reasons that recall, in part, the circumstances surrounding discussions over the Eilat-Ashkelon pipeline, the Egyptian pipeline opened only in early 1977 and has proved its economic worth since. The difficulty in realizing the Egyptian project thus saved the Eilat-Ashkelon pipeline from a competition that would have certainly lessened its economic value. Equally notable is the fact that since July 2003, Israel's pipeline has operated in reverse, conveying oil from Ashkelon to Eilat. For more than a decade, it has provided transport for oil from Russia (Israel's largest current supplier) and Caspian Sea states that is loaded at the Black Sea for Asian destinations, primarily China and India.

After the Fall of the Shah

Historians have thoroughly explored and exposed the story of Israel's search for fuel supplies through the mid-1970s, using Israeli and other documentation. Iran's withdrawal from Israel's fuel economy, in contrast, has yet to receive the same attention and analysis, primarily because the relevant documents remain classified. We therefore cannot present that perspective with the same degree of resolution. Nonetheless, we can point to a number of strategically significant experiences Israel underwent at the time, which confirm that the issue has remained a core agenda item in Jerusalem since the fall of the shah. Let us briefly describe some of these dynamics.

One of the key drivers of Israel's search for energy sources was cost. During the 1970s, especially with the Arab oil boycott that followed the 1973 War, oil prices soared meteorically. In 1967, for example, Israel paid $60 million for oil; in 1973, the price rose to $209 million, and a year later, it reached $629 million. In 1978, it was $775 million, and by 1980, the figure was $1.9 billion. Regarding fuel sources, concerns about the possible termination of Iran's fuel supply were a salient issue during internal debates in Jerusalem well before the overthrow of the shah, and a search for alternatives was underway by early 1972. The alternatives that theoretically existed were also of a lesser quality from Israel's perspective. Oil from the North Sea and Mexico was much "lighter" and less suited to Israel's electricity needs and distillate-production requirements, which had been specifically adapted to Middle Eastern oil even before independence. It also entailed high transport costs. In any event, the balance of Israeli fuel imports during the last year of the "Iranian connection" indicates that of its total consumption of 7.5 million tons, Israel received 4.5 from Iran, 1.5 from Mexico, and 1.5 from the Sinai oil field Alma (which Israel developed over the course of a decade and which remained in Israeli hands after the disengagement agreements of 1975). The remainder came from occasional purchases. One year later, Israel found itself in a hopeless situation, dependent for at least half its consumption needs on uncertain sources. Bribery, for example, became part of the work of Israel's envoys to ensure fuel supplies, as illustrated by one anecdote about conveying a suitcase full of millions of dollars to the president of Gabon, who took the time to count the cash slowly and systematically in the envoys' presence.[8] Israeli assessments at the time were that such dependence was a material threat to national security. Above all, concerns stemmed from the concessions Israel had made in the disengagement (1975) and peace (1979) agreements with Egypt with regard to the oil wells in Sinai. Until that time, those wells had helped Israel meet a substantial portion of its energy needs. In her recently completed PhD dissertation, Efrat Shaoulian-Sopher found that Israel's agreement to return the Egyptian Sinai oil fields to Egypt was a result of Rabin's personal visit in the spring of 1975 to Tehran, to secure personal assurances from the shah that Iran would substitute any oil that would have originated from the Sinai with its own oil.[9]

How did Israel's leaders deal with this difficult state of affairs? Only the general contours of the complex and twisted plot have become known. What we do know is that Israeli political strategy was based on four pillars: securing alternative supplies, particularly from Mexico and Norway; reaching fuel-supply agreements with Egypt after signing the peace treaty; securing guarantees from the United States that it would help the state meet its energy needs in the event of a crisis; and reducing Israel's dependence on oil by gradually shifting to coal for electricity production.

The need for an alternative to Iranian oil was a source of concern for policy makers even when it flowed uninterrupted to Eilat, and particularly with the Arab boycott after the 1973 War. The importance of finding a "parallel," in Eshkol's words, gave the prime minister no rest, and he persistently queried relevant officials on the matter.[10] An internal Foreign Ministry debate in January 1972 addressed the possibility that Egypt might successfully persuade Iran to stop selling fuel to Israel, or that Iran would decide to do so itself, and concluded that Israel needed to find alternatives.[11] Concerns only intensified when Israel learned, through direct communication between the new prime minister, Menachem Begin, and the shah about a month before his fall, that "if the Security Council imposes an oil embargo on Israel, he will join."[12] The course of action that then began to take shape centered on Mexico and the North Sea. Mexico became an additional source of fuel in 1973, when the country first began exporting fuel independently. The volume was initially small because of transportation costs and quality, but by the mid-1980s, it reached 40 percent of Israel's consumption needs. Israel paid dearly for this energy supply but lacked any realistic alternative at the time, especially as Norway declined offers made by Israel during the 1970s. Oslo changed its stance in the early 1980s, when Israel agreed to pay particularly high prices for Norwegian oil. The high transport costs made the value of this source questionable, and indeed, in 1985 Israel suspended imports.

For understandable reasons, Israel wanted a portion (about $1.5 million tons per year) of its fuel supply to continue coming from the Sinai oil wells even after the peace treaty with Egypt obligated it to vacate them. The Egyptians, however, held firmly to their stance: they would be willing to sell oil to Israel after the normalization of relations but were unwilling to commit to quantity or price, which made them a particularly problematic source. Even the United States was unable to dissuade them from this position. Still, Egyptian oil, transacted only in cash, continued to flow unhindered into Israel for decades; even extreme crises such as the Lebanon War have not disrupted cooperation in the energy sector. However, Israel was not sure it could rely on the Egyptians, so it focused on securing US commitments to meet Israel's consumption needs through other sources at reasonable rates. And indeed, the United States provided Israel with such pledges on two important occasions: in 1975, when it signed the Sinai disengagement agreement, and in 1979, when Israel agreed to withdraw from the Sinai Peninsula under the terms of its peace treaty with Egypt. Fortunately for Israel, considering the domestic political obstacles the US administration would face if it ever attempted to meet such an unusual obligation, this arrangement (which officially lasted until November 1994) was never put to the test. Until that time Israeli experts warned not to take very seriously US promises on the provision of oil in times of crisis. Jerusalem's sense of vulnerability regarding the matter of energy sources therefore persisted. Thus, we learn of an internal Foreign Ministry debate in April 1980, which concluded that "no oil-importing country is as dependent as Israel on the soft market for such a high proportion of its fuel supplies. Reliance on uncertain sources for 45% of the supply constitutes a material threat to Israel's national security."[13] We can also understand why, as noted earlier, Israel was willing to relinquish the oil wells of Abu Rudeis as part of the disengagement agreement with Egypt in 1975: Iran was its main supplier at the time. Four years later that fact became a source of unprecedented complications when Israel, while deeply immersed in peace talks with Egypt, had to cope with Iran's sudden departure under Khomeini from its fuel supply map.

Israel was also successful in securing fuel from another source. Two decades earlier it had decided to reduce its dependence on imports by generating electricity using power plants fed by coal as well as fuel oil, and the facility subsequently built in Hadera in 1975 indeed proved its worth as a solution to Eshkol's parallel problem. In terms of price and potential suppliers, coal was a genuine bonanza, especially in light of the strategic relationship Israel formed with South Africa in the mid-1970s, making the latter a major supplier. By 1988, more than half of Israel's electricity was generated by coal, the vast majority of which came from South Africa. It is important to bear in mind, however, that despite its achievements in the energy sector, Israel remained dependent on foreign suppliers.

Future historians with access to Israeli documentation on these and other topics will be able to analyze Israel's efforts to secure energy sources during and since the 1970s within the complex political and economic reality of the "land of milk and honey" but no oil, in which Jerusalem has had to operate since Israel achieved statehood. No doubt they will also explore the dramatic shift that took place in the first decade of the twenty-first century, with the discovery of natural gas along Israel's coast. This discovery has had far-reaching implications. Suffice it to note that in February 2018, Israeli oil production companies and Egyptian companies signed an agreement providing gas to Egypt in quantities that amount to $15 billion over the course of a decade. The State of Israel is expected to receive about 50 percent of the volume of gas contracts, and the royalties and taxes are expected to amount to NIS 2.5–3 billion a year. In many ways, Israel thus became a regional energy supplier at the start of this century.[14]

Since independence, Israel has dedicated itself not only to ensuring a continuous supply of these natural reserves but also to its own demographic fortification. This task has constituted a central pillar of Israel's foreign policy, which is analyzed in the next chapter.

Notes

1. Annand Toprani, "Oil and Grand Strategy: Great Britain and Germany, 1918–1941" (PhD diss., Georgetown University, 2012), 143.

2. "MeKheletz Ad Nir Am—HaNeft SheLo Tarakhnu Legalot" [From Kheletz to Nir Am: The oil we did not bother to discover], *Al HaMishmar Daily*, November 2, 1964.

3. The source for the excerpts and account that follow, until indicated otherwise, is Uri Bialer, *Oil and the Arab-Israeli Conflict* (London, Palgrave, 1999).

4. Uri Bialer, "Fuel Bridge across the Middle East: Israel, Iran, and the Eilat-Ashkelon Oil Pipeline," *Israel Studies* 12, no. 3 (2007): 29–67.

5. Ibid.

6. Yuval Elizur and Eliyahu Salpeter, *Alilot Neft* [Israel's oil adventures] (Tel Aviv, Zmora, 1999).

7. Roham Alvandi and Eliza Gheorghe, "The Shah's Petro-diplomacy with Ceausescu: Iran and Romania in the Era of Détente" (working paper, Cold War International History Project, December 2014).

8. Elizur and Salpeter, *Alilot Neft*.

9. Efrat Shaoulian-Sopher, "Israeli Foreign Policy towards Iran, 1948–1979: Beyond the Realist Account" (PhD diss., London School of Economics, 2017), 308.

10. Elizur and Salpeter, *Alilot Neft*.

11. Vered to foreign minister, January 10, 1972, via Israel State Archives (ISA), file 3247/6 [in Hebrew].

12. Cabinet meeting, March 14, 1979, via ISA [in Hebrew].

13. April 23, 1980, via ISA, file 9087/4 [in Hebrew].

14. Lior Guttman, "Exit Mitzri: Kol Ma SheTsarikh LaDa'at Al Heskem HaGaz Be-15 Milliard Dollar" [Egyptian exit: Everything you need to know about the $15 billion gas agreement], *Kalkalist*, February 20, 2018. On the general issue, see Shouki Stern, "Natural Gas," *Ministry of National Infrastructures* (Jerusalem 2011) [in Hebrew].

7   "Let My People Go"

Fᴩᴏᴍ ɪᴛs ɪɴᴄᴇᴩᴛɪᴏɴ, Zionism had two objectives: saving Jews from oppression and establishing a territorial base for the Jewish people in its ancient homeland. The tension between salvation and *binyan ha'aretz* ("the building of the land"), between the needs of the Diaspora and those of the national base, was a permanent feature of the Zionist enterprise. Although many saw the two missions as complementary, believing that salvation would follow from aliyah and binyan ha'aretz, there was constant disagreement over the prioritization of concrete objectives, which did not always pull in the same direction operationally. The tension manifested, in particular, in internal debates over restrictions on immigration and the practice of selection among those who wanted to make aliyah. During the 1940s immigration policy changed in response to the Holocaust in Europe, which starkly underscored the issue of salvation, on the one hand, and the acute and pressing need to establish the demographic, economic, and military foundation of a state, on the other. These considerations effectively sidelined the question of selection (as reflected, for example, in the inclusion of Jews from Islamic countries in Zionist immigration programs) but did not do away with it altogether. The practice of selection persisted even for countries that permitted aliyah. Sebastian Klor's groundbreaking study on Jewish immigration from Argentina in 1962–1963, for example, reveals that the selective policy of Israeli agencies undeniably shaped the composition of immigrants, most of whom were families and young people.[1]

In any event, the end of the 1948 War placed the issue of immigration and immigrant absorption at the very top of Israel's national agenda, mainly because of the belief that only substantial population growth could ensure the state's survival. International proposals to restrict Jewish immigration as a measure toward resolution of the Arab-Israeli conflict began to emerge after May 1948. Foreign Minister Moshe Sharett explained the state's firm opposition to these proposals by citing the importance of preserving its "lifeblood."[2] Ben-Gurion, who was similarly unequivocal, would routinely cite the latest immigration figures at the outset of weekly Ministry of Defense meetings on military and strategic issues. Nor is there any doubt that the scale of immigration during that period was impressive. Between 1948 and 1951, nearly 690,000 new *olim* (immigrants) arrived, doubling the country's Jewish population. Moreover, Israel's continuous demographic growth since that time stems mainly from frequent waves of

Table 7.1. Immigration to Israel, 1948–2014

Year	Immigrants	Year	Immigrants	Year	Immigrants
2014	26,500	1991	176,100	1969	38,111
2013	16,968	1990	199,516	1968	20,703
2012	16,557	1989	24,050	1967	14,469
2011	16,892	1988	13,034	1966	15,957
2010	16,633	1987	12,965	1965	31,115
2009	14,574	1986	9,505	1964	55,036
2008	13,701	1985	10,642	1963	64,489
2007	18,131	1984	19,981	1962	61,533
2006	19,269	1983	16,906	1961	47,735
2005	21,183	1982	13,723	1960	24,692
2004	20,899	1981	12,599	1959	23,988
2003	23,273	1980	20,428	1958	27,290
2002	33,570	1979	37,222	1957	72,634
2001	43,473	1978	26,394	1956	56,330
2000	60,201	1977	21,429	1955	37,528
1999	76,766	1976	19,754	1954	18,491
1998	56,730	1975	20,028	1953	11,575
1997	66,221	1974	31,979	1952	24,610
1996	70,919	1973	54,886	1951	175,279
1995	76,361	1972	55,888	1950	170,563
1994	79,844	1971	41,930	1949	239,954
1993	76,805	1970	36,750	1948	101,828
1992	77,057				

Total: 3,152,146

Source: Jewish Virtual Library, www.jewishvirtuallibrary.org/total-immigration-to-israel-by-year.

new olim. Between Israel's founding and 2010, some three million Jews immigrated to Israel—60 percent from Europe, 16 percent from Africa, 14 percent from Asia, and the rest from the Americas and Australia. At the end of that period, foreign-born Israelis constituted about one-quarter of the population and one-third of the labor force.

Over the years the immigration rate fluctuated, and countries of origin varied. But immigration never ceased, as table 7.1 illustrates. Most of these immigrants, 1,737,000 in all, arrived in 1948–2005 from Eastern Europe, the Soviet Union, and Russia. Such large-scale immigration required investing energy and effort in Israel's foreign relations, and several studies published over the past decade and a half shed light on these efforts. Given the issue's scope and complexity, this chapter can only outline a few of the main historical contours. It focuses, therefore, on aliyah from those countries that restricted or prohibited emigration and necessitated intervention in various forms by the Foreign Ministry, Israeli secret services, and international Jewish organizations: certain Eastern European countries, the Soviet Union, Iraq, Morocco, and Ethiopia.

The Gates of Eastern Europe

During its early years, most of Israel's aliyah efforts focused on Eastern Bloc countries. In the immediate aftermath of World War II, the Jews who remained in this part of the world were seen as the most important and promising potential immigrant population, especially as their aliyah was seen as an act of salvation (*aliyat hatzalah*, meaning "rescue aliyah"). There were some 40,000 Jews in Czechoslovakia, 200,000 in Hungary, 350,000 in Romania, 50,000 in Bulgaria, and 230,000 in Poland (some of whom were residing in the Soviet Union). Ensuring their emigration before the Iron Curtain fell was a prime operational objective for the Jewish Agency's Executive. By the time Israel achieved independence, the Jewish Agency had managed to smuggle about 250,000 Jews from Central and Eastern Europe into Italy, France, and Germany, through an operation termed the Briha (flight), and nearly 100,000 "illegal" refugees into Mandatory Palestine. After 1948 these efforts continued under conditions that improved in three aspects: removal of the British blockade, the presence in Central and Eastern Europe of official Israeli entities whose primary objective was to promote aliyah, and the increased resources available to Israel in pursuit of this goal. Israel's endeavors led to the aliyah of nearly 300,000 Jews from the Eastern Bloc in 1951. According to estimates at the time, after this massive wave there still remained hundreds of thousands of potential olim in these countries (excluding the Soviet Union). Indeed, recently declassified Communist Party documents from Bucharest reveal, for example, that in the spring of 1950, when it appeared that Romanian authorities were prepared to permit massive emigration, more than 100,000 Jews submitted requests.

What obstacles did Israel face in pursuing this aim, and how did it successfully overcome them? The first obstacle, which Israel encountered in every country where it sought to promote aliyah, was that from an international relations perspective, encouraging emigration from another country is regarded as interference in that country's domestic affairs and a challenge to its sovereignty. It naturally provokes resistance, and all the more so in the post–World War II Eastern Bloc system, which as a matter of principle restricted the internal and external movement of its citizens. More than any other political system at the time, the Eastern Bloc viewed open emigration as a threat to its core existential principles. The second obstacle was the natural suspicion of Soviet and Eastern European leaders, who feared that even though political relations with Israel were growing closer, the latter was still aligned with the Western anti-Communist camp. They were therefore extremely cautious about any unwanted consequences of support for Israel, which included granting permission for mass aliyah. The Polish secret service from early 1948 was thus of the opinion that among Jews, all political groups (except for the Communist Party [PPR]) depended on foreign entities for whom the presence of Jews in Poland was nothing more than a political tool in their hands."[3] Accordingly, the service considered it essential to monitor and surveil the Israeli legation in its capital.[4] Given that these suspicions were also raised openly, it comes as no surprise that Israel Barzilai, Israel's first envoy to Warsaw, encountered difficulties. In a 1950 report, he described how, over the course of "an entire year,"

> my arguments with the Foreign Ministry and other ministers in Poland over aliyah never ceased. This is not a simple matter for them. You can explain a thousand times that aliyah and independence are linked, but they do not accept it. . . . They say, look at the example of France. It has tens of millions of residents and they are still subservient to Truman, and the same for Italy. So how can you, a country of three million, be independent? They have trouble accepting our theory of independence based on strength and aliyah. Yet when you point out that even [if] from their point of view quantity does not ensure independence, a minimal quantity does mean subservience and stagnation; that if Mao Tse Tung had had half a million rather than four million people, the revolution would have been meaningless. And in our situation, lack of quantity means an inability to establish ourselves even at a minimal level.[5]

The solution adopted by Eastern Bloc leaders, therefore, was to permit partial and temporary aliyah on a selective basis, which in turn required Israel to engage in a constant struggle to enable more Jewish emigration.

The third obstacle was Israel's limited freedom of operation. These countries typically placed severe restrictions on the activities and movements of diplomats and foreigners as well as local Jews. Physically smuggling Jews across borders, as practiced during the British Mandate, posed major obstacles for the Israeli establishment in post-1948 Eastern Europe. Despite having an entire organization dedicated to the cause, in 1951 Israel managed to smuggle only forty Jews out of all Eastern Bloc countries, according to Yaakov Kedmi, the former head of Nativ (Israel's liaison bureau for aliyah from the Eastern Bloc, founded in early 1953 and subordinate to the prime minister).[6] Moreover, Israel's physical capacity to absorb massive numbers of olim was extremely limited, as were any resources that could serve as bargaining chips in negotiations on aliyah with those countries.

Without full access to Soviet and East European documents, it is hard to differentiate and assess the relative contributions of Israel and of domestic actors in those countries who provided support for aliyah. It was undoubtedly a combination of the two that led to success, with Israel employing a variety of foreign policy tools in pursuit of this goal. The first of these tools was an effort to reach an understanding, even tacitly, with the Soviet Union to open the gates of Eastern Bloc countries under its control and permit Jewish emigration as a natural and vital element of its fundamental support for the founding of the Jewish state. Meeting with Soviet deputy foreign minister Andrey Vyshinsky in December 1948, Moshe Sharett stressed that Vyshinsky "should clearly understand" the special importance of immigration from that part of the world in the eyes of Israeli leaders:

> When it comes to building our homeland, the Jews of Eastern Europe are the salt of our earth. In the past it was the Jews of Russia. In the period before World War I the Jews of Russia were the majority and the foundation of our immigrant base, and this is still evident today. If you look at who our leaders are, at our government composition, you see that most came from Russia. This does not mean that Jews from other countries have not contributed. We had immigrants from Germany and America who brought a lot of energy and initiative. But if we're talking about a largescale collective effort by masses of people who need to create this pioneering potential physically, with their own bodies, then our greatest reserves lie in the Jews of Eastern Europe.[7]

This was the message conveyed to Soviet representatives even before 1948 and during Israel's first three years as well. No explicit or authoritative reply came from Moscow, but from events that transpired in Eastern Europe, Israel's representatives surmised that Russia's reaction was not negative. State documents recently declassified in Warsaw clearly confirm earlier impressions that Stalin authorized the government of Poland to permit Jewish emigration before 1948 as a way of creating pressure for aliyah and embarrassing the British.[8] After Israel achieved independence, the Soviets maintained this line of thinking for strategic reasons, to ensure Britain's departure from Palestine through the demographic reinforcement of Israel. Today we know that Israel's efforts to pursue its aims through the Communist Bloc leadership also entailed refraining from activities that might trigger a negative Soviet reaction to aliyah from Eastern Europe. One of the interesting conclusions that emerge from declassified Israeli Foreign Ministry documents is that for nearly half a decade, Israel deliberately refrained from actively and openly promoting aliyah from the Soviet Union itself. This concession, frustrating though it was, emerged from an unequivocal assessment that the Soviet Union would categorically prohibit emigration by its Jewish citizens in any event and from the belief that Israeli efforts on behalf of Soviet aliyah might sabotage the likelihood of aliyah from Eastern European countries. Thus, only in 1955 did Israel establish an organization to work—very secretively and cautiously—on behalf of aliyah from the Soviet Union, after it appeared that the gates had closed on mass aliyah from Eastern Europe.

The second and simultaneous political tool Israel employed over the years was a systematic policy of not publicly or visibly associating itself with the Western anti-Communist camp and of refusing to allow the construction of a Western military base on its territory. This policy differed fundamentally from the policy of "nonalignment" or "neutrality" adopted in the 1950s by many third-world states vis-à-vis the then-bipolar international system. This was not an easy policy to maintain, but it was one that Israeli leaders and diplomats often underscored in their meetings with Eastern European and Soviet diplomats, and not only with them. Ben-Gurion explained the basic motivation behind the policy to an American Jewish leader who visited Israel in early 1950 as follows: "We place all our trust in aliyah. Romania is closed but we cannot simply give up on hundreds of thousands of Jews. . . . If there is any chance of bringing Jews from the East . . . we must not abandon them."[9]

Israel's third tool to promote aliyah from this region was close cooperation with the Joint Distribution Committee (JDC). This cooperation was essential because, despite Israel's diplomatic presence in Eastern Europe, the movements and activities of its official representatives were subject to severe restrictions in these countries. In addition, Israel had very limited sources of direct funding for aliyah-related activities during its early years. For these reasons it forged a relationship with the JDC, which grew stronger over time and substantially enhanced Israel's ability to advance the cause of aliyah. It also helped that the JDC was not an official representative of the state and could contribute significantly to activities deemed humanitarian. Moreover, the JDC's activities were a direct extension of a long-standing tradition: in the 1930s it had assisted in the emigration of about 400,000 Jews from Central Europe, and it had continued to provide such assistance as World War II came to an end. In late 1944 JDC representatives began arriving in parts of Europe liberated from Nazi occupation and organizing relief efforts. By 1947 about 700,000 Jews had received support from the JDC, 250,000 of whom were residing in refugee camps in liberated Europe. In addition, the JDC had assisted large numbers of Jews in making aliyah before the founding of Israel. It is particularly relevant for our purposes that the JDC's aid efforts in the late war and postwar period were quite intensive. In 1946 approximately 120,000 Jews in Hungary depended on its aid, as did 65,000 in Poland and more than half of Romania's Jewish population, which numbered 380,000. This JDC tradition naturally extended to cooperation with Israeli state representatives, and their cooperation remained significant until the Cold War led to the committee's expulsion from Romania, Poland, and Bulgaria in 1949, from Czechoslovakia a year later, and from Hungary in 1953. For years after its expulsion, however, the JDC continued to provide financial and logistical assistance in these areas.

Under these circumstances, and given that the majority of Czech and Bulgarian Jews who wanted to make aliyah had done so by May 15, 1948, in its early years Israel focused most of its attention on aliyah from three Eastern Bloc states: Poland, Hungary, and Romania. Israel's political efforts to promote aliyah from these countries, a subject yet to be fully researched, achieved partial success in Romania and Poland and ended in relative failure in Hungary for a combination of reasons. The most important factor was the natural objection of these states' leaders to efforts to encourage their citizens' emigration. These leaders were also quite effective at physically preventing Jews from being smuggled out of their countries. At the same time, recently declassified documents in Eastern Europe reveal that the authorities, with the backing and approval of Kremlin leaders, were interested in establishing homogenous states of a single nationality and were therefore willing to be rid of unreliable elements with national ties to a foreign country that belonged to a hostile political bloc, as well as the elderly and the ill. Indeed, Romanian documents reveal that in 1950 Jewish accountants, plumbers, electricians, and bankers were allowed to emigrate only if they were aged sixty or above.[10] In addition, the measures adopted by these states to permit some degree of Jewish emigration (which were not identical in scope) were a tactical preliminary step that formed part of a continuous policy to implement a strategy aimed at expediting the assimilation of the remaining Jews into local society and culture. Accordingly, this policy required eliminating all Zionist activity in Eastern Europe, and its implementation began in the early 1950s.

Still, the expressions of anti-Semitism evidenced in Eastern Europe after 1945 were most unwelcome in the eyes of local governments. Today we know, for example, that the pogrom against the Jews of Kielce in July 1946 greatly embarrassed the Polish authorities and resulted in their granting permission for massive emigration, which they halted immediately afterward. The popular tendency to associate Jews with Communist rule (because of the large Jewish presence in higher echelons of the Communist Party) also created problems for Eastern European leaders. There is evidence, for example, that during debates of the Romanian Communist Party leadership in 1949, Foreign Minister Ana Pauker (the daughter of a rabbi) and Minister of Finance Vasile Luca proposed that Jews who did not integrate into the new regime be sent to concentration camps. Their proposal received only four votes because the prime minister disagreed, believing that the only solution for these Jews was emigration to Israel. Two Soviet delegates present at the meeting requested time to examine the issue and eventually backed the prime minister's position. Moreover, as Lukasz Krzyzanowski has recently shown, Jewish refugees failed to return to their former home in Poland after 1945 not only because of anti-Semitism but also because of difficulties adapting to the new economic reality.[11]

For these reasons Eastern European leaders did not automatically dismiss the opportunity to be rid of unwanted elements among the Jewish population, especially if they could receive financial compensation in return. After World

War II, Eastern Bloc countries were in great need of foreign currency and certain goods to which they lacked access, and most of Israel's efforts, not surprisingly, focused on this need.

The first technique of persuasion was to secure agreement from the relevant states to allow Jewish emigration in exchange for payment in dollars for each emigrant. This technique had been successful in two instances before the founding of Israel. The first was in 1946, when representatives of HaMossad LeAliyah Bet (a branch of the Jewish paramilitary Haganah that facilitated clandestine immigration) offered Romania payment for fifteen thousand Jews who were then allowed to leave the country. The second was in 1947, with agreements that permitted the transit of tens of thousands of Jews from Romania to Bulgaria and from there to Palestine, as well as aliyah by Bulgarian Jews at fees of $50 to $100 per person. A rough estimate indicates that the two Eastern Bloc countries received $5 million for these deals. In addition, nonnegligible sums went to high-ranking officials in Bulgaria and Romania as bribes to enable the operations. Because of the Jewish Agency's financial difficulties, at least some of these funds came clandestinely from the JDC.

The pre-1948 practice of "greasing the machinery" of aliyah had proved successful, so the practice continued. After achieving independence Israel sought to apply the same technique of persuasion, using the same source of funding. In 1949 Hungary and Romania were offered financial incentives, but this time Israel was only partially successful and only with one of these countries. After lengthy negotiations Israel agreed in September of that year to pay Hungary a ransom of $300 per Jewish immigrant, and Hungary agreed to allow three thousand Jews to leave. Israel acceded to this deal mainly out of hope that it would lead to additional deals with the Eastern Bloc countries at better financial terms, but this hope was not realized. The Hungarians and Romanians refused to sign agreements along the lines of the "Aliyah of 3,000" despite Israel's many attempts to entice them in the early 1950s. Available sources do not indicate that such efforts took place in Poland, yet Polish authorities did demand large sums of money from Jewish emigrants to process their requests—17,000 Polish zlotys per person, which amounted to about a year's salary for a midsized family. Thus, despite the absence of an agreement such as that behind the "Aliyah of 3,000" from Hungary, Poland did demand and eventually receive financial compensation for Jewish aliyah during that period.

The second and more widely used financial technique was trade agreements. These were not based on purely economic logic. During Israel's early years, Eastern European countries could offer Israel very few essential goods and certainly could not offer commercial credit. Nor could Israel sell goods to these countries on a large scale as payment for imports. Nonetheless, Israel's leaders considered it important to cultivate trade relations. One aim was to develop economic leverage so as to redeem Jewish capital in Eastern Europe (a system known as "transfer"—payment for goods purchased by Jewish capital that had been frozen in local banks after World War II). More importantly, Israel sought to provide Eastern Bloc countries with an indirect incentive to permit Jewish emigration, through foreign currency that would actually serve as payment for their "export" to Israel. Between 1949 and 1951, Israel signed trade agreements on a scale of tens of millions of dollars with Poland, Hungary, and Czechoslovakia. For Israel the deals entailed payment in foreign currency, while the Eastern Europeans agreed to accept payment in the form of local Jewish capital. It is hard to assess the impact of these deals on the states' willingness to permit emigration. The only documented evidence of a correlation is the example of Poland permitting a large wave of emigration eight weeks after signing a trade agreement in May 1949. Later Israeli assessments, however, apparently determined that the potential for this economic incentive to ensure aliyah from Hungary, Romania, and Poland was minimal, and efforts to secure such deals abated by the mid-1950s. Thus, it would appear that until 1956 economic relations with these states had no bearing on the issue of aliyah.

The trade agreements Israel signed with Eastern Bloc states during the period of mass aliyah from that region inspired another type of incentive to overcome resistance to Jewish emigration. Bloc states faced economic hardship because of an intensive US campaign to prevent its allies and aid recipients from selling them any of a long list of industrial products, machine equipment, raw material, and even medicines that were defined as "strategic" and therefore potentially useful to the Soviet war effort. This situation provided a tempting opportunity for Israel to serve as an important and clandestine economic bridge for these Eastern European states, an opportunity it could exploit to promote aliyah. The operational concept was simple: Israel could purchase prohibited goods, supposedly for itself, and then export them immediately as transit deals. There was, of course, the risk that the United States would discover this economic pipeline, but Israel decided to use it anyway—a fact that was not publicly known until recently. Declassified documents in Israel's State Archives reveal that such activities took place in Czechoslovakia, Yugoslavia, Hungary, Romania, and Poland in 1949–1951, with Israel "exporting" lead and scrap iron, drilling equipment, industrial diamonds, and medicines. None of these were produced in Israel, of course. To ensure efficiency, Israel established a special company named Haddad to coordinate activities. Undoubtedly there was a demand for transit deals in Eastern Europe during that time, but it is hard to assess precisely how much these deals contributed to the willingness of states to permit Jewish emigration. In any case this economic bridge was suspended in 1951, primarily because of increased US monitoring and growing recognition in Israel that the risk exceeded the likelihood of success but presumably also because the massive aliyah from Eastern Europe came to a halt that year.

During this period, both before and after aliyah halted, Israel had another source of economic leverage. The underlying concept was to provide financial assistance openly to the Diaspora, and covertly to Jewish communities that faced economic hardship, in order to keep their "embers burning" and enable aliyah when the time was ripe. Here too the JDC provided operational channels and some of the funding. A fascinating recent study on these activities, which draws on documents disclosed in Budapest, reveals the full scope of the committee's activities in Hungary (the largest sphere of operations), where about $50 million was invested from the end of World War II through 1953.[12] Although the JDC was the main funder, Israel's Foreign Ministry and the Mossad (foreign intelligence agency) participated in the planning and operations behind the scenes, providing direct financial support and transferring food packages (which could be sold at very high prices) to tens of thousands of Jews in Hungary.

The end of this "Great Aliyah" from Eastern Europe in the early 1950s did not thwart the new state's hopes of reopening the gates of emigration. Its next major successes were in Poland and Romania, to which we now turn.

To Poland and Back

In both absolute and relative terms, no country in the world saw as drastic a reduction in its Jewish population during the mid-twentieth century as Poland. Before World War II, its Jewish population numbered about three million. Most were killed during the Holocaust. After the war only 240,000 remained, some of whom had escaped to the Soviet Union during the war and returned after it ended. In 1945–1946 some of Poland's Jews fled (as part of the abovementioned Briha), further reducing the Jewish population. In the aftermath of prestate illegal immigration and the "Great Aliyah" that included nearly 30,000 Polish Jews, only 70,000 Jews remained in Poland, many of whom wanted to make aliyah. During those years Israel's Foreign Ministry never ceased its efforts to persuade the authorities in Warsaw to reopen the gates it had shut in 1951. Simultaneously, Israeli representatives sought to replicate the 1955 agreement between Poland and West Germany for the return of 20,000 Germans in exchange for goods provided to Poland on long-term credit at good terms. However, Jerusalem's proposals to allow Jewish emigration in exchange for such trade, like other economic proposals, were not fruitful. Poland remained firm in its refusal to permit Jewish emigration.

Against this background Poland's decision in the summer of 1956 to permit mass emigration came as a surprise. In time this wave of immigrants came to be known as the "Gomulka Aliyah" after the secretary-general of the Polish Communist Party whose rise to power in 1956 led to the country's change in policy regarding aliyah. The motives behind this shift are complex, and a detailed exploration is beyond the scope of our discussion.

This shift could certainly, in part, be related to Gomulka's having come to power as a Polish nationalist who sought to demonstrate some degree of independence from the USSR, and to his being an anti-Semite who wanted to rid Poland of the Jews—especially if he could profit from their departure. I mention these factors in the context of Israeli activity. Notably, Israeli representatives played no part in the process that led to this policy change and were completely surprised by it. Nonetheless, they then made concerted efforts to take part in the decision's implementation and the removal of obstacles. These were not simple objectives, given that in just over two years (by the end of 1958), thirty-nine thousand Jews immigrated to Israel (about 60 percent of Poland's total Jewish population), alongside thirteen Polish Jews from the Soviet Union who were covered by a repatriation agreement and whom Warsaw allowed to immigrate to Israel. This wave of aliyah, accordingly, was not an isolated event but a complex, continuous, and multifaceted process. It also inspired no small amount of objections and complications.

Declassified documents from Warsaw and Jerusalem indicate several channels of diplomatic, economic, and informational activity by Israel to ensure the policy's implementation. These activities aimed to address two sources of resistance to aliyah that continuously threatened to put a halt to immigration and thus close what Israel understood to be a very brief and uncertain window of opportunity. The external source of resistance to aliyah was of course the Arab world. The empowerment of Israel, through tens of thousands of new residents, was an anathema to Arab leaders, who voiced their opposition mainly to the Soviet Union. Moreover, Arab relations with Poland and the latter's substantial trade in exports to the Arab world provided tools to pressure Warsaw, which consequently had to tread carefully regarding any matters related to the scope of aliyah. Domestic resistance in Poland stemmed from the belief that Jewish emigration would focus attention on the rampant anti-Semitism in the country and make it look bad in the eyes of the world. In addition, many within Poland strongly criticized any loss of productive citizens, engineers, and specialized professionals whose departure would undermine the economy.

The first measure Israel took to ensure aliyah was a massive increase of its means of transport, which were nowhere near adequate to meet the demand for Jewish immigration. Because Poland's decision had come as a surprise, Israel lacked any capacity for advance preparations on such a scale. Almost all the olim from Poland traveled by train, many from Poland to Czechoslovakia, then to Vienna, then to port cities in Italy or Greece, and finally to Haifa. To avoid the impression of mass emigration, the Polish government allowed the addition of only one railcar for each regular train along this route. The resulting bottlenecks at times comprised more than ten thousand people who had exit permits but lacked means of transport. This lack, alongside apparent reluctance on Poland's part to grant permissions in practice, posed a genuine threat to the operation. When the addition of more railcars and more flights still failed to meet the demand, Israel sought to secure the use of ships, which came at great cost—in one instance Israel covered the costs of airfare for Italian emigrants planning to sail for Australia in exchange for the use of their designated ship. Eventually Israel did manage to cope with its lack of ships.

Much more complicated was the mission of concealing the entire process and scale of this aliyah. The governments of Poland and Israel saw eye to eye in this regard, and the latter took great pains to create an information black-out. This included specifically requesting newspaper editorial boards in Israel not to publish the name of the country from which olim were arriving and not to publish stories in which olim described life in the country they left. Israel also prohibited any citation of articles from the foreign press, and it took it upon itself to persuade foreign news agencies in Poland to refrain from publishing stories on the operation. The blackout could not be absolute, however, given the scale of aliyah, Poland's inability to keep its public under a media blackout, and the large number of information sources. Nonetheless, authorities in Jerusalem devoted a great deal of time and attention to this issue.

Simultaneously Israel also helped Poland conceal the anti-Semitism that had, in fact, been a key factor in its decision to permit Jewish emigration. Israel did so in two ways: it refrained from placing the issue of Poland's anti-Semitism on the global agenda, and it used its position as "the voice of the Jewish people" (as at least Israel saw itself) to silence criticism from foreign sources. In this context, for example, Israel blocked a resolution of the American Jewish Congress protesting the harassment of Poland's Jews, as well as news items of the Polish Catholic news agency that would have reported on the persecution of Jews in the country. This was not a simple policy for Israel to maintain. Moshe Avidan, who was in charge of the embassy in Warsaw, reported to his superiors in Jerusalem in June 1956, "Please, consider carefully if publishing in the Israeli or the Western press about the anti-Semitism is worthwhile. The reasons pro and con: Pro, per-haps it will motivate the [Polish] government to implement vigorous measures to combat the anti-Semitism. Con, the publication might harm chances of aliyah. The Polish government would not want to admit that it is unable or unwilling to terminate the persecution of the Jews and it will fear that a flow of Jewish immi-gration will be interpreted as such."[13]

Another sphere of Israeli activity related to two assumptions that were preva-lent among the Polish leadership and seemed potentially useful. The first was that allowing Jewish emigration could effectively bring Poland closer to the United States, which could have economic advantages. The second was that enlisting Israel's efforts would help "sweep anti-Semitism under the rug"; that is, granting Jews permission to leave could "buy Israel's silence" on the matter and might even lead it to take measures to silence anti-Polish criticism from other sources. Israeli diplomats did not hesitate to exploit these assumptions as leverage and in fact encouraged Polish perceptions (and misconceptions) of the weight US Jewry had in US decision-making and of Israel's own influence over US Jewry. When, in February 1958, Poland received its first line of credit from the United States, totaling $100 million, Warsaw assumed that Israel had played some part. Mutual expectations of continued emigration from Poland and of Israeli assistance in ensuring a positive US attitude toward Poland were thus a key facet of Israeli diplomacy in the context of the Gomulka Aliyah.

Moreover, Jewish immigration has always involved financial interests and concerns. The case of Poland in the late 1950s was no exception. Polish authorities were very sensitive to charges by oppositionist circles that Jewish emigrants were taking their country's best assets, and they placed restrictions on the removal of Jewish property from the country. Israel's embassy in Warsaw, for its part, conducted an information campaign among Jews who were preparing to leave, urging them not to engage in conspicuous consumption before leaving and not to raise the question of Jewish property in Poland after the owners had made aliyah. The embassy also initiated a payment system that granted the authorities twenty dollars for every Jew who left the country.

Another economic measure was the leveraged use of assistance provided by the JDC and other organizations for repatriated Jews returning to Poland from the Soviet Union during those years, some of whom were due to make aliyah. The main concern among Israeli diplomats was that the financial hardship these returnees faced in Poland would lead to an unofficial agreement between it and the Soviet Union to halt the repatriation process. Israel's plan was to offer external assistance using the foreign currency of Jewish aid organizations to "compensate" Poland for the costs it incurred by hosting Jews who would later make aliyah. Israel also conditioned this assistance on an agreement in principle that the repatriates would reside briefly in Poland and be permitted to immigrate to Israel as soon as circumstances permitted. Despite the objections of some of the Jewish community in Poland to the ultimate aim of this process, they had to accept it after Israel intervened at the highest levels of the JDC and ORT (a world-wide Jewish educational network) directorships.

Another major problem that this aliyah from Poland posed for Israel's leaders was its high proportion of disabled and ill immigrants. There is no mystery regarding Poland's interests in this regard. Nor is it hard to imagine why the situation was undesirable from Jerusalem's point of view. Researchers who explored this issue recently discovered a document in which Ben-Gurion voiced the opinion that "one disabled person per family does not constitute a tragedy. But if masses of ill and disabled people start arriving in Israel—this is a different story. The Land of Israel is not a hospital."[14] The initial decision, adopted with the notable support of Foreign Minister Golda Meir, was therefore to give serious thought to a policy of granting entry permits on a selective basis. Katriel Katz, Israel's top envoy to Warsaw at the time, was of the view that Poland's response to such a selective process would endanger aliyah as a whole. His assessment was ultimately decisive, and the open-door policy remained unchanged.

The Polish aliyah of those years included very unorthodox Foreign Ministry involvement in their absorption, triggered by hundreds of Polish olim who planned to seek return visas. No doubt many were disappointed with life in Israel, as the numbers of those who sought to leave was unprecedented for aliyah from Eastern Europe. The danger from Israel's perspective was the impact this would have on the Jews still in Poland who had expressed interest in aliyah. Israel's Foreign Ministry then advised the Ministry of Absorption to adopt a policy of preferential resource allocation for olim from Poland. Thus, in December 1959 Israel's envoy to Warsaw received a message from Jerusalem that "all immigrants from Poland will receive housing immediately upon arrival and will be granted special treatment."[15] The Polish supervisor of consular sections made note of this policy, and in talks with Israeli representatives in Poland, he said that "many immigrants from Poland were pampered by absorption agencies for no objective reason."[16] Naturally, Israel's Foreign Ministry was also concerned about news stories in Poland, particularly in the Communist Jewish magazine *Folks-Sztyme*, with hair-raising accounts of conditions in Israel among those who had immigrated earlier. Israel's leaders decided to fight back by recruiting new immigrants to write "spontaneously" about the rosy reality and their happy lives in Israel.

The consequences of Israeli activity surrounding the Gomulka Aliyah are subject to various interpretations, but there is no denying that the aliyah in and of itself was one of Israel's immigration success stories.

Aliya and Bribery in Bucharest

Israel's efforts to enable aliyah from Romania and sustain it over the years were much more extensive than in the case of Poland. Before Israel's founding, Romanian Jews had constituted the largest and most promising source of potential aliyah in Eastern Europe, and the hope of achieving large-scale immigration from Romania was indeed realized during Israel's early years. According to Israel's Central Bureau of Statistics, from May 15, 1948, through the end of 1951, more than 120,000 Jews made aliyah from Romania. Most arrived in 1950 (46,171) and 1951 (39,046). Notably, however, these figures do not reflect the problems Israel encountered in seeking to promote aliyah from Romania. A recent study based on Romanian documents clearly indicates that the Communist government that presided over Romania after Israel's declaration of independence was opposed in principle to Jewish emigration.[17] Aliyah was seen as a vote of no confidence in the Communist regime and as a negative example for Romania's other residents. Despite this, the basic dynamic that characterized Warsaw's approach to the issue also applied in Bucharest. Both states had fundamental interests that were served by permitting Jewish emigration on a temporary basis and limited scale. In both cases Israel had to race against time to expedite aliyah before the Iron Curtain descended completely, putting a stop to Zionist activity. The main difference in the Romanian case was the success of Jewish organizations and the State of Israel in ensuring large-scale aliyah through financial payments and bribes. The concrete outcome of the "carrot" Israel offered the Polish government might be unclear, but in Romania's case the effect was direct, and the cumulative pre-1948 experience was quite indicative of future events.

Between the end of World War II and the Communist revolution in Romania, many Romanian Jews decided to emigrate. The Romanian authorities, however, conditioned emigration on the payment of a fee for each emigrant according to a multicriteria scale. Representatives of Jewish institutions, in coordination with the Jewish Agency, would transfer these payments to Romanian government agents. Negotiations over the price per emigrant, as well as the fact of the deals themselves, remained a well-guarded secret. The Romanians feared that discovery would be embarrassing, and the Jews feared that it could put a halt to the aliyah. But there is no doubt that this mechanism was at the heart of the process. The form of payment varied over time—equipment and goods, exorbitant costs of transit on Romanian passenger ships, foreign currency deposits in bank accounts in Western Europe, and cash payments. Transit countries such as Bulgaria also charged "passage fees" in foreign currency. The following episode illustrates the spirit of the time and characteristics of the aliyah from Romania.[18]

On Christmas Eve, 1947, a representative of HaMossad LeAliyah Bet arrived at a bridge over the Danube in the Romanian city of Giurgiu, along the Bulgarian border. Romanian authorities demanded exorbitant "exit fees" from each emigrant and asked to see receipts before allowing the emigrants to pass over the bridge. But representatives of HaMossad LeAliyah Bet did not have such receipts. "The banks were closed that day," related Dr. Şlomo Leibovici-Laiş, the "last Mohican" of this clandestine aliyah organization. "The person who saved the immigrants was a wealthy Romanian Jew, Leon Yitzkar. He had foreign currency, obtained legally from selling his wife's diamonds, and had paid the ransom fees to the national bank but was not given a receipt. Fortunately, Yitzkar was personally acquainted with the bank's president and contacted him. [The bank president] opened the bank despite the holiday, and Israeli businessman Efraim Ilin managed to convince a few bank clerks to leave their families and come to the bank. They received their rewards and gave the 15 stamps of approval that were required." Subsequently, one thousand Jews left for Israel on two cargo ships, *Atzma'ut* (Independence) and *Kibbutz Galuyot* (Ingathering of Exiles), which had been purchased specially for this purpose and converted into passenger ships.

The assumption at the time was that conditions would change drastically once a Communist government took hold in Romania. And indeed, emigration initially came to halt. Citizens—Jews as well as non-Jews—were prohibited from leaving, with the limited exception of a few exit visas based on "family unification." Seeking to restart the aliyah process, Israel and various Jewish figures approached the Romanian authorities in the hope of identifying a financial incentive that would convince Romania to cooperate. Simultaneously, Romanian Jews put pressure on the authorities by protesting and demanding exit permits to go to Israel. The solution came in the form of American equipment for oil exploration, which Romania needed but could not access because of the US embargo on Communist countries. The Jewish entities were able to provide used but functional equipment, and in late 1949 the Romanians permitted Jews to register for aliyah, allowing a few thousand to depart each month.

A serious obstacle to Romanian aliyah, as it turned out, was the financing of sea passage. Romania demanded that emigrants be transported using only its own passenger ship, *Transylvania*, and it charged fifty-five dollars for each passenger, double the standard fee on Israeli ships. The JDC, in coordination with the Israeli government, covered the cost of passage. As the number of Jews seeking to make aliyah increased, the Romanians increased the number of voyages and number of passengers per voyage, while also raising the cost of passage by thirty-five dollars. When the JDC's funds ran out, the burden of payment shifted to Israel, whose cabinet then addressed Romania's demand of ninety dollars per person. The idea was floated to slow down Romanian aliyah so as to ease the financial burden, but there were concerns that this measure could put an end to the aliyah altogether. Minister Haim Moshe Shapira voiced a generally accepted view among cabinet members when he said, "We must pay the ransom. We are doing business with thieves."[19] Yet this ransom represented only a portion of the expenses Israel was struggling to cover at the time. The cost of massive immigrant absorption was more than Israel could bear, and it became clear that the Jewish Agency would have to prioritize among olim. Thus, when the Israeli legation in Bucharest received 150,000 immigration requests in early 1949, Israel established a selection policy for Romanian aliyah. Toward the end of that year the Romanian authorities' attitude toward Jewish emigration suddenly changed as well, so that by 1950 the number of immigrants had declined. In 1952 only 3,712 Jews left Romania for Israel, compared with 47,041 in 1950 and 40,625 in 1951, and for 1953–1957 the cumulative total was 1,809. During this time Romanian Jews who had already submitted emigration requests were socially sidelined, dismissed from work or placed in low-paying and low-status jobs, passed up for promotion, and generally ostracized.

The major turning point that enabled Israel to resume operations occurred in the latter half of the 1950s. For various reasons, including the launching of large-scale industrial development plans, Romania wanted to be rid of its Jews and transfer their jobs and homes to other citizens. It was also interested in the financial compensation it would receive for permitting Jewish emigration, which in the post-Stalin era (for reasons yet to be fully researched) received the approval of the new Soviet leader. Available information indicates that in 1958 Nikita Khrushchev visited Romania to sign an agreement withdrawing the Red Army from its territory. During this visit, Gheorghe Gheorghiu-Dej, the authoritarian secretary-general of the Romanian Communist Party, raised the issue of receiving goods from the West in exchange for permitting Jewish immigration to Israel. Khrushchev considered the issue and replied pointedly, "Goods are okay, but not money."[20]

The pioneer who paved the way to "aliyah-purchasing" deals, beginning that very year, was Henry Jacober, a British Jew of Romanian descent. Jacober, who imported goods from Romania to Britain, was on the verge of bankruptcy. Initially without the Israeli government's knowledge, he approached Jews in Western Europe and Israel, offering to acquire exit permits for their relatives in exchange for goods. Over the course of six years, Jacober arranged aliyah for hundreds of Jews. His operation brought Jews to Israel but also earned the latter's criticism because the fees Jacober's associates paid tended to be significantly higher than what Israel was willing to pay, and eventually, in 1965, Israel put a stop to his activities.

In the course of his covert and original operation, about which we have only scattered and sometimes inconsistent knowledge, Jacober advanced Romanian aliyah considerably, not to mention the Romanian farming industry. Initially Jacober, who was also an intelligence service recruit, approached Gheorghe Marcu, a high-ranking officer in the Romanian secret service (Securitate) and Jacober's case officer. Jacober requested an urgent meeting, at which he said that he had been approached by representatives of Israel's secret service, who asked that he convey a proposal to Romania—exit permits for Jews in exchange for payment. The deal was to remain unwritten and secret. Initially the Romanians refused, fearing that the proposal was a provocation, but Jacober persisted and was eventually successful, paving the way to a practice that lasted many years: the purchase of Jews by the government of Israel.

News about the possibility of emigration broke out that year in 1958, generating euphoria and cautious optimism among the Jewish community in Romania. Hordes of people flocked to the Ministry of Interior in central Bucharest. The kilometer-long waiting line was a source of great embarrassment to the authorities, and they dispatched police officers to move people to a side street. From October 1958 to March 1959, a total of 130,000 Jews submitted requests for exit permits. "Prime Minister Ion Gheorghe Maurer and President Petru Groza were stunned," related Leibovici-Laiş. "At their meeting with [Romania's] Chief Rabbi Moses Rosen, they asked him, 'What have we done to the Jews that makes them want to leave?'"[21]

Bucharest faced obvious problems with concealing large-scale Jewish immigration and therefore found it expedient to portray Jewish emigration publicly as a humanitarian operation for the sake of "family unification." On February 25, 1958, it issued an announcement expressing support for Arab countries and denying any immigration deal between Romania and Israel or "other Zionists"; rather, Romania had a humanitarian interest in the unification of families separated during World War II. The announcement also harshly condemned Israel as a tool of American imperialism and denounced international Zionism.

Most Israeli documents regarding these and other affairs involving "covert diplomacy" remain classified for obvious reasons. Similarly, the comprehensive book by Yosef Govrin, Israel's ambassador to Bucharest in the 1980s, *Israeli-Romanian Relations at the End of the Ceauşescu Era* (2001), is careful not to reveal too many details. But foreign sources, primarily journalists, have uncovered fascinating stories based on Romanian documentation exposed after the fall of the Communist regime, interviews with former functionaries of the regime, and memoirs.[22] These sources teach us, though without official Israeli confirmation, that Romania exploited the sale of Jews in various ways and—of special relevance for our purposes—that Israel was a key partner in deals that led to aliyah on a massive scale beginning in the late 1950s. This aliyah continued for years, as table 7.2 illustrates.

Besides his role as initiator, Jacober played a crucial part as mediator. On behalf of Israel, he proposed the construction of a large, highly automated chicken farm in Romania in exchange for allowing five hundred Jewish families to emigrate.[23] Gheorghe Gheorghiu-Dej approved the deal, and the farm was built in the village of Peris near Bucharest. The Romanian leader was extremely impressed when he visited the farm, and he authorized exit permits for the five hundred families. He also requested five more farms of the same quality. By late 1964 the Romanians had received chicken, turkey, pig, sheep, and cattle farms, each equipped with respectively suited slaughterhouses and meatpacking facilities, as well as Mercedes-brand refrigerated transport vehicles. Most impressive was the deal involving uncastrated Landrace pigs, a highly prized and selectively bred Danish pedigree, whose export Denmark prohibited. The farms exported their goods to Western Europe. Romanian journalist Emilia Sercan, who investigated this story, relates that "over the course of seven years Israeli agents smuggled thousands of

Table 7.2. Aliyah from Romania, 1948–1965

Year	Immigrants	Year	Immigrants	Year	Immigrants
1948	24,780	1954	70	1960	9,262
1949	13,602	1955	253	1961	20,800
1950	46,171	1956	729	1962	9,149
1951	39,046	1957	665	1963	11,473
1952	3,759	1958	8,785	1964	24,244
1953	92	1959	9,670	1965	9,817

Source: Hary Kuller, *Buletinul Centrului, Muzeului și Arhivei istorice a evreilor din România* (Bucharest, 2008), 22.

tranquilized wild animals all over Europe in sealed vans and diplomatic cars" (ibid.). Gheorghe Gheorghiu-Dej died in March 1965 and was succeeded by Nicolae Ceaușescu. For a complex mix of reasons, Romania under Ceaușescu became the only Eastern Bloc country not to sever diplomatic ties with Israel after the Six-Day War, which helps explain why aliyah continued during the many years of his rule. The commerce in Jews had been kept so secret that Ceaușescu learned about it only when he came to power. Initially he viewed the matter as scandalous and ordered a halt to the operation, fired the general who oversaw it, and greatly reduced the number of exit permits issued. Two years later he changed his mind. Under Ceaușescu's orders, contact was reestablished with Jacober, and the dismissed Romanian general was reinstated and promoted. This time, however, commerce in goods was not enough. Ceaușescu demanded foreign currency.

The deal with Israeli government representatives, though secret and unwritten, included a detailed payment scale for emigrants. Rates varied in accordance with level of education, occupation, age, family status, state of health, and the like. Candidates for aliyah were divided into four categories: A, B, C, and D. Category A applied to those with academic credentials, Category B to students, Category C to laborers, and Category D to the unemployed and children. The prices were $497 for Category D, $600 for Category C, $1,700 for Category B, and $3,000 for Category A. Higher rates applied to special cases, such as those with specialized training or high-ranking positions in the Romanian government. The quotas and fees for Jews who would be allowed to emigrate were renegotiated annually, with Romania steadily raising the rates. By July 1978 the prices ranged from $2,000 to $50,000 and in some cases reached $250,000.[24]

The success of this trade in Jews whetted Ceaușescu's appetite, and he ordered that parallel tracks be established for the "sale" of Romanian Germans to West Germany and, later, for other minorities as well. These included Greeks, Armenians, and even Romanians who had families in Western countries with the means and will to finance their relatives' emigration. Interestingly, on May 1, 1997, during a visit of German foreign minister Klaus Kinkel in Bucharest, the Romanian foreign minister, Adrian Severin, apologized to Germany and German emigrants from Romania for the sale of German emigrants, yet no such apology was issued to Israel or Jewish emigrants.

The steadily soaring financial payments for each Jew were not enough for Ceaușescu. He demanded and received additional benefits as well. In exchange for exit permits, the State of Israel and Jewish organizations had to support Romania's petition for most-favored-nation status in trade with the United States. Moreover, they had to grant Romania long-term, low-rate loans (in one instance Romania received a loan from a German bank for which Israel paid the interest) and to import unwanted Romanian goods, such as outdated ships for the shipping company Zim. Having established a local arms industry, Ceaușescu also demanded assistance in acquiring modern tanks so that Romania could copy their blueprints and duplicate them. And indeed, Romania acquired the Centurion tank. The Eilat-Ashkelon pipeline, which transported crude oil from Iran, provided Israel with another bargaining chip to promote aliyah. In the late 1960s and early 1970s, Romania's refineries needed particularly large quantities of crude oil, which Iran supplied at appropriate rates. As elaborated earlier, oil was conveyed through the Eilat-Ashkelon pipeline before being loaded onto containers headed to Constanta. Not surprisingly, Romanian-Israeli negotiations over oil during that period always included pressure by Israel on behalf of Jewish emigration.

The payment for exit permits was sometimes by check, deposited in West European banks, but more often in cash using foreign currency. "Sometimes we would redeem Jewish Agency checks in Europe and then pay [the Romanians] in cash," according to Leibovici-Laiş (ibid.). This form of payment could be dangerous at times. One day in 1974, a Romanian citizen was rushing to catch a flight from Zurich to Bucharest. He had arrived late for check-in but waved his diplomatic passport and was allowed to board. When he landed in the Romanian capital, however, he was stunned to realize that the small suitcase he had received in Zurich from a longtime acquaintance was missing. That suitcase contained $1 million in cash. The Romanian general was Gheorgh Marcu, and the money was payment for the aliyah of several thousand Jews from Romania. His Israeli friend was Shaike Dan of the Israeli Mossad and Foreign Ministry, who for decades oversaw clandestine aliyah from Romania. Fortunately for them, Swiss authorities had been monitoring the two, found the suitcase, and returned it to Marcu. But they barred him and his Israeli friend from entering Switzerland again.

Recently available documents also reveal that some of the funds were transferred to secret bank accounts in Switzerland, but neither Israel nor Romania was mentioned in these transactions. As Romania's financial crisis worsened, the "price" of Jews rose. Every time the Romanians failed to meet the terms of the agreement and delayed aliyah, the Israeli government would threaten them with public disclosure of the trade in Jews. During Ceauşescu's final years in power, he had an agreement with Israel to allow Jews from the Soviet Union to fly to Israel via Romania for a fee. According to a senior Israeli official who worked on this issue, Nativ's annual briefings on Jewish immigration from Romania under Ceauşescu typically included talk of "how many Jews we bought this year and how many we'll buy next year." Likewise, Romanian journalists have described how until his final days, Ceauşescu would regularly inquire "how much money has come in from the Jews." Two weeks before he was deposed and not long before he was executed, he received a report on the most recent revenues. Had he received a cumulative summary at the time, he would have learned that under his rule tens of thousands of Jews had been sold in 1968–1989 for a sum total of over $100 million, an amount with double the purchasing power in 2017.[25]

It is clear what Israel gained from these deals: the aliyah of a decisive majority of Romania's Jewry. It is also clear that this Diaspora community was almost completely obliterated as a result. After the Holocaust in Romania and the extermination of North Transylvanian Jewry, there remained about 350,000 Jews in the country. The figure rose to 450,000 in 1947, after the return of refugees from the Soviet Union and elsewhere. After emigration from Romania, the number fell to 170,000 in 1956. By 1992 a total of 15,000 Jews remained, most of whom were elderly and many of whom were married to non-Jews. There is no doubt that behind this phenomenon was a large-scale Israeli operation that still awaits the release of official Israeli and Romanian documentation as well as the historian who will tell the story of "Lasă pe poporul Meu să plece!" ("Let my people go!" in Romanian).

By the Shores of Babylon and the Banks of the Bosporus

Israel also took measures to promote aliyah in parts of the world where, besides lacking diplomatic representation, it was officially an enemy state. For these operations it needed the clandestine services of HaMossad LeAliyah Bet and others. One of the first sites of such activity was Iraq, where the Jewish community after World War II numbered nearly 150,000. These efforts (for which a relatively rich historiography exists) were recognized as one of Israel's crowing achievements in the sphere of aliyah and led to the immigration of nearly the entire community in 1950–1951. For a variety of reasons, beginning in 1949 aliyah from Iraq was identified as aliyat hatzalah (rescue aliyah) and given priority. Israel's efforts on behalf of aliyah from this country focused on two locations: Iraq itself and Iran. Iran's recognition of Israel in early 1950, which entailed intensive covert activity by Israel and bribery of Iran's prime minister to the tune of hundreds of thousands of dollars, was a crucial chapter in the story of aliyah from Iraq.

The main obstacle to aliyah from Iraq, however, was of course the domestic situation in that country: Israeli representatives had to arrive clandestinely and could not operate openly, and Zionist organizations essentially operated as an underground, which severely limited their scope of activities. It is inherently difficult, therefore, to assess the relative contributions to the success of this aliyah on the part of the local Jewish community and Zionist organizations, on the one hand, and of Israel, on the other. Nonetheless, we can point to a number of activities that would naturally be within Israel's sphere of responsibilities. First, Israel's agents in Iraq assisted in organizing massive illegal emigration beginning in the final months of 1949 and through March 1950. Second, this was a covert operation organized and funded by the state, which involved smuggling Iraqi Jews into Iran and from there flying them to Israel. Moreover, shortly after Iran promised to open its doors to Jewish refugees from Iraq, the latter announced that it would permit its Jews to make aliyah. One of the main motives behind this decision (a very problematic step for an Arab country in conflict with Israel to take) was the government's powerlessness to prevent Jews from fleeing along with their capital, and embarrassment on the domestic front as the public learned of its inability to enforce law and order. It preferred, therefore, to control the phenomenon through its legalization. Presumably Iraq's decision was also intended to rid the country of elements that did not contribute to the regime's stability and even undermined it. The authorities in Baghdad, however, mistakenly assumed that only a small number of Jews sought to leave. They were shocked by the collective decision of the entire Jewish community to make aliyah. This decision had taken shape, gradually but turbulently, over the course of a year following the government's announcement.

The Jewish community's decision also came as a surprise to Israel's covert agents in Baghdad and their bosses in Jerusalem. Nor was Israel equipped to absorb such a large immigrant wave at that time. At the same time, the opening of the gates to all who wanted to make aliyah actually played an important part in the operation's success. Responsibility for arranging the aliyah and transfer of Jewish capital fell almost entirely on the state. Israel succeeded in securing Iraq's agreement to allow direct flights from its territory for most of the emigrants. This success resulted, among other factors, from Israeli-Iranian cooperation in refusing to turn Tehran into a temporary base for Iraqi emigrants. The circumstances made it very difficult for Iraq to abide by its decision regarding the rapid departure of only those seen as disruptive to law and order, and they necessitated direct, clandestine contact between Israel's agents and the Iraqi government. Iraq then gave its consent (with the help of some palm greasing of indeterminate amounts), which in due time the prime minister would approve, to allow regular flights to Cyprus, whence the Jews would make aliyah. The operation therefore required diplomatic coordination with Britain, which eventually gave its authorization. Israeli diplomats also tried unsuccessfully to engage the United States. At the start of 1951, Iraq decided to accelerate emigration. The direct and indirect dialogue with Israel that followed led to Iraq's decision, in January 1951, to allow direct flights to Lod, Israel's main airport, which in turn led to the conclusion within six months of what came to be known as "Operation Ezra and Nehemia" (named after the biblical figures who led the Jewish people out of exile in Babylonia to the Land of Israel).

Iraqi Jewry had been identified earlier as "a diaspora under threat of destruction" because of assessments that its situation would deteriorate if Israel did not act quickly to ensure its aliyah. Similar assessments had led to intensive efforts in 1948–1951 in two other countries where smaller Jewish communities were in danger: Libya and Yemen. About thirty thousand Jews were brought to Israel from the former and fifty thousand from the latter. In the case of Yemen, Israel had to conduct indirect negotiations through a representative of the JDC and representatives of the imam in Aden to secure his consent for Jewish emigration. Israel also needed Britain's consent to allow transit because Britain controlled Aden and the main port of egress in the region. In April 1949 the imam did give authorization, primarily for various domestic reasons, after Britain had already responded affirmatively to Israel's request. The JDC undertook a large portion of the funding and organization for this operation, which was termed Magic Carpet. In the Libyan case, Israel needed to conduct negotiations with the British government to receive authorization to operate there, both to put a halt to unregulated immigration to Italy and to initiate direct, regulated immigration from Libya to Israel.

After its founding Israel also sought to ensure aliyah from neighboring Arab countries, resuming efforts that had begun immediately after the end of World War II. In 1945–1946 an operation termed Aliya of the Thousand had brought thirteen hundred Jewish children from Syria. This was a clandestine operation organized by members of the Jewish paramilitary Palmach and Jewish Palestinian agents, with the assistance of immigrants from Syria who had arrived earlier. Another Syrian aliyah project, Lehava (Flame), took place in the late 1950s and is particularly interesting despite the small number of olim involved. Recently released Israel Defense Forces (IDF) documents reveal details about the activities of Intelligence Unit 504 as part of this endeavor. In the course of twenty-five operations between 1959 and 1961, agents from this unit based in Lebanon were recruited to assist in transporting small groups of youths across the Lebanese-Israeli border to Metulah. In all, a total of one hundred Jewish youths were brought to Israel. Shmuel Goren, who served as commander of the unit's northern base, noted in a 2013 television program that the idea did not actually originate with the Israeli establishment:

> It emerged from the circumstances at the time. The Jews in Syria were in a terrible situation. They faced persecution and demands to convert to Islam, and the Jewish youth in Syria itself, in fact, rebelled. This began with groups of youth who arrived in Lebanon from Syria. In Lebanon they reached the Jewish neighborhood of Wadi Abu Jamil . . . where they were taken care of. There was a Jewish woman there named Shula Cohen [a Mossad agent], and she, through her contacts, established contact with agents who worked for us, and they came to us, told us the story, and suggested that we start receiving the Jews through them, for payment. These were Arab agents, Shiites, from Lebanon, who worked with us. . . . And in fact this was a mission they took upon themselves, mainly out of greed.[26]

Another fascinating chapter in the clandestine aliyah of Syrian Jews was written later, not officially by Israel but personally by the Canadian Jewish human rights activist Judy Feld Carr. After the death of her first husband, Dr. Ronald Feld, a foundation was established in his name in 1973. Carr used the funds donated to the foundation to send religious books to Syrian Jews and later to pay ransom fees to Syrian authorities for the release of Syrian Jews. Her covert activities, described in Harold Troper's *The Ransomed of God: The Remarkable Story of One Woman's Role in the Rescue of Syrian Jews* (Toronto, 1999), continued for more than twenty-five years, and she helped rescue more than three thousand Jews from Syria. "It was not easy," recalled Carr. Each case was unique. Since Syrians would only rarely permit an entire family to leave together, she bargained for each family member in turn. And costs varied; an old man generally cost less than a young and single woman, a little boy more than a little girl. "How much for a pregnant woman?"[27] During these years Israel also faced difficulties in arranging aliyah from countries that did not, in principle, prohibit it. One such example was Turkey. At the time of Israel's War of Independence, the secular Turkish government viewed aliyah as a means to the military reinforcement of the Yishuv (prestatehood Jewish community) and IDF, so out of Islamic solidarity with Arab states it suspended permits to emigrate there in November 1948. This restriction did not, however, prevent the emigration of Jews by illegal means. Only a year later did the Turkish authorities relax this prohibition and, with certain restrictions, permit emigration for any Jew who wanted to make aliyah. The result was a massive exodus of Turkey's Jews. They sold or abandoned their property and came to Israel on dozens of ships that made the voyage between Istanbul or Izmir and Haifa. In 1948–1949 about thirty-seven thousand of the seventy-five thousand Jews of Turkey made aliyah. Zionist movements, still operating as an underground, prepared the immigrants. When immigration from Turkey increased, an aliyah bureau (operated by Yishuv envoys) was established in Istanbul. The bureau organized aliyah and collected funds, operating cautiously and clandestinely as an underground. To ensure regular, frequent passage of immigrant ships, agents equipped with sailor's certificates were dispatched to Istanbul. Their role was to assist in making arrangements for aliyah and to accompany the ships.

The story of illegal emigration from Turkey contains a subplot: the smuggling out of hundreds of Turkish draft dodgers, which formed part of a larger logistical operation involving tens of thousands of Jewish immigrants from Turkey. Under Turkish law these young men were prohibited from leaving the country until they had completed their military service. To address this problem, aliyah agents hired Turkish smugglers' boats. Initially each boat would ferry about twenty young men at a time, but later the number reached as many as three hundred per voyage. Most boats left from the port of Izmir and a few from Iskenderun. In one tragic case, twenty-eight young men sailed for Israel on the ship *Varol*, whose captain refused to enter the Haifa port. His passengers had to transfer to a smaller boat, which could hold only twenty, and row into the port. Of the remaining eight who had to swim through the stormy sea, five drowned, and only three reached the shore of Bat Galim. Another smuggling route was via Mersin to Iskenderun. Small groups of olim, assisted by Zionist movement activists, were transported through this route.

Israel's commitment to aliyah required it to conduct operations on a global scale, not just in Europe and the Middle East. This scale is exemplified by two cases from the African continent that deserve our attention: Morocco and Ethiopia.

Rabat and Jerusalem

On the eve of Israel's independence, North African Jewry numbered 480,000: 130,000 in Algeria, 100,000 in Tunisia, and 250,000 in Morocco. Since Israel's founding most of Morocco's Jewry has immigrated to Israel, and this community constitutes the largest aliyah from an Islamic country. Ensuring Moroccan aliyah was one of the most complex missions Israel undertook in the sphere of foreign relations. The operation was unique not only because it largely contravened the basic position of Rabat but also because it entailed a fundamental internal dispute in Jerusalem.

The founding of Israel in 1948 and the destabilization of French rule triggered uncertainty among Moroccan Jews and concerns for their future among Israel's leaders. A series of violent incidents further alarmed the Jewish community and prompted a growing demand to make aliyah, which encountered two obstacles. Emigration from Morocco to Israel remained legal as long as the French were in charge—that is, until 1956. From May 1949, Kadima, the branch of the Jewish Agency responsible for aliyah, could operate freely in Morocco. At the same time, Jews were seen as supportive of the French government, and given the growth of the Moroccan national movement, which threatened to destabilize the country, the authorities were not favorably inclined toward massive Jewish emigration. They therefore permitted only a limited but steady stream of emigrants, who by 1956 totaled eighty-five thousand. And it was not only the French position that curtailed aliyah. In November 1951 the Jewish Agency's liaison office and the government of Israel reached the unusual decision to implement a selection process for Jews from Tunisia and Morocco, permitting aliyah only for those families that would be able to support themselves in Israel. This decision was the focus of a fierce debate that left a lasting mark on history and on the subject's historiography.

The debate manifested, and still manifests, in accusations of a perceived sense of cultural superiority that fueled discrimination against olim from Islamic countries generally and Morocco specifically, primarily on the basis of character and image. From the early 1950s, it was already apparent that mass immigration from Islamic countries, and North Africa in particular, would change the state's demographic composition and threaten the Western, pioneering image of the Yishuv. "There is now, already, a Diaspora in the Land of Israel," said Moshe Kol, a top Jewish Agency official, in a closed debate. "Israel will turn into a land of the Levant."[28] Two years later Nahum Goldmann, chairman of the Jewish Agency's Executive, voiced his objection to the aliyah of Jewish "natives." Such views were also expressed publicly. Chaim Sheba, a Ministry of Health emissary to Morocco, and *Haaretz* reporters Aryeh Gelblum and Amos Elon opposed aliyah from Morocco and often invoked repellant images to dissuade the leadership from "Levantization" of the state. The sense of superiority that Moroccan olim encountered remained an open wound in their formative memory. In his 2016 book *The Moroccans*, former Knesset member Daniel Ben-Simon recalls the remarks of *Davar* editor Hannah Zemer when she hired him as a reporter many years earlier: she "sweetly" asked him, "Why are the Moroccans in Israel so primitive?" Henriette Kalev, today a sociologist, transformed a remark made by an Ashkenazi woman, for whom Kalev had worked when she was cleaning houses, into a slogan and the title of one of her academic articles: "You're So Pretty—You Don't Look Moroccan."[29]

The historiographic counterarguments present an explanatory pyramid that places at the top other, objective reasons for the decision on selection. Among those who believe that selection was necessary, many emphasize the severe difficulties the state faced in absorbing large waves of olim during its early years and the advanced age and poor health of a significant portion of them. Nor did they believe that these countries required aliyat hatzalah in the early 1950s. Finance Minister Levi Eshkol expressed this view when he addressed the Jewish Agency's Executive in February 1955: "Under current conditions we lack the infrastructure and economic capacity to receive more people. . . . When we were not our own state, when an English official was [in charge], there was nothing easier than to approach him with demands. It was wonderful. Today it is we who have to balance the accounts." In his view the accounts necessitated that aliyah be "cut to measure," as Avi Picard describes it in his recent book on this subject.[30] In any event, the government in Israel and its agents in Morocco came under pressure to change this policy as hostilities against Jews increased and it seemed the authorities in Morocco were on the verge of halting Jewish emigration. The pressure had its effect. In his poem "The Gate of Morocco," which appeared in June 1956 in the newspaper *Davar*, poet Natan Alterman expressed it as follows: "The grinding sound of the closing gate added its voice to the debate." Thus, although the policy was not officially revoked, in 1955 the Jewish Agency's Executive allowed three thousand Moroccan olim per month and relaxed the selection criteria. Still, this meant that only about forty thousand of the one hundred thousand Jews who petitioned for aliyah that year actually made it to Israel.

When Morocco closed the door on aliyah in 1956, it reinforced the sense of a missed opportunity among the Israeli leadership. In a retrospective book, Yehuda Braginski, head of the Absorption Department in the Jewish Agency, wrote that "we left 150,000 Jews in Morocco who were longing to make aliyah. They remained in Arab hands, facing an uncertain future, hostages of the Moroccan authorities and a living reminder of Israel's conduct." Eliyahu Dobkin, head of the Aliyah Department, said that "we all lived with the heavy sense of having missed an opportunity to bring tens of thousands of Jews out of Morocco." Zalman Shazar, later to become Israel's third president, spoke of "the heavy cloud hanging over us because we did not take them out when we could. Everyone senses this, whether they speak of it or not."[31] It was clear to all that in the early 1950s the aliyah of North African Jewry was subordinate to the needs of the State of Israel and that the hardship these Jews were facing was a secondary concern.

Whatever the disputes over the past, a consensus emerged within the Israeli establishment that henceforth this aliyah should be viewed as an aliyat hatzalah and pursued clandestinely. The new government in Morocco under King Mohammed V, who had returned from exile in 1956, categorically opposed such an operation for three reasons. The first involved concerns about criticism from Arab states and accusations that Morocco was providing military manpower for the Zionist state. The second reason had to do with Morocco's own need for skilled manpower after the French withdrawal and departure of Europeans. And third, Morocco wanted to prevent the illegal transfer of Jewish emigrants' capital outside of its own borders. Another factor that shaped the new regime's stance was its frustration in trying to monitor and control what was happening in the country—a situation that Israel exploited to organize illegal aliyah operations. Moreover, some Moroccan Jews took a dim view of aliyah, and prominent groups among them competed politically and culturally with Zionism to propose alternative existential solutions that involved integration into Morocco. Among the latter were students of Alliance Israélite Universelle as well as anti-Israel radicals. These circumstances and the Moroccan government's restrictions on legal aliyah explain why in 1956–1958 only about 2,000 Jews, out of a community of 170,000, arrived in Israel, with exit permits issued on an individual basis. Many more required the assistance of covert aliyah operations.

During those years the regime's anti-Zionist stance became more extreme, and Jews often faced violence. In 1959 the government outlawed Zionism, defining it as a severe crime, and a year later one-third of Alliance Israélite Universelle schools were nationalized. These developments intensified the pressure for emigration and increased Israel's clandestine involvement, which took several forms. The first was illegal, covert aliyah that began as early as 1956 under the supervision of the Mossad operating from its base in Marseilles, which smuggled many agents into Morocco (to conduct a variety of activities, including massive passport forgery), and of the Aliyah Department of the Jewish Agency. An underground organization of Moroccan Zionists named HaMisgeret (the Framework) was intensely active on the ground, identifying, organizing, and transporting Jews who wanted to make aliyah. Although Jews were also smuggled by land—through Spanish Morocco and Algeria—the main route involved departing the country secretly by sea toward Spain (Gibraltar) and from there by ship to Marseilles, Naples, and finally Israel. The operations required the consent of Britain and Spain, which was secured behind the scenes and, in Madrid's case, complicated by lack of diplomatic relations. By 1960 about one hundred small ships had made this voyage, each ferrying a few dozen refugees. The illegal aliyah organized by the Jewish underground in Morocco and the Mossad comprised 8,700 olim in 1957, 1,800 in 1958, 3,300 in 1959, 4,100 in 1960, and 11,500 in 1961. In operational terms these were substantial achievements, requiring intensive activity on Israel's part. Nonetheless, these efforts could not satisfy the growing demand, so in parallel Israel sought an agreement with Moroccan authorities to permit legal aliyah.

Because Israel did not have official relations with Morocco, it sought to enlist the World Jewish Congress (WJC) in conducting negotiations on aliyah, despite the opposing views of Foreign Minister Golda Meir, Aliya Department chief Zalman Shragai, and Mossad director Isser Harel, all of whom viewed the WJC as an organization of "Jews without roots."[32] The WJC had established ties with Morocco's leadership years before that state had achieved independence, publicly supporting Moroccan independence under this new leadership during the struggle over global public opinion of the mid-1950s. The WJC had also been heavily involved in establishing political contact between Israeli diplomats and Moroccan nationalists during the mid-1950s, in making it possible for Kadima to operate systematically once Rabat gave its approval, and in facilitating Rabat's decision in 1955 to appoint Jewish community activist Dr. Leon Ben-Zaken as minister of communications. However, these talks, in which the US ambassador to Rabat, Charles Yost, also participated, were not fruitful. Nor were the attempts by the Mossad to establish indirect contact with Morocco's crown prince Hassan, who was perceived as a moderate, although these attempts did lay a foundation for positive developments some years later. Likewise, a proposal conveyed to Hassan indirectly during his October 1960 visit to New York, through an American Jew with economic ties to Morocco, led nowhere. The proposal would have supported US investment in Morocco in exchange for "flexibility" on aliyah. Hassan did not respond, and the Mossad pursued alternative plans to reach the leadership through other government channels, including Prince Moulay Ali, the king's nephew, with a proposal that included payment of fifteen dollars for every Jewish emigrant. Here too, Israel's efforts were unsuccessful.

Two dramatic events that took place in early 1961 broke this pattern of aliyah. The first occurred on January 9, when the *Pisces/Egoz*, a ship illegally transporting olim to Israel, sank, resulting in the death of forty-three passengers. The tragedy could not be covered up, and it exposed an operation that Morocco, its Jewry, and Israel, each for their own reasons, sought to keep secret. For Morocco the exposure necessitated a more intensive domestic crackdown on Zionist organizations, resulting in the near-total destruction of HaMisgeret, but it also encouraged more Jews to emigrate. At the same time, the incident intensified international pressure on Morocco to permit emigration, while in Israel it was cause for an open Knesset debate. In Jerusalem the event and its repercussions raised doubts about whether to continue covert aliyah operations. In the end Israel decided to continue despite secret assurances from Mohammed V to ease up on legal emigration, and indeed, these assurances were not implemented.

In February 1961 Mohammed's son, Hassan II, came to power, which allowed Israel to revise its strategy completely. A number of factors explain the turnaround resulting from this change in personalities on the Moroccan throne. First, the publicity surrounding the *Pisces/Egoz* and its aftereffects painted a most unwelcome picture from Rabat's perspective. Much more important, evidently, was Hassan's interest in closer relations with the West and his view that it would be wiser for Morocco to permit the emigration of Jews who wanted to leave and whom he considered a dissatisfied, destructive force, while simultaneously making efforts to ensure the loyalty of those who did not wish to leave.

A series of recently declassified documents in the Israel State Archives contains a letter dated February 10, 1961, from the Israeli embassy in Paris to Yohanan

Meroz, director general of the Office of the Foreign Minister under Golda Meir. The letter, citing a credible source, reported that at its most recent meeting the leadership of Morocco's ruling party, Istiqlal, had discussed Jewish emigration and decided that, for a three-month period, any Jew who wanted to leave Morocco would be free to do so.[33] The rationale for this decision was the party leaders' assumption that because many Moroccan Jews had strong ties to Zionism, Morocco's close relations with the United Arab Republic and its shift toward Nasser's policy would lead to internal problems best avoided. It was preferable, therefore, to be rid of the Zionists and allow them to make aliyah. Although the collapse of the Syrian-Egyptian union in September of that year reduced the potential threat of pan-Arab sympathies, the new king remained vulnerable to internal criticism regarding any changes to his father's position on aliyah.

This situation convinced Mossad leaders to open direct communication channels with Hassan for the sake of aliyah. In August 1961 the two states reached an agreement through the mediation of businessmen Dr. Yitzhak Cohen and Sam Ben-Azraff. Under this "compromise agreement," as it was called, Morocco would allow the Israelis to make arrangements on its territory for a collective exodus of families in exchange for financial compensation for the consequent loss to its economy. For every Jew who left, the Israelis paid between $50 and $250, and the fee rose over time as more left. The emigrants were transported by ship at night, clandestinely, so that opposition parties would not exploit the situation to attack the king's close associates. The agreement also officially recognized the right of Jews to emigrate via Europe to the United States or Canada but explicitly not to Israel. In practice, of course, the implications were that once they arrived in Europe, these Jews could immigrate to Israel or, as some did, choose other destinations. According to unconfirmed reports, in addition to financial payments for the easing of emigration restrictions, Israel also provided assistance to Morocco in upgrading its internal security mechanisms and made additional payments. Ultimately, for understandable reasons, Morocco refused to grant the Jewish Agency permission to organize the aliyah but did allow the Hebrew Immigrant Aid Society to do so. From late 1961 through the end of 1964, Operation Yachin, as it was named, brought more than ninety-three thousand Jews to Israel, which left Morocco with a community of some seventy thousand Jews whose living conditions were generally good and who did not express an interest in aliyah at the time. Besides overseeing the physical aspects of the operation, Israel had to maintain secrecy and persuade the king to uphold his commitment when domestic and foreign criticism caused him to waver. There is also evidence that Israel provided assistance to Moroccan olim in overcoming severe restrictions on the export of their capital. Aliyah from Morocco continued in the 1970s and 1980s. It is worth underscoring that the secret, ongoing negotiations on aliyah between Israel and Morocco paved the way to special, albeit discrete, relations between the two states long before official relations were established in 1994. Regarding the aliyah itself, one may conclude that after Israel suspended immigration in the early 1950s and Morocco later prohibited it for half a decade, those Moroccan Jews who had applied to emigrate in 1956 were, eventually, able to realize their dream.

"Bring Me the Jews of Ethiopia"—Operation Moshe

The 1984 aliyah of some seven thousand Ethiopian Jews was unique in Israel's history for several reasons. First, it took place after a period of three decades during which the rights of these Jews to make aliyah was not recognized, despite significant pressure to change that policy. Second, it was a highly dangerous physical operation conducted in complete secrecy hundreds of miles away from Israel in territories of enemy states. And finally, Jewish organizations and individuals outside of Israel as well as the US administration were involved, often very intensively. It is no wonder that Operation Moshe, as it came to be known, received a great deal of media attention. Much more importantly for our purposes, the operation exemplifies and epitomizes much of Israel's modus operandi and internal doubt.

Before immigrating to Israel, Ethiopian Jews numbered about thirty thousand. They constituted a religious and social minority in their country. Many lived in northern and northwestern Ethiopia throughout more than five hundred small villages and amid a largely Christian population, with a few in the cities of Gondar and Addis Ababa. A majority worked in agriculture and maintained self-sufficient households for the most part. Others worked in areas such as blacksmithing, pottery, and weaving, occupations that were considered menial and further diminished their already low social status. More than anything, Jews were distinguishable by their religious and separatist lifestyle, strictly maintained by their priests, or *kesoch*, who also served as leaders of the various communities. The dream of return to Zion was a central motif in the lives of Ethiopian Jews. Yet only in the nineteenth century did they become aware that, besides themselves, there existed a vast Jewish Diaspora across the world. This exposure resulted from an encounter between the community and Joseph Halévy, who came to Ethiopia on behalf of European Jews to verify the truth of claims by the London Society for Promoting Christianity amongst Jews. The latter was a Christian missionary organization that aimed to convert Ethiopian Jews, among others, and publicized its achievements.

The mutual discovery of another community of Jews drew great interest across the Diaspora and inspired many in the Jewish world to take action on behalf of Ethiopia's Jewish community. Specifically, they sought to prevent its extinction given the dangers of living in the midst of a missionary Christian society. The 1904 journey of Dr. Jacques Faitlovitch, who went in search of the Ethiopian Jewish community, marks a turning point in the community's history. Dr. Faitlovitch, a student of Joseph Halévy, endeavored to establish the Ethiopian Jewish community's position among the Jewish communities of the world. His efforts focused on education, the founding of a Jewish school in Addis Ababa, and the creation of an elite leadership by sending young people to be educated in Europe, among other measures. These efforts succeeded in strengthening Ethiopian Jewry, so that it could resist missionary activities in Ethiopia, and helped reinforce the community and consolidate its standing.

The founding of Israel did not have an impact on these Jews because during its early years the state opted not to encourage their aliyah. There were two reasons for this singularly atypical stance: misgivings about whether they were truly Jews and serious doubt—if not complete lack of faith—that this community could adapt to life in Israel. Moreover, until the early 1980s Israel did not view Ethiopian immigration as a case of aliyat hatzalah. The Jewish Agency did, however, decide to assist Ethiopian Jewry, primarily in the area of education, and in the mid-1950s it opened a seminar for Hebrew teachers in Asmara (the current capital of Eritrea). In 1955 two groups of youths, graduates of the Jewish Agency's education program in Ethiopia, came to the Israeli youth village Kfar Batya to study Hebrew, Judaism, and other subjects. Most returned to Ethiopia and served as teachers in village schools established by the Jewish Agency. These developments, alongside the community's growing ties with Diaspora Jewry, raised awareness among Ethiopian Jews regarding the possibility of aliyah and provided a basis for the activism of Jewish organizations and public figures in Israel and around the world who had been trying to promote aliyah from Ethiopia since the early 1950s.

However, the Ministry of Interior under Yosef Burg and the Ministry of Absorption opposed the aliyah of Ethiopian Jews (or Falashim) and regarded activism on their behalf as unacceptable. To reinforce this stance, in January 1973 Dr. Yosef Litvak of the Absorption Ministry's Planning Department prepared a report that, although not officially approved, reflected widely held views among Israeli public servants and society regarding appropriate responses to the community's interest in aliyah. Litvak argued,

The Falashim are, in the view of objective scientific researchers, one of the many peoples that constitute the Ethiopian population. Ethnically and culturally, they are an organic part of the Ethiopian people. . . . Encouraging Falashim to immigrate to Israel could contribute to the phenomenon of Falasha pretenses and put Israeli authorities in a difficult and complicated position. It could also provide material for hostile elements within global public opinion to increase anti-Israel incitement with accusations of "racism" and religious discrimination and oppression and the like. . . . We should not encourage activity on the part of Jewish entities, and certainly not Israeli entities, that aim to cultivate Falasha ties to Israel. Certainly for the Falashim's own good, and also for Israel's own good, any plans for their aliyah to Israel should be completely abandoned.[34]

Israel's negative stance on Ethiopian aliyah remained unchanged for nearly thirty years after independence. Paradoxically, this stance solidified after the establishment of diplomatic ties between Israel and Ethiopia. Notably, in the 1950s Israel sought to establish ties with peripheral states in the Middle East as important elements of its security policy. Accordingly, Ben-Gurion invested a great deal of effort in building strategic bridges with Tehran, Ankara, and Addis Ababa. Relations with Ethiopia also had a crucial economic aspect because of the latter's proximity to the Red Sea, which served as a channel for maritime transit linking Eilat to the East. This transit included the fuel tankers that provided most of Israel's supply. In the late 1950s, Israel therefore began to assist Ethiopia through projects related to agriculture, medicine, and development. In 1966 an Israeli military delegation of one hundred arrived in Addis Ababa. This was the second-largest military delegation to visit Ethiopia after the US delegation. During those years Ethiopia received more Israeli aid than did any other African country. Israel also trained Ethiopia's special forces for combat against the Eritrean nationalist movement, which perhaps surprisingly did not impede Israel's access to the Eritrean Red Sea port of Massawa.

Israel's interest in preserving strategic relations with Ethiopia only reinforced its excuses for passivity on matters of aliyah. In the 1960s and 1970s, the Israeli political and military establishment resisted any official involvement on behalf of Jewish emigration from Ethiopia. In 1963, for example, the idea of establishing a public committee to promote Ethiopian aliyah surfaced, and Aryeh Levin at the Israeli Consulate in Addis Ababa responded with the following suggestions: Ethiopian aliyah should not be on the national agenda; Ethiopian Jews should not be brought to Israel as long as their Jewishness remained unresolved; the Embassy of Israel in Ethiopia should refer matters relating to Ethiopian Jews to the Conference of Jewish Organizations, where the Foreign Ministry should have veto rights; and Israel's assistance to Ethiopian Jews should focus only on improving their social conditions, with the aim of having them remain in Ethiopia. The perception was that any deviation from these guidelines could trigger a negative reaction by the local government, which consistently opposed Israeli aliyah activity, and it would unnecessarily complicate matters for the sake of a marginal issue. This strategic outlook only grew stronger in the early 1970s, when Ethiopia did not immediately join the many other African countries severing diplomatic ties with Israel and thus became, albeit briefly, an important and almost exclusive gateway to the "Black Continent."

Israel's position did not change even when the state's religious establishment recognized the Jewish identity of Ethiopian Jews. In February 1973 Israel's chief Sephardic rabbi, Ovadia Yosef, affirmed that they were Jews and called for their aliyah. Whereas most of the prominent twentieth-century halachic (Jewish law) scholars doubted that the Falashim were Jews, Ovadia Yosef relied on the writings of two fifteenth-century rabbis who argued that these were members of the Tribe of Dan, which Ashur had sent into exile when the Kingdom of Israel was destroyed in the First Temple era. Two years later Israel's chief Ashkenazi rabbi, Shlomo Goren, adopted this position as well, and in March 1975 an interministerial committee determined that Ethiopian Jews had the right to Israeli citizenship under the Law of Return. Despite these developments, however, the government of Israel took no active measures on behalf of Ethiopian aliyah during this time. Given that the halachic excuse became invalid after the early 1970s, the reasons for Israel's inaction presumably lie in the two other factors cited (reluctance to cope with the challenges of absorption and alienation, and concerns about complicating relations with the Ethiopian government). At the same time, these developments did significantly galvanize Israeli and international organizations working on behalf of Ethiopian aliyah, and they resonated with Israeli and Jewish media in Israel and across the world. Prominent among the international organizations was the American Association for Ethiopian Jews (AAEJ). These groups intensified their efforts to pressure the Israeli government and Jewish Agency to take action, at least symbolically, on behalf of Ethiopian aliyah. Additional pressure came from small groups of Jewish refugees who had managed, with great difficulty and at tremendous sacrifice, to escape Ethiopia during that period and reach Israel. Israel's response to these refugees was to grant entry permits, as tourists, to a small number of community members. Once in Israel, they had to undergo a strict conversion process, only after which they received recognition as Jews and full rights as olim.

Two unforeseen events in the 1970s lay behind the substantive shift in Israel's stance. The first was internal changes in Ethiopia that provided Israel with an opportunity to recompense the authorities in a meaningful way. In 1973, under pressure from the African Union, Ethiopia had severed diplomatic ties with Israel, a year before the military coup that replaced the regime of Emperor Haile Selassie with the revolutionary Marxist government of General Mengistu Haile Mariam. Cooperation with Israel certainly did not accord with Mengistu's international orientation, but he was facing a massive rebel uprising in the north and military confrontation with neighboring Somalia in the south. He needed military aid, and acutely so after relations worsened with the United States, Ethiopia's main arms supplier until then. Toward this end he began to explore the option of turning to Israel. The second development was the election of Menachem Begin as prime minister of Israel. At his first meeting with Mossad chief Yitzhak Hofi,

Begin issued an emotional plea—"Bring me the Jews of Ethiopia"—and he was consistent thereafter in promoting their aliyah.[35] The situation in Ethiopia convinced Begin to use this opportunity to support a deal involving the exchange of Israeli arms for Jewish emigration, despite the consistent stance of Ethiopia's leaders opposing intervention in its domestic affairs. According to Uri Lubrani, who had served as Israel's ambassador to Addis Ababa, Mengistu did not want to let Israel anywhere near the country's Jews because he feared that "we would take them away." Lubrani added, "The emperor's secretary, with whom I was on friendly terms, told me at the time, 'Ethiopia cannot afford to lose one iota of its genius.'"[36]

Mengistu's openness to the plan therefore removed a key obstacle to its implementation. But it did not completely quell Israel's political qualms regarding military ties with the revolutionary government in Addis Ababa. After all, Somalia, which had the support of the United States, Western European states, Saudi Arabia, and Egypt, was at war with Ethiopia, which in turn had the support of the Soviet Union, Communist China, and East Germany. Israel therefore had to persuade its ally, the United States, of the crucial nature of the deal. During his first visit to the United States as prime minister in 1977, Menachem Begin met with President Carter and secured his agreement. Over the course of late 1977 and early 1978, Israel and Ethiopia then sealed the deal. From the outset this arrangement had been problematic for Israel because Mengistu, though agreeing in principle to permit Jewish emigration, refused to specify any figures. As it turned out, the numbers were indeed quite small, and the Israeli Air Force planes that carried out the operation ended up transporting only a few dozen or hundred olim per flight. Israel sought to change this situation by increasing its military aid, but these efforts were stalled when Foreign Minister Moshe Dayan mentioned Israel's support for Ethiopia at a press conference in Zurich in February 1978. The revelation prompted Mengistu, whose foreign policy was decisively pro-Communist, to sever contact with Israel and remove its military presence from his country. Another factor behind his decision was that Libya and South Yemen, Islamic countries that had previously supported Eritrea, began to provide aid to Ethiopia, where Soviet influence was increasing, thus reducing the importance of Israel's military aid.

Presumably this state of affairs would have put an end to Israeli activity on behalf of Ethiopian aliyah, but new developments in Ethiopia soon revived Israel's efforts. The bloody civil war and severe famine in the country triggered a massive flight of Ethiopians to Sudan, where they sought refuge. Among these refugees were Jews, which reinforced the position of those in Israel who insisted that this was a case of aliyat hatzalah, and they ultimately succeeded in tipping the balance in Jerusalem. The flight to Sudan also sparked an idea that took shape among agents of the Mossad and a few Ethiopian refugees who had managed to reach Israel in a very tortuous way: to encourage the illegal exodus of Jews from Ethiopia to Sudan so as to facilitate their aliyah. The initial attempt to carry out such an operation, on a small scale, was successful. Under the guise of a humanitarian aid organization for Christians, civilian planes flew a small number of Ethiopian Jewish refugees who had reached Khartoum to Nairobi, then Athens, and, finally, Israel. As it happens, the Mossad had to operate on a much larger scale when thousands of Jewish refugees began flooding into Sudan's border regions after the news had spread among Jews that they could make aliyah from there.

This situation required Israel to make unconventional decisions. The first was whether to endanger thousands of people by having them make the unpredictable journey from Ethiopia to Sudan. The key question here was whether Israel as a state could take such a responsibility and a risk, and the answer it reached, with all its implications, was affirmative. The second decision related to the dispatch of large numbers of Israeli agents to Sudan, a hostile country that did not recognize Israel, in order to carry out operations that would expose them. The Mossad decided to take this risk. And finally, Israel had to resolve the problem of providing rapid transport for the thousands of Ethiopian Jews flooding into Sudan. In the early 1980s, covert Israeli-Ethiopian relations apparently revived slightly, which facilitated Israeli operations somewhat. According to some of the reports, in 1983 Israel even provided Ethiopia with Soviet military equipment confiscated from the Palestine Liberation Organization in the Lebanon War, and this paved the way for Israeli military advisors and Mossad agents to return to Addis Ababa.

Israel's initial proposal for implementation of its plans reads like fiction: to build a holiday village on the shores of Sudan, which would in fact serve as a base for routine operations using land and sea transport. Its location, more than a thousand kilometers from the government center in Khartoum, would allow for secrecy. Thus, in early 1980 a Mossad agent, under the guise of a European businessman, approached the Sudanese Ministry of Tourism with a proposal to build a holiday village, which of course entailed financial investment, and Khartoum gave its approval. Once established, the holiday resort, named Aros, attracted tourists from around the world. "It was indescribably busy," recalls Emanuel Alon, an agent of the Mossad and the special ops unit of Israel's navy, who oversaw construction of the resort. "Every week we would raise the rates so as to reduce demand, and the opposite would happen. The demand only increased."[37] The undercover operations increased as well. Rabbi Shalom Sharon of Kiryat Gat, author of the book *From Sinai to Ethiopia*, recalls the unforgettable moment of aliyah after his long journey: "In the middle of the night Mossad agents came and put us on trucks, about 150 people per truck. Soon we reached the Red Sea. . . . Looking at the vast sea, I felt absolutely terrified, until suddenly there appeared men in rubber boats and they hugged me."[38] Through this maritime operation,

named Home Port, one thousand Ethiopian Jews made aliyah by way of the ficti-
tious holiday resort. It took eight sea voyages and two Hercules airlifts to bring
them from the shores of the Red Sea in Sudan to Sharm El Sheikh in Egypt, where
they boarded planes to their final destination—Israel.

This scale could not, however, meet the growing demand as thousands of
Jews continued to flee from Ethiopia to Sudan. The trek was extremely grueling and life-threatening. According to some estimates, more than four thousand
Jews died on the journey and in refugee camps in Sudan. To organize and oversee these human masses, therefore, Israel had to change its modes of operation.
The solution—building refugee camps not far from Khartoum and airlifting olim
from there—was supremely problematic and required cooperation with Sudan's
leaders. Initially Israel tried to establish contact independently, but Sudan's president rejected all offers. Efforts to engage Egypt, which had friendly relations with
Sudan, failed to secure Cairo's agreement. Israel then decided to try another indirect approach, through the United States, which was on good terms with Sudan
and viewed it as a moderate, pragmatic country. Indeed, Sudan was a recipient
of US economic aid. Israel had information that then–vice president George H.
W. Bush was planning to visit Khartoum, and it made contact through one of his
Jewish aides. At the time the US administration was also under independent Jewish American pressure to provide humanitarian assistance to Ethiopian Jewish
refugees in Sudan. Eventually Bush secured the agreement of Sudan's president
to allow the operation (at an unknown price).

Subsequently, the Americans, cooperating behind the scenes with Israeli
representatives, worked closely with senior Sudanese officials to formulate the
plan. They decided that the operation would use a single European commercial airline and that it must remain secret. Under no circumstances could it be
known that the government of Sudan was cooperating with the "Zionist entity."
At this stage Jews from Belgium also entered the picture. The founding owner of
Trans European Airways (TEA), George Gutelman, whose father had survived
the Holocaust and whose mother had died at Auschwitz, donated the use of his
planes and pilots for the operation. He received legal authorization to fly thousands of "passengers"—with no passport or ticket—from Belgium's minister of
justice, a Jew by the name of Jean Gol. In all, Gutelman's airline transported
thousands of Jews from Khartoum to Israel by way of Belgium.

The final fifteen scheduled TEA flights were unable to carry out their mission, because in January 1985 the chairman of the Jewish Agency leaked the story
to the media. Moreover, Prime Minister Shimon Peres later took the liberty
of disclosing information about the undercover operation during a conversation with Canadian donors. His remarks subsequently reached the media and
ultimately appeared in the *New York Times*. At a press conference later, Peres

confirmed that flights were arriving from Sudan and requested that those present not discuss the matter. A few hours afterward, Operation Moshe came to a permanent halt.

Later that year Peres did successfully arrange aliyah for the hundreds of remaining Jews stranded in refugee camps in Sudan through a cooperative endeavor with then-president Bush named Operation Sheba. The United States contributed to this operation by relaxing Sudan's foreign debt, which stood at $9 billion, and by providing US aid planes for transport from Sudan. In 1989 Israel and Ethiopia renewed diplomatic relations, after the change in balance of power with the end of the Cold War and the cessation of continued support Ethiopia was due to receive from the Soviet Union. As a result, Ethiopia began to look to the West and to Israel, which provided the latter with an opening to renew aliyah efforts. During negotiations conducted behind the scenes, with US mediation and the participation of prominent American Jewish leaders, Addis Ababa requested arms and money in exchange for its cooperation. Lubrani conducted complex negotiations with Mengistu and his emissary Kassa Kebede. Because the Americans supported the rebels who opposed Mengistu, Prime Minister Shamir instructed Lubrani "not to pay Mengistu with anything that shoots."[39] Jerusalem's initial offer to Ethiopia, therefore, was for desalination plants, but this did not satisfy Addis Ababa.

In late May 1991, just days before Addis Ababa fell to the rebels, Mengistu fled Ethiopia and found refuge in Zimbabwe. Negotiations between Israel and Ethiopia, exhausting as they were, had intensified when it became apparent that the regime was likely to fall. Eventually Israel reached an agreement with Mengistu's representatives to allow Jewish emigration in exchange for a bribe of some $35 million (raised through American Jewish donations) and asylum in the United States for several senior officials. That same month, over the course of two days a massive airlift known as Operation Shlomo brought 14,310 Jews, who had gathered for this purpose in Addis Ababa, to Israel. The operation required eighteen Israeli Air Force planes, twenty-three El Al planes, and one Ethiopian Airlines plane. As soon as it commenced, the agreed-upon bribe was deposited in account number 1094-7839 at the City Bank of New York. But Mengistu and his associates never had the chance to enjoy this money. The US government immediately froze the account and transferred the funds to the new government in Addis Ababa.

At a diplomatic reception in the capital immediately after the operation, an Ethiopian dignitary voiced his opinion to Asher Naim, an Israeli Foreign Ministry official who had actively participated in events leading up to Operation Shlomo. The dignitary was impressed not only with the level of execution but even more so with the extensive diplomatic efforts and massive financial investment required. "That is a People to which I would like to belong," said the

Table 7.3. Aliyah from Ethiopia and Total Aliyah to Israel, 1948–2013

Years	Ethiopian-born immigrants	Total immigration to Israel
1948–51	10	687,624
1952–60	59	297,138
1961–71	98	427,828
1972–79	306	267,580
1980–89	16,965	153,833
1990–99	39,651	956,319
2000–04	14,859	181,505
2005	3,571	21,180
2006	3,595	19,269
2007	3,607	18,131
2008	1,570	13,701
2009	243	14,574
2010	1,652	16,633
2011	2,666	16,892
2012	2,432	16,557
2013	450	16,968

Source: Israeli Central Bureau of Statistics, *Immigrants, by Period of Immigration, Country of Birth and Last Country of Residence*, Statistical Abstract of Israel, no. 58.

Ethiopian. "For that," replied the Israeli, "you need to take a [preparatory] course that includes two thousand years of exile."[40]

Operation Moshe, a daring undertaking that paved the way for Operation Shlomo, exposes much of the problematique Israel faced and its modus operandi in the area of aliyah. Although immigration from Ethiopia never reached the numbers of other immigrant waves (see table 7.3), the story of aliyah from Ethiopia provides powerful evidence of the centrality and multidimensionality of the issue in Israeli foreign policy.

Silent Route: Early Aliyah from the Soviet Union

Aliyah from the Soviet Union constituted the largest and most complex of all immigration operations in Israel's history. The numbers reveal important facts about this aliyah. According to the 1939 census, a total of 3,020,000 Jews lived within the pre–World War II borders of the Soviet Union, and at least 2,100,000 lived in territories that were later captured by Germany. When Operation Barbarossa began, on June 22, 1941, there were roughly 5,250,000 Jews living in the Soviet Union, accounting for more than half of European Jewry. During World War II, nearly 3,000,000 Jews were slaughtered in the Soviet Union—that is, about half of all the Jews killed in the Holocaust. After this bloody chapter in history, a total of 2,267,814 Jews remained in the Soviet Union, according to the 1959 census.

According to data on aliyah from the Soviet Union since Israel's founding, there were a few dozen olim in 1950, 33,000 in 1973, 185,000 in 1990, and 50,000 from Russia in 2012. The total figure was about 1,250,000, which accounts for more than one-third of all olim during this period. The Soviet census of early 1989 indicates that the Jewish population had declined to 1,458,000. This figure continued to fall with the massive immigration that followed the collapse of the Soviet Union.

Another background element, not represented in the dry data of course, is the pressure, anti-Semitism, and persecution to which the regime subjected Jews, which peaked with threats of actual annihilation toward the end of the Stalin era but did not disappear under his successors. These practices manifested in various forms, both institutional and societal. For two-thirds of the twentieth century, therefore, Soviet Jewish life was characterized by threat of mass annihilation, oppression based on nationality, communal and individual hardship, and massive emigration to Israel.

The literature on this aliyah, spanning a history of more than sixty years, is vast and multidimensional, and we cannot do it justice here. The following analysis therefore focuses only on key aspects of Israeli foreign policy as it relates to aliyah from the Soviet Union during the first two decades of statehood, with emphasis on Israel's actions as well as areas where Israel refrained from acting. One important initial observation is that when the Soviet Union and Israel were cementing their diplomatic relations in mid-1948, they did not fully appreciate the significance of the Jewish dimension of their relationship. The Soviets did not view Jews as a relevant factor in their foreign policy, in part because they believed that Jewish citizens of the Soviet Union had largely adapted to the norms of the "Soviet man," whose identity was Soviet and culture Russian. Consequently they also consistently refused to recognize Israel as the national state of its Jewish residents, and they viewed any foreign intervention in matters related to Soviet Jews as conspiratorial and aggressive.

In May 1954 the Soviet first deputy premier, Anastas Mikoyan, told a visiting delegation of the French Socialist Party in Moscow that "we do not encourage aliyah, because Israel is a capitalist American enclave and anti-Soviet stronghold. Nevertheless, we do not prevent and will not prevent the emigration of those who want to leave—but there are none: the Jews of the Soviet Union have no interest in immigrating to Israel."[41] In operative terms, by basing its relations with Israel solely on geostrategic considerations and realpolitik, the Soviet Union not only underestimated Jewish enthusiasm over the establishment in 1948 of an Israeli legation in Moscow but also misjudged Israel's stance on Soviet Jewish aliyah.

There is no doubt that Soviet support from early 1947 for the establishment of a Jewish state in Palestine was an important driver of national Jewish awakening in the Soviet Union. Shortly after Foreign Minister Gromyko announced this support, a commemoration for Jewish writer Mendele Mocher Sforim took place in Moscow. At the event, the chairman of the Jewish Anti-Fascist Committee, Shlomo Mikhoels, stated that during Mendele's time there was no answer to the question presented in his book *The Travels of Benjamin III*: Where does the road to the Land of Israel lead? Yet now, Mikhoels asserted, Gromyko had provided the answer from the podium of the United Nations. The one thousand members of the audience gave a long standing ovation.[42] Jewish enthusiasm over meetings with Golda Meir (then Meyerson), Israel's first minister plenipotentiary to Moscow, was equally strong. The Soviet response to this awakening was firm and uncompromising. It included executions, imprisonment, the prohibition of any contact between Jewish citizens and Israeli diplomats, and a lengthy article in *Pravda* by Jewish writer Ilya Ehrenburg in September 1948. Ehrenburg asserted that there was absolutely no connection between Jews living in "socialist" countries and the State of Israel or their kin who lived there. In February 1949 Israel's envoy to Moscow was summoned to the Soviet Foreign Ministry, where Deputy Foreign Minister Valerian Zorin officially notified him that his delegation's activities to promote Soviet aliyah were illegal and in breach of diplomatic conduct. Shortly thereafter, for reasons apparently unrelated to the founding of Israel, Stalin sealed the fate of the remaining Soviet Jewish cultural institutions, dooming them to extinction.

These developments presented Israel with a political, moral, and ideological dilemma. On the one hand, Soviet support for Israel's establishment and its struggle for recognition within and beyond the United Nations was a vital asset during the early years of statehood. Reducing the points of friction, which included the issue of aliyah, was therefore a clear operational objective for Jerusalem. On the other hand, it goes without saying that Israel was not prepared to accept a Soviet prohibition on aliyah or the ever-growing threat of disconnection from Soviet Jews. Moreover, as Nati Cantorovich describes in his doctoral dissertation, domestic Soviet developments had the effect of reducing long-standing divisions within the Zionist leadership. Some leaders, including Chaim Weizmann, had long given up on Soviet Jews as candidates for aliyah, believing they had assimilated into Soviet society and culture, while others continued to view Soviet Jewry as flesh of their flesh and a potential source of aliyah once the Soviet government gave its authorization.[43] During the first two years of statehood, however, it became clear to Israel's leaders that the potential for Soviet aliyah was tremendous. Foreigners who visited the Soviet Union during the late 1950s estimated that half a million or more Jews were ready and willing to make aliyah if they had the chance. Even Ehrenburg, who was famously cautious on all matters

Jewish, said that if the gates were to open, one hundred thousand Jews would make aliyah. Israel's leadership was also aware, at least in part, of the anti-Semitic campaign that threatened Jewish extinction culturally and even physically, and therefore demanded, more than ever, political and other forms of action. Jerusalem decided on a way forward, but it was fraught with complication and internal contradiction.

Despite the clear and decisive message from Moscow, during its early years Israel did on several occasions raise the issue of aliyah with Soviet diplomats. For example, during her first meeting with Vyshinsky in January 1949, Golda Meir asked whether children or the elderly who had relatives in Israel might be allowed to make aliyah. In December of that year, Sharett suggested to Yakov Malik, head of the Soviet Union's permanent mission to the United Nations, that the Soviets permit a few tens of thousands of Jews to emigrate. Similarly, a recently disclosed report sent from the Soviet legation in Tel Aviv to the Foreign Ministry in Moscow in early 1950 notes that Ben-Gurion repeatedly stressed that Israel would not give up on aliyah from the Soviet Union. But these facts hide a different truth: Israel actually refrained from making aliyah a central issue in its diplomacy, and only half a decade after achieving independence did it create an organization that would deal, albeit clandestinely, with Soviet aliyah. This delay, whose significance we should not underestimate, resulted from several factors: the negative Soviet response to Israel's requests, Israel's inability to undertake large-scale action in the Soviet Union, its concerns about the impact that strong pressure on the Soviet Union could have on mass aliyah from Eastern Europe, and the Cold War superpower confrontation, which reduced the likelihood of both US support for Israel and Soviet acquiescence on this matter. There is no doubt that these circumstances generated considerable frustration among Israeli policy makers, as Moshe Sharett expressed poetically in a letter to the Israeli minister plenipotentiary in Moscow in March 1950:

> Your final report has arrived and unleashed a new torrent of profound fear as to what is happening and what is about to happen to Soviet Jewry. We stand helpless and forlorn before this fate.
>
> As I write this we have managed to bring about the deliverance of a Jewry that similarly appeared doomed to total severance from the body of the people and quivered helplessly in the talons of an obsessive regime. I refer to the decision of the Iraqi government to permit the emigration of Jews to Israel. This surprising turn-about was reached thanks to our unceasing efforts. Here in the land of unenlightened zealotry and ruthless despotism, we succeeded in penetrating into its very bowels, maintaining a living connection and acting. . . . In the Soviet Union we can only observe and take note, and this too only fragmentarily and partially.
>
> From time to time the thought recurs of traveling to Moscow to get the highest rung of the ladder. But serious doubts still mitigate against such

moves: will we be allowed to arrive? And if so—will the effort bear any fruit? Or shall we fail and lose? And in the meantime who knows what price we will pay for this daring attempt in other parts of our international arena? Such are the thoughts that must be considered and which forestall initiative. . . . The tragedy of Soviet Jewry infinitely objects my spirit and darkened all our sky.[44]

Because of the constraints under which Israel had to operate, it directed most of its efforts during its early years only toward establishing and maintaining links with Soviet Jewry. Among other reasons, it sought to keep the embers of national identity burning so as to facilitate aliyah when the time was ripe. Moreover, in the course of consolidating this policy, from the outset Jerusalem understood the importance of raising global awareness regarding the plight of Soviet Jews. In May 1956, Nehemiah Levanon (who later became head of Nativ) formulated the basic principles of Israel's policy, the first of which held that Soviet Jewry was an asset to the people of Israel and the State of Israel and that "its heart still beats with love for Zion and we should struggle on behalf of this Jewry with all our might." The second principle related to the aims of the struggle: to "inform world Jewry and the world as a whole that there is a Jewish and humanitarian problem in this part of the world, which demands a solution" and to "persuade Jews and non-Jews that struggling to maintain the unique character of Jews living in communist countries is worthwhile."[45]

There may have been consensus in Israel regarding the end, but there was substantial disagreement over one aspect of the means.[46] Although the prevailing desire in Jerusalem was to avoid bringing the Cold War into the struggle for aliyah, some demanded "removing the gloves" when it came to Israel's part in the operation. In their view it would be obvious to the Soviets that the initiative and direction came from Israel, and as Levanon framed it, hiding Israel's involvement would be "needless and pointless." Following this line, Mossad chief Isser Harel demanded a "high-level Israeli initiative . . . making full and open use of the propaganda potential." Shaul Avigur, the head of Nativ, also sided firmly with "a public stance in each and every forum, without hiding ourselves; we should present ourselves under the motto of Moses, 'Let my people go.'" However, Foreign Minister Sharett opposed such an open stance and decreed a strategy of caution, avoidance of any impression of hostility toward the Soviet Union, neutrality vis-à-vis the Cold War, and nonintervention in internal Soviet affairs. Accordingly, a public relations organization named Bar was established to recruit known moderates, Communist socialists, and supporters of the Soviet Union. Israel requested that its partners in this endeavor not touch on matters of domestic Soviet politics and not establish contact with dissidents in the Soviet Union. Activities in the West also had to follow this line and maintain anonymity, avoiding any public association with the government of Israel. Indeed, it deserves emphasizing that in this context no tension emerged between Moscow and Jerusalem.

Conflict was inevitable, however, in relation to Nativ's other activities—namely, those directed from the inner depths of the Israeli embassy in Moscow, which was under constant surveillance and scrutiny. The grand scale of Israel's operation could not elude hidden microphones, physical surveillance, and government cameras. In the late 1950s, an internal report of the Central Committee of the Soviet Communist Party asserted that even the Hebrew Bible and prayer books were nationalistic and racist. It claimed that they served as a basis for Israel's aggressive imperialistic policy and undermined the integration of Soviet Jewry into society because they preached the superiority of Jews as the chosen people. The Soviet leadership acted with vigor on this report, imprisoning or expelling Israeli representatives and persecuting local Jews. Notably, from Israel's perspective, providing material and maintaining contact with Jews were only ever intermediate steps. The aim had always been to bring these Jews from the Soviet Union to Israel. After Moscow's harsh reaction, however, the focus of Israel's efforts shifted to maintaining ties with Soviet Jewry.

Conducting such Israeli activities inside the Soviet Union was extremely problematic. As Yaakov Roi, author of the most authoritative and comprehensive work on the struggle for Soviet aliyah, explains,

> Interaction with Jews took place not only at synagogues, although that was the regular venue for exclusively Jewish gatherings. Israeli diplomats, and Nativ representatives in particular, sought Jews out in any public forum in hopes of speaking with them, though cautiously and guardedly. They tried to draw the attention of Jewish passersby on the street, in shops and restaurants, on public transportation, in public parks, at exhibitions, and at the theater, by carrying El Al bags, having a Hebrew newspaper poking out of their pocket, or speaking loudly in Hebrew. The appearance of embassy cars bearing an Israeli flag in various, including remote, cities would also attract attention and excitement. Reaction to official Israeli presence varied from fear and avoidance to excitement and enthusiasm that was also replaced within minutes by anxiety. After receiving a "souvenir" from Israel (a coin, stamp, musical lighter, calendar, or even [Israeli] chocolate or cigarettes) the Jew would quickly vanish. The aim of all this was to gauge the mood on the Jewish street and convey an unmediated greeting from Israel.[47]

Large numbers of Jews received a wide range of goods and material through these encounters. In 1961, for example, embassy staff, some of whom worked for Nativ, made no fewer than sixty-eight visits beyond Moscow, reaching forty-two cities throughout the Soviet Union. In one year during the 1960s, they distributed more than 2,000 religious texts and 1,600 other books, 350 copies of a Russian-language

Israeli periodical (*Vestnik Israeliya*), 400 prayer shawls, and thousands of post-cards, stamps, Bezalel Arts Academy souvenirs, and coins.

Nativ also worked intensively on renewing ties between Israeli citizens and their family members who remained in the Soviet Union but had lost contact during the Stalin era. Toward this end, Nativ provided the JDC with addresses for delivery of food and clothing packages. According to Ralph Goldman, chief executive of the JDC (1976–1988), Soviet refuseniks would receive special packages of American goods that were in high demand on the black market: "For every $100 of goods we purchased, they could receive $400–$800, which gave them enough to live on for eight months."[48] From mid-1954 to the end of 1955, Nativ delivered six hundred such packages to more than four hundred recipients, including many who resided in Siberia and the far north.

As part of its publicity campaign among Soviet Jews, Bar spread the word through daily broadcasts on a Russian-language radio station, Kol Zion LaGola (The Voice of Zion to the Diaspora). The broadcasts focused exclusively on Jewish matters, avoiding talk of the situation in the Soviet Union or government policy.

Nativ invested much effort over the years in producing literary material especially suited to Jewish needs, and Hebrew-language study material in particular. Avigur viewed the latter as a key tool in preparing Jews for aliyah, as anyone making the effort to learn Hebrew would be looking toward Israel. Publications included specially designed dictionaries and Hebrew textbooks, one of which (*The Hebrew Language*, by Shlomo Kodesh) was printed in pocket size on fine paper to facilitate distribution without undue attention. The calendars made it possible to convey information about Israel, as well as prayers, pictures, and texts. A years-long project that began in the early 1960s produced Russian translations of many books dealing with Jewish and Israeli history and culture. The first of this collection was Leon Uris's *Exodus*. Western tourists would distribute these books after receiving them from Nativ messengers or by mail.

Another aspect of Nativ's activities was the promotion of tourism to the Soviet Union among Israeli Jews with dual citizenship. They provided a vital channel for communication with Soviet Jews, information about developments affecting Soviet Jewry, and delivery of books and money.

Despite their fundamental opposition to aliyah, the Soviets did permit limited emigration to Israel after Stalin's death, primarily in the context of family unification: 50 Jews in 1954, 100 in 1955, 750 in 1956, 12 in 1958, 7 in 1959, 1,400 in 1965, and 1,900 in 1966. Anyone who wanted to emigrate had to undergo a lengthy, tedious, unpredictable, and potentially very risky process of scrutiny. Candidates were required to have a *vizov*, an invitation or petition from Israeli citizens. In both Israel and the Soviet Union, Nativ was heavily involved in providing behind-the-scenes assistance for legal emigration. Golda Meir hinted at the scale of this activity in a 1960 report to the Knesset, which noted that to date

Israeli citizens had submitted nearly ten thousand petitions that included a commitment to take in their relatives from the Soviet Union.

Throughout these years, Bar worked to raise international awareness regarding the plight of Soviet Jewry and promote calls for their release. The Western general public knew little of this plight for two reasons. First, the Soviet government was careful not to generate headlines in this regard, and second, communication between Soviet Jews and the West was problematic. In the mid-1950s, this situation changed when three distinct groups in various countries began to speak out on behalf of Soviet Jewry: prominent political figures, progressive government leaders, and Jewish organizations. Intellectuals such as Raymond Aron and Manès Sperber in France and Jose Luis Romano in Argentina denounced Moscow's policy toward Jews. In April 1963 British philosopher Bertrand Russel issued a public letter to Khrushchev decrying the Soviet decision to apply the death sentence to Jews found guilty of financial crimes. Three years later, after visiting the Soviet Union, Holocaust survivor Elie Wiesel wrote a book titled *The Jews of Silence*, which in time became a well-known manifesto condemning the Soviet oppression of Jews. Jewish groups organized international conferences, the first of which took place in September 1960 with the participation of forty Jewish and non-Jewish intellectuals from fourteen countries. Similar conferences followed in 1961 in Italy, 1963 in Britain and Latin America, 1964 in Belgium, and 1965 in Scandinavia. Most prominent was the American Jewish Conference on Soviet Jewry, founded in Washington in 1964 as a coordinating body for dozens of Jewish groups advocating on behalf of Soviet Jews. The 1963 Socialist International Congress passed a resolution publicly condemning anti-Semitism in the Soviet Union. Local politicians also conveyed the message directly to Moscow in ways that made headlines, such as during Khrushchev's 1956 visit to Britain, or through approaches by the Canadian and Norwegian foreign ministers some years later. Communist leaders, too, raised their voices against the Soviet oppression of Jews.

It remained a well-kept secret for many years that Bar was responsible for much of this public activity from its base in Tel Aviv, through emissaries in Europe and the United States. Not only did the organization successfully conceal its own involvement to a large extent, but it also took great pains to keep non-Israelis who were engaged in these operations, including aliyah activists, from learning that Jerusalem was directing matters. The historiographic result was that for many years the connection between Israeli foreign policy and Jewish as well as non-Jewish advocacy on behalf of Soviet Jewry remained shrouded in obscurity. The names and activities of many contributors to the cause also remained buried, including Meir Rosenne, later the ambassador to Paris and Washington; Dr. Yoram Dinstein, later the president of Tel Aviv University; Baruch Eyal, a senior member of the Scientific Council at the Prime Minister's

Office; Yaka Yanai, who served in Washington; Yehoshua Pratt, who served in London, New York, and Washington; and Sarah Frankel, first a reporter for Voice of Israel and later an aliyah emissary to New York.

In the aftermath of the Six-Day War, the Soviet Union cut diplomatic ties with Israel in 1967, thus eliminating Nativ's local base of operations and necessitating a massive change in Bar's modus operandi. Paradoxically, aliyah figures remained low when Israel had diplomatic relations with the Soviet Union and was working to promote immigration. Nonetheless, according to Yaacov Ro'i, had Israel abandoned its commitment to Soviet Jewry before the Six-Day War, the Kremlin would not have severed relations in June 1967.[49] However, the consensus explanation for Moscow's breaking of diplomatic relations with Israel was that Brezhnev was not ready to go to war with Israel but felt he had to do something or lose Moscow's position in the Middle East. In any event, aliyah operations increased significantly after relations were severed. Among the causes of this change were internal developments in the Soviet Union, Moscow's militant anti-Israel stance and virtually unconditional support for the Arab position, a more proactive role on the part of Soviet Jewry seeking permission to emigrate, greater involvement by international Jewish organizations, the nascent superpower détente that made it possible to enlist the US administration on behalf of Soviet aliyah, and the emergence of the UN as an important forum for human rights advocacy in the Soviet Union, among other places. The outcome was a proliferation of activities related to Jewish emigration from the Soviet Union, which were now no longer in Israel's exclusive domain. This situation created unfamiliar constraints for Jerusalem as well as options for new forms of activity, ultimately forcing it to abandon the policy of quiet diplomacy.

Several factors contributed to this policy shift. Zionist activists in the Soviet Union and Soviet olim threatened the liaison bureau that they would take matters into their own hands if Israel did not change its official policy. Moreover, the Soviet Union's failure to abide by its promises of permitting family unification had generated widespread disappointment. Jewish American advocacy groups that rejected Israel's policy on Soviet aliyah further compounded the pressure. There was also a general impression that quiet diplomacy had run its course without yielding the anticipated results, and the entities responsible for operations on behalf of Soviet Jewry took a "tactical retreat" so as to restore calm and maintain control over the situation. The ultimate turning point in official Israeli policy regarding public advocacy for Soviet Jewry occurred in the autumn of 1969, when Prime Minister Golda Meir brought a petition signed by eighteen Jewish families from Georgia to the attention of the Knesset and the public in Israel and overseas. Additional momentum came from a February 1971 conference in Brussels, with the participation of 760 delegates from thirty-eight countries who represented the major Jewish communities campaigning on behalf of Soviet Jews. The campaign in Israel played a decisive part as well, when it managed to overcome extreme reluctance among Soviet olim and enlist Zionist activists to advocate on behalf of their brethren who were still hoping to make aliyah. Despite the criticism and subsequent policy shift, however, it is hard to avoid the conclusion that Israeli operations within and outside the Soviet Union before 1967 did in fact help lay the foundation for what followed. Between 1969 and 1985, some 266,000 Jews left the Soviet Union, of whom 164,000 made aliyah. Ultimately, in the late 1980s and early 1990s, the dream of fully "open gates" was realized.

This cursory survey of some of Israel's efforts to promote aliyah since achieving statehood demonstrates that it did indeed fulfill Herzl's vision: that the State of Jews serve as a refuge and homeland for the Jews of the world. "Let my people go" was anything but an empty slogan. It was a political directive in every sense and a core element of Israeli foreign policy.

Notes

1. Sebastian Klor, "HaAliya MeArgentina BaShanim 1962–1963 BeTsel Parashat Eichmann" [Argentinian aliyah during 1962–1963 in the shadow of the Eichmann affair], *Iyunim Bitkumat Israel* [Studies in Israeli and modern Jewish society] 25 (2015): 437–66.

2. *Davar Davur* [The spoken word] (Tel Aviv, Sharett Heritage Society, 2013), 83.

3. See Marcos Silber and Szymon Rudnicki, eds., *Te'udot LeYakhasei Israel Polin, 1945–1967* [Documents on Israeli-Polish relations, 1945–1967] (Jerusalem, Government Printer, 2009).

4. Ibid., 230.

5. Ibid., 260.

6. Private information.

7. *Davar Davur*, 86.

8. Albert Kaganovitch, "Stalin's Great Power Politics, the Return of Jewish Refugees to Poland, and Continued Migration to Palestine, 1944–1946," *Holocaust and Genocide Studies* 26, no. 1 (2012): 59–94.

9. Uri Bialer, "Ben-Gurion VeShe'elat HaOrientatsia HaBenle'umit Shel Israel, 1948–1956" [Ben-Gurion and Israel's international orientation, 1948–1956], in *Atsma'ut: 50 HaShanim HaRishonot* [Independence: The first fifty years], ed. Anita Shapira (Jerusalem, Shazar Institute, 1998), 217–44.

10. Magdalena Ionescu, "The Jewish Emigration from Romania in the Context of Israel's Creation," *Valahian Journal of Historical Studies* 15 (2011): 119–36.

11. Lukasz Krzyzanowski, "An Ordinary Polish Town: The Homecoming of Holocaust Survivors to Kalisz in the Immediate Aftermath of the War," *European History Quarterly* 48, no. 1 (2018): 92–112.

12. Zachary Paul Levine, "Concealed in the Open: Recipients of International Clandestine Jewish Aid in Early 1950s Hungary," *AHEA: E-journal of the American Hungarian Educators Association* 5 (2012), http://ahea.net/e-journal/volume-5-2012.

13. Marcos Silber, "Foreigners or Co-nationals? Israel, Poland, and Polish Jewry (1948–1967)," *Journal of Israeli History* 29, no. 2 (2010): 213–32.

14. Aviva Lori, "Gam Lanu Ze Lo Haya Kal" [It wasn't easy for us either], *Haaretz Daily*, March 2, 2013.

15. Makhleket Mizrakh Eropa El HaTsirut BeVarsha [East European Desk to the Legation in Warsaw], December 30, 1959, via Israel State Archives (ISA), file 3118/19.

16. Reshef LeMahkleket Mizrakh Eropa [Reshef to the East European Desk], February 3, 1959, via ISA, file 3118/20.

17. See Magdalena Ionescu, "The Jewish Emigration from Romania in the Context of Israel's Creation," *Valahian Journal of Historical Studies* 15 (Summer 2011). 119–136.

18. The quotations that follow are from Igal Avidan, "LeKol Ish Yesh Mekhir: Kakh Makhra Memshelet Romania et HaYehudim" [Everyone has a price: How the Romanian government sold the Jews], *Israel HaYom*, September 27, 2013.

19. Dvora Hacohen, *Olim BeSe'arah: HaAliyah HaGdola VeKlitatah BeIsrael, 1948–1953* [Immigrants in turmoil: Mass immigration to Israel and its repercussions, 1948–1953] (Jerusalem, Yad Ben Zvi, 1994).

20. Avidan, "LeKol Ish Yesh Mekhir."

21. Ibid.

22. See, in particular, Ion Mihai Pacepa, *Red Horizon, Chronicles of a Communist Spy Chief* (London, Gateway Books, 1987); Radu Loanid, *The Ransom of the Jews: The Story of the Extraordinary Secret Bargain Between Romania and Israel* (London, Ivan R. Dee, Publisher, 2005).

23. Avidan, "LeKol Ish Yesh Mekhir," 1–3.

24. Ibid.

25. Ibid.

26. Michal Reshef, "HaMivtsa HaSodi Shel Ha'alat Yehudei Damesek LeIsrael Nekhsaf" [The secret operation to bring the Jews of Damascus to Israel is exposed], *Walla*, April 16, 2013.

27. Encyclopedia of Jewish Women https://jwa.org/encyclopedia/article/carr-judy-feld.

28. Avi Picard, *Olim BeMesorah: Mediniyut Israel Klapei Aliyatam Shel Yehudei Tsfon Africa, 1951–1956* [Cut to measure: Israel's policies regarding the aliyah of North African Jews, 1951–1956] (Sde Boqer, Ben Gurion Heritage Center 2013). 102 This is the source for the quotations that follow until noted otherwise.

29. Henriette Dahan Kalev, "You're So Pretty—You Don't Look Moroccan," *Israel Studies* 6, no. 1 (2001): 1–14.

30. Picard Olim BeNesorah, 36. See also Avi Picard, "Reshitah shel HaAliyah HaSelectivit BiShnot HaHamishim" [The beginning of the selective immigration in the 1950s], *Iyunim Bitkumat Israel* 9 (Sede Boker) (1999): 338–94, which is the source for the following information until otherwise cited.

31. Picard, *Cut to Measure*, 339.

32. See Michael Laskier, *Israel VeHaAliyah MiTsfon Africa, 1948–1970* [Israel and the aliya from North Africa, 1948–1970] (Sede Boker, Ben Gurion Heritage Center, 2006), 416. Pages 186–289 are the source for quotations that follow unless noted otherwise.

33. See the collection of documents published in 2014 by Israel's State Archive under the title *Mivtsa Yachin: Khamishim Shana LeHa'alat Yehudei Morocco* [Operation Yachin: Fifty years since the aliyah of Morocco's Jews]. http://israelidocuments.blogspot.com/2014/12/50 .html.

34. Menachem Waldman, *Me'ever LeNaharei Kush: Yehudei Etiopia VeHaAm HaYehudi* [Beyond the rivers of Ethiopia: The Jews of Ethiopia and the Jewish people] (Tel Aviv, Ministry for Defence, 1989).

35. Gad Shimron, *Havi'u Li Et Yehudei Etiopia* [Bring me the Jews of Ethiopia] (Tel Aviv, Hed Artzi 1998).

36. Tal Bashan, interview with Uri Lubrani, *Maariv*, December 30, 2013 [in Hebrew].

37. Uri Perednik, "Shloshim Shana LeMivtsa Moshe" [Thirty years since Operation Moshe], *Mida*, November 20, 2014.

38. Ibid.

39. Tali Bashan, "Hasipur HAmiti Meacharei Hazalat Hayehudim: Kach Hitnahel Mivza Shlomo" ["The true story behind saving the Jews: This is how Operation Solomon was conducted"], *Maariv*, May 23, 2015.

40. Asher Naim, "Mivtsa Shlomo" [Operation Solomon], in *Misrad HaHuts: Hamishim HaShanim HaRishonot* [The Foreign Ministry: The first fifty years], ed. Moshe Yegar, et al. (Jerusalem, 2002), 667.

41. A. Eshel to Y. Avidar, May 24, 1956, in *Te'udot LeMediniyut HaKhuts Shel Israel* [Israeli oreign policy documents], vol. 11 (Jerusalem, Governmnt Printer, 2007/2008), document 262.

42. Yaacov Ro'i, *Yehudei Rusia BaMe'ah HaEsrim: HaSugiya HaYehudit BeYahasei Brit HaMo'atsot-Israel* [The Jews of Russia in the twentieth century: The Jewish question in Soviet-Israeli relations], vol. 3 (Ra'anana, The Open University, 2014), 8.

43. Nati Cantorovich, "Mutsi'ut o Mishala? HaYishuv HaYehudi BeEretz Israel U-Vrit HaMo'atsot, 1933–1945" [Reality or wish? The Jewish Yishuv in Palestine (Eretz-Israel) and the Soviet Union, 1933–1945] (PhD diss., Tel Aviv University, 2012).

44. March 8, 1950, via ISA, file 2514/1.

45. Ro'i, *Yehudei Rusia BaMe'ah HaEsrim*, 156.

46. The following is based until otherwise indicated on Yaacov Ro'i "The Jewish Question as an Element in Soviet-Israeli Relations" draft paper privately held [n.d.], 17–18 [in Hebrew].

47. Ro'i, *Yehudei Rusia BaMe'ah HaEsrim*, 22.

48. Ofer Aderet, "Meah Shanim LeMa'an HaAm HaYehudi" [A hundred years for the sake of the Jewish people], *Haaretz*, November 20, 2014.

49. Ro'i, *Yehudei Rusia BaMe'ah HaEsrim*, 158.

Part III
Strategic Relations

8 France—Weapons Recognition and Grandeur

In the autumn of 1955, French Minister of the Interior Maurice Bourgès-Maunoury described the rationale of strategic relations between Paris and Jerusalem as "waves of the Mediterranean Sea lapping at the shores of France and Israel with the same frequency."[1]

The geographical dimension—often invoked as a means of analyzing the significance of events that transpired in the 1950s as they relate to other circumstantial and temporal contexts—cannot possibly encompass the complexity of dynamics with which the French statesman and his interlocutors had to contend. Many questions remain unanswered, and this chapter attempts to address them. These include the following: What were the historical aspects, from Israel's perspective, of diplomatic relations with France? What did the state seek to achieve through these relations? What obstacles did it have to confront? How did it navigate them? Finally, what is its historical balance in this sense? The limited scope of this study compels us to focus primarily on the period leading up to the Six-Day War and to explore two of the main objectives of Israeli foreign policy in the context of France: recognition and weapons.

Zionist Diplomacy and France before Statehood

Historical Background

One of the guiding principles of Herzl's political activity and of the World Zionist Organization was the axiom that only support from at least one international power would pave the way toward its ultimate goal—a sanctuary for Jews in Eretz Israel. Herzl personally failed to achieve this, but the concept continued to draw followers even after his departure from the political stage. It further gained ground as a practical option with the outbreak of World War I, which marked the decline and eventual end of Ottoman rule in Palestine. At the same time, two foci of political activity aimed at drawing international support actually became nonoptions for Zionist diplomacy in 1914. In general, the war made it difficult for the movement to operate as a global political actor, given that its followers were scattered across countries at war with each other. Moreover, the management of the World Zionist Organization was then in Berlin, but because of the war all its Russian representatives had to depart, leaving only representatives of the German movement. The large presence of Jewish soldiers, including many volunteers, in the Russian Empire did not improve the attitude of the Russian government toward the Jews. The Russian army high command, under Nikolai Nikolaevich, uncle of Czar Nicholas II, publicly accused the Jews of treason and spying for the enemy. Consequently, Russian army commanders began expelling entire Jewish communities from areas near the front. The political options available to the Zionist movement therefore centered on only two states, which were in competition for influence and control over the Middle East: France and England.

Both realized that the Jews could help them end the war and that it was therefore in their own interest to recognize and support them. The British Balfour Declaration of 1917 was one outcome of this realization. What is often forgotten is that six months earlier, France had issued a comparable, and extraordinary, statement. On June 4 of the same year, the secretary-general of the Quai d'Orsay (French Foreign Ministry), Jules Cambon, sent the following dispatch to Nahum Sokolow, who was engaged at the time in extensive diplomatic activity on behalf of the Zionist movement:

> You were good enough to present the project to which you are devoting your efforts, which has for its object the development of Jewish colonization in Palestine. You consider that, circumstances permitting, and the independence of the Holy Places being safeguarded on the other hand, it would be a deed of justice and of reparation to assist, by the protection of the Allied Powers, in the renaissance of the Jewish nationality in that Land from which the people of Israel were exiled so many centuries ago. The French Government, which entered this present war to defend a people wrongfully attacked, and which continues the struggle to assure the victory of right over might, can but feel sympathy for your cause, the triumph of which is bound up with that of the Allies. I am happy to give you herewith such assurance.[2]

The "Cambon Declaration" did not ultimately yield any political results. Among other factors, the League of Nations decided to grant a mandate to Britain for Palestine and to France for Syria and Lebanon. The Zionist leadership naturally chose Britain as the nearly exclusive axis of its diplomacy, and symbolically, the pro-British Chaim Weizmann replaced the pro-French Sokolow as soon as the war ended. Britain, for its part, would henceforth have to navigate between its commitment to the Jews and its political interests in the region, which required increased consideration of the Arab side. France had no such commitments and therefore demonstrated a clear and consistent preference for the latter.

The 1930s provided ample evidence that the fatalistic approach adopted by the Zionist movement, when it decided not to challenge the Quai d'Orsay's stance, was the right and rational choice. Nor did France's political stance change after the rise to power of a radical leftist socialist front under the leadership of Leon

Blum, in whose government Marius Moutet, a loyal ally of the Zionist movement, served as minister of the colonies. In 1938 Moshe Sharett, then head of the Jewish Agency's Political Department, therefore concluded, "France is so uninterested in continuing our project in Eretz Israel that it will become a source of pressure on Britain that works to our disadvantage. There is some basis for the reverse hypothesis: we do indeed have friends in France, including one very good friend who headed the government and remains influential. . . . But [Blum] does not decide what France's state interests should be."[3] Indeed, from Jerusalem's point of view, France's political record during the 1930s spoke for itself quite clearly and unambiguously. It included, among other things, a lack of support for the 1937 Peel Commission partition plan; the salient anti-Semitic argument, heard throughout the Quai d'Orsay, that "a Jewish state would soon become a base for Jewish imperialism in the East"[4]; refusal to take action against the mufti's anti-Semitic broadcasts from Beirut; and rejection of Zionist initiatives to establish a large, multinational Jewish legion.

Statecraft in the Dark

This state of affairs began to change somewhat, from the Zionist perspective, during World War II. The Vichy regime, established after the French defeat of May 1940, was a radical anti-Jewish organization from its inception and therefore unfit as a potential negotiating partner. Nor could it be expected to meet Zionist aspirations of international support for its settlement enterprise in Palestine. Britain remained the central arena for diplomatic activity by the Jewish Agency, but shock waves within the international system, especially those that caused a rift between the Vichy regime and the "Free France" movement led by de Gaulle, provided opportunities to forge contact with the latter, which the Jewish Agency was later able to exploit upon the cessation of hostilities. A relatively large number of Jews participated in various units of the underground, including its upper echelons, and the agency maintained continuous contact with political leaders in the French underground based in France and England. The French Resistance (*La Résistance*) included many individuals who came to hold senior political positions in the aftermath of World War II and during the 1950s and who provided support to Israel during those years. Prominent among these were Georges-Augustin Bidault, Maurice Bourgès-Maunoury, General Maurice Challe, and Guy Mollet. A large number of Jews held positions at the Free French headquarters in London, including jurist René Cassin, Pierre Mendès France, and sociologist Raymond Aron. As the representative of a "nonstate," France's London-based leadership-in-exile was in great need of vast assistance of any kind, and thus the Zionist movement, the Jewish Agency, and global and American Jewish organizations served as one of its lifelines, albeit a relatively minor one.

The exiled leadership had aims that exceeded the political sphere. It hoped to receive operational support from the Yishuv in the course of its struggle against the Vichy regime, which still controlled Syria and Lebanon. The Jewish Agency indeed provided such assistance, which included extensive sharing of intelligence, propaganda through Radio Levant France Libre (Levant Free French Radio, which relocated to the home of David HaCohen, a Haganah leader, in Haifa in October 1940), and an active role in the French-British invasion of Syria in 1941–1942, during which Moshe Dayan lost his left eye. In the opinion of Benjamin Pinkus, a prominent scholar in the field, these activities and the resulting contact with other Jews evidently created a dichotomy for de Gaulle: the apparent success of the Zionist enterprise in terms of progress and development, on the one hand, and the need to take the "masses of Damascus" into consideration because of their importance for French national interests, on the other.[5] In any event Ben-Gurion's remarks during a May 1944 concert in Tel Aviv come as no surprise: "A terrible catastrophe befell France, but it also experienced a great miracle—General de Gaulle, [who] redeemed France's honor. France will play an important role after the war, and it will provide assistance for the Jewish People in Eretz Israel."[6] The half decade that elapsed after this declaration decidedly put it to the test. Another factor that almost certainly contributed to this expectation was that Britain's attempts to neutralize French influence in the Middle East both angered and offended de Gaulle, a fact of which Zionist leaders were fully aware.

One of the interesting facts about post–World War II Zionist diplomacy is that London to a large extent lost its centrality. Britain, of course, remained important because it was the seat of Mandatory government in Palestine and the dominant power in the Middle East, but in practical terms the Jewish Agency needed a base of operations across the English Channel, on the continent, from which it could organize and conduct operations it viewed as critical to the fate of the Yishuv, many of which blatantly defied British policy. New York served successfully as a base of operations for the fund-raising needed to support the ever-expanding Zionist enterprise, but it was too far away from the European arena and the Yishuv. From mid-1945, therefore, Paris became the operational base of the Zionist movement's international struggle. Ben-Gurion often stayed there for long periods, overseeing the political and diplomatic affairs of the Zionist movement from his hotel room at Le Royal Monceau.

Zionist activity comprised, first and foremost, the establishment of a "Haganah headquarters" in Paris in mid-1946, with the following aims: Rescuing Jews by doing away with the diaspora, establishing a network for self-defense in all Jewish population centers, training and drilling units of immigrants to reinforce the Haganah in Eretz Israel, assisting the Mossad LeAliyah Bet in matters of training and security, forming communication networks, engaging in public relations, and fundraising (Hadari 1991). The Jewish Agency also established a political base in the French capital, where Moshe Sneh, commander of the Haganah in Palestine at the time, also officiated clandestinely from a hotel room at the Hôtel Metropol under guise of a travel agent. A connection network with Israel was established via radio stations operated by French Jews. In addition, an operation base was established in Marseilles, near which transit camps were built for hundreds of anticipated immigrants.

In his book *Second Exodu*,[7] Zeev (Venia) Hadari reveals the full spectrum of Mossad activities undertaken from Paris and Marseilles. In early 1946, Mossad decided on four courses of action: acquisition of large ships; expansion of the field of operations through additional ports of passage in Europe and the Balkans; a renewed effort to solicit funding from the JDC, select institutions, and other Yishuv sources; and acquisition of loans from private entities in the United States and European countries. The Mossad LeAliyah Bet's activities in France had a direct and considerable impact. Sixteen of the sixty-four ships that made their way from Europe to Palestine transported no fewer than sixteen thousand immigrants, out of seventy thousand who arrived in Israel during 1946–1948.

Of course, these figures do not reflect the impact that the organization's activities had across the entire European continent. In addition to the direct efforts of aliyah activists, their success was undoubtedly due to the extensive network of connections that they established within and beyond France at the time, as well as the fact that French authorities and figures overlooked or even directly assisted these efforts. Notably, the French government included many members of the Free France movement who had served in the anti-Nazi underground during World War II and were now accessible thanks to the contacts established earlier by Yishuv representatives. These personal contacts with state authorities—such as the security services, the Ministry of the Interior, the Ministry of Transport, and other government ministries—allowed Mossad emissaries to extend their network to include officials at the middle, lower, and local levels. The Yishuv's "statecraft in the dark" made frequent and very fruitful use of these contacts. Representatives of the Mossad and their local operational collaborators, some of whom were also involved in criminal activity, were immune to arrest. Moreover, they shared the encryption code of the Mossad LeAliyah Bet with various security services that were monitoring the British agents then in France, and this collaboration was extremely helpful in concealing Zionist activity. According to Yigal Allon, one of the prominent Mossad activists at the time, "We traveled around France as if we were on a legal Haganah base, and the French authorities regarded us as allies. Our ships would undergo maintenance at the Marseilles ports in preparation for their next voyage. Everyone showed solidarity: the port workers, food service providers, and lawyers we needed for various documents, all went out of their way to help us. We were surrounded by love and human warmth."[8]

Israel's emissaries did not hesitate to adopt disguises or seek assistance from Jews in the French underworld. Mordechai Gichon of the Jewish Agency, who later became a leading figure in Israel's intelligence services and eventually a classics professor at Tel Aviv University, related in an interview that during the latter 1940s, "we needed local currency. I was instructed to go to Paris and receive a large sum of money from a Jew who had been a member of HaShomer HaTza'ir [a socialist Zionist youth movement]. His bodyguards met me at a luxury hotel, like out of a Hollywood movie . . . and brought me to a room where he was sitting in a red silk robe. He opened the closet near his bed, which was full of bills, offered them to Gichon and said, 'Blessed are your deeds. Peace be upon Israel.'"[9]

However, this covert cooperation did not escape the eyes of the British, who exerted heavy pressure on the French government and turned the issue into an international problem that muddied relations between the two countries. Indeed, British foreign secretary Ernest Bevin, in a meeting with French prime minister Paul Ramadier in June 1947, spoke in blunt terms that bordered on a threat when he explained that both the Arabs and the Jews were affected by the question of Palestine, "and I am sure that the French authorities' tolerance of Jewish immigration will have negative repercussions in French North Africa."[10] The confrontation culminated a month later in the well-known affair of the illegal immigrant ship *Exodus*. At the same time, a dispute was playing out behind the scenes between the French Foreign Ministry, which supported the British demand that immigrants disembark and be detained in Cyprus, and the French Ministry of the Interior, supported by public opinion sympathetic to immigrants and covert Zionist efforts, which opposed the British stance. As a result of these two clashes, France eventually decided that it would not force clandestine immigrants to disembark but that those who decided to do so "would enjoy all the liberties that France offers to anyone seeking asylum [in France]—a traditional sanctuary for refugees—a country whose citizens have always fought for individual liberty."[11] The prominent publicity that certain aspects of the affair received provides an indication of the operational success of the Yishuv and of the widespread support in France for the Zionist movement.

This success bore other fruit as well. In February 1948, when war in Palestine was imminent, a secret meeting of Haganah representatives took place in Europe, at which the organization set as one of its goals the mobilization of "all possible forces in Europe, to undergo training in preparation for a military response during the decisive struggle for the defense of Eretz Israel."[12] Subsequently some ten thousand individuals received military training at Haganah camps in Marseilles (with tacit approval from the relevant authorities), and half of these trainees ultimately joined the combat in Palestine. France also supported the Zionist movement in its procurement efforts. In December 1947, the United States had imposed a ban on the export of arms and military equipment to countries involved in the conflict in Palestine. The embargo became official UN policy in June 1948 and remained so until August 1949. Although France officially supported this policy, in practice it did not take pains to implement it, and for a brief period, particularly during the critical months of April and May 1948, France approved arms shipments to the Yishuv on a cash basis. This "green light" allowed Israel to receive thirty 30 mm cannons, artillery shells, twelve 120 mm mortars, twenty-five 20 mm cannons, ten Hotchkiss H35 tanks, and 75 mm cannons from France by June of that year. Moreover, Dakota C-47 Skytrain planes carrying large quantities of weapons purchased in Czechoslovakia made their way to Israel through French seaports and airports. Aside from these arms shipments to the Yishuv, in late May 1948 France also supplied ETZEL (the National Military Organization in the Land of Israel) with 5,000 English rifles, 250 Sten Mark II pistols, fifty 18 mm mortars, 5,000 shells for these mortars, and several tons of explosives. The IDF, however, captured these arms in June of that year, in an affair that bears the name of the immigrant ship that was transporting this cache—the *Altalena*.

Ben-Gurion and other Zionist leaders undoubtedly approved of these efforts to actualize the operational and material objectives of promoting aliyah and acquiring arms from or via France in the three years after World War II. In matters related to public diplomacy, however, the primary objective of securing international recognition became particularly critical and pragmatically imperative during this period. Political recognition by France was thus a matter of paramount importance, but in this regard delegates of the Jewish Agency and the young state encountered significant obstacles that, to some extent, foreshadowed upcoming developments.

The Struggle for UN Recognition

The 1946 British decision to withdraw from Palestine, thus leaving it to the UN to resolve the problems resulting from the Mandate's termination, further spurred the Zionist struggle for recognition, which peaked during the early months of the following year. France was, as noted, an important focal point of this effort, despite its political decline in the aftermath of World War II. Yet the path toward securing French support was difficult and complex. France had a range of multifaceted considerations that informed its policy on the question of Palestine. Although it lost its hold on Syria and Lebanon in 1946, the notion of a political, economic, and historical connection to the Levant and Egypt remained important for France. Forty-eight percent of the foreign investments in Egypt at the time—amounting to 120 million francs—were attributable to France, which also retained its colonies in Muslim North Africa as well as many connections throughout the Arab world. On the one hand, the national awakening underway in that world, particularly surrounding the founding of the Arab League, posed a clear threat to French interests in the region, but on the other, it also had a strong interest in seeing the British hold in the region weaken. From the French perspective, as reflected in the words of its diplomats, the British Empire was on the verge of bankruptcy. For France this seemed an opportunity to rectify its standing after its humiliating expulsion from the Levant by Britain toward the end of World War II and to conquer or reconquer various strongholds in the Middle East. Yet its diplomatic ties with London could not be dismissed, especially regarding a security alliance against the Soviet Union in which the United States was expected to be the first violinist.

Jewish influence on the United States and French dependence on US economic aid necessitated great caution on France's part, particularly given that the two superpowers supported the partition plan for Palestine. It would have been very difficult for Paris to promote any policy that categorically opposed that of Moscow and Washington. Finally, the question of Jewish refugees and displaced persons in Europe, and above all the Holocaust, added a weighty moral dimension to France's deliberations. Moreover, the French political system during the second half of the 1940s was quite unstable, and matters of national interest often remained unresolved. During the period in question, no fewer than nine governments were formed in France, encompassing nearly all ideologies along the political spectrum. Three Socialists, two Radicals, and two representatives of the Popular Republican Movement held the post of prime minister over this period. Their attitude toward Israel varied and frequently shifted. For example, the Popular Republican Movement, a Catholic party, embodied two trends in respect to the "Zionist cause": supporters and opponents of Israel. The main issues dividing them also related to matters of great importance for Israel, such as the Christian holy places in Palestine, the question of Jerusalem, and the property of the French Catholic Church in Israel. Even the Socialists who supported Israel in principle were divided over the significance of the "Jewish factor." Furthermore, this political discord in effect underscored the traditional stance of the Quai d'Orsay, which was opposed in principle to any cooperation with the leadership of the Zionist movement. Despite tactical changes over the years, the Quai d'Orsay was largely consistent in prioritizing the Muslim political bloc over Israel in light of France's interests in the region and in maintaining a presence in French North Africa. At the same time, declassified French documents reveal that certain figures in this ministry did in fact support the Zionist cause based on local and primarily global French interests. Among these supporters were the director of the European Division, the French general consul in Jerusalem, and the French ambassador to the United States.[13]

Structurally, Israel had one consistent basis of support within the French government. The security challenges facing the regime—the domestic Communist threat, the Soviet Union and the Eastern bloc, and the severe threat of revolt in Algeria—provided a rich foundation for cooperation in matters of security. Leading figures in the French security services therefore often adopted distinctly pro-Israel positions based on history, the justice embodied in the Zionist struggle for a solution to the Jewish problem, and vital French interests. Finally, after World War II, the Jews of France evidently had little electoral influence on Paris's policy regarding Jerusalem, in part because of the relative weakness of the French "Jewish voice." Unlike Jews in the United States, who accounted for 3 percent of the population at the time, French Jews constituted only 1 percent of the general population. Additionally, in contrast to the United States, where the voter participation rate among Jews was higher than the average for the general population, in France these rates were equivalent. Moreover, unlike the American Jewish vote, the Jewish vote in France was scattered, spanning the entire political spectrum. Certain facts were also evident to the Zionist diplomats and those who succeeded them in various political posts in Paris: that the House of Representatives of the Fifth French Republic had little influence, and that there existed an inherent norm in French society that sought to blur the differences among various ethnic groups and, given France's centralized Jacobean heritage, viewed any dual identity in a negative light. Accordingly, in 1954 the Israeli ambassador to France, Yaacov Tsur, observed, "Jewish public opinion has no influence on political life."[14] One significant exception, however, was a 1947 appeal to the French government by the Conseil Représentatif des Institutions Juives de France (CRIF, the umbrella organization of Jewish groups in France) requesting support for the establishment of Israel. Against this intricate background, the Zionist movement launched a large-scale two-year campaign aimed at influencing the French position, which began with the British decision to withdraw from Palestine and lasted until November 1947, when the UN adopted the recommendation to establish both a Jewish and an Arab state. Ultimately, France supported this recommendation. Can one therefore conclude that this French support is attributable to the Zionist campaign? Today we know that the Zionist course of action drew primarily on personal contacts established years earlier in France and that emotion and morality played a part, as confirmed by Idit Zartal's study on the socialist ties between the two states during the early days of Israel's statehood.[15]

In retrospect, however, it is no less evident that despite these diplomatic advantages, France was quite reserved in its approach to the new state. Even before this approach crystallized, there were indications of French reservations regarding its vote on the partition plan. Moreover, indeed, the French position threated to sabotage the vote altogether from the Zionist perspective. Initially France held that a resolution could not be imposed on the parties to the conflict. Later it sought to postpone the vote to pursue a compromise agreement that would accommodate Arab concerns. Only when it was unable to propose an alternative solution did France vote in favor of the partition plan and the establishment of a Jewish state in Palestine. In the words of Moshe Sharett, "France became [the state to be held] responsible if the unstable majority [in support of a Jewish state] dissolved and the sun set on the Jewish state before it ever rose."[16]

More significant for our purposes was the length of time it took France to recognize the Jewish state (or even offer de facto recognition)—nine months after the founding of Israel and after most Western states as well as the Eastern Bloc states had already recognized the new state. Recognition by France was in fact one of the first important tests that Israel faced in the sphere of international relations. From the latter half of 1948, it conducted these relations, in contravention of classic Zionist diplomacy, on the basis of raison d'état and the ability to exert influence outside the political, moral, or ethical arenas. This chapter of history highlights many aspects of Israeli foreign policy during its early years and therefore warrants further analysis.

Raison d'État—Israel's Diplomatic Objectives from 1948

Political Recognition

After Israel's declaration of independence in May 1948, the United States and the Soviet Union, as well as several other states, hastened to recognize Israel on a de facto basis. The Israeli Foreign Ministry, expecting that France would also be supportive, sent an official request to this effect one day after Israel's declaration. Israel's expectations were based on the belief that France shared common interests in the struggle against British rule and the Arab League, as well as the French values of traditional support for national liberation movements, France's aid to the Yishuv, and France's affirmative vote on the partition plan. It therefore came as a bitter surprise for Sharett and his associates when their request failed to elicit a positive response. What they did not know was that on May 19 the French cabinet had in fact discussed the question of Israel's recognition and concluded, "The necessary conditions for recognition under international law have not yet been met."[17] Nor did Jerusalem later realize that France had political reasons for refusing to endanger its relations with the Arabs and that these considerations underpinned its legal reasoning. Also noteworthy was that Britain declined to recognize Israel at this time, and recognition by France was therefore liable to harm the latter in its struggle against the former for influence in the region. In any event, the explicit legal requirements presented by France as conditions for recognition created a challenging political test for the young Jewish state. For France's part, these requirements served as leverage to compel Israel to grant its institutions the special rights they had previously enjoyed under Ottoman and British rule.

Historical circumstances had made it possible for France to attain special status in the Ottoman Empire, where it acted as a representative and patron of

Christianity generally and Catholicism specifically from the eighteenth century onward. Its status enabled Paris to defend Catholic institutions, and the sultan therefore granted certain privileges to French institutions—initially to places of worship and monasteries, and eventually to schools and hospitals as well. In view of France's special status, non-French institutions also sought and received patronage. The special status granted to these institutions first took the form of concessions that allowed them to function properly and protect their constituents in the face of a generally hostile Muslim environment. The aim of such privileges was to prevent trespass or disruption on the part of local administrative authorities. Over time these concessions also came to include fiscal benefits (such as exemption from customs duties for certain commodities and from government and municipal taxes for certain assets owned by the institutions) as well as educational benefits related to the operation of schools. Lack of clarity surrounding some of these arrangements and France's efforts to extend them led to the 1901 and 1913 agreements that defined those arrangements, which were signed under French pressure. With the dissolution of the Ottoman Empire after World War I, France lost its status as a patron of non-French institutions, but it remained particularly sensitive to the rights of its own institutions, which served as a gateway for political and cultural involvement and became all the more important as its strategic role in the region declined. French political leaders and public citizens, regardless of party affiliation or religious belief, shared this sensitivity. Although the British were displeased with some of these rights, they did not take any meaningful action to have them rescinded. France therefore retained its special concessions in Palestine during the Mandate era as well.

The partition plan, which proposed two independent states in Palestine, threatened to jeopardize France's privileges. France was especially concerned about the rights of its nearly seventy institutions in the Jewish state. These included thirty-six schools attended by some eight thousand students and some forty cultural, religious, health care, and charity institutions in Jerusalem itself. The issue was both emotionally charged and politically important for France. As a Catholic country, France wanted its Christian institutions in the Holy Land to operate smoothly, and the French public was sensitive to any threat in this regard. French institutions also served as a bridgehead for cultural influence, and the Quai d'Orsay was therefore determined to use its diplomatic advantage to compel Israel to respect France's rights. Moreover, Paris had traditionally participated in the defense of Christian holy places that it sought to protect. As such, it was a strong supporter of the plan to internationalize Jerusalem, a position that only strengthened its standing at the Vatican. Notably, the French authorities at the time spoke only of the "Tel Aviv government," and France had three specific demands: compensation for damage to its institutions during Israel's War of Independence and the complete removal of any military presence from

French institutions; exemption from customs duties and taxes for its institutions in Israel, as well as autonomy in the area of education; and the granting of special status to France in defense of the holy places. France further demanded Israel's withdrawal from Lebanese villages along the Israeli-Lebanese border captured by Israeli forces. France was unequivocal and unwavering in its position, as indicated by its refusal to support Israel's admission to the United Nations in December 1948.

The Quai d'Orsay's preconditions for recognition were nearly impossible for Israel to meet. As a fledgling state whose sovereignty was frequently challenged, it actively avoided making any publicly evident concessions. Moreover, despite the freedom of religion and worship to which Israel committed itself in its Declaration of Independence, it was extremely anxious about missionary activity within its jurisdiction. Recently declassified documents in the State Archives in Jerusalem reveal that, on the one hand, Israel upheld its commitment by not adopting blatantly antimissionary legislation, but on the other hand, it granted no such freedom of action to Christian missionaries as a matter of practice. In mid-1948, for example, the Dutch consul sought permission from Israel's prime minister for Christian missionaries to operate in Israel. Ben-Gurion's reply was twofold: "I said that under the laws of the state, you have complete freedom of operation in Israel. But I also expressed my hope that if they work among Jews, they will again fail as they failed before."[18] Israeli authorities undoubtedly contributed to the implementation of this approach over the years. The various churches in Israel were aware of the situation, which inevitably became a regular obstacle for Israeli diplomacy in its efforts to build political bridges with them.

The demands France posed in mid-1948 were hardly the first time Israel had to address this issue. In their struggle for recognition at the United Nations in 1947–1948, Jewish Agency representatives were well aware of the great importance France attached to its privileges, especially respecting Christian religious and educational institutions. As such, and because France's political support was considered particularly important, the agency's delegate in Paris declared on July 13, 1947, that the Zionist leadership intended to respect France's rights under the international agreements it had reached with the Ottoman Empire and Britain. This, however, was not enough to satisfy the French, who eventually conditioned their recognition of Israel (a matter of utmost importance for the country's leaders because of the struggle they anticipated over Israel's entry into the UN) on a signed agreement that would guarantee their rights. Negotiations between the two sides, which commenced with the onset of the 1948 War, were fraught with confrontations. Military considerations initially made it difficult for Israel to withdraw from its outposts inside French institutions (notably the Notre-Dame building in Jerusalem), while France was blatant "to the point of insult" in its demands in other areas—a full list of which it officially presented to Israel in late August 1948. The French consul in Jerusalem submitted these demands on behalf of four hospitals, eighteen clinics, two hospices, six nunneries and charities, and three secondary schools, four seminaries for priests, thirty-nine colleges, and multiple schools, girls' hostels, and orphanages housing twelve thousand students in all, including students in the Alliance school system (Bialer, *Cross*, 115–120, which is the source for the following analysis until otherwise indicated). The Ministry of Religious Affairs representative who received this list found it difficult to accept and reported to his superiors that "in actuality we are being asked to leave the education of our Christian citizens in the hands of French educational institutions" that would benefit from "far more rights than those enjoyed by Jewish and state schools and educational institutions." Beyond that disparity and the implicit challenge to its jurisdiction, Israel was concerned that any acquiescence to France's demands would open the door for other states to issue demands that Israel would have difficulty meeting. Nonetheless, Israeli authorities hoped that France would be satisfied with a general declaration guaranteeing its interests and rights, as delivered by the Israeli emissary in Paris, Maurice Fischer, in a letter dated September 6, 1948. However, these expectations were dashed. France reiterated its demands in subsequent contacts between Jerusalem and Paris—a clear hint that if these demands were not met, it would not recognize Israel. Paris further recommended seeking a formulation of its rights that would not appear as a challenge to Israeli sovereignty, and it proposed that Israel accept them through an official exchange of letters, such as the exchange between France and the Ottoman Empire in 1903.

Jerusalem saw no difficulty in committing itself to withdraw from French sites or provide compensation for damages, but it regarded other demands, now more starkly stated than originally presented, as untenable. These required that Israel guarantee the rights of French institutions to an extent that would grant those entities immunity from any future constitutional laws or amendments to them. Less problematic for Israel were the demands that Israel grant France the same preferences that it might in the future decide to grant to a third state or to the pope and that it submit any disputes regarding the interpretation of their agreement to the appropriate international court. Accordingly, the response of Israel's foreign minister, which had the prime minister's approval, expressed a willingness to negotiate regarding the "just demands of France" but made no prior commitment regarding a special or permanent status quo arrangement for the French institutions. Sharett saw the French demand as being intended "to restore a regime of capitulations" and categorically rejected any type of ultimatum "that would not have occurred to France to demand from some other country in the world." In a letter dated January 24, Ambassador Fischer informed the Quai d'Orsay that Israel was willing to enter into negotiations regarding French rights and promised that France would have the same rights as any future third party or the pope. Jean Chauvel, secretary-general of the Quai d'Orsay, replied, expressing agreement to such negotiations. Their correspondence, which came to be known as the Fischer-Chauvel Agreement, was in fact nothing more than an expression of mutual willingness to enter into negotiations on the matter. France, however, regarded the positive aspects of Israel's position as fulfillment of its own conditions for recognition.

Ultimately, these negotiations never took place for one simple reason: vagueness suited both sides. Israel realized that a detailed discussion on implementation of the "Fischer-Chauvel Agreement" could yield only two possible and very undesirable outcomes: to acquiesce to French demands and commit to what the Foreign Ministry later termed "absurd concessions such as the Turks made in 1901" or "to fight with the French over something they view as a sacred matter of principle." For its part, France was willing to accept the existing ambiguity because in practical terms its institutions continued to receive the benefits and exemptions they had enjoyed during the Mandatory era, Israel was refraining from any interference in Christian schools, and its Committee for the Admission of Christian Clerics to Israel was relatively flexible about admitting French clergy under the Fischer-Chauvel Agreement. Unsurprisingly, therefore, authoritative internal Israeli assessments from that time found that "in fact, French institutions are enjoying greater concessions and privileges than those they enjoyed at any time in the past." In any event, France consequently recognized Israel on a de facto basis on January 24, 1949, and after Israel's acceptance into the UN four months later, it recognized Israel on a de jure basis as well. The armistice talks between Israel and its neighbors that took place in Rhodes had provided France with the rationale it needed to recognize Israel fully without appearing to turn its back on the Arabs. France also hoped that this step would make it easier for it to advance its interests in Jerusalem.

It should be noted, however, that the initial, positive position of France regarding the Fischer-Chauvel Agreement was not uniformly or consistently acceptable among the French. During the French-Israeli strategic "honeymoon"—from the mid-1950s in particular—differences of opinion occasionally surfaced, making it easier for France to apply effective pressure on Jerusalem in relevant areas. Israel's ambassador to France, Walter Eytan, who in his previous position had personally witnessed these matters, told a Foreign Ministry official that "in protecting the rights of the monasteries, [Pierre-Eugène] Gilbert [the French ambassador to Israel in the mid-1950s] was always very forceful—and always successful. For who would refuse Gilbert anything? The nuns ran [to him] for every small matter, and he rushed to bring the matter to the Quai d'Orsay." The best illustration of Israel's determination to avoid any conflict with the French, despite their growing demands, took place in 1957, when Israel rescinded the law that exempted religious, charitable, and educational institutions as well as hospitals from paying taxes and customs. In contrast to all other foreign religious institutions, the French continued to enjoy their traditional rights. Israel's willingness to act against its own law was influenced by political as well as economic considerations: the fiscal concessions "did not pose an intolerable burden on the state treasury." Moreover, discrimination in favor of French institutions was largely justifiable because these were Catholic entities and therefore did not pose an overt challenge to other religious groups in Israel, such as the Protestants. On other matters, however, Israel refused to concede. In 1950, for example, the French demanded that the Mandate-era practice of permitting residential rights and issuing visas for French clergy be upheld. At the same time, the fact that the French did not insist on legal recourse in the framework of the Fischer-Chauvel Agreement indicates that they were satisfied with the status quo.

This pattern evidently ended in late 1963, after an affair that came to be titled "On People and Pigs" in internal Israeli correspondence. A year earlier, Israel had adopted a law that prohibited pig breeding except in certain areas around Nazareth and the Galilee and in scientific research centers and public zoos. In October 1963, it came to the attention of Israel's Ministry of the Interior, during its efforts to enforce this law, that a French convent in Ein Karem, Les Filles de la Charité, which cared for hundreds of special-needs children, was raising forty pigs. The deputy minister of the interior, a member of Israel's National Religious Party, became deeply immersed in the issue, ordered that the monastery remove its pigpen, and intended to implement this order as a matter of immediacy. The convent's Mother Superior told the ministry's representatives that the pigs provided the main source of food for the children and that the convent could not exist without its pigpen. She further informed them that she would not have the pen removed but would instead "alert the entire world" if Israeli authorities acted on their threats. The convent did indeed raise such an alarm, which reached the ears of French diplomats. They, in turn, brought the matter to the attention of the Quai d'Orsay, thus launching a series of negotiations that preoccupied the Ministry of the Interior, the Ministry of Religious Affairs, and the entire government for nearly five weeks, until the matter was resolved. In their appeal to Israel's foreign minister, the French stressed the point that Israel's order contravened the Fischer-Chauvel Agreement. In Paris, the French foreign minister telephoned the Israeli ambassador and told him "with gravity and sincere concern" that he had received "a notice from a senior Catholic figure regarding the forty-seven pigs" and that although "this is a minor matter . . . [it could] gradually erode the goodwill towards Israel that, to his delight, had been developing among church circles in recent years." The Israeli government subsequently decided to suspend immediate implementation of the order for the time being to reach a "satisfactory settlement."

The Foreign Ministry in Jerusalem was well aware of the damage that would result from a clash with France over "forty-seven pigs that provide food for nuns"—especially in view of the affair's media appeal and inevitable publicity in the worldwide Catholic press—unless forcefully thwarted. As Israel's ambassador to France framed the issue, "Every French monastery or convent in Israel has a 'head office' of sorts in France (and certainly in Rome as well). Moreover, it is only natural that every little issue becomes magnified. By the time the story . . . about the pigs . . . reaches Rome, their number will swell to three hundred." For understandable reasons, however the Israeli Foreign Ministry did not want to see this affair trigger a legal and political debate regarding interpretation of the Fischer-Chauvel Agreement. The government's first approach, therefore, was to persuade the Ministry of the Interior to concede the case of the "Ein Karem pigs" through an administrative order in accordance with the law. The ministry, however, refused to comply, while the French in Israel and Paris adopted a firm stance and demonstrated no willingness to reach a practical compromise in light of "Israeli [heresy], especially the political and legal [defiance of the Fischer-Chauvel Agreement]." The Israeli embassy in France therefore concluded that "[this agreement, which] was always a myth . . . has [today] become very real for the French side" and could lead to a "dangerous deterioration" in relations between the two countries. During a consultation on November 27 among the prime minister, the interior minister, and the acting foreign minister, they decided not to implement the order to confiscate and destroy the pigs in Ein Karem as long as the meat was used solely for the convent's residents. Thus, there would be "no danger to the Jewish residents of the state." This message would be conveyed to the government of France, emphasizing that the decision had been reached in view of the friendly relations between the parties "rather than their legal arguments." Shortly thereafter, another condition for overlooking the presence of pigs in Ein Karem emerged: their pen would have to be confined to the convent and must not be visible from the outside. At the same time, Israel actively avoided engaging in official discussion of the Fischer-Chauvel Agreement. Despite the Quai d'Orsay's dissatisfaction with Israel's evasion, it evidently agreed in early December 1963 to lay the affair to rest.

If Paris had any concerns that the "swine affair" reflected Israeli disregard for this agreement, the years that followed proved otherwise. On several occasions, Jerusalem displayed exceptional flexibility in responding to French requests related to its religious institutions. These included an exemption from travel tax for monks, after this exemption had been abolished in 1962 for all clergy and foreign residents who paid for their travel with foreign currency; recognition of laissez-passer certificates issued to Arab members of the church by the French Consulate in Jerusalem; exemption from customs for vehicles belonging to the French clergy; and the accreditation of a French school in Jaffa. The agreement continued to constrain Israel's freedom of action even after the Six-Day War and became a source of grievances among other church leaders, who objected to the discrimination. Israel justified its discrimination by claiming that it was adhering to status quo strategy and practice in respect to the Christian communities and therefore had to honor the historical privileges enshrined in international treaties. Its adherence to this strategy also had pragmatic motives: Israel had a clear interest in maintaining the Mandatory practice of recognizing a fixed number of Christian denominations (not including the Protestants) and not allowing this number to grow.

Weapons: Israel and the Middle East Arms Race

One of the more complex problems Israel faced from the outset was the need to ensure an arms supply. Four factors, which have remained largely unchanged throughout Israel's existence, contributed to this complexity. First, the state was born in wartime, and the Arabs' consistent refusal to accept its existence made military conflict a permanent feature of national life. Second, Israel was not technologically capable of producing the weapons systems it needed, at least not during its first few decades, and therefore depended on foreign supplies. Third, the superpowers were the main source of these supplies, and they typically conditioned any arms deals on their own global and regional political interests, which did not necessarily work in Israel's favor. Finally, arms purchases entailed a financial burden that limited the state's ability to satisfy its military needs. These basic facts were evident even before, though especially after, independence.

In the six months between the UN's acceptance of UNSCOP's recommendation for the establishment of a Jewish state in Palestine and the recommendation's implementation, Israel had to cope with three international developments that limited its ability to purchase arms. The first was an American embargo on the sale of arms to the region, which came into effect in December 1947; the second was a similar measure by the British in February 1948; and the third was a complete ban on such sales, announced by the Security Council in late May of that year. The common goal of these measures was to minimize the military power of the belligerents and thereby help expedite the end of the armed conflict. In hindsight, we can safely conclude that this goal was not reached in respect to the Jewish side. While the Arab armies (except Syria) relied on British weapons and support systems and therefore suffered because of the embargo, the Jewish population began to prepare itself as early as the summer of 1945 and was relatively successful in smuggling weapons systems from various sources. In early 1948, it acquired considerable quantities of Czech weapons, which proved to be highly valuable during the critical early stages of the war. The Soviets, besides declining to sell arms to the Jews, neither hindered nor provided logistical support for the Czech weapons transports to Palestine via Hungary and Yugoslavia; Israel therefore faced numerous difficulties that stemmed directly from lack of explicit instruction by Moscow with respect to this effort. Still, one of the key factors in Israel's eventual victory was, indeed, its military superiority over the Arabs in the area of arms supplies, especially for infantry and artillery units, and it maintained its firepower superiority after armistice agreements were reached in mid-1949. A British assessment conducted late that year reviewing the various arsenals of tanks, artillery, and aircraft in the Middle East refutes any possible depiction of Israel as "David against Goliath," even taking into account the cumulative might of the entire Arab camp, let alone individual countries. Compounding the situation were Arab military demoralization, on the one side, and Israel's strategic decision to prioritize immigrant absorption, on the other. Both factors explain why Israel was so interested, toward the end of the war, in maintaining the status quo military balance—an extension of the UN embargo would not have been detrimental to Israel.

Israel's efforts at persuasion failed, however, and in August 1949, the embargo was lifted, mainly because of Britain's strategic regional interests in rearming its allies in the Arab world, which accorded with the global aims of the United States. The sale of surplus and outdated weapons also generated economic profit. Various arms deals with Arab countries thus began to take shape and fueled an unchecked arms race, given the ongoing Arab-Israeli conflict that threatened regional stability and raised concerns among major powers, particularly the United States. The result was an agreement—in the form of a joint US, British, and French statement issued in May 1950—permitting the controlled and coordinated export of arms to states in the region, in conjunction with the creation of mechanisms to facilitate such export. The architects of this policy were actually Britain and the United States, with France included mainly to prevent it from freely arming Syria. The international embargo on arms exports was thus replaced with joint superpower oversight over regional arms supplies, an arrangement that lasted for about half a decade.

These arrangements were, of course, less than ideal for Israel. They forced it, for the first time in its history, to operate along two parallel and interrelated tracks, which in turn became cornerstones of its diplomacy in this area. One of these was Israel's effort, beginning in late 1949, to reduce Arab procurements, mainly through political persuasion directed at Britain and the United States. The second was its attempt to prevent any loss of its relative standing in this regard by buying weapons that, after the cessation of arms shipments from Czechoslovakia in 1950, could come only from Western sources. In both of these areas, the potential for and effectiveness of Israeli action was limited during half a decade for a number of reasons. The United States consistently refused to sell major weapons systems to Middle Eastern countries and confined itself with sales to countries identified as having little military potential. From Jerusalem's perspective, the joint superpower oversight mechanisms for provision of arms to the Middle East created a unified Anglo-French-American political front, which, at least until 1955, took pains to preserve what it saw as a strategic balance between Israel and the Arab states. Although Israel did not accept their interpretation of this balance (which was based on a comparison between it and each of the Arab countries separately), it found it difficult to break through this front. Finally, as noted, Israel had limited financial means for procurement, but it still refused to accept certain US conditions for acquisition without compensation that involved supervision and possible restrictions on use. In any event, Israel's activities in this area indicate that the state of affairs, although inconvenient and at times threatening, did not pose existential security problems.

The situation changed, and radically so, only with the signing of the Czech-Egyptian arms deal in late 1955. Until then, Israel's efforts to prevent Arab states from procuring arms and to ensure its own foreign supplies (about which little is known because Israeli defense establishment documents are unavailable) were less vigorous than during other times and did not lead to any significant breakthroughs. Although Israel consistently protested arms deals with the Arab countries (particularly the sale of British Centurion tanks to Egypt), these deals did not actually raise existential concerns. Given the lack of any detailed studies from the superpowers' perspective, it is difficult to assess the actual impact of Israeli pressure on Anglo-American decisions to supply arms to the Arab world during the first half of the 1950s, although Israel's own assessments concluded that its efforts were, in some cases, effective. They did indeed bear fruit in the tactical sense in the United States, France, and Britain: during this period the three powers provided Israel with ancillary military equipment and outmoded weapons systems, some of which was damaged and most of which comprised surplus weaponry from World War II. Israel's few successful acquisitions of relatively advanced systems gave it no advantage, as these were mainly a by-product of the superpowers' decisions to arm the Arab side. In late 1952, for example, Britain independently approved the sale of Gloster Meteor T.7 jet planes to Israel, primarily so as to counterbalance its previous decision to supply such aircraft to Arabs states (mainly Egypt but also Syria and Lebanon, among others) in order to buttress its political standing in the region. The British-French competition over weapons sales to the Levant provided an opportunity for Israel, in 1954, to obtain a number of large Howitzers and AMX tank destroyers from Paris, which was selling these arms to Arab countries at the time. However, this competition did not provide sufficient grounds for France to fulfill its promises of supplying Israel with modern high-quality Mystère planes, which the Arabs lacked, by the close of 1955.

In late September of that year, the regional military balance shifted radically for the first time, to Israel's detriment, after a massive arms deal between Czechoslovakia and Egypt. The deal was intended to reinforce the Egyptian army by

providing it with some 100 fighter jets, 50 bombers, 230 tanks, 100 tank destroyers, 140 field guns, 300 antitank guns, 2 destroyers, 12 torpedoes, and 6 subma-
rines. Policy makers in Jerusalem were astonished not only by the magnitude of
this deal, amounting to roughly $200 million and undermining the entire West-
ern system of oversight, but also by the quality of much of this Soviet weaponry,
which far outstripped the quality of Israel's arsenals. The figures painted a fright-
ening picture at Israel's military headquarters. In the autumn of 1955, the IDF
had only thirty fighter jets. After implementation of the new arms deal, the ratio
of aircraft fleet size between the IDF and the Arab armies would stand at 1:10 in
favor of the latter, and the relative balance of Israeli-Egyptian armored forces
compared to the Egyptian armored system was expected to be comparable upon
conclusion of the transaction. For the first time since the initial stages of the 1948
War, Israel's military leaders believed the country to be in existential danger.
Restoring the military balance of armaments therefore became a prime strategic
objective for Israel and remained so for about a year. Israel directed its efforts
simultaneously at the United States and France, given that Britain appeared
unreceptive. A little-known request by Israel for military aid from the Soviet
Union had received a negative response. In addition, the only realistic option for
counterbalancing the modern Soviet tanks that Egypt had received (excluding
the British Centurions that some Arab countries had acquired by then) was the
Patton tank. Likewise, the most advanced Western jet planes at the time were the
French Mystère 4, whose sale required approval from the United States because
it had funded the plane's production for NATO, and the American Cyber F-86,
which was produced outside US borders. Israel also believed that the United
States would be willing to grant it credit so that it could implement a procurement plan that, in turn, necessitated a significantly larger defense budget. Finally,
Israel hoped that the ties formed between the Israeli defense establishment and
the French military in 1954–1955 could translate into currency for arms acquisition, given that Nasser's growing influence presented both Israel and France with
a common, increasingly powerful enemy.

Israel's hopes of a positive US response were dashed. In mid-December
1955 the State Department rejected a large purchase request under the pretext
of Israeli aggression during its "Operation Kinneret." In fact, the US decision
masked a broader set of political considerations. The diplomatic pressure then
exerted by Israel over the next three months eventually persuaded the United
States to supply it with several defensive weapons systems and to authorize the
sale of twenty-four French Mystère 4 jets to Israel, while Britain agreed to sell
one hundred old Sherman M4 tanks and two old, renovated warships. Canada
also promised to supply cyber aircraft, but ultimately this sale did not materialize. In all, Israel could not but view the US response as negative, and it therefore accelerated efforts to forge contacts with France, which led to a series of

arms deals beginning shortly after the announcement of the Czech-Egyptian agreement.

The rise to power in France in January 1956 of Guy Mollet, who had distinctly pro-Israel leanings, and the positive US decision on the sale of French planes accelerated the arms transfers, which took place in April 1956. During this period, the ties between the Israeli and French military establishments also grew stronger, leading to strategic understandings that expedited the process even before Nasser nationalized the Suez Canal in July. From France's perspective, these developments overrode any reservations related to US approval. The extent of aid to Israel was quite substantial. It requested and received about seventy Mystère 4 jets, two hundred AMX-13 tanks, forty-eight Sherman tanks, eighteen artillery guns, half-tracks, ammunition, and more. Since it was clear from the outset that it would take Egypt some time to receive and incorporate the Soviet weapons, Israel regarded its arms deals with France as a necessary and immediate response to the situation. Indeed, the immediate threat posed by the Czech deal largely dissipated by late 1956. It would be difficult, therefore, to characterize Israel's efforts to procure weapons from France during this period as anything other than successful. No doubt some of this success is attributable to French interests, some of which were circumstantial (for example, the cancellation of an Indian purchase order for two hundred Mystère jets naturally led France to seek alternative buyers) and some of which were enduring, such as the financial compensation and the development of its arms industry (the systems purchased by Israel involved cash transactions and enriched France's treasury by about $100 million in 1955–1956). For the most part, however, France viewed Israel as a means to putting the brakes on Nasser's support for the anti-French revolt in Algeria, although in time it became evident that this support was actually much less than imagined and was limited mainly to rhetoric and radio broadcasts by the Egyptian leader. Nevertheless, Israel's efforts in this area were of great value in persuading potential French allies and creating a basis for military cooperation between the two from late 1955 to mid-1956. Israel fully exploited the fragmentation of France's government and the potential to forge personal and atypical contacts within the French defense establishment, thereby circumventing the Quai d'Orsay. It managed to dispel doubts and navigate its way among more than a few influential opponents. The relationship that took shape in 1955–1956 became the basis for a strategic alliance in the context of the Sinai Campaign and continued to bear fruit for more than a decade.

Alongside these strategic factors and motives, the personal dimension undoubtedly played a role. Until de Gaulle's rise to power in 1958, for example, Shimon Peres had a room in the Office of the Prime Minister, arranged by George Elgosi, a Jewish economist of Algerian heritage who served as advisor to the French government. From his personal office, Peres corresponded, had telephone conversations, and established a continuous physical presence that greatly facilitated Israel's activities in Paris. Likewise, the personal dimension on the French side is illustrated, for example, by a retrospective lecture on France and the Sinai Campaign delivered by Maurice Bourgès-Maunoury at the Ben-Gurion Heritage Institute in 1986. He enthusiastically described the joy and sense of conspiracy against an evil enemy that he had felt in 1956, which brought to mind his underground activities during World War II.[19] Among other indicators of this relationship, the Israeli Air Force as it stood on the eve of the Sinai Campaign was composed largely of French aircraft. Even more significant was the fact that after the Sinai Campaign, in 1959, Israel requested and received top-of-the-line French planes—the Super Mystère—and signed an agreement to purchase seventy-two Mirage planes that began arriving in 1962, only two years after their introduction into French service. The Mirage was the first European plane capable of exceeding Mach 2 (that is, twice the speed of sound), and for Israel it was a necessary means of contending with the Soviet MiG-21 fighter jet that Egypt, Syria, and Iraq received in the 1960s.

It is an open secret that French military aid to Israel comprised more than conventional weaponry. France was indisputably Israel's major backer when the latter sought to implement the course of action that Ben-Gurion had conceived as early as 1949 for the development of a nuclear program. By the early 1950s, preliminary talks with France toward this end were already underway. France was concurrently pursuing its own nuclear option and investing heavily in the necessary research and development. Accordingly, and under the advice of Ernst David Bergmann, a leading Israeli nuclear scientist, Ben-Gurion decided to send young scientists to France to prepare them for the eventual fulfillment of his vision. One of the important contributing factors in this arrangement was the Jewish heritage of several senior French scientists. Another was France's expectation that cooperation with Israel on research and development would allow it to obtain assistance for its nuclear program from scientists based in the United States, such as Robert Oppenheimer and Edward Teller. Israel's efforts to prove that it could "deliver the goods" met with considerable success, particularly when its scientists managed to develop innovative processes for the production of heavy water and the extraction of uranium from phosphates discovered in the Negev. In 1954, France purchased the technology for the latter for 60 million francs, although in practice it actually implemented the former. Under their arrangement, France also agreed to allow Israeli scientists to visit its reactors. All of these activities combined to create an important foundation for what was to come.

During preparations for the Sinai Campaign in September 1956, Peres held talks with the French Atomic Energy Commission, headed by Pierre Guillaumat and Francis Perrin, at which he appealed for assistance in the construction of a twenty-four-megawatt reactor. It was inferable from his request that Israel wanted to produce nuclear weapons as a means of existential defense. This did not deter Guillaumat, who had economic motives for seeking an agreement with Israel. Perrin initially hesitated for ideological reasons but eventually conceded. Some weeks later, at what became known as the Sèvres meeting, Peres managed to obtain the consent of the French political leadership (Mollet and Foreign Minister Christian Pineau).

The agreement that emerged, though perhaps not a reward per se for Israel's willingness to participate in the campaign against Egypt, nonetheless reflected an exceptional closeness between the two states. It should be noted that assistance to another country's civil nuclear program was considered a legitimate practice at the time, and in fact, Canada had already assisted India in constructing a nuclear reactor. Israel's specific requirements, however, were aimed at the construction of a chemical facility for plutonium separation—a fact that, if discovered, could trigger a US reaction that would in turn jeopardize the French nuclear program itself. France was therefore reluctant to implement the agreement and began to do so only in September 1957. Work on the reactor in Dimona eventually began under the de Gaulle administration, after the term of Israel's most loyal French governmental ally, Maurice Bourgès-Maunoury, came to an end. Under de Gaulle, however, one of France's primary objectives in developing a nuclear capability was the demonstrable grandeur such a capability projected, and to that end, it needed substantial American assistance. Such assistance was contingent on France terminating the nuclear cooperation in which it was then engaged with Germany, Italy, and Israel. Consequently, de Gaulle decided to suspend French aid for construction of the Dimona reactor. Immediate implementation of this decision would almost certainly have stymied the Israeli effort for many years. However, French Minister for Energy Jacques Soustelle, a prominent Gaullist and friend of Israel, delayed implementation until 1960. At the end of that year, the parties entered into complex negotiations, during which France agreed to fulfill the terms of its original agreement for a period of ten years, while Israel undertook to return enriched uranium to France so that it would not be used for military purposes. Presumably, the United States was to be made aware of these developments. Israel then sought to evade French oversight by purchasing uranium from other sources, such as Argentina and South Africa. These efforts, however, resulted in France suspending its uranium supplies to Israel in April 1963.

For understandable reasons, Israel has not disclosed documents that would shed light on this aspect of its strategic relations with France. Nevertheless, it is safe to surmise that Paris's willingness to cooperate in the nuclear field, on the one hand, and US efforts to prevent such collaboration, on the other, would have weighed heavily on Israel. France's acquiescence to the "nuclear relationship" was considered an important aspect of their armaments arrangement, and de Gaulle himself promised Ben-Gurion in mid-January 1960 that despite the cessation of nuclear aid, France would continue to equip the Israeli army with new weapons and aircraft. Indeed, for nearly a decade such weaponry continued to flow into Israel, much of it by air. It is not surprising, therefore, to read a testimony by an Israeli pilot revealing that Israeli crews visited France so frequently that French hotel staff began referring to them as "El Al Militaire" in order to distinguish them from regular El Al passengers.[20]

WEAPONS FROM FRANCE: IMPLICATIONS

Several historical and historiographical observations as presented by researchers who had engaged in this issue deserve mention because they provide a broader perspective on the developments described above. The first of these observations relates to the influence of arms deals with France on domestic Israeli politics: in the mid-1950s a continuous but closed-door debate was simmering between one camp headed by Moshe Dayan, which believed, even before the Sinai Campaign, that Israel should launch a war against Egypt, and an opposing camp headed by then prime minister and foreign minister Moshe Sharett. Ben-Gurion wavered between these two camps until at least mid-1956. Dayan saw the French weaponry as a factor that would tip the balance in this debate, arguing that "the sabotage of Egyptian-Israeli relations should be reserved for a later date when Israel, having incorporated the new French weapons, can do so in a calculated and preplanned manner."[21]

The second observation relates to the cards Israel held in its pursuit of French security assistance. There exists a consensus among historians that arms deals with France were the primary aim of bilateral relations and that in the absence of an alternative option in the near term (in fact until the United States began to supply advanced weapons systems in the mid-1960s), and given the challenges posed by massive Soviet engagement in the regional arms race, Jerusalem was prepared to recompense France on a substantial scale. Most importantly, Israel was willing to cooperate in the overthrow of Nasser and expressed its willingness during the negotiations that preceded Nasser's nationalization of the Suez Canal. As Ben-Gurion observed after returning to the premiership in early April 1955, "Nasser is our danger; Nasser is their danger."[22] Concurrently, Peres called for the "activation, despite the occasional displeasure of Quai d'Orsay personnel, of those large pro-Israel forces who believe that the 1,600,000 French [citizens] in Morocco and the 1,600,000 Jews in Israel are two common problems in the Middle East" (Bar-On 1991, 144). A year later, Mordechai Bar-On noted in the chief of staff's diary that the concept crystallized within the Israeli defense establishment when Israel's arms procurers realized that it was necessary to pursue "a bilateral agreement with France in which Israel was no longer the desperate recipient and France the generous provider"; rather, it should be an agreement establishing "genuine cooperation based on mutual support, mutual risk, and mutual benefit."[23] Israel officially presented its perspective at a meeting of the two states' military leaders that took place in Vemars on June 23, 1956. Moshe Dayan, the Israeli chief of staff, explained,

> In taking action against Nasser we would be willing to work with you, if you are willing to work with us. . . . The action can take place in the military and political spheres. The Arab empire that Nasser dreams of will not arise without the subjugation of Israel. . . . We face two critical questions: tanks and planes. . . . [Having] the weapons means that if we are attacked, Nasser will face defeat. I am convinced that eventually he will attack us. . . . What matters to us is whether France is willing to cooperate with us, directly or indirectly, in order to overthrow Nasser and reinforce Israel against an Egyptian attack.[24]

When the Israeli delegation returned from Vemars, Ben-Gurion told its members, "This is a somewhat dangerous adventure. However, what can we do? Our entire existence [has been] so."[25] Shaul Avigur, an advisor to the minister of defense on special matters, also expressed reservation, arguing that Israel could purchase arms without taking on such a commitment. Dayan countered by asserting that "in the past the Jewish People paid a much steeper price for not taking action than for taking action, even if mistaken in retrospect." In any case, the Israeli invasion of Sinai at the start of the campaign and its successful military operations fulfilled one of the parties' commitment to the deal. The Israelis hoped that the other side would meet its obligations, especially in the area of arms supplies, and received nearly immediate assurance to this effect. In a message dated November 15, 1956, France informed Ben-Gurion that Israel could keep the weapons it had received in advance of the campaign, at no cost. In addition, France's and Britain's operational failures in Egypt highlighted Israel's military victory. France's generals and political leaders realized the potential value of the IDF. In 1957, the arms deals signed over the preceding two years were fully implemented, and all the French governments of that year agreed to supply Israel with weapons of every type on a regular basis.

One of the interesting facts that emerged from later studies is that the vast quantities of arms Israel received from France by mid-1956 effectively neutralized the threat posed by Egypt's enhanced military capability. This was one of major factors that allowed Ben-Gurion to overcome his reluctance and support a three-pronged military initiative against Nasser, which served as the basis for subsequent cooperation with France, particularly in the area of arms supplies on a scale and of a quality that Israel required for its defense. In so doing, the "Old Man" was effectively actualizing an earlier assessment by one of Israel's more brilliant and lesser-known diplomats, Emile Najar, who in 1956 expressed an axiomatic convention in Jerusalem, writing that "only the country which supplied arms worthy of that term would have the privilege and opportunity to find a listening ear among Israel's leaders."[26] Such considerations were also a salient factor in Israel's decision to comply with French demands that it withdraw from Sinai in early 1957. Speaking to Moshe Dayan, Ben-Gurion described his concerns that Paris would "abandon Israel, leaving it alone and unarmed."[27] France's unilateral decision to continue to supply Israel with arms for about another decade gave it a strategic and political edge in its relations with Israel, and a good deal of testimonial evidence confirms that many of Jerusalem's important decisions regarding various bilateral and multilateral relationships were shaped by this dynamic. In the area of foreign policy, for example, when African states united in the early 1960s to condemn France's nuclear tests in the Sahara, Israel opted to support France. During a meeting of the Knesset plenum on June 26, 1962, in the presence of Foreign Minister Golda Meir, Israel Barzilai of MAPAM, who had served as ambassador to Poland years earlier, noted, "The Foreign Ministry did not always maintain a balance. For example, with respect to nuclear tests in the Sahara, Israel's stated policy should have led it to oppose such tests or at least, out of respect for France, abstain when the UN voted on the matter. But it did not object, it did not abstain, and it created resentment among various African countries."[28] Also notable in this context was Israel's acceptance of several decisions made by France in the area of bilateral economic relations, such as the purchase of fuel tankers from Japan, construction of the Ashdod port, and the sale of Renault cars in Israel. In all these cases, France demanded special consideration of its economic interests and pressured Israel, successfully for the most part, to accept its stance in light of the all-important military aid that continued to flow into the country. A similar dynamic informed Israel's concessions on cultural agreements with France, after the latter demanded and received extra privileges in matters related to the French language and culture in Israel, including the option of studying French as one's main second language in Israel's high schools. During a cabinet meeting in early December 1959, Ben-Gurion explained that "France is not in Israel's pocket"[29] and that the importance of relations with France stemmed from the latter's provision of arms that were essential for survival; hence, questions related to French political or economic policy were marginal as long as France continued to sell arms to Israel. At the same time, Ben-Gurion warned against assuming that France would always be willing to supply Israel with arms.[30] (See his comments to the Foreign Policy Committee of Mapai on June 27, 1957, Mapai Archive.)

After assuming office in 1958, de Gaulle formulated a strategy deliberately aimed at cultivating closer ties with the Arab states, third-world countries, and the Soviet Union. This policy involved a dramatic and surprising decision to withdraw from Algeria (per the 1962 Évian Accords). As Gadi Heimann demonstrated in his comprehensive study on the subject, this decision reduced but did not put an end to France's strategic cooperation with Israel, which continued for another half decade after the accords were signed.[31] Israel had more than a hint of the new atmosphere in the Élysée when, contrary to expectations, France refused to support to its efforts in 1962–1964 to join the European Economic Community.

De Gaulle further honed and underscored the French approach by insisting that the two states' strategic relationship remain secret, as exemplified by France's stubborn refusal to allow any of its ministers, even the most junior, to visit Israel. When a scheduled visit by André Malraux, the minister of culture under de Gaulle, was canceled in December 1966 on the grounds of illness, Abba Eban told the Knesset Foreign Affairs and Defense Committee, "They owe us a state visit, but every time Malraux nears the plane, he faints and collapses."[32] France had made its approach clear as early as February 1955. Its ambassador to Tel Aviv at the time, Pierre Gilbert, advised Israel to make do with the facts of their strategic relations and not to overburden France with demands for public acknowledgment, adding that "not every romance has to lead to marriage."[33] From Israel's perspective the heart of the issue in this romance was its own armament, and toward that end it was willing, until 1967, to concede on a range of matters. It therefore accepted the French stance, which allowed it to receive large-scale but covert military aid while requiring it to maintain discretion in the public sphere and project a measure of coldness in the diplomatic arena. It should be noted, however, that anytime Israel perceived a major military threat beyond its borders, it permitted itself a freedom of action that risked jeopardizing France's willingness to extend military aid. Examples include Israel's military confrontation with Syria in the early 1960s and, most notably, its refusal to abide by de Gaulle's demand on the eve of the Six-Day War that it not launch a first strike. Foreign Ministry Director General Aryeh Levavi verbalized the Israeli approach when he informed the French ambassador to Israel, Bertrand Edmond Rochereau de La Sablière, in late June 1967 that "you believe we are the aggressor, but what could we do when our kibbutzim are being bombed, when our radar picks up enemy planes, when Egyptian tanks begin to flank Eilat? . . . Israel is not the France of 1914 that could afford to retreat ten kilometers. Keep in mind how much weaponry was aimed at us. Their goal was to destroy us. Israel had never before faced such danger."[34]

The arms deals with Israel also benefited France. In 1959, French sales accounted for 54 percent of Israel's worldwide arms purchases. The figure declined slightly in the following years, but after Israel's acquisition of Mirage jets in 1962, France's share rose to a record 65 percent. Israel had to pay a steep price for these transactions, particularly as they usually involved immediate payment in cash, which also increased their significance for France. The major arms deal of June 1956, for example, amounted to $80 million, on top of the $20 million Israel had paid during the preceding year. That deal required Israel to allocate no less than one-fifth of the state budget for this purpose. It should be noted in this context that the cost of the modern, advanced weapons systems purchased in 1956–1956 was significantly higher than the cost of arms purchased in the early 1950s. The Mystère jet, for example, cost nearly twenty times as much as the Mustang plane. Thus, Israel's large purchase orders in the 1950s and early to mid-1960s were a source of considerable income for France.

Israel's scheduled arms purchases for 1957–1958 totaled $120 million. At the same time, the difficult economic situation in France during those years resulted in a reduced military budget, which in turn meant fewer orders from the French aerospace industry. This made the export of existing aircraft stockpiles a matter of vital importance. Moreover, the sale of French arms to a state whose military forces had demonstrated the superiority of these arms created an incentive to sell arms to other countries. In particular, Israel's successful use of French weapons systems against the Soviet weaponry in Arab possession was a matter of paramount strategic importance for the French. France naturally decided therefore to maintain close relations with Israel in this area. Besides aircraft, Israel also bought some eighty Sherman tanks, antitank missiles, and three torpedo ships from France in 1957–1958. In 1962, the two states signed a major arms deal for the sale of Mirage jets. The precise financial figures that formed part of these and other transactions are not accessible, but we do know that the total value of such deals between 1955 and 1967 reached $600 million—the 2016 equivalent of $5 billion. There can be no doubt, therefore, that France had a strong economic and strategic interest in selling arms to Israel.

The form of payment on Israel's part was not strictly financial. Israel also reimbursed France through intelligence sharing. The two states had been cooperating in this area since at least the mid-1950s. The French security services, Direction de la Surveillance du Territoire (DST), had preexisting ties with Israel's Mossad, especially in the area of illegal immigration from North Africa and the self-defense organization located there (Gonen). Additionally, Israel provided France with intelligence that related to areas beyond the Middle East. Later, the French sought and received Israeli intelligence related to Egypt and the rebellion in Algeria, which Israel had obtained in 1955. According to Moti Golani, one of Israel's prominent experts on the Sinai Campaign and its background, Israel's ability to provide relevant intelligence on this issue was a crucial component of its alliance with France.[35] Of particular note, the French had full diplomatic relations with Egypt, which constrained their ability to take any action against it—hence the importance of potential intelligence and sabotage operations by Israel. French-Israeli cooperation included French-commissioned Israeli reconnaissance flights over Sinai, intelligence on naval maneuvers in the eastern Mediterranean, and the exchange of information relevant to covert action against

Algerian leaders in Europe. One of their planned (but never implemented) operations was targeted against supporters of the revolt on the coast of Tripoli. It was to be carried out by a French unit with the assistance of an Israeli infiltrator disguised as an Arab, whose role was to make the necessary arrangements on the ground and lead the French forces to the target. However, when France sought Israel's cooperation for assassinations in Damascus and Cairo, Ben-Gurion and Dayan refused to comply lest Israel later be held solely responsible. Although French expectations exceeded Israeli capabilities (a misconception that Israel did not try to correct, according to the former head of Military Intelligence, Yehoshafat Harkabi[36]), and despite the Israeli chief of staff's concerns about information leaking to the Arabs, Ben-Gurion gave these activities a green light. Senior intelligence officers from both sides thus continued to meet twice a year until the early 1960s, when France pulled out of Algeria. It should be noted that after the Vemars agreement, Israeli cooperation with France fell into two administrative categories: on the "credit" side, termed "high tide" or "the French invasion," were weapons deals conducted by the Ministry of Defense, while on the "debit" side, termed "olive," were intelligence sharing and military cooperation against Egypt and the rebels in Algeria, which were solely the responsibility of the chief of staff.

Another issue that deserves attention is the strategic and political significance of Israel's arms deals with France: What, if any, impact did these deals have on Israel's overall strategic orientation during its first two decades? Did Israel expect that France's massive military support would ensure its survival? The facts (to be analyzed in a later chapter) that Israel failed to obtain weapons from the United States during this period and that its successes in the French political and military arena largely alleviated or prevented its strategic isolation have contributed to a historiographical outlook that views Israel as having adopted a "European orientation" in place of an "American orientation." This scholarship focuses on the defense establishment, Moshe Dayan, and especially Shimon Peres as the main proponents of that orientation.

A close examination of Israeli documents from the same period, however, presents a more complex picture. First, there was a consensus in Israel regarding the centrality, power, and military, political, and economic influence of the United States in the global arena at the time. Israel also had an important political asset in the United States in the form of a Jewish population whose influence was much stronger than that of the Jewish community in France. Second, several of Israel's top foreign policy officials regarded France as, at best, a second-rate superpower that had suffered defeat during World War II and was desperately struggling to regain the status it had enjoyed in Europe before May 1940. Jerusalem was well aware that the United States and Britain refused to include France in their plans to establish security organizations in the Middle East. Indeed, one senior Foreign Ministry official described France as a "broken branch," whereas the two Anglo-Saxon powers remained "masters of the Middle East." Third, Foreign Ministry personnel who followed the basic outlook of their minister (and, briefly, prime minister), Moshe Sharett, were acutely aware of the erstwhile circumstances that had given rise to strategic ties with France and the latter's willingness to sell arms. Israel's ambassador to Paris at the time, Yaakov Tzur, wrote to Abba Eban on May 22, 1956, that "despite our achievements—and they are by no means insignificant—I do not predict a rosy future for Israel among wide circles in France. The Algerian struggle has placed in our hand a card and aroused a wave of admiration for Israel among wide circles in France. Yet in truth, this is admiration born [out of] desperation. . . . Sympathy for Israel and honest concern for its fate are diluted by the fear of chasm between France and the Arab world."[37] His assessment was apparently based on something he had heard three months earlier from Pierre Maillard of the Quai d'Orsay's Middle East Department, who observed that the friendship between France and Israel was "based solely on the blood spilled in North Africa and bound to change at any moment."[38]

Moreover, although Ben-Gurion appreciated and welcomed France's willingness to provide military aid, and indeed had authorized the strategic cooperation that led to the Sinai Campaign, he was both skeptical and wary as to the nature of the relationship that emerged. For obvious reasons he voiced this skepticism only behind closed doors, never publicly. He presented his strategic assessment at a meeting of the secret foreign affairs committee of his party, Mapai, on June 27, 1957, where he compared the United States with France in terms of their relations with Israel. As a matter of principle, he categorically prioritized relations with Washington, and one of his key arguments in this regard centered on France. He predicted that France would never back Israel in confrontations with the rest of the world because French-Israeli relations would necessarily be limited to "brief and isolated" periods, in part because they were of an "underground" nature and defied the stance of the Quai d'Orsay.[39] Nevertheless, Israel's prime minister did not want to jeopardize the positive aspects of relations with France by explicitly naming the United States as Israel's sole strategic priority. Washington's consistent and absolute refusal to sell strategic weapons systems to Israel until 1965, and its opposition to an Israeli nuclear program during the 1960s, made him receptive to the "window of opportunity" for armament that France provided. Until his resignation in 1963, therefore, he was perfectly willing to exploit the French option to the extent possible. Even in the absence of documents on the subject, one may reasonably assume that French nuclear aid, which lasted until the early 1960s, was also an important consideration. At the same time, however, Ben-Gurion objected to Peres's proposal that efforts to purchase US arms be suspended lest France take offense and revoke its agreement to supply Israel with practically any weapons it wanted. The prime minister definitively rejected an assessment by Peres that predicted a long-lasting friendship with France.

Supporters of the prevailing outlook included senior IDF officers such as Ezer Weizmann, commander of the Israel Air Force, who from 1958 effectively determined the military acquisition policy and who later prioritized the purchase of Mirage jets; Chaim Herzog, the head of Military Intelligence, who was in charge of intelligence sharing with the French defense establishment; and later, Chief of Staff Zvi Tzur. The acquisition of US weapons was their "heart's desire" but "far from achievable."[40] Declassified Israeli documents reveal that throughout this period a fierce internal debate raged between the Ministry of Defense (including Shimon Peres, who became deputy defense minister in 1959), which supported pursuing and extending Ben-Gurion's policy, and those who recommended an alternative independent Israeli initiative.

The leading opponent of Peres's approach from the mid-1950s was Foreign Minister Golda Meir. Although, like the prime minister, she viewed the arms deals with France very favorably, she had no doubt that eventually the United States should and must take its place. She therefore not only rejected the prioritization of France as an ally but also sought to promote an alternative approach that would guide Israel toward a US orientation in all aspects, including military acquisition. Chief of Staff Haim Laskov and the head of the Operations Directorate, Yitzhak Rabin, backed her approach, mainly because they preferred US to French weaponry (except for Mirage planes) and did not believe that French arms could provide a sufficient response to the Soviet arms in Egypt's possession. France's most advanced tank at the time was the MX-13, which was inferior to the US Patton and vastly so to the Soviet T-54 and T-55 tanks. Changes that took place in the mid-1960s made it possible to pursue the policy Golda Meir had unsuccessfully been trying to promote for nearly a decade: Ben-Gurion vacated his post and was replaced by Eshkol, who had considerable experience in economics. The new prime minister viewed with great concern the high cost of military acquisition from France and sought to avoid risking everything on one endeavor. Rabin, now chief of staff, also leaned toward Golda Meir's approach. Other indicators of a new chapter in Israel's history of military procurement include the United States' de facto acceptance of Israel's nuclear program, its willingness to provide Israel with strategic weapons systems beginning in 1965, and the increasingly cooler nature of defense ties with France, culminating with Paris's decision to impose an arms embargo on Israel two years later.

AFTER THE FACT

France's willingness to serve as Israel's main arms supplier and to continue to do so when it reentered the Arab world under de Gaulle was the most tangible and important indicator for Jerusalem of French support for the Jewish state. However, this "wonderful friendship," in the words of one Israeli historian, ended in mid-1967, when France suspended its military aid (which it has not

renewed to date). The shift in French policy manifested in France's nonfulfill-
ment of the Mirage arms deal, a painful blow for Jerusalem that left fifty planes
earmarked for Israel in the Dassault warehouses after the Six-Day War, and in
the nondelivery of naval missile carriers for which Israel had already paid. The
termination of military aid served as definitive proof in Israel's eyes that its
wonderful friendship with France was over and could not be revived. That year
Paris also adopted a strategic approach to the Arab-Israeli conflict that Jerusalem regarded as particularly hostile. De Gaulle refused to ease the embargo,
and, notwithstanding Israel's success in salvaging some of the weapons it
was intended to receive, he would not budge on the matter of policy. According to a report Israel received regarding a meeting between de Gaulle and the
US ambassador in January 1968, the general stated that "they gave [Israel] 100
planes with which it conquered vast Arab lands. If I give them 50 Mirages, they
will conquer Damascus and Cairo."[41] It is worth underscoring in this context
that Israel had been quite confident that French arms supplies would continue,
and de Gaulle's embargo therefore had a devastating impact. In fact, some days
before the signing ceremony in Tel Aviv for the Mirage purchase agreement,
an aide of Defense Minister Zvi Dinstein proposed the inclusion of a clause
that would bind Dassault to the agreement and protect Israel in the event of
an embargo. The aide received a reprimand: "You're crazy. The French would
never do that."[42] Israel indeed had difficulty coming to terms with the unyielding and continuing nature of the embargo. As Moshe Dayan stated during a
meeting in July 1968 with Prime Minister Levi Eshkol, "After the war, many of
us did not want to believe our own ears [when we heard] that France would not
deliver the Mirage planes for which we had paid."[43] However, the facts became
blatantly evident when the French president intensified the embargo in January
1969 after Israel's military action in Lebanon. French hostility in this regard
took other tangible forms as well: the refusal by President George Pompidou,
who succeeded de Gaulle six months later, to lift the embargo was compounded
by Paris's decision to sell more than one hundred Mirage planes to Libya.
Despite—indeed, because of—the embargo, in December 1969 Israel smuggled
five missile carrier boats out of the Cherbourg port, triggering a particularly
acute diplomatic incident that led to the expulsion from Paris of Major General Mordechai Limon, head of the Defense Ministry's acquisition delegation.
Furthermore, during the Yom Kippur War, the French government prevented
the United States from fueling the aircraft carriers that were delivering arms to
Israel. When France eventually decided—in 1974, after the election of President
Valery Giscard d'Estaing—to lift the embargo officially, Israel had already opted
to purchase all its advanced military equipment from the United States under
particularly favorable financial terms. During the 1970s and early 1980s, moreover, France helped in the construction of an Iraqi nuclear reactor in Osirak,

sparking official Israeli protest. Israel's subsequent bombing of the facility in June 1981 further exacerbated tensions between the two countries.

The 1967 French arms embargo was initially very traumatic for Israel, not only because it came as a shock but also because it came into effect before Israel was able to ensure a sufficiently varied and sizable US option. As such, the direct blow to Israel should not be underestimated, especially given that two years later, Britain, under Arab pressure, cancelled a major deal for the sale of advanced Chieftain tanks, thus leaving Israel with a large void in its artillery arsenals. The British and French measures therefore had a significant impact on Jerusalem, which has manifested in decisions reached since the late 1960s to develop a military industry as swiftly as possible in order to reduce Israel's risky dependence on foreign arms suppliers. The implementation of this enduring policy over the course of four decades reached such a massive scale that in 2007 Israel sold $6 billion worth of arms, making it the fourth-largest arms exporter, surpassed only by the United States, Russia, and France. The geographical spread of these sales tells us quite a bit about Israel's political priorities. In 2016, for example, the volume of exports to European countries reached $1.8 billion, far exceeding sales to North America ($1.3 billion), Latin America ($550 million), and Africa ($275 million), although still less than the volume of defense exports to Asian countries ($2.6 billion).[44]

No doubt Ben-Gurion would have found it hard to believe that Israel would be in this position today. However, Shimon Peres, who played a key role in promoting and developing Israel's military industry, was a true believer. In any case, it would not be an overstatement to say that French weapons, especially aircraft, enabled the IDF to achieve its greatest victory—namely, the Six-Day War. Nor is there any dispute among historians regarding France's crucial role in transforming Israel into a nuclear power. Alongside its cultivation of French ties, Israel invested many years and much energy into building strategic relationships with liberated African states—a topic explored in the next chapter.

Notes

1. Moti Golani, "Iskat Neshek o Brit? Perek BeYakhasei Israel Tzarfat" [Arms deal or alliance? A chapter in Israel-France relations, April–July 1956], in *Nof Moladeto* [The landscape of his country], ed. Israel Bartal, Yossi Ben-Artzi, and Elchanan Reiner (Jerusalem, Magnes, 2005), 515–32.

2. "The Cambon Letter," Wickipedia, https://en.wikipedia.org/wiki/Cambon_letter.

3. Moshe Sharett, *Political Diary*, vol. 3 (Tel Aviv, Maariv, 1971), 16.

4. Benjamin Pinkus, *MeAmbivalentiyut LeBrit Bilti Ktuva: Israel, Tzarfat VeYehudei Tzarfat, 1947–1957* [From ambivalence to an unwritten alliance: Israel, France, and the Jews of France, 1947–1957] (Sde Boker, Ben Gurion Heritage Institute, 2005), 47.

5. Eliezer Yapo, "De Gaulle VeHaYehudim, 1940–1943" [De Gaulle and the Jews, 1940–1943]. (Gesher, 1986, 116) [in Hebrew].

6. Moshe Perlman, *David Ben-Gurion* (Tel Aviv, Zmora Dvir, 1987), 108.

7. See also Irit Keynan, *Holocaust Survivors and the Emissaries from Eretz-Israel: Germany, 1945–1948* (Tel Aviv, Am Oved, 1995); Zartal, *From Catastrophe to Power: The Holocaust Survivors and the Emergence of Israel* (Berkeley, University of California Press, 1998); Menachem Shelah, *The Yugoslav Connection: Illegal Immigration of Jewish Refugees to Palestine through Yugoslavia, 1938–1948* (Tel Aviv, Am Oved, 1994), on which the following analysis is based until otherwise indicated.

8. Miriam Rosman, *Yahasei Tzarfat-Israel MeKum HaMedina Ad LeParashiyat Sfinot Cherbourg* [Relations between France and Israel from the founding of the state until the affair of the Cherbourg ships] (Tel Aviv, Resling, 2014).

9. Ofer Aderet, "Im Mekhonot Ktiva VeKartisiyot: HaIsh SheYasad Et HaMekhkar HaModi'ini BeTzahal" [With a typewriter and index cards: The man who founded intelligence research in the IDF], *Haaretz*, September 29, 2016.

10. Aviva Halamish, *Exodus: HaSipur HaAmiti* [*Exodus*: The true story] (Tel Aviv, Am Oved, 1990), 64.

11. Pinkus, *MeAmbivalentiyut LeBrit Bilti Ktuva*, 85.

12. Yaacov Markovitzky, *Gahelet Lohemet: Giyus LaAretz BeMilhemet HaAtzma'ut* [Fighting/burning embers: Foreign recruits in the War of Independence] (Tel Aviv, Ministry for Defence, 1995), 39.

13. Gadi Heimann, *Sofa Shel Yedidut Mufla'ah* [The end of a wonderful friendship] (Jerusalem, Magnes, 2015); Pinkus, *MeAmbivalentiyut LeBrit Bilti Ktuva*, 144.

14. Heimann, *Sofa Shel Yedidut Mufla'ah*, 11.

15. Idit Zartal, "HaKesher HaSotzialisti: Sotzialistim Tzarfati'im VeHaMiflagah HaSotzialistit HaTzarfatit—Yakhasam LaTzionut Erev Hakamat HaMedina" [The Socialist connection: French Socialists and the French Socialist Party—their relation to Zionism on the eve of the establishment of the state], in *Yahadut Tzarfat, HaTzionut VeMedinat Israel* [French Jewry, Zionism, and the State of Israel], ed. Benjamin Pinkus and Doris Bensimon (Sde Boker, Ben Gurion Heritage Institute, 1992), 178–98.

16. Moshe Sharett, *BeSha'ar HaUmot* [At the gate of the nations] (Tel Aviv, Am Oved, 1958).

17. Pinkus, *MeAmbivalentiyut LeBrit Bilti Ktuva*, 169.

18. Uri Bialer, *A Cross in the Star of David: The Christian World in Israel's Foreign Policy, 1948–1967* (Jerusalem, Yad Ben Zvi, 2006) [in Hebrew]. Unless noted otherwise, this is the source for the quotations that follow. For a detailed analysis of the issue, particularly from the French perspective, see Pinkus, *MeAmbivalentiyut LeBrit Bilti Ktuva*, 156–91.

19. I am grateful to Professor Ilan Troen for this information.

20. Asher Orkaby, "The 1964 Israeli Airlift to Yemen and the Expansion of Weapons Diplomacy," *Diplomacy and Statecraft* 26, no. 4 (2015): 659–67.

21. Moti Golani, "Iskat Neshek o Brit," 525.

22. April 10, 1955, via Israel State Archives, file 2539/16/B.

23. Ibid.

24. Moshe Dayan, *Avnei Derekh* [Milestones] (Tel Aviv, Idanim, 1976), 206.

25. Ben-Gurion's diary, July 17, 1956, via Ben-Gurion Heritage Archives. This is the source for the following citation.

26. Zach Levey, "French-Israeli Strategic Relations, 1950–1956: The Strategic Dimension." In Simon C. Smith, ed., *Reassessing Suez 1956: New Perspectives on the Crisis and Its Aftermath* (New York, Routledge, 2008), 106.

27. Ben-Gurion's diary, February 28, 1957, Ben-Gurion Heritage Archive.

28. Proceedings of the Knesset, plenum no. 147 of the Fifth Knesset. On Mapam, see Tal Elmaliach, *Yesterday's People* (Beer Shava, Ben Gurion Heritage Institute, 2018) [in Hebrew].

29. Heimann, *Sofa Shel Yedidut Mufla'ah*, 95.

30. See his comments to the Foreign Policy Committee of Mapai on June 27, 1957, Mapai Archive.

31. Heimann, *Sofa Shel Yedidut Mufla'ah*.

32. Ibid., 143–44.

33. Moshe Sharett at the meeting of the Knesset Foreign Affairs and Defense Committee, March 22, 1955, via Israel State Archives.

34. Heimann, *Sofa Shel Yedidut Mufla'ah*, 219.

35. Golani, "Iskat Neshek o Brit."

36. Personal oral communication.

37. Levey, 102.

38. Ibid., 103.

39. Ibid., 105.

40. Yossi Goldstein, "France or the US? The Struggle to Change Israel's Foreign Policy Orientation, 1956–1964," *Israel Journal of Foreign Affairs* 4, no. 2 (2010): 99–113.

41. Heimann, *Sofa Shel Yedidut Mufla'ah*, 204–26.

42. Personal communication.

43. Yitzhak Greenberg, "Heibetim Kalkali'im U-Vitkhoni'im BaHakhlatot LeYatzer Matos VeTank BeIsrael" [Economic and security aspects of decisions to produce aircraft and tanks], *Iyunim Bitkumat Israel* 12 (2002): 79.

44. Eili Rettig and Yotam Rosner, "The Crises of Europe Offer Opportunity for the Israeli Arms Industry," *INSS Insight*, August 17, 2017.

9 Sub-Saharan Africa—Failed Expectations

Raison d'État—between Realpolitik and the Ideal

Among the most interesting chapters in the history of Israel's foreign relations is that of its relations during the 1950s and 1960s with sub-Saharan African countries. The background, motives, and later transformations that these ties underwent make them unique in many aspects: Israel was among the first states to provide aid to sub-Saharan African countries as soon as they achieved independence (primarily in the form of training for personnel rather than financial assistance), which, contrary to the utilitarian "realpolitik" interests that characterized most Israeli foreign relations decisions, stemmed from ideological and humanitarian as well as economic and self-serving considerations. Moreover, the differences of opinion among Israel's policy makers regarding sub-Saharan Africa were often quite strong, which had an impact on the policy's implementation. And finally, relations between Israel and Africa were subject to vicissitudes and dramatic swings, shifting from intensely friendly relations in the 1960s to a near-absolute and comprehensive severing of diplomatic ties by dozens of African states in the 1970s, on a scale unprecedented in the history of Israel's relations with other countries. The historiography surrounding this subject is quite rich and can now draw on declassified state documents from various sources in Israel and around the world. Given the limited scope of this study, I focus only on three issues in relation to Israel's early years, from the late 1950s until the Yom Kippur War: examination of Israeli objectives, analysis of two of the measures adopted by the state in pursuit of these objectives, and identification of the reasons for and implications of what came to be seen, in retrospect, as failure.

In her memoirs, Golda Meir devoted much attention to these relations. Her official status as foreign minister at the time, her personal involvement and prominent role in shaping the relations, and her frankness justify quoting her here:

> During 1957 and 1958, I would look around me at the UN and think to myself that we have no family here, no one shares our language or our past. . . . And in fact we do not belong anywhere or with anyone other than ourselves. . . . But the world was not composed only of Europeans and Asians; there were also the rising nations of Africa that were on the verge of attaining independence, and Israel could and wanted to give a great deal to the black states in the making.

Like them, we had shared a foreign ruler, and like them we had to learn on our own how to redeem our country, how to grow crops in our fields, how to irrigate, how to raise chickens, how to live together, and how to defend ourselves.[1]

The foreign minister, who played a crucial role in formulating and implementing Israeli policy in this area, in part because it provided fertile ground for the ministry she headed, stressed the state's twofold motivation—its cold political calculations as well as its altruistic and principled motivation: "Did we enter Africa because we wanted to gain votes at the UN? Yes, of course this was one of our motives, and absolutely a significant one, which I never hid from the world, from myself or from the Africans. But this was far from being the most important motive, though certainly not marginal. The main reason for our African adventure was that we had something we wanted to convey to nations that were younger and even less experienced than we were."[2] Notably, the cold analyses by foreign experts who examined Israel's objectives in sub-Saharan Africa have usually overlooked or minimized the moral and principled aspect of its aims. A retrospective intelligence report prepared by the US State Department in late 1973 found, for example, that "Israel's careful wooing of African nations in the 1960s was designed to assure support in the UN; to guarantee access to raw materials; in some cases to meet strategic needs; and most importantly, to project an image of Israel as a dynamic friend of the third world."[3]

Although the political aspects of Israel's strategy in this area are clear, they deserve further elaboration. Three developments had a dramatic impact on Israeli policy regarding sub-Saharan Africa. The first was an event that took place on another continent altogether—in faraway Indonesia. Toward the end of 1954, plans were underway for an international conference of third-world countries, with the aim of establishing a third, Afro-Asian bloc within the map of international relations delineated by the two superpowers, the United States and the Soviet Union, in conjunction with their official allies. The organizers decided to convene the conference in Bandung, Indonesia, in April 1955. On December 29, 1954, they issued a joint communiqué announcing the aims of the conference and listing the twenty-nine Asian and African countries invited to attend. Those not invited included North Korea, South Korea, South Africa, Australia, New Zealand, the Mongolian People's Republic, the Republic of China (Taiwan), and Israel. The five prime ministers of India, Pakistan, Burma, Ceylon, and Indonesia met to consult in Bogor and decided not to invite Israel, in light of an Arab ultimatum that all thirteen Muslim countries (nine of which were Arab) would boycott the conference should Israel participate. The decision stemmed, as well, from the organizers' interest in compensating Pakistani prime minister Muhammad Ali Jinnah for agreeing to the inclusion of the People's Republic of China among the invitees. On April 21 the conference's preparatory committee approved a recommendation, which was adopted as a resolution by the conference plenary upon concluding three days later. The resolution held that, given the current tension in the Middle East arising from the situation in Palestine and in view of the consequent threat to world peace, the Asian-African Conference was declaring its support for the rights of Palestine's Arabs and calling for implementation of the UN resolutions on Palestine and for peaceful resolution of the question of Palestine. The resolution embodied a fundamentally anti-Israel stance and clashed directly with the state's efforts to secure international recognition of the facts on the ground following the 1948 War.

The architects of Israeli foreign policy viewed these developments as an additional and highly significant threat. The Bandung Conference gave Arab states two important advantages over Jerusalem. First, Israel's standing in Asia took a severe blow, delaying by decades the establishment of diplomatic ties with the major and most influential Asian states. Second, relations between Arab states and Asian states were strengthened. Within a year after the conference, Egypt and other Arab countries established diplomatic ties with Indonesia, Burma, India, Japan, and most significantly, the People's Republic of China. Once Nasser became a central figure in the Asian-African bloc, the UN, and other fora, the Arabs turned into a dominant group in that bloc. The Bandung Conference thus marked a watershed moment, or breaking point, in relations between Israel and the entire third world.

Moshe Sharett viewed this conference as "a new demonstration of Israel's isolation and the consolidation of a massive front against us, encompassing most of the human race." He feared that "Israel's sense of isolation and alienation from the rest of the world would worsen and intensify throughout the country."[4] Given the sense of defeat that followed the Bandung Conference, Sharett managed to secure government approval for the establishment of diplomatic ties with China on the grounds—which, as noted above, soon proved to be false—that such relations would serve as "compensation for the damage caused by the Bandung Conference."[5] The conference continued to preoccupy Sharett afterward until his resignation from government. He feared that the Bandung Conference would be followed by a second conference to which Israel would not be invited, thus increasing its political isolation. Ultimately the Bandung Conference did not undermine preexisting bilateral ties between Israel and certain individual Asian states or the formation of ties with additional states, but it did establish the fundamental principle that Israel was not accepted in any forum of the third world or the nonaligned states. This capitulation to the threat of an Arab boycott became a highly significant precedent at subsequent Afro-Asian conferences. Accordingly, Israel was not invited to any such gathering of Afro-Asian or nonaligned states. The only issue debated at these conferences regarding Israel was the intensity of condemnation. Israel's marginal diplomatic presence in Asia in

1954 reinforced this state of affairs, as it had only five legations at the time—in Burma, Japan, Thailand, India, and the Philippines—none of which had the status of an embassy.

The sense of siege that permeated Israel's leadership stemmed, as well, from the broader Palestinian context of the events at Bandung, which only exacerbated the situation for Israel. During the early to mid-1950s, Israel's "working hypothesis" (formulated, as noted, years earlier) took hold—namely, that the Arab world had not come to terms with the status quo following the 1948 War and that it was pursuing a number of courses aimed at reinstating the status quo ante. The leadership was therefore certain that the Arabs would not hesitate to employ military means against Israel the moment they believed they had attained military superiority. As such, they saw a second round of hostilities between Israel and the Arab states as a near-certain future scenario. The covert diplomacy that took place at the time for the sake of political arrangements, particularly in the Egyptian context, did nothing to lessen, and in fact reinforced, this assessment. A solid majority of Israel's leaders did not view Egypt's qualified consent to engage in dialogue with Israel as genuine acceptance of the latter's existence. They argued that it should be seen in the context of the overall Arab inclination to deny Israel's gains after the 1948 War. From their perspective, the Arab world had resorted to political means in pursuit of its aims only because it lacked the necessary military means. Indeed, in its contacts with the major powers—particularly the United States and Britain in the context of their 1954–1955 "Alpha Plan" aimed at removing the Negev from Israeli jurisdiction—Israel realized to its dismay that the superpowers essentially accepted the Arab stance (namely, that the status quo after the 1948 War did not constitute a permanent arrangement between Israel and the Arab world). From Jerusalem's perspective the Western powers seemed committed to the position that Israel must accept a change in the status quo in the context of any political arrangement with the Arab world. In its struggle to preserve the gains it had achieved in the 1948 War, Israel faced what it saw as an array of Arab as well as international forces of considerable power. The tone set by the Bandung Conference therefore correlated with the sense of pessimism in other areas as well. The need to deal with this political siege, which also manifested in refusal by the major powers (excluding France) to form strategic ties with Israel, naturally mandated a response. Moreover, although the reasons were not strictly financial, Israel's diplomatic representation abroad during the early 1950s comprised only seven embassies—six in Europe and one in North America—which reinforced the sense of siege.

The third element of Israeli policy vis-à-vis sub-Saharan Africa emerged as a result of developments that had far-reaching implications within the continent itself. As we know, after World War I the European powers redrew the map of sub-Saharan Africa. Thus, Britain became the colonial ruler in the Sudan,

Uganda, Kenya, British Somaliland, Malawi, Zambia (Northern Rhodesia), Zimbabwe (Southern Rhodesia), Botswana, Nigeria, the Gold Coast (Ghana), Sierra Leone, Gambia, and Tanzania; France ruled over Chad, the (French) Congo, Gabon, Niger, Mali (French Sudan), Mauritania, Senegal, Guinea, Burkina Faso, the Ivory Coast, and Madagascar; Portugal took control over Mozambique, Angola, and Guinea-Bissau; and Belgium took the (Belgian) Congo, Rwanda, and Burundi. However, Europe began to lose its hold on Africa after World War II. Within a quarter of a century, the decolonization process was completed, as table 9.1 illustrates.

Britain was the first to have its colonial ties with Africa severed, followed by France in the 1960s and Portugal in the 1970s. The cumulative impact in the international political arena became starkly evident by the 1960s, when independent African nations came to represent no fewer than a quarter of UN member states—far more than in Latin America or Asia. Of this group, thirty-three were new states in sub-Saharan Africa. Two of these (Ghana and Guinea) were admitted to the UN in 1957–1958, seventeen in 1960, and fourteen in 1961–1968.

The implications for Israel of this dramatic growth of the United Nations were complex. For one, it gave rise to a new international reality with several dozen states that had not existed in November 1947 (when Africa had only two

Table 9.1. Africa's Decolonization Timetable

Country	Year	Colonizer
South Africa	1910	UK
Egypt	1922	UK
Ethiopia (not originally colonized but occupied by Italy in 1936)	1941	Italy
Libya	1951	UK
Sudan	1956	UK/Egypt
Morocco	1956	France
Tunisia	1956	France
Ghana	1957	UK
Guinea	1958	France
Cameroon	1960	France
Senegal	1960	France
Togo	1960	France
Mali	1960	France
Madagascar	1960	France
Congo (Kinshasa)	1960	Belgium
Somalia	1960	Britain

Table 9.1. (*continued*)

Country	Year	Colonizer
Benin	1960	France
Niger	1960	France
Burkina Faso	1960	France
Cote d'Ivoire	1960	France
Chad	1960	France
Central Africa Republic	1960	France
Congo (Brazzaville)	1960	France
Gabon	1960	France
Nigeria	1960	UK
Mauritania	1960	France
Sierra Leon	1961	UK
Tanzania	1961	UK
Burundi	1962	Belgium
Rwanda	1962	Belgium
Algeria	1962	France
Uganda	1963	UK
Kenya	1963	UK
Malawi	1964	UK
Zambia	1964	UK
Gambia	1965	UK
Botswana	1966	UK
Lesotho	1966	UK
Mauritius	1968	UK
Swaziland	1968	UK
Equatorial Guinea	1968	Spain
Guinea-Bissau	1973	Portugal
Mozambique	1975	Portugal
Cape Verde	1975	Portugal
Comoros	1975	France
Sao Tome and Principe	1975	Portugal
Angola	1975	Portugal
Western Sahara	1976	Spain
Seychelles	1976	UK
Djibouti	1977	France
Zimbabwe	1980	UK
Namibia	1990	South Africa
Eritrea	1993	Ethiopia

Source: http://sites.middlebury.edu/global60s/2013/09/26/africa-decolonization-timeline-2/, courtesy of Prof. Sujata Moorti.

independent states, Liberia and Ethiopia), which as a group could pose a serious threat within the international organization, specifically with respect to the Arab-Israeli conflict as well as UN recognition of Israel and the latter's membership in the organization. The ominous writing on the wall, in Israel's view, came in the form of a resolution adopted at the Casablanca Conference in January 1961. The gathering included relatively radical African states (notably Egypt, Libya, Morocco, and Algeria), and its aim was to counterbalance the "Brazzaville Bloc" formed a year earlier by eleven moderate African states. The final declaration of the Casablanca Conference harshly denounced Israel as "an instrument of imperialism and neo-colonialism not only in the Middle East but in Asia and Africa as well" and called for "the reinstatement of the legitimate rights of Palestine's Arabs." Egypt's Gamal Abdel Nasser viewed the declaration as a victory, in particular because it "transformed the Palestinian issue into an African problem."[6] At the same time, because the sub-Saharan African states were geographically disconnected and distant from Israel, did not historically have a political stance on the conflict, and needed large-scale aid to translate their nominal independence into reality, they offered a potential source of support that could dramatically improve Israel's political standing, especially in the United Nations. It was only natural therefore that Israel sought to transform this potential into reality. Ehud Avriel, one of the architects of Israel's activities in Africa and its first ambassador to Ghana (1957–1960), described Prime Minister David Ben-Gurion's continuing alarm in response to the hostile Bandung resolutions. In the spring of 1957, when Ghana achieved independence, Ben-Gurion asked Avriel to establish an Israeli legation there, explaining that "we must break out of the [circle of Arab hostility surrounding us] and build bridges to the emerging nations on the Black continent. We [cannot] allow a situation similar to [what emerged in] our relations with most Asian nations to develop, [when] we were excluded from the Bandung Afro-Asian conference in 1955. Burma, at the pinnacle of her prestige, was our friend. But almost every other nation on the continent we shared was not."[7]

Israel's publicly stated aims regarding the official positions of these African states toward itself at both the bilateral and the multilateral international levels, which historians have long recognized, were not the only considerations guiding Jerusalem. Later studies have found that beneath the surface and outside the public eye, the Israeli defense establishment took measures to advance strategic objectives that many regarded as no less important. Several of the new African states, for example, controlled maritime corridors and flight paths of strategic value to Israel, and a few of these states bordered on Arab states hostile to Israel. The situation posed a threat yet also presented a great temptation. In an earlier chapter, we discussed the port of Eilat as a conduit for Iranian oil. Eritrea and Ethiopia, located near the Red Sea coast and Bab al-Mandab, were geographically close to Israel. Maintaining good relations with Ethiopia, which controlled Eritrea during the 1960s, was therefore an important means of ensuring Israel's sole passageway for this oil. The ports of Mombasa in Kenya and Dar es Salaam in Tanzania were key maritime stations on the way to the Far East and South Africa. Likewise, Israeli airline flights to eastern and South Africa relied on the goodwill of African states and permission to transit through their airspace. And of course, an Israeli presence in Ethiopia, Uganda, and Kenya, which bordered Arab countries, was an element of security and intelligence activities. The question (further elaborated below) of which interests were most important—the public ones pursued mainly by the Foreign Ministry or the hidden ones within the purview of the defense establishment—greatly preoccupied policy makers in Jerusalem because of its inevitable and critical operational implications.

Achievements and Means

The end result was an intensive, wide-ranging Israeli policy that lasted more than a decade and a half, aimed at fostering relations with sub-Saharan African countries. It is important to note, however, that these countries were never at the top of Jerusalem's international agenda. The primary objective of Israeli foreign policy has always been to ensure the existence and security of the state. Accordingly, the priority states were those that could provide weapons for its defense (Czechoslovakia in 1948, France and Britain in the 1950s, the Federal Republic of Germany in the 1960s, and the United States from the mid-1960s onward), those with the power to deter a state hostile to Israel (the United States), and those that might join an anti-Israel coalition and supply weapons to Arab states (the Soviet Union, the United States, France, and Britain). A second objective of Israel's foreign policy was to secure economic aid and maintain extensive trade relations with developed markets so as to ensure the growth of the Israeli economy and reduce its large trade deficit. In this context, the decisive importance of the United States and the European Economic Community compared with the marginality of Africa is evident: in the late 1960s, trade with African countries did not exceed 3 percent of the total volume of Israeli trade. That marginality was also evident on the African side: Ethiopia, for example, a key country in Israeli foreign relations, purchased only about 3 percent of its imports from Israel and sold it roughly 2 percent of its exports. Finally, Israel had a strong interest in maintaining contact with the largest Jewish communities in the world in order to promote immigration, raise capital, and enlist political support. Even in this respect, as Benyamin Neuberger pointed out, "the United States, the Soviet Union, France, and Britain were more important to Israel than the Democratic Republic of Congo or Kenya."[8] This pyramidal distinction explains why relations with sub-Saharan African countries were perceived as a secondary objective intended, on the one hand, to thwart organized activity against Israel in the UN General Assembly and Security Council (whether by countering it through a bloc of states or by vetoing extreme anti-Israel resolutions such as its expulsion from the UN, economic sanctions, military embargoes, and military intervention), and on the other hand, to advance Israel's strategic security interests.

Other, less important factors also made relations with sub-Saharan Africa a political objective for Israel. Many African states had a Muslim majority or sizable Muslim minority, and cooperation with them could help prevent the political Arab-Israeli conflict from becoming conflict with the entire Muslim world. Moreover, there were those in Israel who viewed the new African states as a bridge to peace. A prevailing perspective, which seems rather naive retrospectively, held that "the road to Cairo passes through Bamako [the capital of Mali]."[9] Some therefore believed (wrongly, in hindsight) that mediators from Africa and Asia would be more acceptable to the Arabs and regarded as fair because they had liberated themselves from the colonial past.

Many in Israel also had a sense of solidarity and shared fate with the Africans. Ben-Gurion and Foreign Minister Golda Meir often spoke in those days of a "moral duty" and "historic mission." Historians who have examined the relevant documents are united in affirming the authenticity of these sentiments. The perspective of Israel's leaders, as projected in public and other statements from this period, was one of sacrifice by the Jewish people, who, having suffered racial discrimination, contempt, and humiliation, could identify with the people of Africa and their history. Their shared experience as former colonies that had recently achieved independence and were striving to implement it fully was another significant factor in Israel's view, as was the receptivity among many African leaders who welcomed Israel's initiative and its efforts (as a new state undergoing economic, social, political, and military development) to establish close ties. Many among these leaders saw Zionism and the national Jewish revival as a model and a source of inspiration for the revival of black nationalism and the liberation of Africa. Some even referred to their own movement as "black Zionism." African intellectuals, too, drew this comparison and voiced sympathy for Zionism and Israel.

Unsurprisingly, therefore, the history books tell us that between 1957 and 1973 Israel devoted considerable diplomatic energy to cultivating political ties with African states. Its efforts included the unusual practice (by Foreign Ministry standards) of sending large numbers of unofficial Israeli delegates to African countries even before they had achieved independence, to pave the way to the establishment of official relations. Accordingly, this "twilight period" saw the dispatch of Raphael Rupin to Tanganyika, Hannan Yavor to Ghana, Yaakov Dori (Israel's first chief of staff) to Kenya, Arye Oded to Uganda, and others to Nigeria, Senegal, and the Ivory Coast, all of which were on the verge of attaining independence. At the time neither the region itself nor its leaders were well known, which sometimes resulted in awkward situations. As Arye Oded relates, one such incident centered on Milton Obote, who later became Uganda's first prime minister. In early August 1960, the Histadrut received a telegram from Austria's association of trade unions announcing that a Ugandan leader named Milton Obote was visiting them and was interested in visiting Israel as well. They advised acceding to his request given that, in their view, he would play a central role once Uganda gained independence. The guest arrived in Israel for a week-long visit, where he met with senior Foreign Ministry officials and discussed plans for cooperation. After he departed for Sweden, Israel learned that the man was an imposter and a scam artist.[10]

Israel's Foreign Ministry decided, for understandable reasons, to establish a special research branch devoted to Africa, annexed to the Asia Department, which consequently expanded significantly. The relatively large number of official visits to Africa by Israeli leaders during those years is another indication of the state's priorities and concerted efforts: Foreign Minister Golda Meir visited Africa in early 1958 and again four times during the following decade. In June 1959 Shimon Peres, director general of the Ministry of Defense, visited Ghana and Guinea. In October 1962 Minister of Labor Yigal Alon visited Uganda, and the following year he conducted additional visits to Kenya, Uganda, Tanganyika, and Zanzibar. In August 1962 President Yitzhak Ben-Zvi visited five West African states, and in June 1966 Prime Minister Levi Eshkol visited Senegal, the Ivory Coast, Liberia, Congo, Kinshasa, Madagascar, Uganda, and Kenya. Reciprocally, dozens of African heads of state visited Israel in 1960–1963. These included the presidents of Upper Volta, Liberia, the Ivory Coast, the Central African Republic, Togo, Cameroon, and the Congo.

The public and official results of these efforts manifested, during the heyday of Israeli-African relations, in all these countries (apart from Mauritania and Somalia, which joined the Arab League) forming diplomatic relations with Israel, thus also rejecting the fundamental Arab position on the Arab-Israeli conflict. Israel had representative offices in thirty-three African countries—more than any other state except the United States. This was due, inter alia, to an explicit policy that gave priority to the establishment of an official Israeli presence in every African state that attained independence, regardless of its size or importance or of the expenses involved in establishing a legation. These facts also explain why between 1957 and 1973, there were no fewer than 150 Israelis serving in official positions in Africa, many as ambassadors, in addition to a few hundred more in administrative and logistical positions. Reciprocally, in 1972 there were twelve African embassies in Israel, half of them in Jerusalem.

These figures reflect Israel's undeniable success in breaking the nonrecognition boycott it had faced since achieving statehood. Beyond this core objective, Israel's efforts yielded another, albeit temporary, result. Until the Six-Day War, African states usually resisted being drawn into the Middle East conflict or abiding by Arab dictates. In a few instances, they even took measures to mitigate anti-Israel resolutions within international organizations, such as at the first conference of independent African states in Accra, the capital of Ghana, in 1958; at the All-African Peoples Conference that took place in the same city six months later; and at the second Conference of Independent African States in Addis Ababa in June 1960. According to Oded, during the early days of the Organisation of African Unity (OAU), the Africans were usually able to withstand Arab demands for the condemnation of Israel, stressing that the organization must focus on resolving African problems and that the Arab-Israeli conflict was outside its purview.[11] Jerusalem naturally viewed the OAU's noncondemnation of Israel as the fruit of its own diplomatic efforts. Initially these efforts also bore fruit at the UN. In 1961, for example, a year after the first wave of independent states emerged in Africa, eleven of the twenty African UN member states voted in favor of draft resolutions favorable to Israel. Nine of these states were also among the resolutions' sponsors. Only four states supported pro-Arab draft resolutions at the time: Ghana, Guinea, Mali, and Nigeria. Furthermore, when Israel proposed a draft resolution in 1961 calling for direct negotiations to resolve the Arab-Israeli conflict, it received widespread support among sub-Saharan African states. And in June 1967, in the immediate aftermath of the Six-Day War, a sizable number of African states helped thwart a draft resolution calling for Israel's immediate withdrawal from all territories captured during the war. As we know, however, this pattern changed dramatically after 1967.

Israel's intensive activity in Africa also explains another factor that was often no less important than the overt and official diplomatic support it received until the late 1960s. For years Israel cooperated closely behind the scenes "with many African states, including Uganda, Ethiopia, Kenya, Nigeria, and Chad," according to Neuberger. He adds,

> Israel's image in Africa did not correspond with its actual power, size, or global importance. Chaim Weizmann, Israel's first president, advised Israeli ambassadors across the world not to draw unnecessary attention to Israel's geographic or demographic size. And indeed, the success of Israeli diplomacy in this regard exceeded expectations. During the 1960s the prevailing image of Israel in Africa was one of a mid-sized power, on par with France, Britain, and China. Many [African] countries formed a picture of Israel . . . as a state that could "move mountains" in the US Congress and the White House, able to secure any credit, grant, or investment it needed. Thus Israel managed to project a "diplomatic presence" far beyond its size and importance. There were years during which, in diplomatic terms, Israel was the smallest state with the largest presence in Africa.[12]

These developments explain why, notwithstanding anti-Israel votes by African states in international organizations such as the UN, UNESCO, and the International Labor Organization (which gained momentum beginning in the mid-1960s), Israel maintained covertly friendly relations with those states at the bilateral level, especially in matters of security. Evidently, their overtly unfriendly relations were in many cases a cover for close ties at the pragmatic level. There can be no doubt that, at least from the late 1950s until the late 1960s, Israel enjoyed a positive reputation among African elites. Hard evidence and specific details are, of course, difficult to obtain. But Zach Levey offers some indication of the validity of this claim, which historians of Israeli-African relations have long recognized: a 1962 survey conducted in Paris among three hundred students from francophone African states, asking which country they most admired, ranked Israel in third place (12.4%), after the Soviet Union (25%) and China (20%) and ahead of Cuba (12%), France (8%), and the United States (3.3%).[13]

Israel's success in this regard lasted more than a decade, beginning with its establishment of diplomatic ties with Ghana in 1957, for reasons that go beyond the scope of our discussion. It is also difficult to assess the effectiveness of Israel's efforts on the basis of currently available information, particularly given that, unlike Israel, sub-Saharan states have not disclosed internal state documents that can authoritatively shed light or provide greater detail regarding the considerations, policy making, and assessments of their leaders in this area. I have chosen, therefore, to focus on the Israeli perspective, with attention to two non-diplomatic sources of leverage in Israel's foreign policy first employed extensively in the African context. These points of leverage are important because of their key role vis-à-vis Africa, as well as the foundation they provided, through trial and error during the 1950s and 1960s, for what then became a traditional means Israel has used to advance its international interests. The first of these was technical and technological aid, primarily in the areas of agriculture and local infrastructure, and the second was military aid. An analysis of both these means is enlightening and relevant to our purposes, among other reasons because they represent two conflicting approaches to Israel's strategic priorities in Africa, as well as the different perspectives of the responsible political and bureaucratic entities—the Foreign Ministry and the defense establishment—that shaped the entire process.

The operational elements of the concept of using such aid for political purposes were laid in 1953, in the context of Israel's relations with Burma. During the tenure of Israel's first ambassador to that country, David HaCohen, Israel sent experts to Rangoon and hosted Burmese citizens who came for training in various civilian matters. Applying this technique across dozens of African states naturally required a great deal more resources and planning, in conjunction with a designated responsible entity. It also gave rise to differences of opinion, such as emerged in 1958 between the Office of the Prime Minister, under Theodor "Teddy" Kollek, and the Foreign Ministry, under Golda Meir, regarding the provision of aid. The different positions reflected conflicting political considerations and principles as well as personal interests and disputes. They also indicate the great importance ascribed at the time to activities in Africa. Ultimately the foreign minister succeeded in convincing the prime minister of the validity of her view by arguing that Kollek's approach, which entailed cooperation with American foundations such as the Ford Foundation and the Rockefeller Family Fund, "could lead to our vilification by those [in Africa] who seek to portray us as agents of Western imperialism"—a core argument of Israel's opponents in sub-Saharan Africa.[14] In 1960, accordingly, the Foreign Ministry established an "Agency for International Aid and Cooperation." A year later it dropped the word *Aid* for fear that the Africans would consider it condescending, adopting the name "Agency for International Development Cooperation" (MASHAV—Makhlaka LeShituf Beinleumi). The agency also dealt with eleven Asian states and twenty-three Latin American states, but most of its work during those years focused on thirty-eight African states. Israel's prioritization is also reflected in the fact that 70 percent of its civilian foreign aid during this period went to Africa.

The disputes noted above were not limited to organizational questions. Internal debates over the prime objective of Israel's aid programs continued for years. There were those, such as Prime Minister Ben-Gurion, who stressed the moral and humanitarian aspect of this aid, refraining (presumably for political reasons as well) from publicly discussing the state's operational and practical objectives. Others, evidently including most of the senior officials responsible for the issue as well as the foreign minister herself, did not deny that there were political as well as moral considerations. Hanan Aynor, one of the main Foreign Ministry officials in this area, told the Israeli legation in Washington in 1970 that MASHAV's activities "even under difficult political circumstances [are] first and foremost a spearhead for economic and cultural as well as security and political interests . . . [and] there is also a strong sociological and psychological factor. The Israeli public is willing to provide aid [through] MASHAV not only in order to assist Africa but also to prove its humanitarianism to itself."[15] A decade later he stated before the Israel-Africa Friendship Association, "Let us be completely honest. . . . This thing [MASHAV] was not entirely altruistic. . . . We were surrounded by an Arab chokehold, and we skipped over it through friendship with the Africans."[16] Ultimately, therefore, this friendship proved critical. In explaining its political basis to the Knesset Foreign Affairs and Defense Committee in 1972, the director general of the Foreign Ministry argued that its principles were "not to focus on specific states, however important, but to work with any state that approaches Israel for aid" and "not to condition this aid on political factors, but to expect that the aid would lead to greater understanding of Israel's situation and promote friendly relations."[17] The defense establishment, in contrast, maintained a consistent utilitarian approach grounded in realpolitik. Shmuel Avi-Ad, a defense official at the time, argued in an interview with Ronen Bergman that "we had very little, if any, humanitarian or ideological motives. We were all experienced enough to realise that the NAHAL [a paramilitary program combining military service with the creation of agricultural settlements], GADNA [a premilitary program for Israeli youth] and MASHAV projects were only a smokescreen of ideology and politically correct verbiage which was a cover for our enthusiasm to penetrate Africa."[18]

In any event, there is no disputing the scope of Israeli aid to Africa. Between 1960 and 1968, Israel signed cooperation agreements with twenty-one African countries and initiated approximately two hundred development plans. The bulk of MASHAV's activities was in the field of agriculture, the main economic sector of most sub-Saharan African countries; other areas of activity included health care, community development, and education, as well as cooperatives and trade unions. For economic reasons, most of the courses Israel offered took place in the country that sought assistance, and only a few in Israel. A number of Israeli experts resided in these countries for two or three years, and others remained for several weeks, usually to provide consultation or conduct surveys. During the first year of MASHAV's operations, in 1958, sixty African students arrived in Israel, and eighty Israeli experts (excluding IDF personnel) traveled to Africa. By 1971, nearly three thousand specialists from Israel had undertaken assignments in Africa (compared with only five hundred in Asia and Central America), while Israel hosted some seven thousand trainees from Africa, mainly in the field of agriculture. Besides the activities it organized directly, the Foreign Ministry also supervised the operations of two Israeli agencies that provided aid to developing nations. The first was the Afro-Asian Institute for Labor, Development, and Cooperative Studies, established by the Histadrut in 1960. By 1972 the institute had conducted sixty-two courses in Israel and twenty-four on-site courses abroad, attended by close to four thousand students. The second agency, operated by the Foreign Ministry, was Carmel—the Golda Meir International Training Center, established a year later. Among other activities, the center established a school for social work in Kenya, the first of its kind on the continent, where hundreds of young women were trained. The Foreign Ministry also worked with the Eye Clinic at Hadassah Medical School to establish eye clinics in several African countries, including Liberia, Kenya, and Swaziland, and ran "eye camps" where Israeli doctors treated hundreds of people afflicted with blindness and gave them back their sight. Throughout this period African doctors received training as residents at Hadassah Hospital. Notably, Israel's civilian aid to sub-Saharan Africa received America's blessing in the form of a $7 million grant in 1965.

Israel's activities in Africa thus diverged significantly from traditional diplomatic activities. The experience of using foreign aid as a political instrument proved to be extremely valuable, and Israel frequently employed this instrument albeit on a smaller scale, even after the era of intensive Israeli-African relations came to an end in the early 1970s.

The Israeli leadership regarded it as only natural to supplement civilian aid with military aid for sub-Saharan Africa. A few preliminary remarks are in order. Because Israel did not produce its own major weapons systems, it depended on foreign arms suppliers, with all the attendant problems, as illustrated above in relation to France. The option of selling such systems was of course quite limited during the state's early years, as was Israel's financial capacity to fund military aid programs. At the same time, the security needs of African states did not entail large-scale military aid, which made it possible to operate relatively modest but effective programs openly. In the military sphere, as in the case of MASHAV's activities, Burma was the first country with which Israel engaged in military training and the sale of arms, primarily light weapons. The first customers in Africa were Ethiopia and Ghana. A special unit dedicated to this issue began operating within the Ministry of Defense in the mid-1950s. By mid-1966 it had sent some 170 military experts to Africa, of whom 29 served in Ethiopia, 29 in Uganda, 28 in the Ivory Coast, 17 in the Central African Republic, 15 in Tanzania, 10 in Dahomey, 10 in Zaire, 9 in Malawi, 7 in Chad, 5 in Sierra Leone, 5 in Togo, 3 in Liberia, 2 in Madagascar, and 2 in Senegal. In 1964 military aid activities took place in all these countries, as well as Guinea, Gabon, Cameroon, Niger, Upper Volta, Congo, Zambia, and Zaire. Among other activities, this aid took the form of the training of units in Africa and Israel, in an effort to replicate the practices of Israel's GADNA and NAHAL, as well as arms sales on a scale that reached $200 million between the Six-Day War and 1972. This sum, though not negligible—indeed, it reflects both Israel's economic interest and Africa's needs—was but a small part of the "heavy" armament of sub-Saharan Africa during those years. The figures reveal that between 1957 and 1975, foreign powers sold these African states 313 jet planes, some of which were for training purposes only. Israel's portion comprised only three planes, one of which was a fighter plane delivered personally to Idi Amin as a gift. During this period Africans purchased 1,250 slower planes, 18 of which Israel provided, and 1,787 armored vehicles, of which Israel provided 46, including 22 outdated Sherman tanks. I was unable to find detailed information about light weapons exports, which Israel would have had little difficulty in providing. Such arms were of vital importance for sub-Saharan African states, and presumably their sales were on a more massive scale. Only recently was it revealed that in order to transport these arms to Africa, Israel went to great lengths to acquire a "long aerodynamic arm."[19] In concrete operational terms, according to Asher Orkaby, these activities focused on clandestinely and independently converting the B-377 Stratocruiser passenger jet by adding parts from the 97-C jet (so as to circumvent the prohibition on purchasing US military carrier jets). The plane, which was first used in 1964 (in a military airlift to the deposed government of Yemen), could reach African states without refueling.[20] That capability evidently served Israel well: it exported arms to ten African states—Ethiopia, Ghana, Kenya, Congo-Kinsasha, Dahomey, the Malagasy Republic, Sierra Leone, Tanzania, Uganda, and Upper Volta—and transported arms to rebels in the Sudan.

This rough outline reveals only a fragment of Israel's security-related activities in sub-Saharan Africa, without explaining how its objectives and modes of action often generated fierce internal conflict. While there was agreement within the political echelon and between it and the Foreign Ministry regarding official policy—namely, that the aim of Israel's activities was to guide and foster an official and open friendship between African states and Israel—at the bilateral and multilateral levels they were fiercely divided regarding many aspects of the military aid programs as carried out by the defense establishment. Defense officials consistently held that the most effective and promising way to realize Israel's aims was not through civilian and humanitarian aid but primarily through military aid, a core element of which was the provision of assistance to local leaders facing domestic enemies and rivals. Nahum Karni, who headed the Africa aid unit in the Defense Ministry, explained the advantages of such aid to his superiors in late 1964: "This military training project gives me the leverage with which I could reach all the sources of power in the country: the Prime Minister, the Chief of Staff, and others. . . . Influence in these countries is centered in the hands of a small party and [once you are dealing with military and intelligence] they must take you into consideration."[21] Karni was intimately familiar with the situation in Africa, as was Reuven Merhav, a Mossad official who operated in Kenya. Merhav spoke with an Israeli researcher about the permanently open door of President Jomo Kenyatta when it came to contact with Israel in matters of security. "Merhav was bribing the commander of the presidential guard, so he updated the times when he could see the president very easily."[22] In his assessment, "to arrange the same kind of meeting [with Kenyatta] through the foreign affairs ministry would take months." David Kimche, another architect of Israel's clandestine activity in sub-Saharan Africa, told one historian about the value of such aid during this period, relative to civilian aid: "It cost us the same amount of money to send over to Addis an expert on hen houses or an instructor on intelligence gathering. The latter would end up meeting the Emperor. The former would end up in a hen house. It's obvious what our first choice was. Intelligence liaisons were the fastest way to foster an intimate relationship."[23] This prioritization indeed yielded significant results, including a decision by the president of the Ivory Coast to include a Mossad representative in all his travels abroad and to entrust his personal security both at home and abroad to Israeli security personnel. Likewise, the Ugandan government agreed to a joint action with Mossad agents to break into the Egyptian Embassy in Uganda and steal a large number of classified documents, including, in particular, encryption codes that made it possible for Israel to learn about Cairo's covert actions across the world.

To understand this key dimension of Israeli activity, it is important to bear in mind, as Bergman analyzed in his unpublished doctoral dissertation, that Israeli intelligence, and the Mossad in particular, had two clear objectives in relation to Africa, both of which deviated from official Israeli policy. The first was to use African territory, through a variety of means, as a back door to the agency's own main goal—namely, addressing the Arab world's hostility beyond the continent and, from 1967, that of the Soviet Union as well. It is hardly surprising that for the Mossad, Africa hardly represented an aim in itself; it was rather "an unexpected gateway to this world."[24] The second objective was to cultivate personal appreciation and a sense of gratitude toward Israel, especially in the area of personal security for African leaders. Toward this end Israel made extensive use of intelligence and other clandestine tools. The operational objectives, as Bergman outlined them, included the following: the use of Africa as a base for recruiting and mobilizing agents in the Arab world, its use as a base for signals intelligence (SIGINT) vis-à-vis this world (one of the crowning achievements in this regard was the establishment of an electronic intelligence gathering station in Eritrea), the monitoring of anti-Israel terrorist activities originating in Africa and of Arab and Soviet activities on the continent, the use of intelligence originating in and beyond Africa in pursuit of objectives both there and elsewhere (primarily through intelligence sharing with the CIA), and the use of operations in Africa as a means of compelling Arab states to divert armed forces designated for war against Israel by redirecting them elsewhere—as in the case of Egypt and Sudan.

Conspicuously absent from this list is the aim of ensuring an overt, official pro-Israel position at the bilateral and multilateral levels on the part of African states, whereas matters of security and intelligence topped the list. Several factors made Africa perfectly suited to the Mossad's standard operating procedures: its geographic proximity to Israel (by sea, land, and air); easy access to the thirty-three African states that recognized Israel, which in turn allowed relatively convenient access to additional states; and what turned out to be very fertile ground for covert activity on behalf of unstable local authorities that had difficulty enforcing law and order and needed foreign assistance in various forms so as to assert control. That assistance included the payment of regular bribes to the governor of Eritrea, Ras Asrate Kassa (code-named "Mofet"—meaning "role model"—by the Mossad), and to General Kebede Gabre, Ethiopia's national security minister; a $2 million loan to President Tombalbaye of Chad (which was never refunded); direct aid to Idi Amin for the military coup that ousted President Obota and placed Amin in power (this included help transporting Ugandan military units stationed in Greece to participate in the fighting); and large sums of money that the Mossad transferred to Amin, partly via the customary practice of using false-bottomed suitcases. The Mossad's approach of raison d'état above all else directed these activities and, in many instances, was highly effective. Uri

Lubrani, who served as ambassador to Ethiopia while continuing to work for the state's secret services, explained the Mossad's rather consistent disregard for Western personal and political moral codes: "There is nothing to be done. You cannot be a saint and choose your partners and your enemies. It is very easy to preach without understanding the price that would have been paid. Anyone who does not play by the rules gets taken off the chessboard."[25]

Thus, Africa provided the Mossad with an important base of operations to pursue its objectives on the continent itself (including intelligence gathering on the OAU) as well as beyond it (primarily in the Middle East and the Arab world)—such as during the war in Yemen and the Sudanese civil war. A good deal has been written about the Yemeni case, drawing on non-Israeli sources. The Sudanese case received significant exposure only recently, when David Ben-Uziel (code-named "Tarzan") was granted permission to publish his memoirs.[26] "Tarzan" was a Mossad agent who played a critical role in this operation, code-named "Mezuzah." His book includes fascinating details about the operation, launched in 1969, in which Ethiopia, Uganda, and Kenya participated. By providing assistance to local rebels through the airlift of essential medical and military equipment, among other means, the operation was intended to prevent cooperation between Sudanese units and the Egyptian army (which was engaged in the "War of Attrition" with Israel at the time) and to confine these units to the south. During those years the Mossad was engaged in creating a "peripheral alliance" with Iran, Turkey, and Ethiopia, which focused to a large extent on intelligence sharing and covert operations with these states. Sub-Saharan Africa offered many fruitful sources and modes of operation to advance this alliance.

These factors also explain why the region became a focal point for Mossad activities. Three states on the continent served as the primary bases of operation—Ethiopia, Kenya, and the Ivory Coast—later joined by Zaire, Tanzania, and Chad, where the Mossad also had permanent delegations. I was unable to locate comprehensive data on the Israeli agents associated with these activities. We can, however, draw some conclusions from a 1960 report by a Foreign Ministry official noting that the Israeli delegation in Addis Ababa (which included many Mossad operatives) numbered one hundred that year, and from the fact that a year later there were two hundred Israelis residing in Ethiopia, comprising the second-largest Israeli diplomatic presence after that in the United States. From the information available, we note that Israel's security delegation to Ethiopia numbered sixty in 1965. Also worth noting in this context is Bergman's argument that Africa's importance and the scope of existing and potential activities on the continent made it a vital station on the career path of many senior Mossad officials during the 1960s and early 1970s.[27] As someone who spent much of his early academic career exploring British archives, I see an interesting parallel between the Israeli presence in Africa and the imperial British presence in India: both these vast and relatively open lands provided significant learning opportunities and training grounds, greatly enriching the operational experience of administrative and intelligence elites and thus making service in these countries a professional prerequisite.

Israel's security-related activities in sub-Saharan Africa were inevitably quite costly. Naturally, therefore, it sought financial support from the United States, some of which it received openly. But as Bergman noted in his study, these funds represented only a small portion of the US support to Israel in this field of activity, which evidently also served CIA objectives in the area. At the time the issue was regarded as "highly classified," and even Israel's chief of staff, among others, was not privy to this information. In early December 1964, then–chief of staff Yitzhak Rabin addressed the issue of Israeli operations in Africa at a cost of $17 million, noting that "not all of it comes from the Israeli taxpayers." It is not surprising, therefore, that Israeli and US documents on this matter remain classified. Nonetheless, according to retrospective Israeli intelligence assessments, US funding covered at least 40 percent of the cost of Israel's operations (mainly in the area of security). The US interest was multifaceted and, according to Israeli assessments, included the use of Israel for the indirect pursuit of objectives potentially perceived as imperialistic if openly ascribed to the United States, as well as a shared perception of the Soviet, and at times Arab, enemy.

Yet another factor was Israel's arms sales, which fueled competition with other states operating in sub-Saharan Africa. These sales generated conflict, such as with Britain, yet also facilitated coordination and cooperation, such as with the French in the Central African Republic. They frequently sparked clashes between the defense establishment, which considered arms sales a prime objective, and the Foreign Ministry, whose considerations were primarily political.

Israel's Foreign Ministry refused to adopt the full spectrum of Mossad goals and certainly did not support its brazen modes of operation. Likewise, it rejected what it viewed as blatant interference in the internal affairs of African countries and the deployments of an excessive security network. The ministry also objected to what it regarded as the establishment of facts of the ground without regard for political considerations and without coordination with the ministry itself on the part of the Mossad and the defense establishment. It was highly critical of the defense establishment's practice of cultivating close ties with dictators who violated the human rights of their own citizens, such as Jan Bedel Bokassa and David Dacko of the Central African Republic, Kwame Nkrumah of Ghana, Joseph Mobuto of Congo-Zaire, and Milton Obote and Idi Amin of Uganda. When all these African states abruptly severed their ties with Israel, it came as a harsh and unexpected blow, unforeseen by Mossad operatives, and triggered fierce retrospective criticism of the Israeli defense establishment by the Foreign

Ministry. An April 1972 letter from Israel's ambassador in Nairobi, Reuven Dafni, to his superiors reveals only the tip of the iceberg:

> How can the Mossad people excuse the lack of even the slightest guess that this kind of thing might happen? How could the head of [the] military delega-tion, who not once bluntly stated that he practically owns [Idi] Amin neither feel nor see even the smallest change in Amin's attitude towards Israel? . . . It seems to me that we are compelled to undertake a comprehensive and harsh self-examination regarding our entire African enterprise, with special empha-sis on our military operation. What happened in Uganda reinforces beyond expectation the opinion of those—myself among them—who saw our military operation as too much of a risk and as a heavy burden for a country like ours.... It is unthinkable that an ambassador would not know what the head of the mili-tary delegation and the head of the Mossad in the same country are doing.[28]

The letter also illustrates an important episode in the confrontation that had begun to form years earlier and still exists between the Foreign Ministry and the defense establishment. The clash, in terms of perspective and modes of operation, between what internal correspondence referred to as "Jerusalem" (the seat of the Foreign Ministry) and "Tel Aviv" (the home base of the defense establishment), between the political and the military outlook, and between diplomats and gen-erals, has continued to this day.

Fiasco

The golden age of Israel's diplomatic relations with sub-Saharan African states was relatively short-lived. Most of these states severed their ties with Israel between the Six-Day War in 1967 and the Yom Kippur War in 1973. In early 1972 Israel still had diplomatic representation in thirty-two African countries. By January 1974 only five of these countries still maintained official relations with Israel. The first African state to sever ties in the immediate aftermath of the Six-Day War was Guinea, followed by Uganda in 1972. While Israel's relations with the former were not particularly warm, Uganda had represented the "jewel in the crown," at least in the eyes of the Israeli defense establishment. The Mossad viewed the loss of this relationship as no less than catastrophic. Israeli experts at the time concluded that Idi Amin's main motive for severing ties was Israel's rejection of his request for advanced military equipment, such as the Phantom jets with which he intended to attack Tanzania and capture the port of Tanga so as not to be dependent on the port of Mombasa in Kenya. The manner in which Amin severed ties was particularly harsh, going out of his way to express his new position: in July 1972 he granted the Palestine Liberation Organization the very premises that had previously housed the Israeli Embassy, and in September of that year he sent a memo to the UN secretary-general justifying Hitler's policy of exterminating the Jews. The second wave came toward the end of that year, when Chad, Niger, Mali, and Congo Brazzaville announced they were cutting ties with Israel. The remaining twenty-one states severed relations during and immediately after the 1973 war (as listed below), thus concluding the greatest diplomatic disaster Israel has ever known.

This avalanche was preceded by a stark erosion of Israel's diplomatic standing in Africa during 1967–1970. African involvement in the Arab-Israeli conflict began to increase in 1968 in response to Arab pressure, as expressed in resolutions of the OAU (where there were more than a few Arab delegations) and in the voting records of African states at the UN. The trend first began at the organization's summit meeting in Addis Ababa in 1970, when it was officially decided to introduce a separate agenda item on the Middle East under the heading "Continued Aggression towards Egypt." The trend intensified later that year when the UN General Assembly convened, at which time twenty-one states supported Arab draft resolutions, with nine states abstaining and only two opposing. It peaked in 1971, when four African presidents visited the Middle East, including Israel, with the aim of mediating between Israel and Egypt. In the aftermath of this visit, the OAU concluded that Israel was responsible for the failure of the mission led by Gunnar Valfrid Jarring, a representative of the UN secretary-general, who had attempted to mediate between the two sides.

These developments—or writing on the wall, in retrospect—sparked intense controversy in Israel. Foreign Ministry field personnel were the first to sense an impending political earthquake, and the conclusions they drew were quite radical. In January 1970 Israel's ambassador to the Central African Republic asserted that Israel had failed to achieve its aims in Africa and suggested that aid to countries that spoke out or voted against Israel be terminated. In mid-December of that year, the ambassador to Liberia voiced an even stronger stance:

> If the African countries do not serve our interests, there is no point in consoling ourselves with [the maintenance of] bilateral political or cultural ties. Diplomatic relations are too expensive to allow us to settle for personal friendship with African leaders if it does not bring us the desired results. . . . The blow dealt us during the last General Assembly teaches us that we must change our way of thinking. We are too small and too poor to allow ourselves to be the fifth state, after four major powers, in terms of the number of embassies in the world. Let us therefore be realistic. . . . We must stop our obsequiousness at the doors of [African] foreign ministries and our pleas to be seen and understood . . . and free up resources for activities that are effective and beneficial to us.[29]

That same week the ambassador to Uganda transmitted the following message: "After licking our wounds following the defeat at the UN, each of us is castigating himself for being a failure and disappointment. . . . We resume the gray day-to-day life of increasing MASHAV aid to one country or another, the endless efforts to invite important guests, the dissemination of public relations material, and of course we once again attend cocktail parties and happily invite for dinner those under whose orders we were dealt such a blow in New York." He concluded by recommending that Israel suspend these activities and drastically reassess its strategy.[30]

On the other side of the divide were two groups that, while understanding the severity of the blow suffered in the international arena, actually urged increasing Israel's activities in Africa as a way of overcoming the crisis. To justify this approach—which was eventually, though temporarily, accepted—Foreign Minister Eban and leaders of the defense establishment underscored the fact that the overall network of bilateral relations with Africa remained intact and even showed clear signs of expanding. As the director of the Africa Department in the Foreign Ministry asserted in a January 1971 briefing to legations, "The votes of African states in international fora and on issues relating to the Middle East do not reflect the actual state of bilateral relations . . . which are distinctly characterized by much cordiality and fruitful cooperation on various, and sometimes delicate, matters."[31] These matters would certainly have included security and intelligence. Indeed, much of the activity in this area—especially during this period—was driven by the preponderance of evidence affirming Israel's capability, as demonstrated during the Six-Day War. The lessons learned from this dual reality, as far as defense officials were concerned, only reinforced their view of the relative unimportance of African states' official positions, as opposed to the importance of security and intelligence for these states. Consequently, in 1968–1972 defense and security officials did not advise that Israel lower its profile with respect to sub-Saharan Africa. Nevertheless, later events left no alternative.

The conclusions drawn at the organizational, political, and security levels were naturally related to lessons learned. As Oded suggests, we can now point to three clusters of reasons why African states severed ties with Israel en masse during the early 1970s: political, general, and those related to Israeli actions.[32] The first reason in the political cluster was the fact that six Arab states—Egypt, Sudan, Libya, Tunisia, Morocco, and Algeria—all members of the OAU, initiated and promoted various resolutions against Israel, especially after its conquest of Egyptian lands in 1967 and Egyptian territories in Africa itself during the 1973 War. For deep-rooted colonial and postcolonial reasons, sub-Saharan African states were universally opposed to the conquest of territories. The Arab states exploited African countries' concerns about the military might of South Africa and Rhodesia, as well as their fears that other African countries would try to seize one another's territories in the context of various border disputes. Furthermore, many African leaders viewed the Sinai Peninsula, captured by Israel in 1967, as part of Africa. Their subsequent demands that Israel withdraw went unanswered, which goes a large way toward explaining some of the African states' reactions. The Islamic factor, too, undoubtedly amplified the situation. About a third of the continent's inhabitants are Muslim, and several sub-Saharan states have a

Muslim majority (Mali, Guinea, Senegal, and Niger), while the others (Ethiopia, Tanzania, Cameroon, and Kenya) have a large Muslim minority. Until the late 1960s, they generally avoided involvement in the Arab-Israeli conflict, but this changed after an incident of arson at the Al-Aqsa mosque in 1969 and the formation around this time of the Organization of Islamic Cooperation, whose anti-Israel initiatives received Arab support. Israel was also the focus of political hostility on the part of the Soviet Union and the Soviet bloc in Africa. These states engaged in intensive anti-Israel propaganda after severing diplomatic relations in 1967, which placed Israeli ambassadors in a defensive position. Above all, African states were influenced by the financial incentives that Saudi Arabia and Libya offered them during the early 1970s, as well as the ever-increasing power of Arab states at the United Nations during this period.

Although not a direct cause, additional overriding factors and dynamics created the influential backdrop against which African states cut ties with Israel. The latter's image among sub-Saharan African states underwent a transformation beginning in the late 1960s. Until 1967 these states viewed Israel as a small country surrounded by enemies, which had successfully managed to create and cultivate a modern industry and advanced agriculture and was willing to share its knowledge and experience with them. The Six-Day War demonstrated Israel's power but at the same time highlighted its character as an occupying state identified with imperialism, which justified the view of Israel not as a third-world country but as a "white superpower." Israel's ever-stronger strategic alliance with the United States had two contradictory consequences in this regard. On the one hand, it reinforced the image of Israel as capable of securing important aid for itself and its allies from this superpower, but on the other hand it solidified the image of Israel as a capitalist-imperialist spearhead. Nor did the shift to the left on the part of several African leaders—including Julius Kambarage Nyerere—or the strengthening of ties with the Soviet Union and China work to Israel's favor. Historians are, however, united in the view that Israel itself also played a part in this diplomatic disaster. They point to several factors: the delayed effect of deteriorating relations during 1968–1972, which dampened Israeli enthusiasm for its diplomatic activities in Africa and thwarted its creativity; more than a few catastrophic failures in the area of civilian aid, such as the collapse of a cotton farm in northern Tanzania; the shortcomings of several Israeli companies, including one that failed to make a newly constructed meat factory in Chad operational; and the instabilities and revolutions in sub-Saharan Africa, which undercut Israel's initial enthusiasm. The military aid supplied by Israel undoubtedly had a twofold impact: on the one hand it reinforced a positive image of the state, but on the other it provided detractors with proof of Israel's blatant intervention in domestic affairs. Table 9.2 shows Israel's understanding of the specific reasons behind each African state's decision to sever ties.

Table 9.2. Severance of Relations between African Countries and Israel

Country	Date	Main Reasons
Guinea	June 6, 1967	E, C
Uganda	March 30, 1972	A, B, D
Chad	November 28, 1972	A, B
Congo	December 31, 1972	E, A
Niger	January 5, 1973	B, A
Mali	January 5, 1973	E, B, A
Burundi	May 16, 1973	A, C
Togo	September 21, 1973	A, C
Zaire	October 4, 1973	C, A
Rwanda	October 8, 1973	C, A
Benin	October 9, 1973	E, C
Burkina Faso	October 10, 1973	C, E
Cameroon	October 13, 1973	C, D
Equatorial Guinea	October 14, 1973	C
Tanzania	October 19, 1973	C, D
Madagascar	October 20, 1973	C, A
Central African Republic	October 21, 1973	C, A
Ethiopia	October 23, 1973	C
Nigeria	October 25, 1973	D, C
Gambia	October 26, 1973	C, B
Zambia	October 26, 1973	C
Sierra Leone	October 27, 1973	C
Ghana	October 28, 1973	C
Senegal	October 28, 1973	C, B
Gabon	October 29, 1973	C
Kenya	November 1, 1973	C
Liberia	November 2, 1973	C
Cote d'Ivoire	November 8, 1973	C
Botswana	November 12, 1973	C
Mauritius	June 15, 1976	C

Key to the main reasons for severing relations
A. Financial inducement, generally accompanied by poor economic and internal conditions in the severing state
B. The Muslim factor
C. Solidarity with African Egypt (either willingly or under Arab pressure)
D. Aspiration of the leader of the severing country to assume a leadership position in Africa
E. Radical regime or Communist bloc influence

Source: Arye Oded, "Africa in Israeli Foreign Policy," *Israel Studies* 15, no. 3 (2010).

New Relations

Whatever the actual reasons, the severing of ties greatly reinforced the view among Israeli policy makers that African states had essentially turned their backs on Israel because of monetary enticements offered by Arabs and that their leaders were spineless and unreliable. The term *betrayal* was bandied about in the Israeli media when discussing the African states' decision, and years later the press was still harshly criticizing Israel's leadership for its overly optimistic expectations in the course of its African adventure. Headlines and editorials reinforced the displeasure openly voiced by politicians, including during Knesset debates. Menachem Begin, one of the fiercest critics, chastised the government even before the diplomatic avalanche came to an end. During a meeting of the Knesset Foreign Affairs and Security Committee in mid-June 1972, Begin proclaimed, "They spit on us, and we say that it's raining."[33]

The sense of failure naturally gave rise to a dramatic shift in Israeli policy toward the white government in South Africa. Until the early 1970s, those who opposed political and strategic ties with South Africa (because of Israel's relations with black African states) had the upper hand. The collapse of the network Israel had tried to build tipped the balance in favor of the other side, and henceforth—until the collapse of the apartheid regime in 1994—South Africa became a crucial African ally. The relationship offered Israel new opportunities for large-scale arms sales. In the summer of 1988, for example, it sold South Africa sixty Kfir jets no longer in use by its own air force. The jets, after being comprehensively upgraded, were incorporated into the South African air force under the name "Cheetah C." The deal amounted to an unprecedented $1.7 billion. Outwardly the project was described as an initiative of the South African aerospace industry (named "Atlas" at the time), which was also credited as the project's first contractor. Israel's involvement was downplayed, although details surfaced here and there. In fact, much of the work took place at Israel's aerospace facility in Lod and other Israeli facilities that provided subsystems and components. The South African deal later allowed Israel's aerospace industry to emerge from a state of crisis after the cancellation of the "Lavi" project in the summer of 1987.

At the same time—inevitably, given the lack of official diplomatic relations and the lessons learned from events of the early 1970s—Israel adopted a very low profile on the continent itself. Its efforts focused on a relatively small number of locations, on a far smaller scale than before. MASHAV activities and the number of civilian experts who visited sub-Saharan Africa decreased significantly (in 2008 Israel had only four representatives in three countries—Ethiopia, Senegal, and South Africa). Yet the state continued to pursue these activities by offering training—in Israel—for citizens of many countries, including African nations. In 2008, for example, Israel received 2,762 trainees from 110 states, 688 of whom came from 35 African states. Israel also made a concerted effort to improve its international image by cultivating its ties with the UN, the World Bank, and various international philanthropic organizations. These activities, though they remained a political tool aimed at regaining access to sub-Saharan Africa, decreased significantly in scale during the following years. MASHAV's overall aid budget in 2010 was only $10 million, representing 0.068 percent of the gross national product—well below the rate during the 1960s as well as the average among OECD states, which totaled 0.28 percent that year.

Israel's security-related activity continued to decrease after the mass severing of ties, and after a brief spell of military ties with Ethiopia in 1975 ended, Kenya remained the last active, and isolated, stronghold in this area. As we know from various publications, absent cooperation with this country it would have been impossible to rescue the Israeli hostages in Entebbe, Uganda, a year later. The Mossad's extensive contracts with its counterpart in Nairobi enabled Israel to receive permission in 1970 for two Boeing jets (for command-and-control and as an airborne hospital) and four additional carrier planes to participate in the operation. They also facilitated cooperation behind the back of Kenya's president, Jomo Kenyatta. The day after the operation, Israel's ambassador in Washington, Simcha Dinitz, told Secretary of State Henry Kissinger that Kenyatta had been left out of the loop. Interestingly, Israel also prepared itself for two potential scenarios that did not ultimately materialize: ground-based reinforcements in Entebbe via planes that would land in Kenya, and military aid to Kenya in a clash with Uganda if Idi Amin were to seek revenge in the aftermath of the rescue operation.

At that time Israel officially terminated its military aid to sub-Saharan African states in general, presumably as a direct result of lessons learned from the traumatic experience of 1972–1973. Officially, only three states—the Democratic Republic of Congo, Liberia, and Cameroon—continued to receive arms from Israel and briefly to receive military aid as a reward for the courage demonstrated by renewing relations. Notably, this state of affairs, which characterized the late 1970s and the 1980s, changed dramatically during the following decade. One should keep in mind that since the early 1990s, arms exports have been a critical source of foreign currency for Israel. A substantial portion of these arms (as well as training) was and is destined for Africa, which reopened its diplomatic doors to Israel in the 1990s—this time by way of deals forged by private Israeli companies, albeit with the approval and oversight of the Ministry of Defense. According to the Ministry's Defense Assistance Department, of the total number of arms sales in 2014 (about $5.5 billion), defense contractors' deals accounted for $318 million, compared with $223 million in 2013.

In the twenty-first century the value of contracts signed by Israeli arms exporters with African countries has risen nearly every year: $71 million in 2009,

$77 million in 2010, $127 million in 2011, $107 million in 2012, and $223 million in 2013. Only a future historian with access to the relevant documents might be able to shed light on the curious correlation between these data and Israel's political relations with African states over the past two decades.

For a decade after 1975 and the diplomatic avalanche, Israel had no official ties with most of the states in Africa. But it still maintained extensive relations in practice with several important ones, as no African state was in conflict with Israel at the bilateral level. At the same time, however, Africa was becoming more active in the areas of politics, economy, Islam, and public relations. In the political sphere, a vast network of Arab embassies emerged, with a presence in nearly every African country. In terms of propaganda, the Arabs spotlighted Israel's relations with South Africa, especially in the military nuclear arena, arguing that the two states threatened the security of African countries—Israel from the north and South Africa from the south. These efforts culminated in the UN General Assembly resolution of 1975, supported by most African states, condemning Zionism as a form of racism. In the economic sphere, Arab financial institutions emerged, offering aid to Africa. Examples include the United Fund for Aid to Africa and the Arab Bank for Economic Development in Africa.

This intensive, multifaceted range of activities in Africa was sufficient to forestall any renewal of relations for a decade and, subsequently, to delay the renewal process. A shift in relations between Arabs and Africans, as well as developments in Israel and the Middle East, eventually foiled the Arabs' efforts, and African states began reestablishing diplomatic ties with Israel. The process itself was quite gradual, lasting approximately two decades, as table 9.3 illustrates.

Among the factors that led to this revival of Israeli-African ties were Africa's disappointment in relation to Arab promises of financial assistance, Israel's withdrawal from the Sinai, the establishment of diplomatic relations with Egypt, the Oslo Accords, and the peace treaty with Jordan. This time Israel adopted a different approach, more practical and modest in its expectations than that of the 1960s. The new approach is characteristic of Israel's relationship with the forty-one African states with which it had diplomatic ties in 2011. The scope, political objectives, and energy invested by Israel come nowhere near those of four decades ago. Relations have undoubtedly been "normalized." As Neuberger argued, "It is hard not to conclude that the lost romanticism and idealism in Israel's relations with African states also tells us a great deal about the substantive difference between [idealist] Israel of the 1950s and [realist] Israel of the twenty-first century."[34]

Finally, we must examine the issue in the broader context of Israeli foreign relations. The severing of ties with sub-Saharan Africa was actually the second phase of the process of Israel's international isolation, which began with the stance adopted by the Soviet Union and the entire Eastern bloc immediately

Table 9.3. Renewal or Establishment of Relations between African Countries and Israel

Country	Date of renewal or establishment of relations	Establishment (E) or renewal country (R)
Egypt	March 26, 1979	E
Zaire	May 12, 1982	R
Liberia	August 13, 1983	R
Cote d'Ivoire	December 16, 1985	R
Cameroon	August 26, 1986	R
Togo	June 9, 1987	R
Kenya	December 23, 1988	R
Central African Republic	January 16, 1989	R
Ethiopia	November 3, 1989	R
Congo	July 14, 1991	R
Zambia	December 25, 1991	R
Angola	April 16, 1992	E
Nigeria	May 4, 1992	R
Sierra Leone	May 27, 1992	R
Seychelles	June 30, 1992	E
Benin	July 17, 1992	R
Gambia	September 14, 1992	R
Eritrea	May 24, 1993	E
Mozambique	July 26, 1993	E
Gabon	September 29, 1993	R
Mauritius	September 29, 1993	R
Burkina Faso	October 4, 1993	R
Sao Tome and Principe	November 16, 1993	E
Zimbabwe	November 26, 1993	E
Equatorial Guinea	December 5, 1993	R
Botswana	December 7, 1993	R
Namibia	January 21, 1994	E
Madagascar	January 27, 1994	R
Guinea-Bissau	March 10, 1994	E
Uganda	July 26, 1994	R
Cape Verde	July 27, 1994	E
Senegal	August 4, 1994	R
Ghana	August 9, 1994	R
Rwanda	October 10, 1994	R
Tanzania	February 24, 1995	R
Burundi	March 1, 1995	R

Source: Oded, "Africa in Israeli Foreign Policy."

after the Six-Day War. Thus, in 1973, Jerusalem faced the greatest political defeat in its history, when during the course of five years nearly forty states revoked recognition—more than the number of states that had supported Israel's creation in November 1947 at the UN. The painful culmination of these developments, from Israel's perspective, was the 1975 resolution equating Zionism with racism. These events were extremely traumatic for the Israeli leadership and underscored the vital importance of persisting in the efforts begun in 1948 to remove the stain of nonrecognition. It succeeded somewhat after forging diplomatic ties with Egypt and Jordan and launching negotiations with the Palestinians. Until then, as the next chapter describes, Washington was practically the only international player that mitigated Jerusalem's painful political isolation.

Notes

1. Golda Meir, *Khayai* [My life] (Tel Aviv, Maariv, 1975), 229.
2. Ibid., 230.
3. "Zaire/Israel," intelligence note, Bureau of Intelligence and Research, US State Department, October 12, 1973, NARA NND 969032.
4. Moshe Sharett, *Yoman Ishi* [Personal diary], vol. 6 (Tel Aviv, Maariv, 1978), 1722.
5. April 19, 1955. Israel State Archive ISA 2384\14.
6. Colin Legum, *Pan-Africanism* (New York, Praeger, 1962), 188.
7. Ehud Avriel, "Some Minute Circumstances (Memoir)," *Jerusalem Quarterly* 14 (1980): 28–40, cited in Arye Oded, "Africa in Israeli Foreign Policy—Expectations and Disenchantment: Historical and Diplomatic Aspects," *Israel Studies* 15, no. 3 (2010): 121–42.
8. Benyamin Neuberger, *Africa BeYakhasim HaBeinleumi'im* [Africa in international relations] (Raanana, The Open University, 2011), 146.
9. Ibid., 149.
10. Arye Oded, *Africa VeIsrael* [Africa and Israel] (Jerusalem, Magnes, 2011), 16.
11. Arye Oded, "Israel VeAfrica—Heibetin Histori'im VePoliti'im" [Israel and Africa—historical and political aspects], in *Misrad HaHutz—50 HaShanim HaRishonot* [Ministry of Foreign Affairs—the first 50 years], ed. Arye Oded, Yosef Govrin, and Moshe Yagar (Jerusalem, 2002), 618.
12. Neuberger, *Africa*, 158.
13. Zach Levey, *Israel in Africa, 1956–1976* (Leiden, Republic of Letters, 2012), 210.
14. Oded, *Africa VeIsrael*, 30.
15. Ibid., 33–34.
16. Ibid.
17. Ibid., 35.
18. Ronen Bergman, "Israel and Africa: Military and Intelligence Liaisons" (PhD diss., University of Cambridge, 2007), 90. For information on Israeli intelligence and the Arab-Israeli conflict at that time, see Amos Gilboa's bulky biography of Aharon Yariv, *Mr Intelligence—Arale Yariv* (Tel Aviv, Yediot, 2013) [in Hebrew].

19. Asher Orkaby, "The 1964 Israeli Airlift to Yemen and the Expansion of Weapons Diplomacy," *Diplomacy and Statecraft* 26, no. 4 (2015): 659–77.

20. Ibid.

21. Bergman, "Israel and Africa," 94. This PhD dissertation is the source of the following account and quotes until otherwise indicated.

22. Ibid., 108.

23. Ibid., 89–90.

24. Ibid., 157.

25. Ibid., 131.

26. David Ben-Uziel, *BeShlikhut HaMossad LeDrom Sudan, 196--1971: Pirkei Yoman Mivtza* [On a Mossad mission to South Sudan, 1969–1971: Chapters from an operations log] (Tel Aviv, 2016). On the "peripheral alliance" in Israel's foreign policy, see Yossi Alpher, *Periphery: Israel's Search for Middle East Allies* (Lanham, MD, Routledge, 2015); Jean-Loup Samaan, *Israel's Foreign Policy beyond the Arab World: Engaging the Periphery* (London, Routledge, 2017); Noa Schonmann, *Israel's Phantom Pact: Foreign Policy on the Periphery of the Middle East* (London, Tauris, 2018).

27. For more on this perspective, see Bergman, "Israel and Africa," chaps. 3, 9, and 10.

28. Bergman, "Israel and Africa," 269.

29. Oded, *Africa VeIsrael*, 68. The following analysis is based on Oded, *Africa VeIsrael*, 151–63, and Yegar et al., Ministry for Foreign Affairs, 620–22.

30. Ibid.

31. Ibid.

32. Ibid.

33. Oded, "Africa in Israeli Foreign Policy." *Israel Studies*, 15, no. 3 (2010).

34. Neuberger, *Africa*, 165–66.

10 The United States—the Chosen Venue

History and Historiography

Israel's special relationship with France only partially and temporarily fulfilled Herzl's diplomatic mandate of finding a major power to back the Zionist movement. The state did not begin to receive full superpower support until the late 1960s, when it became an ally of the United States in the full sense of the word—diplomatically, politically, militarily-strategically, and economically—forming a bond that continues and still grows strong. Thus, one often hears claims that Israel's ties with the United States are at the core of its foreign and defense policy. Indeed, among veteran Foreign Ministry officials it is taken as a given that "no Israeli emissary is worthy of the title 'experienced diplomat' unless he has served in Washington."[1]

These relations—of utmost importance for Jerusalem and among the more prominent in US diplomacy as well—have enjoyed a particularly rich historiography, which serves well as our point of departure. The historical research on this subject in relation to the American side is vast, embodying a number of conventions and controversies, and the first and most prominent theme in the orthodox literature revolves around a view expressed by President John Kennedy in late December 1962: "The United States . . . has a special relationship with Israel . . . really comparable only to [that] which it has with Britain."[2] Fifteen years later President Carter asserted that "we have a special relationship with Israel. It's absolutely critical that no one in our country or around the world ever doubt that our number one commitment in the Middle East is to protect the right of Israel to exist, to exist permanently, and to exist in peace."[3]

This view also featured prominently in statements by two US presidential candidates during the 2008 race. Barack Obama declared at the time that his commitment to Israel was intended "to make sure that the bond between the United States and Israel is unbreakable today, unbreakable tomorrow—and unbreakable forever."[4] Senator John McCain stated at the same opportunity that "we are the most natural of allies and like Israel itself—that alliance is forever."[5] The exceptional nature of this relationship was evident recently in a proclamation titled "The Death of Shimon Peres" issued by President Obama on September 29,

2016, ordering that all US flags across the country and in diplomatic missions around the globe be lowered to half-staff.

The existing literature also emphasizes common interests as well as values and ideals as the basic elements of these relations. As Jonathan Rynhold framed it, "Support for Israel goes beyond an empirical calculation of US interests. This is because the relationship is grounded on deep cultural foundations."[6] The literature further highlights the fact that the special treatment Israel receives has made it the world's leading recipient of US military and civilian aid: over the course of six decades, from independence until 2008, Israel received the monumental sum of $113 billion. Eight years later, the United States pledged to provide Israel with $38 billion in aid over the following ten years. By 2017, the US had provided Israel with aid totaling 125 billion new Israeli shekels (NIS), and the figure is expected to reach NIS 179 billion by the end of the next decade. This exceeds the amount of aid provided to any other country since World War II.[7] These figures explain why the literature has identified a pattern of "patron-client relations" between the two countries, with the United States as major grantor, particularly in strategic areas, and Israel providing input through its policy on the Arab-Israeli conflict and in the form of military cooperation.

At the same time, scholars have focused not only on agreements between the two countries but also on confrontations, which according to Rynhold have not diminished over the years: "While this special relationship continues to endure, beneath the surface those foundations are shifting in conflicting directions. For in the first decade of the twenty-first century, a paradox has emerged in the way America relates to Israel. On the one hand, Americans identify with Israel and sympathy for Israel is widespread, surging to new heights. On the other hand, Americans are increasingly divided about the Arab-Israeli conflict, and this division increasingly aligns with the major political, ideological, and religious divides in America."[8] The academic and public debate in the United States reveals intense disagreement around the interpretation of other issues as well. The question of why such a special relationship exists in the first place has received a variety of explanations. Some observers relate it to evangelical support for Israel, during the past three decades in particular, while others emphasize shared democratic principles. There are also those who point to the ideological partnership between the Israeli Right and Republican "New Conservatives" as the main explanation for this phenomenon. Within academia, there are currently three main types of interpretation: the first underscores the US national interest, the second highlights the role of the pro-Israel lobby, and the third emphasizes American political culture. The first approach, accordingly, centers on national security considerations that emphasize US recognition of Israel as a security asset. The corresponding analyses also highlight disputes that have arisen regarding this question during various administrations, as well as the perspective that Israel is actually a burden. Alongside those who answered this question in the affirmative, there were always detractors. Among the first to give voice to the negative perspective was George Kennan, then head of the planning division in the State Department. In January 1948 he argued that Arab hostility and the Arab states' opposition to the partition plan and establishment of a Jewish state prevented the United States from supporting Jewish aspirations, and that the vast and insurmountable differences between Jews and Arabs would inevitably destabilize and disrupt the entire Middle East. Kennan also predicted that any future Jewish state would be dependent on external political and military aid, which at the time only the United States could provide. In the view of this experienced and influential US diplomat, such a commitment did not serve the US national interest.[9]

As we know, Israel's strategic ties with the United States solidified only after the Six-Day War. One of the factors that delayed the formation of this alliance was the reverberations from Kennan's assessment. American political support for Israel peaked in 1948, under President Truman, when the United States backed the founding of the state. In the years that followed, however, under Eisenhower and Dulles, relations turned and remained chilly. The United States refused to supply Israel with arms, and the economic aid that it provided during those years did not deviate substantially from what was customary at the time. During the 1950s the United States was indeed interested in maintaining Israel's stability and provided modest economic aid toward this end, for which Jerusalem had to pay through the partial loss of its own economic freedom, a decline in standing in the international market, and presumably a loss of political status. Reparations from Germany (albeit with US support) provided Israel's main base of economic support and played a part in saving the state from the existential economic threat it faced at the time. Direct, substantial US aid began to arrive only during the late 1960s and early 1970s. At the same time, however, the United States refused to include Israel in plans for the establishment of international defense organizations in the Middle East and applied various forms of pressure aimed at softening its stance on the Arab-Israeli conflict. A salient dispute among historians relates to the timing of and reasons behind the shift that led to the special relationship—whether it occurred during the Kennedy or Johnson administration, or perhaps even during Eisenhower's second term. This controversy underscores the vast differences among various US presidents and administrations with respect to Israel. The topic has remained a subject of academic analysis, which aims to differentiate the individual contributions of subsequent presidents (Nixon, Carter, Reagan, Bush, and Obama) to US-Israel relations. The current literature emphasizes vicissitudes in US policy toward Israel that nonetheless tended to move in a generally linear direction.

The Jewish lobby has also been a focus of historiographical dispute, specifically the question of who is driving whom: Is it the "tail" (Jews and pro-Zionist pressure groups in the United States) wagging the "dog" (the presidents) or vice versa, as John Mearsheimer and Stephen Walt argue in a study that sparked a great deal of controversy.[10]

The extent of Jewish engagement in the bilateral US-Israel relationship is also a matter of debate. Emily Alice Katz, who explores the cultural aspect of American Jewry in this context, including the extensive promotion and consumption of Israel in the American cultural realm, concludes that "Israel served as an increasingly significant touchstone in the American Jewish imagination in the decades after Israel's founding."[11] Others have a different view. Dov Waxman, for example, suggests in his new book on Israel's place in the American Jewish community that "In a fundamental shift, growing numbers of American Jews have become less willing to unquestioningly support Israel and more willing to publicly criticize its government. More than ever before, American Jews are arguing about Israeli policies, and many, especially younger ones, are becoming uncomfortable with Israel's treatment of Palestinians. . . . Israel is fast becoming a source of disunity for American Jewry. . . . A new era of American Jewish conflict over Israel is replacing the old era of solidarity."[12]

The third interpretation, too, is a matter of controversy—between proponents of the rationalist-materialist, neorealist, neoliberal, and Marxist paradigms, who emphasize the "hard" elements of foreign policy and tend to dismiss the influence of political culture, on the one hand, and conservatives and others who highlight "soft" factors, on the other; between those who emphasize considerations of foreign policy and those who stress domestic policy; between those who focus on the objective factors of realpolitik and those who concentrate on the personal facets of US presidents. Other scholars have examined the transformation that the pro-Israel lobby underwent. Samuel Taylor, for example, distinguishes between the first wave of this lobby, which "focused primarily on the security concerns of the Israeli state, often ignored, dodged, or outright rejected the notion of a sovereign Palestinian state [and] emphasized, above all else, the 'Jewish' nature of the state," and "the 'new' Pro-Israel camp, [which] tends to focus primarily on achieving 'peace' in Israel-Palestine, accepts a Palestinian state as a requisite in achieving this 'peace'[and] emphasizes, above all else, the 'liberal' and 'democratic' nature of the Israeli state."[13]

The vast and wide-ranging literature on US-Israeli relations explores these disputes and examines the US interest in its relationship with Israel during times of acute regional conflict, times of war, and the processes of concluding peace treaties in which the United States was often intensely involved (and which, at least in one instance—the 1973 War—nearly sparked a nuclear confrontation with the Soviet Union). There is also an immense, in-depth, and continuously expanding body of declassified historical material in the United States, Israel, and many other countries, which has become available and informs this field of research. Rynhold's authoritative study, for example, includes a twenty-seven-page bibliography with some five hundred entries. Dennis Ross's recent book on US-Israeli relations, *Doomed to Succeed*, lists an even larger number of references.[14]

At the same time, however, the historiography is blatantly disproportionate in its representation of the American as opposed to the Israeli perspective. Although the topic naturally requires exploring both points of view, the many volumes devoted to the subject address it mainly from the perspective of Washington looking outward, offering rich material for enlightening analyses in this context. Conversely, studies that explore Israeli policy—that is, the perspective of Jerusalem looking outward—and in particular its consistent core elements over time, are few. The academic studies in this area do indeed contribute to a better understanding of the issue, but they are too limited in number to generate differing schools of thought or materially different approaches worthy of exploration in themselves.

This disproportionality has several possible explanations. The first and perhaps most significant is the mundane reality of demographics. The topic naturally engages a larger number of citizens as well as pressure groups, institutes of higher education, and academic specialists in the United States than in Israel. For all these individuals and entities, the primary and overriding perspective is of course the American one. No doubt the more liberal American approach to declassification of state documents is also a factor. We know that a large number of Israel's historical documents dealing with military and intelligence issues remain classified even after three decades have passed, and the trend (among national security authorities) is to increase rather than relax secrecy. Moreover, large numbers of American politicians and state functionaries have made a practice out of writing their memoirs, some of which focus on US-Israeli relations. The figure among Israelis pales in comparison. Rare examples include Moshe Bitan's eye-opening memoir,[15] in which he analyzes his role as deputy director general of the Foreign Ministry, particularly in shaping relations with the United States, and the highly detailed political biography of Zalman Shoval, Israel's ambassador to Washington in 1990–1993.[16] We must also account for the language barrier facing many American and other academic researchers, who cannot examine the steadily growing body of Hebrew-language documents available in Israel. And finally, given the exceptional importance of this relationship for the very existence of the state, there is a peculiar dearth of academics who specialize in this area at Israeli universities—fewer than half a dozen.

But perhaps most interesting and relevant to understanding the phenomenon is the conceptual perspective adopted in writing about the issue. The characteristics of US-Israeli relations dictated that most of the time it was Washington rather than Jerusalem that held the keys: the asymmetry of a superpower and a small state, the enormous economic and military disparity, the difference in global standing and influence, and the fact that Israel was traditionally the seeker of aid while the United States was the one that provided or denied such aid. As Yaacov Bar-Siman-Tov explains, "The notion of a special relationship should be considered mainly from the US point of view because of the asymmetrical interdependence of the relationship. Fluctuations in the relationship have been primarily resolved from US assessments of global and regional factors, rather than shifts in Israel's interests or behavior."[17]

This is the prevailing perspective among scholars in the field, most of whom are American. Prominent examples include Isaac Alteras, who examined US-Israeli relations under Eisenhower,[18] and Warren Bass, who explored the origins of the strategic alliance that formed under Kennedy.[19] Israelis, too, have adopted this outlook, as exemplified by Abraham Ben-Zvi in his comprehensive studies on the formative periods of these relations.[20] Even Israeli diplomats have come to accept this perspective, as Hanan Bar-On, a senior official in the Foreign Ministry and a former political envoy in Washington, illustrated. In an eye-opening retrospective spanning fifty years of diplomatic relations between Israel and the United States, he asserts that it was more appropriate to focus on the American rather than the Israeli perspective, adding that "relations between two states that are so different in size and power cannot be symmetrical, and Israel's dependence on the United States is self-evident."[21]

That approach, it is important to note, misses the opportunity for any crosscutting historical analysis of the complex fundamental problems that have preoccupied Israeli policy makers since the founding of the state, as summarized by Noam Kochavi:

> How should Jerusalem conduct itself, when the White House knowingly adopts a policy that Jerusalem views as a threat to national security? Is it possible to predict, with some degree of reliability, the balance of profits and losses for Israel if it decides to publicly and blatantly oppose the US president and the White House? Moreover, when a substantial (and legitimate) dispute arises within the Israeli leadership regarding basic questions of policy, is it appropriate to reveal the dispute to the US leadership and "invite" its intervention, which might tip the balance one way or another? And finally, in the event of a dispute between Jerusalem and Washington, is it legitimate for Jewish leaders, in conjunction with the [US] government, to apply pressure on Israel? Or are American Jewish leaders obligated, under all circumstances, to act on Israel's behalf and exert pressure on Washington?[22]

An exceptional book in this regard is *Fishing with the President: The Rise of the Diplomatic Spin* by former Israeli diplomat Yitzhak Oren.[23] Drawing on both experience and documentation, Oren explores the dividing line between the theatrical posturing of leaders and actual policy in four cases: the loan guarantees crisis, Israel's willingness to participate in the Madrid Summit, the expulsion of Hamas leaders, and the approval of loan guarantees.

Two lesser-known facts are worth noting in this context. First, we still await a comprehensive, in-depth study of the evolution of Israeli policy (as distinct from the American one) in this area since 1948. Second, there already exists a solid foundation for such research thanks to Joseph Heller's thorough and pioneering study, *Israel and the Cold War*[24] (covering the years preceding the Six-Day War), and to the more recent publication by Natan Aridan, *Advocating for Israel: Diplomats and Lobbyists from Truman to Nixon*[25] (covering later years as well).

In light of the historiographic focus on the American perspective and relative neglect of the Israeli point of view, and given the overall aim of this book as well as limitations in scope, I have decided to concentrate in the remainder of this chapter on the Israeli perspective as it relates to a central and singular issue in the foreign policy of both states. Doing so allows us to examine several differing Israeli approaches to an issue that has yet to be comprehensively summarized and analyzed: Israel's struggle for American recognition of its right to possess nuclear weapons, from the early 1950s until after the Six-Day War. The topic has enjoyed more than a little historiographic coverage, despite the secrecy imposed by both sides. Existing studies on the physical development of Israel's nuclear capability still have many gaps and await the historian who can access state documents. Avner Cohen, a leading researcher in this field, has opined that Israel's near-absolute secrecy entirely undermines historical research on the issue.[26] In any event, our concise presentation of this political episode highlights an important aspect of the overall pattern of relations between the two countries: despite being a superpower, the United States often failed to impose its will on little Israel.

Nuclear Weapons for Israel

The main driving force behind Israel's decision to develop a nuclear capability was, as noted, Ben-Gurion's existential fear for the future of the state. In November 1948, presumably before the decision was made, he wrote in his diary, "Will there be an end? Even if the war ends now . . . will a peace treaty be concluded? Has there been a war that was not preceded by peace? We need to look not at resolutions and documents but at historical reality, what is our reality? We defeated the Arab nations . . . 600,000 overcame 3 million. Will they soon forget?"[27] Besides a categorical *no* in response to this question, the "old man" felt that Israel must proceed on the assumption that the circumstances that prevailed during the 1948 War would not repeat themselves in the future; rather, he was certain, future circumstances would pose even greater challenges for Israel in a military confrontation with the Arab states. In his view the ongoing truce since the end of the 1948 War was only temporary and had to be exploited to prepare for a second round of hostilities that would be imposed on Israel. He continued to feel this way even after Israel's remarkable victory in the Six-Day War. For years after retiring as prime minister, Ben-Gurion observed that he was not certain that this would be the "final war," adding that the Six-Day War "is not the last battle. . . . That is the difference between our victory and their potential victory, and if they defeat us, they will destroy us."[28] He also believed that modern battlefield changes would introduce advanced weapons systems into the region, which—even if Israel emerged victorious—would exact a heavy and painful toll for states seeking to conduct a Western lifestyle as a "normal" civil society. Accordingly, the reconstruction process for Israel following every war would be successively more difficult and would take longer. And finally, although he placed great value on strategic ties with major powers, the Sinai Campaign of 1956 (during and after which the United States blatantly turned its back on Britain, its traditional ally) increased his skepticism regarding their dependability. Therefore, and given that Israel would have to face these threats for the foreseeable future, Ben-Gurion decided very early on the nuclear option. Aside from these decisive conclusions, the Israeli leader left no further explanation among publicly available documents regarding his regional military-strategic analysis and his prognosis for state of affairs after Israel acquired nuclear weapons, especially given the possibility that the Arabs would follow suit. Nor did he reveal his thoughts on the question of whether nuclear weapons would allow for drastic cuts in conventional weaponry. He also remained silent on the overriding question of whether nuclear weapons could in time lead the Arabs to accept Israel's existence, or whether it would become a "Samson" option, as one analyst framed the issue.[29]

At the same time, the "old man" could not avoid making practical strategic decisions, in light of three major developments that took place in the late 1950s and early 1960s. The first was the formation, followed by the destabilization, of the nuclear alliance between Israel and France. The second was the construction of the reactor in Dimona, which symbolized the actualization of Israel's military nuclear capability. The third, and related, development was the effort by the United States to dissuade Israel from fully realizing this option. As we now know, Israel began taking concrete steps to implement its decision, primarily in the field of nuclear development for peaceful purposes, around the mid-1950s, when the French-Israeli connection solidified, and continued briefly under de Gaulle. The agreements signed between the two states obligated France to provide uranium and technical and industrial support for the construction of a civil reactor as well as a plant for plutonium production. The official agreed-upon aim was to construct a research facility for peaceful uses of nuclear energy, and in late October 1957 Israel pledged that if the nature of activity shifted from research for civilian purposes to military purposes, France would be entitled to terminate aid and cease cooperation. In subsequent years France also applied great pressure on Israel to disclose its nuclear activities, threatening that it would place the latter under international oversight. In mid-May 1960, accordingly, the French government—keen on receiving nuclear assistance from the United States, which in turn fiercely opposed nuclear proliferation—informed Israel that international oversight of its nuclear activities would be mandatory. These developments conflicted with the actual and original aim of Israel's nuclear program, namely, the cultivation of a military nuclear capability. A collision seemed inevitable and indeed took place when Shimon Peres, as director general of the Ministry of Defense, visited Paris in early June of that year, and again a few days later during a meeting between de Gaulle and Ben-Gurion. The stance Israel adopted during these encounters reflects a policy that continued to manifest in various forms during subsequent years. The overall tone of Israel's initial approach indicates an attempt at evasion, which it evidently and mistakenly thought might be possible, as its research had not yet reached the stage that would allow (or necessitate) deciding on the direction of further activity. Peres also rejected the demand for international oversight, proposing instead a more lax form of supervision by the European Atomic Energy Community (EAEC or Euratom). Ben-Gurion, for his part, sought to make de Gaulle understand the basis for Israel's dire forecast regarding a future war with Egypt, "in which Jews would fight to the death. Even if we win, the cost would be unbearable. Israel cannot afford such a loss after such a large portion of the Jewish People have already been annihilated by the Nazis."[30] As a practical matter, however, Ben-Gurion agreed that Israel would refrain from using the plutonium produced at Dimona for military purposes.

Yet the French persisted. In early August 1960, Foreign Minister Maurice Couve de Murville conveyed France's position on oversight to Israel and made compliance a condition for further support. Israel made it clear that it would not accept international oversight, and the French in turn announced that they would terminate cooperation within a few months. This turn of events "left Israel out in the cold" and exposed the difficulties and risks in maintaining the military nature of its nuclear program. Ultimately, French Minister of Energy Jacques Soustelle, a Gaullist and friend of Israel, delayed the implementation of France's decision, and negotiations resumed toward the end of that year, at which time France agreed to fulfill the terms of its agreement while Israel committed itself to returning enriched uranium to France so that it could not be used for military purposes. The Americans were to be kept informed of these developments. Israel subsequently sought to evade French oversight by purchasing from other suppliers, such as Argentina and South Africa. Consequently, in April 1963 France cut off uranium supplies to Israel.

The Internal Scene

This development, perhaps more than anything else, explains the echoes (albeit few in number) that remain in writings about the internal debate that raged in the Israeli government during those years surrounding the question "Where are we headed?" in the nuclear arena. Despite the dearth of available documentation, recent studies have revealed that from the early 1950s fierce disputes already existed within Israel's leadership and scientific community regarding the nuclear option, and these disputes only intensified over time. The disagreement itself touched on complex issues that surfaced in the early 1960s and became a point of contention between Israel and the United States. As such, these issues deserve further examination, and we can extract a few salient points from the available documentation regarding supporters and opponents of the nuclear option. First, the documentation not only confirms the consensus behind Ben-Gurion but also provides detail regarding the complex measures taken to implement this decision even before 1960. The evidence is unmistakably clear about Ben-Gurion's personal, political, and ideological commitment to this implementation—operationally as well as politically—despite the fierce opposition he encountered. In the former sphere, he was assisted mainly by Ernst Bergmann, and in the latter by Shimon Peres. One of the important measures in the operational sphere was the complete concentration of the issue in the Office of the Prime Minister and the Ministry of Defense, with the Foreign Ministry largely neutralized. Beginning in 1955, notably, the Israeli Embassy in Washington was prohibited from having any nuclear contacts in the United States. Because of the compartmentalization of all nuclear activities—including related financial aspects—and their concentration in the hands of three individuals, the Ministry of Finance was also excluded from direct engagement. Those involved in the issue circumvented the state budget and often kept the cabinet itself in the dark regarding their activities. Ben-Gurion, Peres, and Bergmann were, in essence, working intensely to advance nuclear research and development for military rather than civilian purposes. They also consistently refused to reimburse their nuclear suppliers in the form of external oversight, and for this reason they preferred French over American assistance. The veil of secrecy behind which these three pursued the issue certainly played to their favor in confrontations with opponents of Ben-Gurion's position. The available information demonstrates indisputably that not everyone accepted his and Peres's diagnosis or prognosis. These disagreements led to the resignation of the entire Israel Atomic Energy Commission except its chief, Ernst Bergmann. Some of the commission members were senior scientists who opposed the nuclear option, doubted its value, questioned its cost, and feared it would lead to "brain drain" for Israel in the scientific realm. Some even saw Bergmann as a Doctor Strangelove[31] of sorts—irresponsible and unprofessional—and regarded the senior operational agent alongside him, director general of the Ministry of Defense Shimon Peres, as working hand in hand with French nationalists precisely at a time when the struggle against nuclear proliferation and the threat of nuclear war was at its peak.[32] Bergmann himself, it should be noted, firmly believed that nuclear proliferation was unpreventable and saw the Chinese nuclear test of October 16, 1964, as irrefutable proof of his position. In a rare interview with the Israeli newspaper *Ma'ariv* in April 1965, he argued that "we are facing a very rapid expansion of the nuclear club; those who believe that East and West have reached an agreement on the proliferation of nuclear weapons are very naïve; the Chinese atomic bomb has changed the situation in the world and it is about time that they understand it."[33] At the time Bergmann was also among those most deeply immersed in clandestine cooperation with Taiwan, which in turn was linked to both countries' efforts to secretly develop a nuclear option. Their ambitions clashed with the firmly negative American stance, as Yitzhak Shichor revealed in a recent study, and with opposition on the part of Israel's Foreign Ministry (which was not always in the loop regarding Bergmann's adventures in this area).[34]

Moral, economic, and practical considerations, on the other hand, led to skepticism among many university researchers. Today we know that during the mid-1950s some of Israel's leading scientists—including Israel Dostrovsky, Igal Talmi, and Aharon Katzir from the Weizmann Institute—were in favor of acquiring a nuclear reactor from the United States for energy production and research purposes, and they were fully aware that the latter conditioned such a deal on a commitment to refrain from nuclear activities for military purposes. That condition was, as noted, the main reason that Bergmann preferred French assistance.

Nor did the internal dispute bypass the defense establishment. In April 1959, while discussing Israel's nuclear research, Meyer Weisgal, director of the Weizmann Institute, told Britain's ambassador to Israel that

> There had for some time been a heated argument within the Ministry of Defense as to whether Israel should or should not try to acquire the atomic bomb. Brigadier [Dan] Tolkowsky, who was moved on last year from heading the Air Force to be a "planner" in the Ministry, had apparently been set to carry out a review of Israel's atomic policy. He had concluded that it would be foolish for Israel to try and get an atomic bomb, both because of the expense and because even if Israel were successful, the Soviet Union would undoubtedly arm the Arab countries in similar fashion. Tolkowsky's view was supported by the majority of senior professional soldiers in Israel who thought it wise that the Middle East should be kept bomb-free. Peres on the other hand was extremely keen to have the bomb and had been saying he was sure that he would get it from the French.[35]

Finally, the issue was also the focus of an internal political confrontation. During the mid-1950s several prominent members of MAPAI itself opposed Ben-Gurion's pursuit of a nuclear capability, among them Moshe Sharett, Pinchas Sapir, and Foreign Minister Golda Meir, who feared that a confrontation with the United States over the reactor in Dimona at the start of her term could damage US-Israeli relations, as did Isser Harel, head of the Mossad. The latter two advised Ben-Gurion to adopt certain measures, the practical outcome of which, according to biographer Michael Bar-Zohar, would have been "the elimination" of Israel's nuclear program.[36]

MAPAI's political rivals, especially within Ahdut HaAvoda, also criticized the "old man's" nuclear plans. Yigal Allon, in particular, persistently raised pointed questions about the implications of Israel becoming a nuclear power, including the international opposition it would trigger; the anticipated Arab reaction of making every effort to acquire such weaponry as well; Israel's lack of a second-strike capability, which would accelerate the arms race; and the inherent instability of the Arab world, which could lead to a nuclear holocaust. According to Avner Cohen, Ahdut HaAvoda ministers Yigal Allon and Yisrael Galili claimed that it was necessary to maintain a "technological edge" in the nuclear field, "but we must be careful not to bring about, with [our] own hands, denuclearization of the region. . . . They believed that if we become a nuclear state, as Peres and later Dayan wanted, then it was inevitable that the entire Middle East would become nuclear [armed]; that if Israel became nuclear, then it would not be possible to prevent the other side from acquiring its own nuclear weapons. Sooner or later, a nuclear arms race would ensue, and that was their nightmare."[37] Ben-Gurion also drew criticism from members of the Israeli establishment who supported the Dimona project. The most prominent critic was Shimon Peres himself, who at the time advocated the radically hawkish view that the State of Israel should openly join the nuclear club, as France had done only three years earlier. Peres, who was greatly influenced by the ideas of the French strategist Pierre Marie Gallois regarding the importance of an independent nuclear deterrent, openly advocated a substantial revision of Israel's security concept, with the IDF transformed into a technologically advanced military based primarily on nuclear weapons and outer space rather than conventional arms. All in all, Ben-Gurion often had to navigate tricky, uncertain waters and overcome manifold internal obstacles in pursuit of his nuclear vision.

Three comments are in order regarding the internal Israeli debate and its implications for relations with the United States during the 1960s. The first is that although the debate was apparently intense, it took place relatively quietly and discreetly. Of particular note, even those who did not support the Dimona project generally refrained from overt defiance or internal instigation against Israel's development of a nuclear option. "There is no doubt," notes Yehuda Ben-Meir, "that for [years] there was a consensus among all the Zionist parties to refrain from public debate on the nuclear issue and to avoid almost any public reference to the issue. Presumably this indicates some sort of rapprochement among the parties. . . . But it involved not only the parties. Remarkably, the Israeli media also accepted this consensus . . . and exercised great restraint in its handling of the issue."[38] The public's acquiescence in maintaining secrecy evidently stemmed from a broad-based agreement with the establishment's view that the Arabs sought to destroy Israel, from the prevailing assessment that the realization of this threat was not an impossibility, and finally from the intense respect that Ben-Gurion and his positions enjoyed in the realm of security, even among those who opposed his views.

Second, as it happened, the internal debate and opposition to Ben-Gurion's policy gained momentum and came to the public eye in 1960, after American U-2 reconnaissance aircraft, flying above the interception range of the Israeli Air Force, discovered that suspicious construction was underway southeast of Be'er Sheva. In early March 1960, Israel received an official query about the nature of these structures, to which it responded that they constituted a textile factory. A few months later, Israel informed the United States that the facilities were intended for metallurgical research related to a university network under construction in the Negev. Experts in the CIA were not convinced of the veracity of these responses, and in the first week of December of that year, CIA chief Allen Dulles reported that Israel was building a nuclear complex in the Negev, with French assistance, including a reactor capable of producing plutonium for military uses. Besides its attempts at evasion, Israel also tried to convey its fears of annihilation as a rationale for US assistance, without mentioning its covert nuclear activities at this stage. In mid-March 1960, Ben-Gurion made a concerted effort to explain to President Eisenhower that Egyptian president Nasser's goal was the destruction of the State of Israel and extermination of its Jewish community—just as Hitler had done to six million Jews—a threat that in his view would be realized within a few years unless Israel received weapons for its defense from the United States.

Third, evidently the Americans were well aware of the debate in Israel between proponents and opponents of the nuclear option, and the arguments raised in this debate did influence the US position. Indeed, the US Embassy in Tel Aviv routinely provided Washington with detailed reports on Israel's internal disputes in this area.

Facing Washington

In any event, Washington eventually began exerting diplomatic pressure on Israel. On December 9 of that year, US Secretary of State Christian Archibald

Herter expressed to the Israeli ambassador, Avraham Harman, the grave concern of the United States regarding Israel's nuclear activities and its attempts to conceal them from the Americans. The evidently unprepared Israeli diplomat was shown detailed satellite photos of the Dimona reactor and presented with an expert US assessment of the cost of this very big project—roughly $80 million.[39] On the previous day, CIA chief Allen Dulles had told the National Security Council that in order to fund such an expensive project, Israel was using donations from Jewish individuals and organizations in the United States who then enjoyed a tax exemption for their contributions. Herter informed Harman that when the facts came to bear, they would have a devastating effect on the Middle East and on American interests. As such, the United States sought his confirmation that the reactor was intended solely for civilian purposes. Herter also noted that the Soviet Union had accused the United States of being a "silent partner" in building the reactor, that there was concern the Soviet Union might be driven to provide nuclear assistance to states in its camp, and that the United States opposed the proliferation of nuclear weapons, especially in the "powder keg" of the Middle East. As a direct result of these developments, Israel's nuclear activity came to light in the international media a week later. These leaks, which included photographs of the reactor, came from American sources, in the view of Zaki Shalom. The leaks themselves, according to Israeli assessments, were intended to create a hostile international atmosphere focused on Israel, which would pave the way for massive pressure to shut down the Dimona project.[40]

This event forced Israel to confront the US pressure and formulate an operational strategy, which had been lacking for nearly a decade. The first step was to remove, in part, the veil of secrecy surrounding its nuclear project—first and foremost with respect to the United States. On December 20, therefore, Harman provided Herter with information about the reactor in Dimona, including details about its size, an assessment that its construction would be completed within about four years with French and "other" assistance, and a pledge that it was intended for scientific research purposes that would in the future serve to advance civilian economic development. On the following day, Ben-Gurion disclosed the existence of the Dimona project before the Knesset, emphasizing that it was intended "solely for peaceful purposes." The motive behind this false and convoluted statement was that Israel could not at this stage acknowledge the true nature of its nuclear program, as such a declaration would have obliged the superpowers, and the United States foremost, to apply heavy pressure on Jerusalem to allow close inspection of its "textile enterprise" in Dimona, something Ben-Gurion had regarded as taboo since the 1950s.

To reinforce its message and lend it credibility, Jerusalem established two channels of indirect communication with Washington by way of Canadian diplomats. A day before Ben-Gurion's dramatic declaration at the Knesset, the director general of the Prime Minister's Office, Teddy Kollek, a close associate of his superior with many contacts among American officials, met with the Canadian ambassador to Israel. Kollek admitted that Israel's leaders had discussed the issue of nuclear weapons on more than one occasion, that the political decision remained firmly negative, and that the veil of secrecy that had been imposed over the reactor's construction constituted "unforgivable foolishness" on the part of Israeli authorities.[41] On the same day, the Israeli ambassador in Ottawa, Yaakov Herzog, also a well-known "Ben-Gurionist," met with Canadian Foreign Ministry officials and confessed that the revelations about the reactor were causing Israel discomfort, for which he blamed Israel's own "mania for secrecy."[42] This gentle self-flagellation was presumably intended to convey to the Americans, through their traditional allies the Canadians, that Israel had no reason to conceal its activities at the reactor.

In pragmatic terms, Israel intended this message to calm the spirits in Washington, curtail further public—and what Jerusalem viewed as concrete—discussion of the issue, and enable rapprochement to proceed by way of quiet diplomacy. From the US point of view, talks between the two were intended to convey a singular message: Israel must not cultivate any illusions that it would be permitted to continue its nuclear activities undisturbed. The message also enabled outgoing President Eisenhower's administration to avoid the need for drastic, far-reaching measures in advance of President-Elect Kennedy's entry into office. Such measures would, in any event, have exceeded Eisenhower's authority at this point. At the time the US government also had a strong interest in maintaining calm within the Arab world in the aftermath of Ben-Gurion's declaration. A public rebuke of Israel would have confirmed that it was on the verge of crossing the nuclear threshold, which would have reduced US options vis-à-vis Israel in the diplomatic sphere. Ultimately, therefore, the parties agreed to avoid any public discussion of the issue for the time being. Before two weeks had passed, however, a confrontation erupted.

On January 4, 1961, the US ambassador to Israel met with Ben-Gurion and Foreign Minister Golda Meir and demanded that "by midnight" they provide answers to four questions: What would Israel do with the plutonium produced at the reactor? Would Israel agree to inspections by representatives of the Atomic Energy Commission or of friendly countries? What was Jerusalem's position on the implementation of International Atomic Energy Agency (IAEA) safeguards? And was its highest political echelon willing to make unequivocal commitments regarding the nature and objectives of the Dimona project? Israel tried to soften the tone of this message by extending the deadline for answers and inviting the US ambassador to meet with Ben-Gurion in Sde Boker. It rejected the demand regarding the IAEA (until other members of the international community accepted safeguards as well) and explained that the plutonium produced at Dimona would be returned, as required, to France. It agreed to allow inspections only by representatives of friendly states: "We do not want hostile countries stirring our pot."[43] Israel also expressed willingness to provide the administration with an unequivocal commitment that the reactor would not be used for the production of nuclear weapons. However, Jerusalem's resistance in the face of US pressure for more information was already evident at this stage. Ben-Gurion's instructions to Foreign Ministry officials were quite brazen, considering how dependent Israel was on the United States at the time. He ordered his subordinates to make it clear to their interlocutors that "there are certain things we do not want you to know about. You will simply have to accept that."[44] Yet the pressure to formulate understandings and reach an agreement came not only from Washington. Ben-Gurion was concerned that the new US administration, once firmly established, would easily be able to take measures unfavorable to the Dimona project. Against this backdrop, Jerusalem decided to request a summit meeting between Kennedy and Ben-Gurion. In preparation for this meeting, on May 30, 1961, Israel dispatched a series of messages to Washington that were intended to pave the way specifically for future foreign inspections of the facility. Secrecy was also mandatory for other reasons: Israel's move was not unrelated to precarious political developments on the domestic front, with the MAPAI leadership facing the aftereffects of what came to be known as the "Lavon affair."[45]

The major threat in Israel's view was that international inspections might expose the reactor to public scrutiny, directly or indirectly, through the Soviet Union. Alongside the negative stance Israel adopted, Ben-Gurion fully understood that an inspection of Dimona would be a precondition for Kennedy to consent to a meeting with him. In a clever maneuver, he therefore agreed to have two American scientists of the Atomic Energy Commission visit the plant in advance of his own meeting with the American president. In retrospect we can surmise that this brief inspection, which took place in mid-May, was unlikely to have included all the facilities in the complex. In any event, the report submitted by the scientists highlighted the civil purposes, or "atoms for peace," nature, of the project, and recommended that another inspection take place the following year to ensure that no change had occurred in this regard. It also noted, however, that Israel was capable at the time of producing a "small nuclear weapon." This report, which one State Department official later described as an "acquittal" based on lack of evidence, undoubtedly served Israel well.

An interesting historical question is why the US administration accepted this conclusion. Even more mysterious is the praise the report received from Kennedy during his meeting with Ben-Gurion and his soft-toned responses to the latter's argument that because Israel's nuclear project was a cooperative endeavor with France, further inspections by American scientists were not necessary. Most puzzling of all is Ben-Gurion's assertion that even though the reactor was intended for peaceful purposes, within three or four years Israel might be interested in building a plutonium separation plant (a step toward nuclear weapons production).

The complete, and only recently declassified, protocol of the Kennedy–Ben-Gurion meeting at the Waldorf Astoria Hotel in New York reveals that the Israeli leader's message was that "for now" the reactor was intended only for peaceful uses, "but we shall see what happens in the Middle East." The message was vague not only in the textual sense. A review of the transcript indicates that Ben-Gurion spoke "quickly and softly," making it difficult for the transcriber to follow and for Kennedy to pose concrete questions. "Ben-Gurion was swallowing his words. It was hard for me to hear and understand exactly what was being said, also because of his accent." In his selection of words and manner of speech, Ben-Gurion, in the view of Israeli historian Avner Cohen, "created a vagueness of sorts, knowingly or unknowingly, so that it would not appear in retrospect that he was blatantly lying to the president."[46]

Israel therefore responded with a very qualified *yes* to the American demands of early January 1961, while Kennedy voiced no reservations. The understanding between the two leaders also provided that American government officials would conduct annual inspections of Dimona and that Jerusalem would not object to the findings being shared with Egypt. The reasons underpinning the American approach presumably stemmed from several factors: the positive steps taken by Israel; the young and inexperienced Kennedy's reluctance to engage in a frontal confrontation with the "old man"; Kennedy's impression of the latter's commitment to the nuclear project and opposition to international inspections; concern about dramatically upsetting the Israeli political system, which was absorbed in the Lavon Affair; and above all, the more pressing problems the United States was facing at the time, such as Cuba.

Israel's acrobatic maneuvers, aimed mainly at obscuring its nuclear intentions, were successful. The United States accepted this state of vagueness for a few months, until the situation changed radically after the consolidation of an assessment in Washington that Israel was indeed seeking nuclear weapons. In October 1961, the CIA completed a National Intelligence Estimate on Israel, which unequivocally concluded that the true aim of the reactor at Dimona was the production of nuclear weapons: "At the very least, we believe that Israel is developing its nuclear facilities in such a way that it will be able to produce nuclear weapons quickly . . . should Israel decide to do so"—in the language of the document.[47] The forecast was that by 1965 or 1966, Israel would have enough nuclear material for two bombs. These findings correlated, in the CIA's view, with Israel's postponement of inspections in mid-1962.

After repeated delays, in September 1962 Jerusalem permitted two representatives of the US Atomic Energy Commission, who were in Israel for a semiannual inspection of the reactor at Nahal Sorek, to visit Dimona. But the unusual nature of this visit suggests that Israel was deliberately concealing something. The two Americans had arrived for a routine inspection at the Nahal Sorek Nuclear Research Center. The scientific director of the reactor, Dr. Yuval Ne'eman (later the president of Tel Aviv University and the minister of science during the Begin administration), decided to take advantage of the inspectors' presence for a "trip" to the Dead Sea.[48] As they passed Dimona on their way back, Ne'eman—seemingly spontaneously—suggested they drop by for an unannounced visit. He told his guests that he would be able to arrange a meeting for them with the facility's director. The inspectors agreed, but when they reached Dimona the director was apparently "not in," and instead a few of the senior engineers took them on a brief tour (extremely brief compared with inspections as stipulated by the guidelines). The American representatives noted in their report that on concluding this lightning tour, the Israelis invited them to return the following morning. This actually led them to wonder whether the whole thing was a stunt, as the Israelis knew that the inspectors were due to fly back to the United States that morning and that the next flight would not be not until four days later. Whatever the case, the forty-minute inspection was very incomplete; it did not include entry into all the buildings or examination of all the machinery and equipment.

At the end of the day, Israel did in fact achieve its goal: the inspectors were impressed, and their report described Dimona as a reactor for research purposes rather than plutonium production. CIA officials who reviewed the findings at a later date, however, raised doubts about the credibility of the brief tour. One senior official said that "basic intelligence requirements" had not been met and that there was a lack of congruence between the results of the first and second visits to the reactor with respect to the use attributed to certain equipment. The report presented in Washington therefore recommended, not surprisingly, that the Dimona facility be inspected more closely. The American embassy in Tel Aviv did not, however, need such special oversight to determine, in early 1963, that Israel's nuclear activity at that stage was aimed at acquiring nuclear knowledge that could in the future be used for economic as well as military purposes and that, under current conditions and given Israel's current capacity, it would be able to conduct a nuclear weapons test within six to eight years and to assemble a substantial nuclear arsenal—*frappe nucláire*—within twelve years.

The second factor behind the change in the US position on Israel's nuclear armament was undoubtedly the domestic and international political prestige President Kennedy enjoyed after his success in preventing a nuclear showdown in Cuba in late 1962, alongside Ben-Gurion's loss of standing following the Lavon affair (which, as noted, was not unrelated to internal criticism of Israel's nuclear policy). The result of this new situation was, according to Zaki Shalom, a shift in the American approach from one that permitted Israel a "low profile" to one that delivered "a blow aimed at twisting its arm."[49]

Subsequently, a highly classified memorandum dated March 26, 1963, by McGeorge "Mac" Bundy, national security advisor to President Kennedy, gave orders on behalf of the president to take urgent measures to clarify the nature of Israel's nuclear program, including a comprehensive survey of the reactor, with the aim of forestalling Israel's acquisition of a nuclear weapons capability. Notably, before adopting this policy, the US president had sought information about Dimona from senior Israeli officials. Toward this end he "accidentally" met with Shimon Peres so as to "make his acquaintance" when Peres was in Washington on April 1, 1963, to negotiate the purchase of American Hawk missiles.

The reason Kennedy wanted to meet Peres was highly political—to express his strong opposition to nuclear proliferation in general and his personal concern about the Israeli nuclear program in particular. He wanted to hear about Israel's genuine intentions directly from Peres, and evidently he also wanted to create a situation in which Peres would have to provide personal assurances that Israel would exercise restraint, as Ben-Gurion had provided the American president two years earlier—that is, that Israel did not intend to develop nuclear weapons. Peres was surprised when this seemingly spontaneous meeting turned into something approaching an interrogation under caution, as Kennedy began to bombard him with pointed questions regarding Israel's nuclear intentions. "I was amazed," Peres said. "I was not prepared for this, I did not know how to respond to him, and then somehow I recovered and said that I could assure him that we would not be the first to introduce nuclear weapons into the region."[50] This "improvised response," as Peres used to tell it, eventually became and has remained the official policy of Israel, serving it well for years. Interestingly, it was Ben-Gurion, not Peres, who in a closed meeting with newspaper editors in 1962 coined the phrase "We will not be the first to introduce nuclear weapons into the region." Peres was thus echoing the framing of the issue in terms of the interface between politics and security in Israel that year, and thus, in the words of Avner Cohen, "a compromise was reached in the spirit of opacity."

From Kennedy's perspective, there was nothing opaque about Peres's remarks. They constituted an official Israeli commitment not to develop nuclear weapons. Kennedy's ambitions, however, were not limited to extracting promises from Israel. The administration sought, first and foremost, to ensure that it received credible information about developments at Dimona as a preliminary condition for enforcing restrictions on Israel's nuclear activities. In concrete terms, Kennedy sought full oversight, beyond inspections. In May 1963, therefore, Washington informed Israel that it was interested in conducting two such inspections a year. The demand stunned Ben-Gurion, who told the ambassador in Tel Aviv that it constituted a violation of Israeli sovereignty and that Israel was not "an outgrowth of the United States." This time confrontation was unavoidable, and Ben-Gurion succeeded only in delaying the deadline for a response, stressing that his foreign minister, Golda Meir, was in the hospital at the time. On matters of substance, however, Ben-Gurion was unsuccessful. The American administration was well aware of the "chain of arguments" Israel had begun to voice since late 1961, which were intended to "trap" it and neutralize its pressure in the nuclear sphere. These included the following demands: that the magnitude of the existential threat posed by the Arab world be recognized; that the United States stand behind its declarations that it would not allow the destruction of the State of Israel; that it actualize its moral, political, and legal obligations toward Israel; and that if it could not fulfill all these conditions, then it should at least allow Israel to defend itself. In an effort to weaken Israel's position, the United States counterargued that Israel's nuclear activities were a matter of global concern constituting a responsibility on the part of the United States, which therefore refused to adopt a liberal approach based on reciprocity in its relations with Israel. The dramatic shift in US policy was also behind the US ambassador's unequivocal message to Ben-Gurion that the administration would not tolerate any "procrastination" on the part of the Israeli leader.

Thus Ben-Gurion faced one of the most difficult political dilemmas Israel had known to date. Despite the discouraging US clarifications and negative responses, he decided to enter into negotiations over four of Israel's earlier demands: complete demilitarization of the West Bank in the event that King Hussein's regime collapsed; a bilateral defense pact between Israel and the United States; modern, advanced weapons to be supplied by the United States; and agreement on a comprehensive plan for the disarmament of the Middle East. Ben-Gurion would certainly have known that the United States could not respond to all or even some of these demands. Indeed, his hope was that this would facilitate negotiations in which the United States would be more flexible regarding Dimona. But Israel's stance was completely transparent to the Americans, and in a meeting between Meir and the American ambassador in Tel Aviv on May 14, 1963, the United States once again demanded that Israel allow semiannual inspections of the facility, with the first one to take place later that year. Ben-Gurion tried to employ the entire arsenal of familiar Israeli arguments, but the American diplomat rejected them all, adding cynically that the Americans were insisting on more frequent inspections because Israel had earned itself a reputation as "quick builders."[51] One indication of the magnitude of the dilemma Israel faced was that the "old man" decided to use one of the last weapons at his disposal: he referred the issue to the cabinet, whose subsequent review of the matter remains classified to this day.

To forestall Israel's typical procrastination, on May 19 Kennedy sent a personal cable to Ben-Gurion. In one of the harshest messages a US president has ever delivered to an Israeli premier, Kennedy asserted that although the United

States was committed to Israel's security, "this [American] commitment and this support [for Israel] would be seriously jeopardized in the public opinion of this country and of the West if it should be thought that this Government was unable to obtain reliable information on a subject as vital to peace as the question of Israel's efforts in the nuclear field."[52] Ben-Gurion's response, delivered to Kennedy on May 27, reiterated most of the points Israel had raised previously. The only change in Israel's posture was its acquiescence to annual US inspections of Dimona beginning in late 1963, when the agreement on inspections binding Israel to France would no longer be in force. The "old man" thus opted to dig in his heels, despite the dire situation. Evidently sometime in the summer of 1963, he came to terms with the fact that the United States was determined to impose strict safeguards on Dimona, which in his view would thwart Israel's nuclear program. Moreover, he realized then that he would not be able to garner enough domestic political support for his position and that even those who were willing to maintain secrecy surrounding the Dimona project would oppose any action that might lead to Israel's complete international isolation.

Eshkol Takes Over

On June 16, 1963, Ben-Gurion therefore announced his resignation to his cabinet. Although he did not elaborate on his reasons, in Zaki Shalom's view it was the loss of domestic support for Dimona that tipped the balance, rather than the heavy pressure applied by Kennedy (as reflected in a harsh letter sent just one day earlier, which was never delivered to Ben-Gurion because of his resignation). In any event, despite Kennedy's explicit refusal to allow any more delays in providing authoritative answers on the part of Ben-Gurion's successor—Levi Eshkol—the new Israeli leader did succeed in "buying" a little time. But Kennedy's terms were now more severe and included an express demand that American scientists be allowed free access to all sites at Dimona, as well as enough time for a thorough inspection. The US president's tone conveyed a clear threat: refusal on Israel's part would be "detrimental to its welfare."

Eskhol's response, delivered in writing and verbally in mid-July and mid-August of 1963, was a typical expression of his traditional policy of "tiptoeing between the tulips" without conceding on matters of principle. At the same time, and in line with efforts to persuade the US government to provide security assurances for Israel, he agreed to additional inspections of the reactor beginning in June 1964, when the American representatives would be allowed to examine the fuel production process. This was a positive development from the American point of view, of course, but other factors also influenced the formation of the "low profile" approach toward Israel that Kennedy maintained until the end of his term. The first was Egypt's vehement refusal to concede to US demands to allow inspection of and provide detailed information about its nuclear program, thus reinforcing one of Israel's main justifications for its own nuclear program. Related to this were US concerns that exerting overt pressure on Israel might create the impression in Cairo that Israel was indeed close to obtaining nuclear weapons and that it was therefore in Egypt's interest to launch a preventive war as soon as possible. The second factor was Israel's independent (and apparently temporary) decision to reduce the scope of construction and further development at Dimona upon commencement of Eshkol's tenure, as confirmed by American intelligence experts. Third, and especially important, was the US administration's assessment that a frontal confrontation with Eshkol over the nuclear issue could result in Ben-Gurion, with his uncompromising position, returning to the premiership. "Eshkol himself," according to Zaki Shalom, "was well aware of the US administration's concerns. Throughout his term he was able to exploit its almost obsessive fears of Ben-Gurion returning to leadership in order to ease the pressure on himself." In this sense "wittingly or unwittingly, Ben-Gurion was enlisted to help Eshkol realize [the project]."[53]

The domestic criticism of Eshkol on nuclear matters, including harsh accusations that he was sacrificing Israeli security interests by conceding to US demands, was indeed a central theme of the anti-Eshkol propaganda spread by Ben-Gurion and his colleagues long after he had left office. At an informal gathering on September 21, 1965, Shimon Peres asserted that "Eshkol intended to sell Dimona." Nor were right-wing circles above the fray: an editorial in the newspaper *Herut*, published on October 15, 1965, voiced extreme displeasure over Eshkol's willingness to accept the American demands regarding inspections of Dimona. The Israeli political left, too, voiced fierce criticism in this regard, and during a meeting of MAPAM's political committee on April 13, 1965, Meir Ya'ari referred to Israel's efforts in the area of nonconventional arms and explained that "we must make every effort to arm ourselves if everyone around us is arming themselves." Against this background, on July 4, 1964, Foreign Ministry official Moshe Bitan delivered a message to the US ambassador in Tel Aviv, indirectly conveying the extensive freedom of action the prime minister enjoyed in this context. "We received news," wrote Bitan,

> from scientists in various friendly countries, informing us that your colleagues in Washington are telling their colleagues that regular US inspections of Dimona are underway. The Prime Minister takes this matter very seriously, and he requests that you explain to your government that this is not possible. It could place him in a very difficult position domestically and force him to reconsider the entire issue. . . . In the context of our internal power relations, the issue of US inspections is one of the most difficult problems we face, and the Prime Minister is liable to find himself at a dead-end.[54]

It is therefore hardly surprising that in a memorandum from Dean Rusk to members of the American Congressional Committee on the eve of their visit to Israel in September 1965, the secretary of state reminded them that RAFI (a center-left political party in Israel founded by the former prime minister in 1965) had criticized Eshkol and his government fiercely over the issue of inspections at Dimona and urged that they therefore exercise extreme caution when discussing this sensitive matter.

Fourth, the Americans expected that international efforts to achieve a nuclear test ban treaty, which were in full force at the time, would exert indirect pressure on Israel to relax its position. Israel had no difficulty conveying encouraging messages to Washington in this regard. At the same time, the concept of regional nuclear disarmament placed the Eshkol government, like Ben-Gurion's, in a difficult position. It could not directly and publicly reject an idea that it seemingly had no reason to oppose. After all, if Israel did not have nuclear weapons and had no intention of producing them, then why should it oppose the idea of disarmament, which guarantees full equality between Israel and the Arab states? On the other hand, from Israel's perspective these developments threatened the continuation of the Dimona project. Under these circumstances, Eshkol employed a clever and sophisticated tactic that was typical of his political approach: public expressions of support in principle for the concept of disarmament alongside conditions that would make its actual realization impossible. As events unfolded, however, Israel received the extended deadline it sought in the aftermath of President Kennedy's assassination on November 22, 1963.

The new American president, preoccupied with domestic affairs (the civil rights struggle at home and the Vietnam War abroad) sidelined the Israeli nuclear issue but did not remove it from Washington's political agenda entirely. Discussions between the two resumed in early 1964, and in keeping with its promises, Israel approved a visit by representatives of the American administration to Dimona on January 18. This time the visit lasted about twelve hours and included an inspection of all the "significant sites," after which the representatives issued a report that contained both "acceptable" and "serious" findings. Although they estimated that within two years the reactor's facilities would be able to produce a sizable quantity of uranium, they found no facilities for plutonium production. They also concluded that Israel lacked a nuclear weapons capability at present, but they recommended that periodic inspections continue to take place because they believed that Israel's aim was to be able to produce a small number of nuclear weapons quickly, should it decide to do so. In all, the assessment conveyed the impression that in the not-too-distant future Israel would be able to produce nuclear weapons.

Johnson's reaction to these findings marked a clear shift from his predecessor's position. The new president understood Israel's security concerns, given the military imbalance between Israel and the Arab world, and was in fact beginning to formulate a position that developed into a central facet of his approach to Israel—as a Cold War ally. He told Israel that the Dimona project should be discussed during Eshkol's upcoming visit to Washington. In practical terms Johnson wanted Israel to adopt measures that would reduce Egypt's fears of its nuclearization while at the same serving as a message to the United States itself. However, Eshkol joined his predecessor in rejecting these demands. Israel's position stemmed from its assessment that it should not allay Nasser's concerns regarding its own military capability, if that capability could deter him from launching war. The Israelis also mistrusted the Egyptian leader and feared that he might exploit any information he received regarding US-Israeli nuclear talks.

Despite Johnson's frustration on receiving Israel's message of early March 1964, the US response did not raise the issue of inspections of Dimona, and Jerusalem took this as a sign of encouragement. Apparently this was not an accidental oversight. Presumably the administration concluded that in light of Israel's domestic situation, it should not be pressured to sign an agreement linking nuclear issues with the security guarantees it had been seeking since Ben-Gurion's time. Rather, it was best to reach discreet verbal understandings among the highest political echelons. From discussions of Israel's missile program with American representatives in the weeks preceding his visit to Washington, Eshkol learned that the United States was refraining from raising the issue of Dimona. Acting against his own foreign minister, Golda Meir, Eshkol agreed to refrain from acquiring missiles if Nasser suspended his missile program and provided substantive proof in this regard.

These developments provided a comfortable backdrop for Eshkol's visit to the United States in June 1964, which marked the first time in Israel's history that its prime minister was officially invited to Washington. The records of this meeting reflect a moderate US stance on the matter of Dimona and clearly indicate that the issue was not a priority for the administration. Although the president reiterated US concerns regarding nuclear proliferation generally, and in the Israeli and Egyptian context specifically, his reference to the project lacked any threat. One may surmise that his restrained position stemmed partly from internal considerations relating to himself and Levi Eshkol. In advance of this meeting, the prime minister had sought to convey to the Americans—through his ambassador to Washington, Efi Evron—that his visit to the United States could prove decisive for his continuing premiership, because it was important that he return from Washington with political gains and that no pressure be exerted on him regarding inspections of the reactor. Against this background, the US government evidently concluded that it would be best to use "silk gloves" in dealing with Eshkol and not to exert excessive pressure on him. Moreover, in a frank conversation with Shimon Peres, the president's advisor made it clear that the administration had a strong interest in Eshkol continuing to serve as prime minister, thus hinting that Peres should not support Ben-Gurion's efforts to undermine Eshkol.

The Israeli prime minister, for his part, rewarded the American president for recognizing Israel's security needs: shortly after the Eshkol-Kennedy meeting, Israel's deputy defense minister informed US secretary of state William Phillips Talbot that Israel had agreed to allow the American administration to reassure Nasser about developments at Dimona, as long as it did not tell the Egyptian leader anything about the inspections.

Despite the favorable outcome of this meeting from Israel's point of view, the US administration continued to pressure Israel on the matter of effective oversight over Dimona. But as both countries were preoccupied with elections, they agreed that the next official inspection of the reactor would take place on January 30, 1965, which it duly did, lasting ten hours. The delegation reached the conclusion that it had had enough time to determine the true nature of activities at the reactor and that it had found no evidence of any intent to develop nuclear weapons in the immediate future, but that the extent of development and production necessitated continued monitoring at intervals not to exceed one year. It did, however, recommend responding in the affirmative to Eshkol's request that the next inspection be postponed until after the Knesset elections in November 1965.

In late February 1965, two official emissaries of President Johnson, Averell Harriman and Robert Komer, visited Israel. The president had authorized them to discuss a range of issues with the Israeli leadership, including a commitment that it would not develop nuclear weapons and that it would accept international safeguards at all its nuclear facilities. In contrast to the atmosphere during Eshkol's visit to the United States, this time the American message was firm and unequivocal. The emissaries informed Eshkol that the president was personally committed to the issue and determined to use all the means at his disposal to secure Israel's consent to his demands. Eshkol, refusing to acquiesce, asked the emissaries "to leave out" the demand for safeguards but hinted that Israel would be willing to confirm that it did not intend to develop nuclear weapons.[55] He also stressed that the only term he was willing to accept, and for which he would seek his government's approval, was a reaffirmation of Israel's commitment not to be the first to introduce nuclear weapons into the region. The Israeli premier refused to concede any further, especially on the matters of international inspections and an explicit Israeli commitment not to develop a military nuclear option in the future, even in exchange for a memorandum of understanding that would facilitate Israel's procurement of American tanks by way of West Germany. The Ben-Gurionist approach thus continued to resonate, as reflected in Eshkol's negative attitude toward Washington's implied concessions on the issue of conventional arms in exchange for Israeli concessions on the nuclear issue.

The US representatives understood the constraints they faced: "We demand detailed commitments on matters that are most vital to their security in return for our vague commitments. We can threaten them again [by saying] that if they do not meet our demands, then we will have to act against them, but the threat will not be credible as long as the president does not want to sever relations with Israel at this time."[56] Moreover, they concluded that Eshkol did not have a great deal of maneuverability and would not be able to respond favorably to the American demands. Their conclusion was further informed by the knowledge that Israeli officials had not fulfilled all of the prime minister's instructions in organizing the tour of the reactor and had in fact, at their own initiative, cut it short. Harriman therefore recommended initiating a dialogue that could pave the way to compromise, a course of action that Secretary of State Rusk and other State Department experts blatantly rejected. It should be noted that Eshkol's uncompromising stance apparently stemmed from personal conversations with Harriman, which led him to believe that President Johnson would not support harsh measures against Israel as a means of compelling it to accept inspections.

Under these circumstances, Johnson decided to delay addressing the Dimona issue, and it was not until March 10, 1965, that the parties concluded a memorandum of understanding on the matter of Israel's nuclear activity. Besides reaffirming the US commitment to Israel's independence and territorial integrity and responding favorably to Israel's request for American weapons, the agreement officially stipulated that Israel would not be the first to introduce nuclear weapons into its conflict with the Arabs. The limited scope of this agreement indicated an official retreat from the previous American position on Israel's nuclear activities and, in the latter's view, constituted a major achievement. US documents confirm this interpretation by underscoring that the memorandum of understanding fell far short of what opponents in the administration thought was appropriate and essential—that is, to bring the nuclear project at Dimona to a halt. The same individuals also stressed their assessment that Israel had for years been deceiving the administration regarding its nuclear plans. Rusk himself was of the opinion that lack of official oversight over the reactor would undermine the credibility of the global struggle led by the United States to prevent the spread of nuclear weapons. Nevertheless, the administration refrained from applying massive pressure on Israel in this area, and in particular from conditioning Israel's weapons procurement needs on compliance in the nuclear arena. This reluctance is evident in the detailed arms purchase agreement subsequently signed between the two countries, which included 220 tanks, 250 upgrade kits for Patton tanks already in the possession of the IDF, and 48 Skyhawk fighter planes. As Olivia Sohns argues in a recent doctoral dissertation, Johnson adopted a strategic approach that was evidently informed, among other factors, by the value he ascribed to Israel as Cold War ally—a clear departure from Kennedy's general approach to Israel.[57]

In any case, the memorandum of understanding significantly reduced the likelihood of Israel agreeing to substantial US oversight over Dimona. Eshkol, encouraged by the agreement, found the courage to tell William Phillips Talbot, the State Department representative who visited Israel in mid-April 1965, that Israel could not refrain "forever" from developing nuclear weapons in the absence of a defense pact with the United States: "We have no choice but to try to learn everything about this (developing a nuclear option) because of our responsibility to [ensure] the survival of the Jewish People."[58] Eshkol had concluded, evidently correctly, that Johnson would not "lose it" over the question of Dimona. Thus, after the American president reiterated the demand that Israel place its nuclear facilities under IAEA safeguards, on May 21, 1965, the Israeli prime minister allowed himself to delay his response for nearly three weeks, at which time he suggested postponing discussion of the president's demands until after the Knesset elections in November of that year. Apparently, he was also unimpressed by the blunt language of the US ambassador to Tel Aviv, Walworth "Wally" Barbour, who in mid-August reasserted the president's demands. The American position on Israel's nuclear activity may therefore be characterized, in the words of Zaki Shalom, as "pragmatic acceptance alongside discreet objection." Accordingly, in December 1965, after the Israeli elections, the Americans renewed their demand to allow an inspection of Dimona. Although Israel agreed in principle, it felt emboldened enough to reject the concept of semiannual inspections, demanding instead that each inspection be negotiated anew. The inspection eventually took place in late March 1966, and its findings were consistent with those of previous visits—that is, the inspectors found no evidence that Israel was developing nuclear weapons. The US-Israeli dialogue on this issue then resumed, yielding a subsequent agreement to conduct an inspection of the reactor on April 22, 1967.

Throughout this period, Israel insisted that as long as it did not conduct a nuclear test and did not openly declare that it possessed nuclear weapons, it could not be regarded as having "introduced" nuclear weapons into the region. In practical terms this meant that there was no impediment to Israel's development of a nuclear option as long as it met these two conditions. The US State Department was not satisfied with this definition of "introduction" and insisted that the very development and production of nuclear weapons by Israel be prohibited. The administration, however, essentially conceded on this point, marking a clear victory for those who supported Ben-Gurion's position, as reinforced by Eshkol, and underscoring the inability of the United States to exert its influence as a superpower over a small, friendly country. The significant fact that shortly before the Six-Day War broke out, Israel had already completed the production of several nuclear bombs inevitably undermined the State Department's position on the "introduction" of nuclear weapons into the region.

"We Will Not Be the First"

Ultimately, this formulation of opacity ("we will not be the first") was implemented in the form of an official, comprehensive political deal with the United States on the nuclear issue.[59] In September 1969 Golda Meir, a staunch rival of

Peres during the late 1950s, met with President Nixon and sealed the deal that granted discreet legitimacy to Israel's nuclear weapons program as a "rainy day" policy (a phrase that Peres particularly liked). The opacity formula was a core element of that deal. Notably, in the course of preparing for this meeting, the US administration had determined in January of that year that Israel already had nuclear weapons and even the ability to deploy long-range surface-to-surface "Jericho" missiles. Moreover, we now know that even before the Israeli prime minister's visit, Nixon's aides had concluded that "we cannot cause or force Israel to completely abandon its plan to integrate a nuclear capability into the IDF's operational defense doctrine within a year and a half, in the absence of complete peace with the Arabs and taking into account domestic political consequences" in advance of the Knesset elections. Moreover, "we cannot force the Israelis to destroy data and components, not to mention the technical knowledge stored in their minds, or the talent for speedy improvisation. Israel's main objective is to have the option of achieving a military nuclear capability at short notice." Furthermore, "for our internal purposes," concluded one of Nixon's aides in July 1969, "we can tolerate Israeli activity that does not reach the stage of complete assembly of an explosive nuclear device. We will also demand that Israel stop procuring Jericho missiles, but this demand will be dropped if we move forward on the nuclear issue." The question of whether Israel would sign the Nuclear Non-Proliferation Treaty (NPT) was considered more problematic.

The precise content of the talks between Nixon and Meir has not been published, but we know that it included an Israeli commitment to maintain the policy of opacity and not to deploy missiles for three years. A year later, Ambassador Rabin informed his interlocutors in Washington that Israel refused to sign the NPT. Instead he proposed a vague formulation that would secretly commit Israel to an implicit version of the agreement. Kissinger recommended that Nixon accept Rabin's formula. The president approved this recommendation and asked Kissinger to inform the Israelis that their response was "acceptable." Kissinger saw this as the end of the discussion; he wrote to Nixon that the United States had pushed the nuclear issue as far as possible. Recently declassified documents reveal that Nixon was the first American president to know about and accept the existence of Israel's nuclear arsenal. According to Avner Cohen (1998), in contrast to his predecessors, Nixon believed that a nuclear-capable Israel coincided with American interests. Kissinger shared this view. The two believed that regional nuclear proliferation was inevitable and that it would be more beneficial for the United States to discreetly help friendly states acquire nuclear weapons than to entangle itself in futile efforts to prevent any proliferation. The understandings reached between Nixon and Meir were fully consistent with this approach, which also explains the delivery of Phantom jets to Israel in September 1969. The two leaders' agreement put an end to US inspections of Dimona, and since its conclusion the United States and Israel have firmly abided by it even in times of hardship and severe crisis.

In an article published several years ago, military commentator Yossi Melman claimed that the first time Israel made preparations to use nuclear weapons was on the eve of the Six-Day War.[60] Concurrent with Israel's internal technical assessment of its capability, Brigadier General Dov Tamari, commander of the General Staff Reconnaissance Unit (Sayeret Matkal), was instructed to prepare a team to be flown by helicopter to the Sinai Peninsula with an unexplained "object." The intention was apparently that the soldiers would place the "object"—Israel's first nuclear device—on a high mountaintop in the Sinai. Melman emphasized that according to the few testimonies and references on the subject, the aim was to threaten use of the device so as to deter Egypt, adding that conceivably Israel also intended to use the device as a last resort if the Egyptian army employed chemical or biological weapons or launched missiles at Israel's population centers, thereby placing the country in existential danger. As it turned out, this situation did not materialize, nor did the remotest possibility that Israel might use its nuclear weapons.

The second occasion on which Israel considered but refrained from using nuclear weapons took place six years later. In October 1973, during the most difficult days of the Yom Kippur War, Golda Meir kept Peres's promise to Kennedy.[61] According to foreign sources, she stood firmly with Yisrael Galili, Yigal Allon, and Chief of Staff David "Dado" Elazar in refusing to introduce the nuclear dimension into the battlefield. Working against her at the time was her own government's defense minister, Moshe Dayan, a prominent advocate in those days, as in earlier days, of overt use of Israel's nuclear deterrent. During the 1960s and 1970s, he often spoke publicly about his support for nuclear armament. Indeed, a few days before the elections of 1965, when questioned on the matter, he asserted that "if it were possible to go to the store and buy atomic weapons, I would support that."[62] The acute military situation at the start of the 1973 War and his assessment that Israel was in effect facing the destruction of the Third Temple made his assessment seem realistic. In any event, Golda Meir told her defense minister to "forget it," and Dayan's nuclear proposals were rejected and removed from the agenda. Israel's nuclear posture remained—and, with US acquiescence, still remains—opaque.

As to Israel's capabilities, according to some assessments Israel had two to thirteen nuclear bombs around the time of the Six-Day War. It is generally assumed that the great leap took place sometime in the early 1970s, when Israel began producing about ten hydrogen bombs per year, each of which (containing four kilograms of plutonium) was at least ten times more powerful than the bomb dropped on Hiroshima at the end of World War II. After former Dimona technician Mordechai Vanunu revealed details about the reactor, sharing information and photographs with the global media, it was estimated that by the mid-1980s Israel had a nuclear arsenal of two hundred weapons. Israel's ballistic missiles capability also made giant strides, and undoubtedly its submarine fleet has contributed significantly to its security by effectively granting it a "second strike capability."

Jerusalem's strategic success was, without a doubt, also shaped by the difficult constraints facing Washington, not all of which we can address here. These included internal, sometimes very substantive, prognostic disagreements, which curtailed the United States' ability and willingness to impose its will on Israel for the sake of what it considered a desirable nuclear arrangement.

The key Israeli decisions on nuclear acquisition had been made by the mid-1950s, and their implementation began in the late 1950s. During that time, the United States had neither provided reliable security guarantees nor developed a committed global nonproliferation policy. As Avner Cohen first demonstrated in 1998, part of the problem was that Washington, because of an intelligence failure, had no idea that the Israelis were about to acquire nuclear weapons. When the problem was finally addressed directly under Kennedy, he tried to exert pressure, eventually reaching an arrangement regarding inspections. In retrospect, however, "it was too little and too late. Israel's nuclear program had already been set in motion."[63] Seven years later, Cohen and William Burr published new findings, revealing that the Eisenhower administration's "discovery" in late 1960 that Israel was secretly constructing a large nuclear complex at Dimona was indeed belated. Moreover, as Alex Bollfras has emphasized, what amounted to an intelligence breakdown by the United States was in fact a tremendous counterintelligence success for Israel. The US failure enabled the fledgling state to buy precious time for the highly vulnerable Dimona project. It could be argued that had the United States discovered Dimona two years earlier, or perhaps even a year earlier, it could have applied political pressure on the two foreign suppliers at the time, France and Norway, which might have thwarted their deals with Israel from the outset.[64]

Israel deserves credit for this state of affairs for other reasons as well. On the one hand, it was consistent and unequivocal in asserting that, given the undeniable existential threats it faced, it was determined to continue the Dimona project. Therefore, it was also largely consistent in its refusal to make significant concessions on the nuclear issue in exchange for conventional weapons from the United States. On the other hand, it chose a strategy of partial cooperation with Washington in order to avoid a direct and open confrontation with the administration. Toward this end it demonstrated a willingness to make partial concessions, without explicitly committing to measures that would limit its freedom of action or jeopardize its plans in the nuclear sphere. The fact that for decades after the collapse of the nuclear deal with France, Israel managed through covert diplomacy to acquire nuclear materials from various non-American sources (including Norway, South Africa, and Argentina)—a topic that awaits its own historian—is another point in Israel's favor. In any case it is clear that Israel has actually achieved its goal. There is no doubt that, from Jerusalem's perspective, the development of a nuclear option represents one of Israel's most remarkable achievements in the area of foreign and defense policy, constituting a fundamental pillar of its relationship with the United States. The arrangement established by the two states in the 1960s has not lost its importance. It remains relevant to this day, especially given the prospect of Iran realizing its nuclear ambitions and the consequent likelihood of nuclear proliferation in the Middle East—a state of affairs that neither Israel nor the United States desires but one with which they might have to come to terms.

Notes

1. Personal source. n.d.

2. Scott McConnel, "The Special Relationship with Israel: Is It Worth the Costs?," Middle East Policy Council, 2017, http://www.mepc.org/special-relationship-israel-it-worth-costs.

3. Israeli Ministry of Foreign Affairs, Press conference with President Carter, May 12, 1977, https://mfa.gov.il/mfa/foreignpolicy/mfadocuments/yearbook2/pages/211%20press%20conference%20with%20president%20carter-%2012%20may.aspx.

4. John Dumbrell and Axel Schäfer, *America's "Special Relationships": Foreign and Domestic Aspects of the Politics of Alliance* (New York, Routledge, 2009), 191.

5. "CQ Transcripts," *Washington Post*, June 2, 2008.

6. Jonathan Rynhold, *The Arab-Israeli Conflict in American Political Culture* (Cambridge, Cambridge University Press, 2015).

7. Charles Freilich, "Hanikhu LeAIPAC, Medubar BeHatzlakha" [Leave AIPAC alone, it's a success], *Haaretz*, April 6, 2017.

8. Rynhold, *The Arab-Israeli Conflict*.

9. George Kennan, "Memorandum by the Director of the Policy Planning George Kennan to the U.S. Secretary of State," Department of State, *Foreign Relations of the United States: The Near East and Africa* 5, no. 2 (Washington, Government Printing Office, 1947): 655–57.

10. John J. Mearsheimer and Stephen M. Walt, *The Israel Lobby and US Foreign Policy* (New York, Farrar, Straus and Giroux, 2008).

11. Emily Alice Katz, *Bringing Zion Home: Israel in American Jewish Culture, 1948–1967* (New York, SUNY Press, 2015).

12. Dov Waxman, *Trouble in the Tribe: The American Jewish Conflict over Israel* (Princeton, Princeton University Press 2016).

13. Samuel Taylor, "American Zionism and the Evolution of 'Pro-Israel' in U.S. Politics," Syracuse University Honors Program Capstone Projects, paper no. 192, 2012.

14. Dennis Ross, *Doomed to Succeed* (New York, Farrar, Straus and Giroux, 2016).

15. Moshe Bitan, *Yoman Medini, 1967–1970* [Political diary, 1967–1970] (Tel Aviv, Olam Hadash, 2014).

16. Zalman Shoval, *Diplomat* [in Hebrew] (Tel Aviv, Yediot, 2016).

17. Yaacov Bar-Siman-Tov, "The United States and Israel since 1948: A 'Special Relationship'?," *Diplomatic History* 22, no. 2 (1998): 231–62.

18. Isaac Alteras, *Eisenhower and Israel: US-Israeli Relations, 1953–1960* (Gainesville, University Press of Florida 1993).

19. Warren Bass, *Support Any Friend: Kennedy's Middle East and the Making of the US-Israel Alliance* (New York, Oxford University Press, 2003).

20. Abraham Ben-Zvi, *Alliance Politics and the Limits of Influence: The Case of the United States and Israel, 1975–1983* (New York, Westview, 1984); Ben-Zvi, *Decade of Transition: Eisenhower, Kennedy, and the Origins of the American-Israeli Alliance* (New York, Columbia University Press 1998).

21. Hanan Bar-On, "Khamisha Asurim Shel Yakhasei Israel-Artzot HaBrit" [Five decades of Israeli-US relations], in *Atzma'ut: 50 HaShanim HaRishonot* [Independence: The first 50 years], ed. Anita Shapira (Jerusalem, Shazar Institute, 1998) 379.

22. Noam Kochavi, "Yomano Shel Moshe Bitan: Keitzad Hitmasdu HaYakhasim HaMeyukhadim Bein Artzot HaBrit LeIsrael" [Moshe Bitan's diary: How the special relationship between the United States and Israel was established], *Cathedra* 163 (2017): 228–29.

23. Yitzhak Oren, *LaDug Im HaNasi: Aliyato Shel HaSpin HaDiplomati* [Fishing with the president: The rise of the diplomatic spin] (Tel Aviv, Rasling, 2014).

24. Joseph Heller, *Israel VeHamilkhama HaKara* [Israel and the Cold War] (Sde Boker, Ben Gurion Heritage Institute, 2010).

25. Natan Aridan, *Advocating for Israel: Diplomats and Lobbyists from Truman to Nixon* (New York, Lexington, 2017).

26. Avner Cohen, "Al HaHistoriographia Shel HaGarin HaIsraeli: Bein Amimut LeBehirut Historit" [On the historiography of the Israeli nuclear [program]: Between opacity and historical clarity], *Israel* 9 (2006), 245–254.

27. Ben-Gurion's diary, November 27, 1948, Ben-Gurion Heritage Institute.

28. Zaki Shalom, *Bein Dimona LeWashington* [Between Dimona and Washington] (Sde Boker, Ben Gurion Heritage Institute, 2004), 11.

29. Seymour Hersh, *The Samson Option* (New York, Random House 1991).

30. Shalom, *Bein Dimona LeWashington*, 39.

31. *Dr. Strangelove* is a 1964 political black comedy film that satirizes the Cold War fears of a nuclear conflict between the Soviet Union and the United States. The story concerns an unhinged United States Air Force general who orders a first strike nuclear attack on the Soviet Union.

32. See Adam Raz, "BaDerekh LeDimona: Reshita Shel HaMakhloket Al Mediniyut HaGarin HaIsraelit" [On the road to Dimona: The origins of the dispute over Israeli nuclear policy], *Politika* (2013): 107–34.

33. Quoted in Adam Raz, *HaMa'avak Al HaPtzatza* [The struggle for the bomb] (Jerusalem, Carmel, 2015), 424.

34. Yitzhak Shichor, "Ernst David Bergmann and Israel's Role in Taiwan's Defense," *Asia Papers* 2 (2016).

35. Quoted in Shlomo Aronson, "Or Khadash Al Doctrinat 'HaMikhse LeYom Sagrir'" [A new light on the "rainy day" doctrine], *Iyunim Bitkumat Israel* 2 (1992): 152.

36. Michael Bar-Zohar, *Ben-Gurion*, vol. 3 (Tel Aviv, Yediot 1977), 1522.

37. Noam Sheizaf, "Dr. Avner Cohen, Khoker HaGarin HaIsraeli Metzig: Prakim Khadashim BeProyekt HaAmum BeYoter BeIsrael" [Dr. Avner Cohen, Israeli nuclear researcher, presents: New chapters in Israel's most opaque project], *Haaretz*, October 21, 2010.

38. Yehuda Ben Meir, "HaIdan HaGarini VeHaTzibur BeIsrael" [The nuclear age and the public in Israel], *Dapei Elazar* 16 (1994): 51–61.

39. Actually, according to Eban, by the early 1960s the cost amounted to $340 million. Adam Raz, "Protocols of Hiding," *Haaretz*, June 16, 2019.

40. Shalom, *Bein Dimona LeWashington*, 45.

41. Ibid., 49.

42. Ibid.

43. Ibid., 53.

44. Ibid., 57.

45. The Lavon affair refers to a covert Israeli operation that failed spectacularly. Code-named Operation Susannah, it was a "false-flag" action undertaken in Egypt in the summer of 1954. A group of Egyptian Jews were recruited by Israeli military intelligence to plant bombs inside Egyptian-, American-, and British-owned civilian targets, cinemas, libraries, and American educational centers. The operation caused no casualties among the population but did cost the lives of four operatives: two cell members who committed suicide after being captured and two operatives who were tried, convicted, and executed by Egypt. The operation became known as the Lavon affair after Israeli defense minister Pinhas Lavon was forced to resign in the aftermath of the incident. Until Lavon's resignation, the incident was euphemistically referred to in Israel as the "Unfortunate Affair" or "Bad Business."

46. Avner Cohen, "Ben Gurion Bala Milim" [Ben Gurion swallowed wods] Haaretz, April 22, 2014 (Hebrew).

47. Ibid.

48. Shalom, *Bein Dimona LeWashington*, 72. This is the source for the quotations that follow unless noted otherwise.

49. Ibid., 70.

50. Avner Cohen, "Mi Himtzi Et HaAmimut HaIsraelit?" [Who invented Israeli opacity?], *Haaretz* (October 6, 2016): 5.

51. Shalom, *Bein Dimona LeWashington*, 81.

52. Ibid., 82.

53. Ibid., 94.

54. Ibid., 138.

55. Ibid., 181.

56. Ibid. 184.

57. Olivia Sohns, "Lyndon Johnson's Arab-Israeli Policies" (PhD diss., Cambridge University, 2014).

58. Shalom, *Bein Dimona LeWashington*, 195.

59. The following analysis is based on Sheizaf, "Dr. Avner Cohen." See also Arnon Gutfeld, "Israel Approaches the Nuclear Threshold: The Controversies in the American Administration Surrounding the Israeli Nuclear Bomb, 1968–1969," *Middle Eastern Studies* 52, no. 5 (2016): 715–36 (until otherwise indicated).

60. Yossi Melman, "HaIm 'HaMahalakh HaMeturaf Shel Golda' BeMilkhemet Yom Kippur Kalal Neshek Garini" [Did 'Golda's crazy move' during the Yom Kippur War include nuclear weapons?], *Haaretz*, October 7, 2010.

61. Adam Raz, "HaParasha HaGarinit Shel Milhemet Yom HaKippurim" [The nuclear affair of the Yom Kippur War], Institute for National Security Studies, January 2014.

62. Adam Raz, "HaParasha HaGarinit Shel Milhemet Yom HaKippurim" [The nuclear affair of the Yom Kippur War], Institute for National Security Studies, January 2014, 102.

63. Cohen, "Israel and the Evolution of US Nonproliferation Policy," and William Burr and Avner Cohen (eds.) "The Battle of the Letters, 1963: John F. Kennedy, David Ben-Gurion, Levi Eshkol, and the U.S. Inspections of Dimona," National Security Archives, Briefing Book no. 671. May 2, 2019 https://nsarchive.gwu.edu/briefing-book/nuclear-vault/2019-05-02/battle -letters-1963-john-f-kennedy-david-ben-gurion-levi-eshkol-us-inspections-dimona.

64. Alex Bollfrass, "Desert Mystery: Intelligence Assessment of Israel's Nuclear Program," *Sources and Methods*, Wilson Center, May 22, 2017.

PART IV
PEACE

.

11   Egypt—Diplomacy under the Shadow of the Sphinx

Here comes the president of Egypt
What great joy to have him visit
Pyramid visions in our eyes
And peace the vision in his pipe
And we said let's make peace
And live as brothers side by side
And he said yes, let's do it
Once you leave the territories

And all will be good . . .
——Excerpts from a popular Israeli song, "And All Will Be Good" (1978)[1]

THE POLITICAL ISOLATION and international alienation of Israel constitute one of the central themes of this book. There is no dispute among scholars that Israel has succeeded—but only to a certain extent—in gaining international recognition. Among other factors, the missing piece of the pie became abundantly clear to Israel's leaders as a consequence of developments that form the core theme of this chapter. Eventually they came to the painful but undeniable realization that Sadat's resounding call of "no more war" before the Knesset in 1977 did not result in its implementation and that more powerful forces were at work, preventing Israel's full acceptance in the Middle East. The case discussed here—a chapter in the history of its relations with Egypt—illustrates and expounds on the problem. The importance of this country lies not only in its physical and demographic dimensions but also in its regional and global standing, as well as its role in driving the anti-Israel agenda even beyond the region, as the Bandung Conference exemplifies. Egypt's ability to maintain a peace treaty with the Jewish state, without implementing the normalization commitments of that treaty, constituted and still constitutes a critical failure from Israel's perspective—a failure to realize the all-important hopes embodied in the Camp David Accords.

On March 26, 1979, Israel realized one of the most important goals of its foreign policy: a peace treaty with Egypt, the largest Arab country. Yet neither of these two countries officially commemorated the twenty-fifth anniversary of this landmark day in their respective histories. The obvious explanation is that relations between the two states have remained limited in scope since the outset, despite the language of article 3 of their peace treaty, which provides that "the normal relationship established between them will include full recognition, diplomatic, economic and cultural relations, [and] termination of economic boycotts and discriminatory barriers to the free movement of people and goods."[2] Thus the phrase *cold peace* has become a common feature of the Israeli, international, academic, and media discourses on the topic. The relationship between Israel and Egypt never turned into the type of normalized, peaceful relations that would facilitate full interaction between the two peoples and their social, economic, and political institutions. Rather, it has remained a diplomatic relationship between the two countries' leaders. In summarizing a decade of these relations, Prime Minister Yitzhak Shamir stated in a live radio broadcast on the Voice of Israel on July 29, 1991, that "normalization has sunk into oblivion. There is no normalization now. So many years after the peace treaty there are no normal trade relations with Israel, there is no cultural cooperation, there is no Egyptian tourism to Israel. It is as if Israel and Egypt were not living in peace but were two absolute alien and estranged countries."[3]

The director general of Israel's Ministry of Defense, David Ivry, was equally definitive when he asserted, a few months later, that "the peace with Egypt is not peace; it is actually a cease-fire that has continued for fifteen years."[4] The major disappointment at the time was, as we shall see, on Israel's part. This chapter analyzes the various explanations that have been offered for this state of affairs from both perspectives, in an effort to address one key question: Given that the strategic and security-related aspects of the agreement (withdrawal from and disarmament of the Sinai) did not generate any major confrontations, why were those aspects of the agreement that relate to civilian normalization not realized between the time of its adoption and the early 1990s? Although the limited scope of this analysis compels us to focus on that particular period, toward the end of the chapter I also briefly attempt to address the significance of changes that have taken place in recent years.

A preliminary comment is in order. Egyptian and Israeli state documents on the matter remain publicly unavailable, which of course affects the studies published in this field as well as their accuracy. This comment applies to the level of detail and precision of the analyses of Egypt's positions and policies and—unlike in previous chapters—those of Israel as well. The following is therefore a selective summary of a particular, though not negligible, perspective as embodied in the secondary literature, which inevitably leaves open many historiographic questions that await future historians.

Cairo's Utilitarian Peace Gesture

To understand this dimension of Israeli-Egyptian peace, it is necessary to examine the determinative material interests of both parties. According to available testimonies, upon assuming office in September 1970, Egypt's new president, Muhammad Anwar el-Sadat, was shocked by the latest national economic figures. He learned that Egypt's foreign debt at the start of the decade had grown by an average of 28 percent, compared with only 13 percent during the previous decade. Moreover, Egypt's nearly exclusive dependence on the Soviet Union for economic and, in particular, military aid was impeding efforts to revive the Egyptian economy. The main source of this growing foreign debt was military expenditure. In 1967–1975 Egypt spent $25 billion (including loans) on military equipment and the financing of wars—the Six-Day War, the War of Attrition, and the Yom Kippur War (which lasted six years for Egypt). Its military spending grew from $1.5 billion in 1971 to more than $6 billion four years later. Moreover, to sustain its armed forces the Egyptian government had to make concessions in many sectors of the economy, which in turn undermined public services and disrupted the country's development projects. The situation was further exacerbated by Egypt's rapid demographic growth, with its population reaching forty million by 1980. As most of the country's land (96 percent) consisted of desert, nearly all its citizens resided along a narrow strip of the Nile Valley and the Delta and were almost entirely dependent on agriculture that was not particularly advanced. The natural population growth reached 1.1 million annually. The challenges of sustaining such a massive human populace were therefore monumental, even during times of peace. In 1974, for example, despite an impressive rise in exports and assistance from the Gulf states, Egypt required more than $1 billion in foreign currency just to feed its population, which left no capital for investments. The generous assistance Egypt received from Arab oil-producing countries was indeed significant but came at a high political cost, as it created a dependence on the Arab world, which in Sadat's view translated into political constraints in the international and regional spheres. This economic state of affairs became a significant threat to the stability of the regime, especially in light of its wars with Israel, which were having an extremely detrimental impact on Egypt's two main sources of income—international tourism and transit fees for the Suez Canal. In fact, the canal had closed for seven years because of military confrontations with Israel in the Sinai. Compounding all of the above was a strong sense of disappointment and humiliation on the part of the Egyptian leadership toward the end of Nasser's term, after the Soviet Union's unsatisfactory response to Egyptian requests for aid and what Cairo viewed as the Soviets' demeaning, unfair, and arbitrary approach. These feelings were at the basis of Sadat's decision to expel twenty-one thousand military advisors in July 1972, a decision that earned him great public admiration but evidently also diminished the Soviets' willingness to provide extensive aid. As of the mid-1970s, however, that decision had not yet earned Sadat access to the US Treasury.

The natural way for Egypt to resolve this crisis was indeed revolutionary: to reach a political agreement with Israel under which the latter would return the Sinai, thus reducing Egypt's military spending as well as the threat of war, and in parallel to cultivate diplomatic relations with the United States as its main source of aid. In retrospect it is evident that Sadat first voiced this new approach openly when he announced his peace initiative before the Egyptian People's Assembly in February 1971. Today we know that Israel's lack of response to this initiative persuaded the president of the necessity of military action, which eventually led to the Yom Kippur War of October 1973. (Israel's failure to respond was based in part on an assessment by its Military Intelligence that Sadat—often labeled "a button on Nasser's suit" in Egypt—was regarded in his country at the time as "an unprincipled opportunist, a demagogue, and a hypocrite who is considered a talentless ignoramus incapable of making his own contribution to policymaking."[5]) In Sadat's view, the disengagement agreement reached on conclusion of the war two years later constituted the first step in a process that would lead—via his visit to Jerusalem and the 1977 Camp David Summit—to a peace treaty in early 1979. The principle driving forces behind this new Egyptian approach were, as noted, domestic economic factors. But one should not underestimate the impact of Egypt's stunning defeat during the Six-Day War, which led Sadat to the realization that it would be impossible to reclaim the Sinai by war. This new approach manifested, first and foremost, in Egypt's recognition of Israel, its severing of strategic military ties with Moscow, and its pursuit of strategic economic ties with Washington.

Indeed, the peace treaty greatly benefited Egypt's economy, as subsequent data bears out. It received the generous annual sum of $2.3 billion from the United States, regained possession of the Sinai oil fields and was able to develop oil fields on the eastern bank of the Gulf of Suez, rehabilitated the cities along the canal that had been devastated by the War of Attrition, successfully attracted large-scale foreign investment, and greatly enhanced its tourist industry (which brought in $6 billion in 2004). Studies have shown that between 1979 and 2007, Egypt's financial returns from its peace treaty with Israel totaled about $12 billion annually.[6]

The Egyptian revolution, however, manifested as a break from past patterns not in terms of basic national goals and interests but mainly in terms of means. Egypt, under Sadat's leadership, decided to pay for the economic and strategic change it sought with currency that was strictly illegal throughout the Arab Middle East at the time. This necessitated official communication with Jerusalem, which was intended primarily to serve Egyptian needs and did not require any prior Israeli response to the demands of other Arab states or the Palestinians. As such, it amounted to a renunciation of the concept of a military struggle with Israel. Although Sadat strongly opposed this argument, Egypt under his leadership did largely decide to "go it alone," thereby breaking what all the Arab countries had viewed as a major historical pan-Arab consensus. On the one hand, their severing of relations with Egypt, after it signed the peace treaty with Israel and the subsequent expulsion of Cairo from the Arab League, represented the price demanded of and paid by Sadat for the new direction Egypt had chosen. On the other hand, unsurprisingly, under his leadership Cairo immediately launched a political initiative aimed at securing its return to the pan-Arab fold. It did so primarily by emphasizing (for both Israeli and Arab audiences) that the restoration of Palestinian rights and the return of all occupied territories remained the cornerstones of its approach to the Arab-Israeli conflict and that a full and just peace throughout the region required Israel to fulfill its obligations. Cairo underscored these points during Sadat's visit to Jerusalem in 1977, on signing the peace treaty two years later, and in numerous declarations since that time.

Sadat and Mubarak

Even though Menachem Begin, as prime minister of Israel, and Anwar Sadat, as president of Egypt, were endorsing the same text when they signed the peace treaty between their two countries in early 1979, they interpreted it differently. Sadat regarded the provision on autonomy, contained in a rider to the treaty (and in the Camp David Accords), as an initial step toward the realization of all the Arab demands, particularly that of the Palestinians for self-determination and political independence, whereas the Israeli leadership committed itself only to the implementation of personal autonomy in the occupied territories, which it viewed as the end of the process. One of the most important and lesser-known issues that divided the two sides relates to the civil aspects of peace. While the military commitments were relatively straightforward and, for the most part, acceptable to both parties, the provisions calling on them to bridge their social, economic, and cultural divides—that is, to "normalize" their relations—were subject to vastly different interpretations. What did Sadat mean when he spoke of peace with Israel? The available literature is unequivocal: the Egyptian president regarded the establishment of peaceful relations as a "necessary evil"; its implementation should be minimized, and it should not overburden the Egyptian people, who would need many years to adjust to the notion of peace with Israel. His original and overriding intent essentially required only an arrangement that would put an end to warfare and allow for normal relations as interpreted and accepted by the Arabs. Elie Podeh framed the issue in terms of the negative: he argued that Egypt had no domestic or regional interest in shifting from a cold peace to a warm peace with Israel. On the contrary, its relations with the Arab world, various domestic political and ideological considerations that persisted and even exacerbated the conflict with Israel, and its long history of confrontation with the latter were factors that in Egypt's view required it to adopt a deliberate policy of "normal" peace—that is, no more than necessary—or what Israel regarded as a cold peace.[7]

The following analysis offers an explanation. As early as December 1971, Sadat stated in an interview with the *Times* that "I will never be able to maintain normal and regular relations with Israel, but I will make peace with it and honor my word after I sign a peace agreement."[8] In July 1975 he told the Egyptian newspaper *Al-Ahram* that "I am willing to approve a peace agreement.... But it is only natural that after twenty-six years of war, hostility, and bloodshed, it is inconceivable that peace can be established from one moment to the next. The most we can achieve is an end to the state of war.... Let us leave future generations to act as they see fit."[9] In his autobiography, published shortly after the Camp David Summit, the Egyptian president stated, "What do [the Israelis] mean by peace? Are they referring to open borders and the establishment of diplomatic relations between Israel and the Arab states? They know that [there] are ... obstacles on the path to peace. After thirty years of conflict with Israel, after four wars, massacres and bloodshed, after hatred and rivalry in every sense, no one in the Arab world today is ready to suddenly open the border, just like that, overnight."[10]

On February 24, 1980, shortly before the arrival of Israel's first ambassador to Cairo, Eliyahu Ben-Elissar, Sadat stated that "it is difficult to make people shed their long-time experiences of failure, bitterness, and suspicion; one cannot train people to change their character," adding that "it is normal to have friendly relations and lukewarm relations, and for people to draw closer when it is beneficial and to drift apart when it is harmful."[11] Sadat was voicing a political stance grounded in the view that normalization would follow from measures to be taken by Israel with respect to the occupied territories and the establishment of a Palestinian entity. That is, normalization was not a self-contained process; rather, it depended on progress in other areas, and in any event it was not a priority for Egypt. Israel's refusal to adopt such measures, as detailed below, served as justification for Egyptian presidents to resist any meaningful implementation of agreed-upon normalization provisions.

Sadat also identified an important psychological factor that reduced the likelihood of Egypt implementing the normalization agreements in the near future: its leaders had not been prepared for such a development, and many even feared it. This explains why from the outset, with the initial contact that led to the 1979 peace treaty, Sadat sought to postpone normalization to a later stage. As time passed he shortened the transition period, eventually having no choice but to succumb to Israeli pressure and agree to immediate normalization. Still, unsurprisingly, the president felt that normalization had been forced on him, and he saw it as an embarrassing and harmful surrender. As Avraham Sela, then head of the Egypt desk for Military Intelligence, predicted in 1979, "Egypt will have an interest in preventing criticism and sanctions on the part of Arabs states as a consequence of 'excessive' friendliness with Israel, beyond what is inevitable as a direct result of signing a treaty with Israel. . . . It is therefore evident that the Egyptian interest within the inter-Arab arena will require Egypt . . . to maintain as 'low' a profile as possible as regards the practical aspects of its peaceful relations with Israel."[12]

Egyptian president Hosni Mubarak, who succeeded Sadat after the latter was assassinated in October 1981, maintained this policy even after Israel withdrew from the Sinai in April of the following year. But according to scholars in the field, he sang a different tune and was more reserved than his predecessor in matters related to normalization and the peace treaty. Amira Oron, an Israeli diplomat who dealt with the economic relationship between Israel and Egypt at the time, found in her study that "Mubarak established an approach according to which . . . relations with Israel should not be cultivated any more than was necessary for the sake of Egypt's interests, foremost among which was the renewal and preservation of relations with Arab states. During the first decade of his presidency . . . the pattern of maintaining a cold peace operated as a salient and important matter of principle that benefited Egypt. This pattern served Egypt's needs of confronting the Arab boycott while rebuilding bridges to Arab states."[13]

During a moment of anger while delivering a speech to students at Cairo University in 1991, Mubarak strayed from his written text and spoke directly from his heart. To the dismay of the Israeli ambassador, who read the speech later, the president asserted,

> Why all this criticism? We were told that the Jews would not carry out the second [phase of] withdrawal, [but] they returned all of the Sinai. The Arabs repeatedly said that the Jews were holding on to Taba and had pulled one over on us, yet we successfully extracted the last grain of sand from their hands. . . . We managed to force them to do what we wanted, we prevailed, and what did we give them in exchange—a piece of paper. We were more clever than they were. We managed to stop them and establish networks that would minimize contact with them. We proved that peace does not mean Jewish control and that we were not obligated to cultivate relations beyond those we sought.[14]

Yossi Ben Aharon, director of Foreign Minister Shamir's office, related that one day they received news that the Egyptian president had reacted angrily upon learning of Israel's demand that he retract the freeze on normalization, shouting, "I am fed up with this word." And "thus," Ben-Aharon added, "more than fifty memos and agreements intended to give real and practical content to the peace treaty with Egypt were buried in the archives of the foreign ministries in Cairo and Jerusalem."[15] This outlook explains Mubarak's systematic refusal to visit Israel, except one visit as vice president and on the occasion of Yizthak Rabin's funeral.

The Egyptian Foreign Ministry

Despite the authoritarian nature of the Egyptian regime and the vast decision-making powers of its president, including in the sphere of normalization with Israel, the administrative body responsible for delineating and implementing normalization in practical terms was the Foreign Ministry. Yet this body rejected the entire concept from the outset because it was aware of the political price Egypt would have to pay for such peace: damage to its relations with the Arab world and its regional standing. Sadat had not heeded these warnings, evidently because he did not regard the implications as being particularly weighty and because he hoped that the talks on autonomy would bear fruit. As a result, before signing the peace treaty with Israel, he had to deal with the challenges posed by no fewer than three senior Egyptian foreign policy makers. Ismail Fahmi and Mahmoud Riad (the secretary-general of the Arab League at the time) resigned because of their opposition to the president's visit to Jerusalem and the peace treaty with Israel. Mohamed Kamel Amr resigned during the Camp David talks, accusing Sadat of failing to ensure a solution to the Palestinian problem. He explained his position in his book *The Lost Peace*: "I reached the end of the road. . . . The problem was not Israel's extremist position, nor was it the United States' submission to Israel, but rather . . . President Sadat himself. He deferred completely to President Carter, who in turn succumbed to Menachem Begin. Any agreement achieved on this basis would be a disaster for Egypt, for the Palestinian people, and for the entire Arab nation."[16] During a briefing shortly before assuming his post, Egypt's first ambassador to Israel, Saad Murtada, received instructions from Sadat, who stressed that the primary aim of the ambassador's mission was to ensure Israel's withdrawal from the Sinai and then to promote negotiations on autonomy. The Egyptian diplomat realized that Egypt's approach conflicted with that of Israel and that the latter aspired to return only a portion of the Arab lands in exchange for a warm peace that would include normalization.

On matters regarding peace with Israel, one of the salient figures in the Egyptian Foreign Ministry was Boutros Boutros-Ghali, who in his capacity as minister of state for foreign affairs from 1977 to 1991 maintained close ties with Egypt's presidents. A Coptic Christian, he was one of the "fathers of peace" with Israel and for years was considered the "guardian" of Israeli diplomats in Cairo. In 1981, while awaiting the arrival of Ezer Weizmann at the Cairo airport, he spoke frankly about his views on normalization with the Israeli ambassador, Ephraim Dowek—himself a native of Cairo. Boutros-Ghali's remarks—which were reminiscent of Nasser's "three-circle theory"—echoed for years in the corridors of the Foreign Ministry and Prime Minister's Office in Jerusalem. Anyone in Israel who was engaged in the issue became familiar with these remarks, and much use was made of them. Accordingly, they deserve a detailed examination:

> It is clear that relations with Egypt are important to Israel; Egypt is the largest country in the Middle East and the natural leader of the region. This is a fact of life that Israel must accept and live with. For Egypt, the relations with Israel are not at all important. Israel is a small state, just a dot on the regional map, with no weight or global significance. We Arabs stupidly inflated it beyond proportion and turned it into a giant. The time has come to return it to its natural proportions, and it is a minuscule state in terms of population, geography, and economy. It exists by virtue of massive aid from the United States and world Jewry, and it will encounter tremendous difficulties when this aid is terminated. Its sources of immigration will also be sealed off when the messianic spirit that brought Jews from all over the world dissipates. . . . For decades we were engaged with Israel, fought against it, and placed it at the center of Arab consciousness and action while neglecting our genuine interests. We saw the world through "Israeli glasses" and Israel became the be-all and end-all for us. We concentrated all our resources on annihilating it and ignored the need to invest in advancing our own peoples educationally and economically. Today, because of the peace, Egypt can free itself of Israel, look at the global map more shrewdly, and pursue goals that embrace the entire world [the restoration of Arab unity, leadership of the Arab nation, the realization of its interests in Africa, and the establishment of its standing among the nonaligned states]. These are our natural markets and the backbone of political support that we must consolidate and lead. Israel has no place in Egypt's plans. We will maintain correct relations, but they will always be marginal for us and will never have priority. We will not allow the Israeli conundrum to overshadow Egypt's genuine interests.[17]

Although Boutros-Ghali was fully aware of the important link between the relations with Israel and US foreign aid to Egypt, his remarks to Dowek clarify his opposition to normalization. From Israel's perspective he represented the "cold peace" that characterized relations between the two states. As Major General Avraham Tamir, head of the IDF Planning Division who oversaw preparations related to the peace treaty in Jerusalem, recalled,

> We often wondered whether the [Egyptian] Foreign Ministry was responsible for failures to implement normalization, by circumventing the agreements and the promises President Sadat had given Prime Minister Begin at each of their summit meetings, or whether there was a tactic of two voices—the calming voice of Sadat, intended to give the impression of all-out progress towards

peace so as to ensure that Israel would withdraw from the Sinai without posing obstacles, and the blunt voice of Boutros-Ghali, who had operational
oversight, which was intended to prove to the Arab states that there would
be no peace until the other problems related to the Arab-Israeli conflict were
resolved on the basis of "Arab consensus."[18]

Other key figures in Mubarak's government also identified with this
approach. Foreign Minister Amr Moussa, a devoted follower of Nasser's pan-Arab
legacy, publicly criticized those Arab states that hastened to establish relations
with Israel, using a term that echoed throughout Arab diplomatic circles, especially during the Oslo process of the 1990s—namely, rashness (*harwalah*). He was
also prominent in Egypt's struggle against Israel's nuclear armament. In practice,
these views reflected Egypt's perspective that Israel was in fact competing with it
for hegemonic status in the Middle East—in contrast to Boutros-Ghali's dismis-
sive view. It is therefore not surprising that Yitzhak Rabin once referred to the
"evil winds" blowing from Egypt's Foreign Ministry under Mousa's leadership.[19]
There is considerable evidence that some of Egypt's ambassadors also adopted
this approach. The most prominent was the second Egyptian ambassador to
Israel, Mohammed Bassiouni, who held Israel responsible for the failure of the
autonomy negotiations. As a result, in his words, he "did not devote a single day
to promoting bilateral relations and did not advance normalization."[20] That failure had already been attributed to Jerusalem in the early 1980s by Egypt's ambassador to the UN, Ahmed Asmat Abdel-Meguid. Shortly before Israel completed
its withdrawal from the Sinai, he enumerated Egypt's terms for comprehensive
peace in the region: an end to the occupation, the return of refugees, the Palestinian right of self-determination on their land, Arab sovereignty over Jerusalem,
the removal of settlements from occupied territories, and the establishment of a
Palestinian state along the 1967 borders—all of which represented positions that
Israeli governments at the time categorically rejected. In any event, the available
documentation indicates unequivocally that influential circles within the Egyptian government viewed normalization as tantamount to a warm peace, to which
it was unconditionally opposed.

Ideological Opposition

Egypt's utilitarian peace did not reflect the internal struggle it was having with
its own deeply rooted ideological perspectives, which, whether based on its Arab
identity or its Islamic heritage, rejected Israel's very existence, not to mention normalization with the latter. Beyond the government's argument linking normalization, or the lack thereof, with Arab political interests (such as the legitimate rights
of Palestinians and borders that would at least theoretically allow for change),
the overall social opposition was independent of any such factors and perhaps

therefore more significant. It was grounded in pan-Arab culture and ideology. Many intellectuals, journalists, and commentators in Cairo fiercely opposed normalization in general, and for Egypt in particular, on this basis. In addition to Islam's theological contempt for Jews as "enemies of God and his Prophet," many in these and other circles were categorically unable to accept Jewish sovereignty in Palestine because the latter constituted *dar al-Islam*, the term used by Muslim scholars to refer to countries where Muslims can practice their religion as the ruling sect while certain religions (Judaism, Christianity, and Sabianism) are only to be tolerated. Many Muslims regarded this concept as a solution in the event of a clash between the Muslim vision and reality. In the words of Jacob Lasner and Ilan Troen, "Were Muslims to comport themselves, the Western imperialists and the Zionist colonizers would surely suffer the fate of previous invaders. That is, they would either become Muslims as did the Mongols or like the Crusaders they would be purged from the Abode of Islam by a reinvigorated Muslim Polity."[21]

Furthermore, throughout these widespread circles normalization was regarded as the imposition of Western cultural and political values, such as secular democracy and globalization, which had been identified as antithetical to Islam and pan-Arabism. Accordingly, there was no bridging the two under any circumstances. The contradiction between them meant that criticism of normalization, rather than being "rational" in strategic or political terms, was "irrational" and unrelenting. Given that peace with Israel represented an intolerable threat to the culture and values of Arab identity as a whole, the conflict with Israel was, in the words of Avraham Sela, "a conflict of survival" [*sira' wuoud*] rather than a "conflict of borders" [*sira' hudoud*].[22] Toward the end of the 1980s, Rivka Yadlin examined the harsh criticism of Israel in the Egyptian press of the time, framing the central question she sought to address as follows: "Is the hostility emanating from these writings intended only as an expression of anti-Israel sentimentality or anti-Zionism as such, rather than an anti-Jewish, anti-Semitic position?"[23] Her well-researched response, in the negative, underscores the significance of ideology in the Egyptian attitude toward normalization. Overall, in the view of Yaakov Amitai, a former Israeli ambassador to Cairo, there was a vast discrepancy between the perspective of Egypt (and Arabs generally), which viewed Judaism solely as a religion, and the Israeli perception of Judaism as both a religion and nationality.[24] Thus, it was inevitable that the Egyptians would be unwilling and unable to accept Zionism or to recognize the validity of Israel's existence and its policy makers' aspirations of normalization.

Notably, although Israel's leaders understood that there were relatively moderate voices among Egypt's intellectuals and educated classes, they believed it was the extremists who set the tone. In any event, whether for political reasons stemming from realpolitik or for ideological reasons, Israel's vision of achieving normalization with Egypt failed the test of reality.

Domestic Egyptian Politics

The principles and perspectives described above, which had an important influence on Egypt's leaders, were driven by several domestic entities that deserve mention. The most persistent were the professional associations, a majority of which were subject to the influence if not the control of religious bodies associated with the Society of the Muslim Brothers (the Muslim Brotherhood). The fact that the Arab states, which did not have relations with Israel, were the focus of economic activity on the part of this movement as well as leftist and Nasserist entities also played a part. During a visit by the Israeli minister of health to Egypt in 1995, his Egyptian counterpart informed him that he wanted to promote cooperation with Israel but that this must take place slowly and cautiously so as not to anger the physicians' union, which was controlled in large part by the Muslim Brotherhood. In his words, he was interested in "industrial calm."[25] Radical Islamist groups, opposition parties, intellectuals, and students also tended to hold critical views of the peace treaty and of normalization in particular.

All of these parties were united in the view that normalization was an aggressive Israeli move aimed at exploiting the resources of Egypt's relatively weaker economy, subjecting it to Israeli hegemony, and undermining Egyptian culture and identity. As such it was "good for the Jews and bad for Egypt."[26] Shimon Shamir, a former Israeli ambassador to Cairo who also served as director of the Israeli Academic Center based there, argued that these parties had several advantages in their clash with the government over relations with Israel. Their claims were essentially ideological and based on "values and symbols that are firmly grounded in Egyptian society. The pan-Arab and Nasserist Islamic arguments against peace are based on assumptions that the Egyptian leadership itself accepts to some extent. In contrast, the government's policy is based on utilitarian considerations that, while they have much validity in practical terms, do not inspire much enthusiasm in the domestic debate. The government spokesmen therefore use weak language and in effect leave the domestic arena in the hands of critics opposed to relations with Israel."[27] Among other reasons, their language was "weak" because it was convenient for Egypt's leaders to use normalization as a bargaining chip, in the form of reward or punishment for Israel's actions.[28] One of the factors that impeded the government's ability to challenge opponents of normalization was that it could not offer its domestic constituency a convincing rationale for its peace policy after Israel withdrew from the Sinai in 1982, and particularly in light of the war in Lebanon that year. According to Shamir, "The decision regarding peace with Israel was, as we know, adopted at the time because of the concrete constraints that resulted from the devastating effects of the conflict. But in order to implement this policy, to make it acceptable and legitimate, Egypt needed a favorable and reasonable conceptual foundation. . . . The reality that emerged from the events in Lebanon left the Egyptian peace policy without a case."[29]

In the view of David Sultan, an Israeli ambassador to Cairo, none of these domestic factors was solely decisive in shaping Egyptian policy toward Israel, but their cumulative effect was significant.[30] He also noted that many anti-Israeli preconceptions gained ground among the Egyptian public during those years. Deputy Prime Minister Hassan al-Tuhami, for example, stated in a newspaper interview in April 1980 that the Jews were "treacherous and hypocritical" and thus it was no wonder that history books regarded them as such.[31] The ambassador frequently encountered the popular belief that there was a map hanging in the Knesset marking the borders of "Greater Israel": from the Nile River in the west to the Euphrates in the east. Another popular rumor held that Israel was deliberately spreading AIDS among Egyptians and poisoning the country's water supply. Fears surrounding Israel's advanced technology and what many saw as its efforts to exploit peace with Egypt to secure regional hegemony also fueled harsh criticism of the peace treaty and its normalization provisions.

Consequently, the concept of normalization came to embody negative connotations across Egypt and throughout the Arab world, a fact of which Jerusalem was acutely aware. This explains why, years later, when the question of relations with Jordan was under review, Israel decided not to use that word, opting instead for terms such as *cooperation* and *peace building*. Likewise, in 2007 the Israeli Foreign Ministry issued official, explicit instructions to its personnel to replace the term *normalization* with the phrase *good neighborliness*.[32]

Diplomatic Life in the Shadow of the Pyramids

Israel's delegates to Cairo arrived in the Egyptian capital with great hopes, but the immediate and consistent reaction they encountered was a cold one, as was their daily diplomatic life. The Egyptians left no room for doubt as to the direction of the political "winds" or as to the actual value, in government eyes, of the official treaty between the two states. Moshe Sasson, Israel's second ambassador to Egypt, attested to this in his memoirs, noting with cautious diplomatic understatement that during his seven years in Cairo, "the moments of pleasure and genuine comfort were relatively few and brief." Conversely, there were "long periods of tension, disagreement, and misunderstanding which I had to work hard to remedy."[33]

Furthermore, his reports on daily life in Cairo, as well as those of his predecessor and successors, generated a strong sense of disappointment in Jerusalem regarding hopes for normalization. Zvi Gabai, political advisor at the Israeli Embassy, described the moment in which this reality hit home: upon the arrival of his entourage in Cairo, the manager of the hotel at which they were scheduled to stay rejected the possibility of security measures, compelling them to improvise; after scrambling to find a place for the night, they located a "tiny, derelict, internally and externally depressing" hotel named the Dreamers, "which was too prosaic for us."[34] Israel's first delegate and, later, third ambassador to Cairo, Ephraim Dowek, also recalled the disappointment that awaited Israeli diplomats: after a premises for the Israeli Embassy had been located, its landlord received a "fat check" covering five years' rent; the following morning, however, the landlord arrived and, with shaking hands, returned the money, claiming that he needed the entire building for his married daughter and pleading that they revoke the lease. "It was obvious," according to Dowek, that he was not operating of his own free will but was in fact "scared to death" of the authorities.[35] Moreover, the security arrangements surrounding the building that was eventually located to house the embassy were so strict that, from the Israeli point of view, they were intended to convey a twofold message: to inform the Israelis that they were unwanted guests and to demonstrate to the Egyptian masses "the segregation of the loathsome" Israeli presence. The attitude toward visitors, recalled Dowek, was "rude and brusque": the authorities would subject them to a lengthy, probing interrogation in order to determine who would be sent home, who could enter the embassy, and who would be summoned for further questioning. "The noose around the neck of Israeli delegates steadily tightened, and at times the sense of suffocation was unbearable."[36] Their feelings of claustrophobia stemmed as well from restrictions on communication during the early years. The embassy's mail was subject to a six-week delay; when Israeli diplomats conducted their own experiment—by posting anonymous letters with no identifying marks, using mailboxes in various neighborhoods throughout Cairo—they discovered that these letters reached their destination within a day.

Dowek further recalled that the attitude of high-ranking officials at the Foreign Ministry and other ministries was "cool and restrained," conveying "suppressed hostility" mixed with "affected correctness" and "Oriental politeness" (Dowek Kzarim, 141)The officials were bound by instructions from above: they were not to befriend Israeli diplomats, not to accept their invitations, not to issue invitations to them, and not to meet with them even on work-related matters. In Israel, too, there were reminders of Egypt's interpretation of normalization. The minimal diplomatic presence at receptions marking Israel's Day of Independence contrasted starkly with events hosted by Egypt's ambassador in Israel to celebrate Egyptian independence, which were attended by the entire senior political echelon, including the president and prime minister as well as most government ministers and an audience of thousands. Besides the social and political noose stemming from Egypt's attitude, Israeli diplomats also encountered a blatant lack of interest on the part of foreign diplomats, who refrained from accepting invitations issued by the Israeli Embassy or issuing invitations to Israelis. This was presumably the result of an unspoken assumption on the part of Egyptian authorities and an interest on the part of foreign dignitaries in avoiding problems in their social and business ties with Egypt.

The physical mobility of Israeli representatives in Cairo was therefore very limited or practically nonexistent. Embassy staff were left with a great deal of time on their hands to read and analyze the Egyptian press, which among themselves they termed their "daily dose of poison."[37] When Israel protested the publication by Egypt's Information Authority of *Mein Kampf* and its presentation at the 1982 Book Fair (the last one to which Israel was invited) as well as the publication of *The Protocols of the Elders of Zion*, it was told that these were "old stocks" predating the peace treaty, which had "accidentally been retrieved from the Authority's storerooms."[38] On one occasion President Mubarak informed a delegation of Jewish leaders from the United States that Israel's participation in book fairs would require extensive security measures and a large presence of security officials, which he wanted to avoid because it would not benefit relations with Israel.[39] Although these remarks did contain an element of truth, Israel's diplomats were skeptical about their sincerity. Nor did the diplomats categorically accept Egypt's defensive argument that it had a free press that was merely voicing its opinions. "Everything is coordinated from above," as one Israeli diplomat stated in summarizing years of contact with the Egyptian media:

> Like an octopus with one head and many arms that move in different directions, giving the false impression that each arm is independent and has a life of its own, so too in the case of Egyptian propaganda instruments. . . . The Minister of Public Relations sits at the top of the pyramid. Every morning he or the director of his office sits down with the chief editors of the various media outlets and instructs them how to convey the events of the previous day as well as the government's positions on salient world affairs. He also gives each media outlet a daily assignment and prescribes the "dosage" for each one so as to avoid "boring" uniformity.[40]

Thus Israel's diplomats in Cairo found themselves on the front line in the state's confrontation with Egypt over normalization. Dowek's illuminating memoirs reflect the lessons these diplomats learned during the first decade of peace with Egypt:

> Without taking unnecessary risks, Egypt deliberately and systematically managed to avoid implementing most of the agreed-upon normalization provisions, and to use them as a powerful instrument for exerting pressure on Israel in the form of "reward and punishment" while sending both positive and negative messages and signals to Israel, the Arabs, and the Egyptian people. Israel's longing for recognition, normal relations, and cordiality, and its obvious willingness to keep paying for the crumbs tossed to it from the normalization table encouraged Egypt to maintain and even increase its use

of this instrument, whose effectiveness proved itself in practical terms. The Egyptians learned that their smile had a price and that Israel was willing to pay this price.[41]

After all, Dowek added, "it was clear that we would not sever relations with Egypt simply because it was not sending us belly dancers."[42]

The message conveyed by Israeli representatives to their superiors in Jerusalem in this regard was clear and consistent. It is interesting but not surprising to read the report of an American diplomat in Cairo to the State Department in Washington, noting that "anyone reading the national Egyptian press, whose editors-in-chief are funded by the government, would form the impression that Egypt was still in a state of war with Israel."[43]

Under these circumstances, the Israelis could only conclude that a voice from on high was directing every media statement and cultural expression. They were deeply offended by the interesting and highly instructive fact, as it relates to normalization, that Israel did not appear on any geographic atlas produced in Egypt, including the atlases used at state-run schools. The entire territory between the Mediterranean Sea and Jordan was labeled as "Palestine." According to these maps, Israel did not even exist. "Every time Israeli diplomats asked that the maps be amended, they were told that this would happen 'when the current inventory of atlases runs out.'"[44] Twenty-five years after the peace treaty was signed, Dowek observed, "the stocks of atlases in Egyptian storerooms have not yet run out, and apparently they never will."[45] Israeli diplomats believed that given the extent of public ignorance, the Egyptian media could play an important role in educating the public and preparing it for peace. Yet it was doing precisely the opposite by "perpetuating the feelings of hostility and hatred towards Israel."[46] Moreover, the authorities contributed to this situation by issuing instructions that prohibited or greatly restricted any dialogue between Israeli representatives in Cairo and newspaper editors. Those few and exceptional members of the press who were allowed contact were required to report to security officials on any meetings with Israeli Embassy staff. Israeli diplomats also learned that one of the reasons for the fierce criticism of the normalization agreement on the part of much of the Egyptian press actually had nothing to do with Israel per se. Rather, it stemmed from the government's need to provide the media with a "valve" to release domestic pressure. As a result, even a relative improvement in the bilateral relationship was not reflected in the media, which maintained its harsh criticism of Israel.

There was one notable exception to Egypt's restrictions in the area of media and culture. The normalization agreement provided for the establishment of Israeli and Egyptian academic centers. The Egyptian center, however, never emerged, while the Israeli center, funded and coordinated by the Israeli Academy of Sciences, failed to achieve most of its intended aims, foremost among which were the provision of support for collaborative studies and the promotion of relations between academics from both countries. One of the main reasons for the center's failing was that the authorities had marked it as an Israeli spy agency, causing Egyptian scientists and intellectuals to fear that participating in the center's activities would sabotage their own relations with wealthy Arab countries, which in turn would cut them off, putting an end to commissions for work and invitations to events. Unsurprisingly, therefore, the first director of the Israeli Academic Center in Cairo, Shimon Shamir, chose to title his memoirs *Saved Leaf* (also translated as *A Newly Plucked Olive Leaf*). The title refers, of course, to the biblical story of Noah and the dove that returned with a plucked olive branch in its mouth as a sign of peace. And the Israeli Academic Center had indeed emerged out of the hope for peace, as symbolized by its activities. But in time it became evident that this was a limited peace and "the Center stood alone, like a 'plucked' leaf—the only silver lining in a relationship rife with disappointment."[47]

Jerusalem's Normalization Efforts

Israel's objectives in signing a peace treaty with Egypt were clear from the outset, and to this day they have not changed significantly. First and foremost, peace eliminated Egypt's role in the cycle of war, thus impeding or even preventing the formation of a coalition against Israel. In addition, the demilitarization of the Sinai would provide Israel with advance warning and reduce the likelihood of a surprise attack by Egypt. Nor would Israel need to maintain a large military presence on the peninsula during peacetime. And indeed, the peace between Egypt and Israel did break the Arab consensus that rejected any pact with Israel, and it gradually divided the Arab states between those that supported a political process to resolve the conflict, such as Morocco and Jordan, and those that sought to maintain and even intensify the conflict, such as Syria and Libya. In this sense Egypt became a key agent in the peace process, with the embassies in each country serving as a practical and symbolic bridge. Finally, there was the hope and expectation that this political and strategic agreement would, as the text itself provided, lead to a series of normalization agreements on civil matters such as transportation, trade, and agriculture. After conducting an internal debate that was quite fierce at times, Israel's leaders decided that the benefits of the treaty justified withdrawal from the entire Sinai and its return to Egypt, as well as the destruction of Yamit and other Israeli settlements in the Sinai and the establishment of an apparatus that would address the question of autonomy for the West Bank and Gaza.

The first time Israel expressed the hope of achieving peace, with normalization as a key element, was in the early 1970s. At a peace conference in Geneva in December 1973, Israeli foreign minister Abba Eban gave explicit voice to this aspiration, emphasizing that lasting peace necessitates the creation of "a new human reality," given that the negotiating governments must define the relations they seek in the economic, commercial, cultural, and political spheres. The intricacies of their mutual relations, according to Eban, will create common interests, and human interaction and regional cooperation will reduce the likelihood of future wars.[48] The unique circumstances of the peace agreement with Egypt gave these general objectives concrete significance, largely because of multilayered Israeli concerns regarding the agreement. Most salient was the often-overlooked fact that this peace was initiated by the adversary, which necessarily raised questions about hidden motives. Moreover, Israeli (and Jewish) history is informed by the precept *kabdehu vekhashdehu* ("respect and suspect"—that is, proceed cautiously in dealing with someone new), which only seemed more relevant after the bitter surprise of October 1973. Also influential were the warnings of Yehoshafat Harkabi—the former head of Military Intelligence, a former defense establishment official, and the leading expert on Arab views regarding their conflict with Israel—who argued that the Arabs' statements about peace were not genuine. Israel's political leadership was accustomed to receiving threatening messages from the Arab world, and other types of messages were often interpreted in this light as well. No less significant is the fact that Israel paid for this peace immediately, in the concrete currency of land, in exchange for a series of promises. Israel's concerns that at some point in the near or distant future it would have lost all its assets without achieving peace were therefore natural and rational.

The Israeli government was specifically concerned about three possibilities that Sasson formulated as follows: "What will be the fate of peace with Egypt if Sadat suddenly disappears or resigns? Will peace still exist after we complete our withdrawal from the Sinai and return jurisdiction over the entire area to Egypt, as required by the treaty? Will this separate peace last if, because of unforeseeable circumstances, Israel is forced to launch war against one of its neighboring Arab states?"[49] Even though, as we shall see, future developments provided relatively favorable answers to these questions, Jerusalem remained concerned, particularly in light of the many calls in Egypt from oppositionist Nasserist and Islamist circles to revoke the peace treaty. Moreover, the Middle East remained a volatile and unpredictable region in which peaceful coexistence between two states, no matter how long it had lasted, could suddenly be destroyed. The possibility of failure therefore continued to hang over the heads of Israeli policy makers. Sasson, for example, explained that one of the reasons he remained in Cairo for seven years (an exceptionally long time in Israeli foreign service) was "the knowledge that if, heaven forbid, something undermines this first peace, achieved with the region's largest Arab state, then we will be destined to live by the sword not just for one generation but many generations, we and our children and our children's children. . . . This was in fact the essence of the challenge I had to face."[50]

In June 1979 the head of the Mossad, Meir Amit, wrote a rare and very significant article titled "The Battle over Peace" in which he presented the solution to Israel's problem in this regard. He held that in light of the peace treaty,

> We need to find a way to break the vicious cycle in which we find ourselves. On the one hand we face Egypt's reluctance to cooperate meaningfully until the Palestinian problem is resolved and negotiations with other Arab countries make progress, while on the other hand we feel that we have relinquished valuable assets . . . in exchange for vague promises. Failure to abide by these promises is likely to increase suspicion and repeat the cycle. The main challenge is to establish a higher level of normalization, beyond the "bare minimum" required for the technical practicalities of official peace. Even if we accept that the Egyptian version of normalization does not necessitate close ties, we face the question: How do we take advantage of current dynamics to enhance the value of [our] part of the package. . . . First of all we must understand the importance of the normalization process in its true sense and accept the fact that without it the treaty is on shaky ground.[51]

Accepting this analysis, the Israeli government called for the formulation and implementation of normalization processes that would expand the base of support for peace within Egyptian society, beyond the ruling elites. In other words, Egypt's interest in peace with Israel—in terms of its civil aspects and foreseeable benefits—should be made clear to the Egyptian people. Israel's aim in this regard was to establish a "positive peace" based on active engagement rather than settle for a "negative peace" that embodied nothing more than refraining from war on the basis of mutual deterrence. In Israel's view, normalization should lead to the "concretization" of Egypt's commitment to peace. Importantly, Israel's normalization efforts were not centered on generating material economic gains from its relations with Egypt; in this regard the Israeli economy was oriented toward the industrialized world rather than the third world. Nor did Israel in any way aspire to seize control over the Egyptian economy. From the outset, Israel's normalization efforts were a "litmus test" of Egypt's political intentions, and at no time were they aimed at the achievement of material gain.

Given these contradictions between Egyptian and Israeli principles and viewpoints, the following questions arise: How did these contradictions translate into action? Of the fifty or so agreements and protocols on normalization (in the form of "agreed minutes" signed by the two sides during the first year of peace), which ones did they implement and in what way?

Business as Usual?

Although the peace treaty explicitly called for normalization across a broad range of areas, it did not provide any blueprints or binding timelines in this regard. That task was left to joint professional committees. However, as soon as these committees began their work, it became clear that a vast gulf existed between the positions of the two sides, both procedurally and substantively. While Israel assigned experts who specialized in the relevant areas to head the corresponding negotiating teams, Egypt tended to dispatch relatively low-level delegations whose expertise was limited to the sphere of negotiations with Israel. From the outset the two sides had divergent points of view. The Israelis focused on substantive matters, seeking the most suitable professional solution, whereas the Egyptians focused on political aspects and sought to minimize any "unnecessary" commitments (even if substantively justifiable) that appeared to conflict with the fundamental government position on normalization with Israel. Nevertheless, before Israel completed its withdrawal from the Sinai, the parties signed a series of normalization agreements that included direct flights between the two states (February 1980), the opening of a commercial terminal in Israel at Nitzana (December 1981), cargo transit (November 1981), the establishment of a direct telephone line between the two countries (September 1981), airmail delivery (April 1982), and mutual commercial insurance (April 1982). Simultaneously Egypt continued to fulfill its earlier commitment of selling Israel two million tons of oil annually, which generated approximately $500 million per year for the former and met a quarter of the latter's consumption needs.

These achievements cannot, however, obscure the basic fact that during the first decade of peace, economic relations remained very limited in scope and entailed only a small number of initiatives. Most of the agreements were not implemented, for a number of objective reasons: the two economies traditionally interacted with different markets (Egypt with the Arab markets and Israel with Europe); the quality and cost of Israeli products were not suited to the Egyptian market, and vice versa; and it took some time to establish stable and credible channels between the two states' respective businesses and entrepreneurs. Above all, though, the limited scale of commercial and economic peace is probably attributable to Egypt's bureaucratic restrictions, most if not all of which were politically based. According to Amira Oron's analysis, Israel nonetheless had high hopes in this area. Many in Israel believed that geographic proximity and land-based contiguity would bridge the Egyptian and Israeli economies despite their differences; in fact, they would complement one another, given Israel's technological know-how and Egypt's cheap yet skilled labor force. There were Egyptian businessmen who shared this optimism and, during the first year of peace, visited the Israeli legation in Cairo to share their "one thousand and one proposals," in Dowek's words.[52] But mutual trade remained deadlocked. The initial available data reveals two basic facts. First, Israelis were more eager to sell than Egyptians were to buy, and second, the figures on the Egyptian side (as well as the Israeli side) are quite underwhelming. They reflect a distinct hesitation to engage with Israel on the part of Egyptian businessmen. This was undoubtedly attributable to Egypt's categorical prohibition on trade between the government sector and Israel (except for oil), which stemmed from the need to ensure the continuity of official trade relations between Egypt and the Arab states, as well as an interest in preventing Israel's entry into Egypt's official economy.

There can be no doubt that Egypt's trade unions also played a part. Their opposition to commerce with Israel evolved into a policy of boycotting any interaction with Israeli agents, with the threat of punitive measures against anyone who violated this policy. Despite this, Israel's representatives in Cairo believed that the regime still disapproved of any commerce with Israel, modest as it may be. In 1981 the government adopted a policy that Dowek dubbed "a tightening of the screws."[53] Egyptian businessmen interested in trade with Israel now had to face complex bureaucratic hurdles (permits, which only the minister of economy could issue, were difficult to attain), interrogation for security clearance, and social and professional exposure. After the launch of Israel's war in Lebanon, which coincided with its withdrawal from the Sinai, Egypt decided not to grant any new permits for import from Israel. The Egyptian authorities also required that any citizens wishing to visit Israel (including for trade purposes) had to obtain a special certificate from the security services—the "yellow permit," as Egyptians and Israeli diplomats called it because of its color. As a consequence, mutual trade decreased drastically, dropping 80 percent. It continued to decline, and by 1989 (the year in which Egypt renewed diplomatic ties with the other Arab states) Israeli exports amounted to only one-fifth of what they had been seven years earlier. From the material available to us, we can safely conclude that the limited scope of the two countries' trade relations resulted primarily from Egypt's interpretation of normalization, which was intended to project its interest in reuniting with the Arab world, minimize Israel's influence, and demonstrate its commitment to the Palestinian cause.

Israel viewed reciprocal tourism as an important element of normalization, which would demonstrate the peaceful nature of its relations with Egypt and serve as leverage for economic cooperation. But the way events unfolded actually highlighted the two sides' differing perspectives. Israel established an elegant travel agency in the heart of the Egyptian capital, headed by a senior tourist official, whereas Egypt never established a comparable agency in Israel. El Al Airlines opened an office in Egypt, which in turn founded Sinai Air, a subsidiary of the national airline, Egypt Air, in order to circumvent a potential Arab boycott or prohibition on flights to Israel. Yet from the outset, Egyptian authorities took several measures to ensure that the number of Egyptians seeking to visit Israel remained small. Egyptians wishing to visit Israel had to deposit their regular passport (which bore a seal stating its validity everywhere except Israel and South Africa) in exchange for a passport valid only for travel to Israel. They also had to obtain the above-mentioned yellow permit. Egyptian authorities indisputably

Table 11.1. Data on Reciprocal Israeli-Egyptian Tourism in 1980–1989

Year	Israeli visitors to Egypt	Egyptian visitors to Israel
1980	14,000	1,886
1981	38,000	2,392
1982	45,000	4,159
1983	63,000	4,400
1984	63,000	4,563
1985	24,575	4,652
1986	32,319	5,598
1987	71,000	5,073
1988	62,902	4,343
1989	122,260	4,235

Source: Oron, "Yakhasei HaShalom Bein Israel LeMitzra'im," 76.

played a major role in minimizing tourism to Israel. According to Dowek, "the tourist agents who worked with Israel were ordered to focus only on bringing Israeli tourists to Egypt" and "to refrain from encouraging Egyptian citizens to visit Israel."[54] The authorities also established several mechanisms for filtering Egyptian tourism to Israel. For example, it would take many weeks to issue exit permits, visas permitted only one entry (which hurt business travel), and Egyptian tourists were subjected to grueling inspections on their return. Mubarak's remarks in a 1991 interview with the Israeli newspaper *Ma'ariv* reflect Egypt's refusal to view reciprocal tourism as a means of rapprochement: "There is nothing to see in Israel. Egypt has thousands of kilometers of wonderful beaches and hundreds of tourist sites that are far superior to those in Israel."[55] Table 11.1 numerically illustrates this disparity in tourism.

There was one area in which normalization, albeit limited, did take place—namely, Israeli agricultural aid—for four important reasons: the fact that Egypt is an agricultural country with a rural population that makes its living from working the land; the increasing rate of Egypt's natural population growth, which requires self-sufficiency to meet the country's growing demand for food; Israel's scientific and technological advancement in this field; and the detrimental desert climate common to both countries. Not coincidentally, therefore, in March 1982 the two signed an agreement that included the formation of an agricultural commission, which continues to operate to this day. The establishment of an agricultural enterprise in the Nile Delta in 1983, their first joint enterprise, as well as smaller initiatives such as the construction of a farm near Ismailia, coincided with Egypt's national interests, and it was therefore only in this area that Israel saw positive developments in the late 1980s. One interesting outcome of this cooperation revolves around the Anna apple, first developed in Israel and acclimatized to Egypt by Israeli and Egyptian agronomists: during that period the Anna apple constituted more than half of Egypt's apple harvest. Nonetheless, cooperation remained limited. During the late 1980s, the number of Egyptians who participated in the ventures of MASHAV ranged from ten to twenty-five annually. Egypt refused to sign aid agreements between the two governments, and the Israeli experts who traveled to Egypt did so under the auspices of private companies that contracted directly with the Egyptian government. Furthermore, agricultural cooperation did not extend beyond the two model farms and a training program that began to take shape toward the end of the decade, although that program was also constrained by political considerations related to other Arab states and to Egypt's unwillingness to appear inferior to Israel or show it preferential treatment.

Nevertheless Peace

Inevitably, this cold peace was a source of disappointment for many in Israel, although there were those, such as Military Intelligence personnel, who had accurately predicted future developments and thus refrained from cultivating false hopes. At the same time, one of the pessimistic forecasts that Israel's military establishment translated into a potential scenario never actually materialized. This fact was and remains one of the most important aspects of the peace agreement, first voiced by Sadat during his speech before the Knesset and reiterated on the same occasion by Begin: "no more war." The assassination of Sadat on October 6, 1981, has not changed this state of affairs. Moreover, the treaty has held its own, despite periods of severe crisis in Israeli-Egyptian relations. One of the important conclusions that Israeli foreign policy architects reached in this regard was that Egypt would not use perceived violations of the peace treaty by Israel as a pretext for war. At the height of the 1982 Lebanon War, Dowek met with Muhammad Abdullah, chairman of the Egyptian Parliament's Foreign Relations Committee, and queried him about his defense minister's implied threats that Egypt would launch war against Israel in response to the latter's invasion of Lebanon. The Egyptian parliamentarian laughed out loud and explained the salient strategic military perspective of Egypt's leaders:

> You should not take such remarks seriously; they are more a sign of weakness than of strength. If Egypt really regarded Israel as an enemy, it would launch war right now and join the efforts to defend Lebanon. But it has rejected all such Arab appeals and opted to maintain peace. . . . The dangers Egypt faces come from other directions, and in any case Israel could easily defeat all the Arab armies put together as it has in the past. It has nuclear weapons and powerful conventional weapons. The entire Sinai is demilitarized, and Israel could reach the Canal within hours. If someone on your side goes crazy and decides to launch war against us, all Egypt could do is to hold out for a few days until the international community intervenes to stop the fighting.[56]

The Egyptians also refrained from using Israel's invasion as a pretext for harsh diplomatic reprisal that would have translated into preparations for war and forced Egypt to confront the question, as framed by Mubarak, "Who would give me the weapons to fight it?"[57]

Ibrahim Saada, editor of the influential daily *Al Akhbar*, expounded candidly on a parallel economic and political perspective prevalent in Cairo at the time:

> Deceiving the Jews is a duty because by their nature they are traitorous and duplicitous. The temptation to revoke the Camp David Accords and expel the Israeli ambassador is great, but we must not give into these feelings. We must carefully consider whether such a step would advance Egypt's national interests. Clearly [Egypt] would be labeled as an aggressor in violation of its international commitments. The West, which has close ties with Israel, would cut off aid to Egypt, stop investing, and suspend trade relations. Israel would be granted legitimacy to invade the Sinai and would quickly seize control of the area, as it is substantively demilitarized. The Canal would again be closed to international transit, which would hurt the cities along the Canal and return them to a state of desolation. The oil wells would fall into Israeli hands, and oil production in the Red Sea would cease. The United States would stop providing us with weaponry to replace outdated Russian arms, and Russia would not come to our aid as it has in the past. The Arabs would not provide us with significant aid . . . [and] would rejoice over Egypt's hardship. In all, not only would Egypt lose about $12 billion annually, it would also find itself without weapons or means of defense. The inevitable conclusion, expressed with "clenched teeth," is that peace with Israel serves Egypt's supreme interests, and unfortunate as it is, Egypt cannot free itself from its contractual obligations towards Israel.[58]

Later developments provide further evidence that Egypt had indeed abandoned war as an element of its relations with Israel. It even engaged in large-scale military cooperation against Hamas and Iran. Intelligence expert Major General Amos Gilead, then director of policy and political-military affairs at the Ministry of Defense, stated in 2009 that relations with Egypt constituted "a cornerstone of Israel's national security." He noted "Egypt's tolerant stance towards Israel during Operation Cast Lead as well as its cooperation in efforts to put an end to smuggling," adding that this state of affairs has important implications beyond the Israeli-Egyptian context: "Without Egypt's leadership, I do not see Jordan maintaining peace with Israel. The Jordanians will not hold out if Egypt deviates from [peace]."[59] Nevertheless, Israeli leaders received a painful reminder of the quality and extent of normalization in its relations with Egypt on September 9, 2011, when several thousand demonstrators attacked the Israeli Embassy in Cairo, seizing control of the building and ransacking many of its offices. The Israeli security staff on the premises, facing peril, were rescued by Egyptian commando forces after the United States applied pressure on Egypt's military leaders to intervene. The Israeli ambassador as well as the embassy staff and their families returned, under escort, to Israel.

Notwithstanding these events, in the aftermath of the "Arab Spring," relations between the two states came to include security cooperation, with US support, in the fight against terrorism, thus actualizing a potential they could not have predicted when they signed the peace treaty. This cooperation explains the recent consent of Israel to the crossing of its border by Egyptian military aircraft in their joint pursuit of terrorists. At the same time, however, according to Israeli diplomats who had served in Cairo, these strengthened strategic ties only appeared to reduce Israel's aspiration for greater civil normalization. As in the past, these diplomats bore firsthand witness to the damaging effects of the lasting cold peace between the two countries. As Yaakov Amitai, a former Israeli ambassador to Egypt, related on his return to Israel in a 2014 interview with *Yediot Akhronot,*

> Every time I wanted some air I would take refuge in a small bookstore. I would search the new titles, political books and novels on Egypt in the modern era, and would dive into them. During my last week in Cairo I paid a farewell visit to a wonderful shop. A few minutes after we, Israeli diplomats and security guards, entered, the shop owner, quite upset, approached me and said that his customers were leaving the store because of me. But in the same breath he said "*birahtak, birahtak,*" meaning, take your time and finish your purchases. I bought a book quickly, with a sour feeling. The awkward situation and the tension that the owner projected while also showing politeness combined to create a lousy feeling that for me reflected, at the deepest personal level, the gulf between the cold nature of peace between us and my hopes."[60]

The current Israeli ambassador to Cairo also had a humiliating experience in early 2017, after attending a performance at the Egyptian National Theater. His presence sparked harsh criticism of the theater's manager for not interrupting the show and expelling the ambassador. "Forty years after Sadat's visit to Israel, the presence of an Israeli ambassador at a show in Egypt still provokes criticism," David Govrin sadly observed at a conference in Tel Aviv on March 21, 2017, where he also offered his professional opinion on the glass-half-full approach, noting that "relations between the two states [currently] have a military footing, but peace requires two feet, one of which provides a civil and economic footing."[61]

Having said that, we should bear in mind that Israel's consistent refusal to pursue the establishment of a Palestinian state or withdraw from the territories captured in 1967 (the West Bank, Gaza Strip, and Golan Heights) amounted, in Egypt's view, to direct responsibility for the failure to achieve normalization. On matters surrounding Israel's invasion of Lebanon, Cairo also came to realize that Jerusalem either gave no weight to considerations of a possible Egyptian military or political response (a question whose answer requires the declassification of

Israeli state documents) or dismissed such considerations as negligible in light of its own security concerns. Particularly notable in this regard was Israel's bombing of the Iraqi nuclear reactor. Despite an assessment by its own Military Intelligence that such an operation would have a devastating effect on Egypt's approach to relations with Israel, the government opted to carry out the operation. A similar dynamic characterized Israel's decision to implement the Golan Heights Law. When he submitted the matter for governmental authorization on December 14, 1981, Menachem Begin argued that "we are not violating the peace treaty with Egypt because that is an agreement between two states and it bears no relation to Syria."[62]

The prime minister would certainly have been aware of the accepted political and military assessment at the time, which, according to Ambassador Yaakov Amitai, held that although implementation of the Golan Law did pose a certain risk, given Egypt's political and security needs, it was not a major one. Indeed, Israel took Cairo's restrained response to the law and to its nine-week siege of Beirut a year later as an important validation of this thesis.

In any event, the failure to realize the vision of normalization still amounts to an outstanding debt from Israel's viewpoint, with wide-ranging repercussions beyond the specific context addressed in this chapter. Peace with Egypt centered, in essence, on a formula that Israel was always reluctant to acknowledge—namely, land for peace. Yet Israel's hope was that the deal it had struck with Egypt and continuous subsequent dialogue would pave the way to peace not only between the states but also between their respective societies, not only between the leaders but also between the two peoples. This was not how events unfolded, though. The lesson for Israel, perhaps, is that it should not foster illusions of the sort that characterized the early years of peace with Egypt: neither the return of territories nor continuous contact were instantly able to obliterate patterns of conduct, ideology, theology, sentiment, or perceptions of identity and of the past, especially in the absence of any breakthrough toward resolution of the Palestinian problem. Such a metamorphosis will take a long time, as Moshe Sasson observed in his memoirs: "Peace building is a matter of prolonged work."[63] Shlomo Gazit, the head of Military Intelligence during Sadat's visit to Israel, reinforced this view with his assertion that "recognition of the right of the Zionist entity to exist in the heart of the Arab-Muslim Middle East might only be possible after several generations of cold peace and normalization."[64] It remains an open question whether the extensive security cooperation currently underway in the fight against ISIS and terrorism in the Sinai has the potential to challenge those conclusions. Nor do we know whether the peace that currently exists in the smoke-filled rooms where security and defense officials meet will last or dissipate. Likewise, only time will tell whether Egypt, as an Arab state, will continue to resist Israel's inclusion as an equal partner in the mapping of Middle Eastern power dynamics, and how long it will continue to use normalization as a sophisticated tool for controlling its relationship with Israel and advancing its ever-changing interests and objectives.

Notes

1. "Yihyeh Tov" [All will be good], lyrics by Yehonatan Geffen, music by David Broza, 1978, courtesy of the Centre for Educational Technology (CET) and David Peretz. See also David Peretz, "Yihyeh Tov," *Tarbut*, December 7, 2014, http://tarbut.cet.ac.il/ShowItem.aspx ?ItemID=8f073b0a-cee9-41cf-aad9-20b2c90ad9ce&lang=HEB.

2. Peace Treaty between Israel and Egypt, March 26, 1979, art. 3, para. 2, http://mfa.gov.il /MFA/ForeignPolicy/Peace/Guide/Pages/Israel-Egypt%20Peace%20Treaty.aspx.

3. Kenneth Stein, "Continuity and Change in Egyptian-Israeli Relations, 1973–97," in *From Rabin to Netanyahu*, ed. Efraim Karsh (London, Frank Cass, 1997), 312.

4. Ibid.

5. Shlomo Nakdimon, "Mekhir HaZilzul HaIsraeli BeAnwar Sadat" [The cost of Israel's disparagement of Anwar Sadat], *Haaretz*, January 23, 2014.

6. Gad Gilbar and Onn Winckler, "The Economic Dividends of Egypt and Jordan from Peace Agreements with Israel," in *The Search for Israeli-Arab Peace*, ed. Edwin Corr, Joseph Ginat, and Shaul Gabbay (Brighton, Sussex Academic Press, 2007), 67.

7. Elie Podeh, "Normal Relations without Normalization: The Evolution of Egyptian-Israeli Relations, 1979–2006—the Politics of Cold Peace," in *The Search for Israeli-Arab Peace*, ed. Edwin Corr, Joseph Ginat, and Shaul Gabbay (Brighton, Sussex Academic Press 2007), 107–29.

8. Rafi Israeli, *Anwar Sadat Al Milkhama VeShalom* [Anwar Sadat on war and peace] (Jerusalem, Magnes 1982), 41.

9. Ibid.

10. Anwar Sadat, *Sipur Khayai* [The story of my life; translated into English as *In Search of Identity*] (Jerusalem, Idanim, 1978), 226.

11. Moshe Gemer, ed., *Tahalikh Nirmul HaYakhasim Bein Israel LeMiztra'im* [The normalization of relations between Israel and Egypt] (Tel Aviv, Shiloah Institute, 1981), 63.

12. Avraham Sela, "HaShalom BeEinei Mitzra'im" [Peace through Egyptian eyes], *Ma'arakhot* 269 (June 1979): 8–13.

13. Amira Oron, "Yakhasei HaShalom Bein Israel LeMitzra'im: HaAsur HaRishon (1980–1989)—Krirut Yedu'ah MiRosh?" [Peace relations between Israel and Egypt: The first decade (1980–1989)—a coldness foretold?] (master's thesis, Hebrew University, 2011), 80.

14. Ephraim Dowek, *U-Vekhol Zot Shalom: Yahasei Israel-Mitzra'im* [Nevertheless peace: Israeli-Egyptian relations] (Tel Aviv, Yediot 1998), 232–33.

15. Moshe Yegar and Arie Oded, eds., *Misrad HaKhutz—50 HaShanim HaRishonot* [The Foreign Ministry—the first 50 years] (Jerusalem, 2002), 170.

16. Oron, "Yakhasei HaShalom Bein Israel LeMitzra'im," 34.

17. Ephraim Dowek, *Ktzarim Diplomati'im* [Diplomatic stories in short] (Jerusalem, private publication, 2007), 176–77.

18. Avraham Tamir, *Khayal Shokher Shalom* [Soldier in search of peace] (Tel Aviv, Yediot 1988), 102.

19. *Yediot Akhronot*, February 14, 1995.

20. Dowek, *Ktzarim Diplomati'im*, 237.

21. Jacob Lasner and Ilan Troen, *Jews and Muslims in the Arab World: Haunted by Pasts Real and Imagined* (Lanham, Rowman & Littlefield, 2007), 6.

22. Avraham Sela, "Policy, Identity and Peacemaking: The Arab Discourse on Peace with Israel," *Israel Studies* 10, no. 2 (2005): 40.

23. Rivka Yadlin, *Genyus Yahir VeOshek: Anti-Tzionut KeAnti-Yahadut BeMitzra'im* [An arrogant oppressive spirit: Anti-Zionism as anti-Judaism in Egypt] (Jerusalem, Shazar Institute, 1987), 15.

24. Personal source. Interview held on January 14, 2017.

25. David Sultan, *Bein Kahir VeYerushala'im: HaNormalizatzia Bein Medinot Arav VeIsrael—HaDugma HaMitzrit* [Between Cairo and Jerusalem: The normalization between Arab states and Israel—the Egyptian case] (Tel Aviv, Tel Aviv University, 2007), 37.

26. Shimon Shamir, *Aleh Taraf: Sipur HaMerkaz HaAcademi HaIsraeli BeKahir* [Saved leaf: The story of the Israeli Academic Center in Cairo] (Tel Aviv, Tel Aviv University, 2016), 128.

27. Quoted in Aluf Hareven, ed., *Od Milkhama O Likrat Shalom* [Another war or the path to peace?] (Jerusalem, Van Leer Institute, 1988), 144.

28. Shamir, *Aleh Taraf*, 129.

29. Ibid.

30. Sultan, *Bein Kahir VeYerushala'im*, 35.

31. Stein, "Continuity and Change," 304.

32. Shimon Shamir, *Aliyato U-Shki'ato Shel HaShalom HaKham Im Yarden: HaMedina'ut HaIsraelit BeYemei Hussein* [The rise and fall of warm peace with Jordan: Israeli statesmanship during the time of Hussein] (Tel Aviv, Ha Kibbutz Ha Meuchad, 2012), 459.

33. Moshe Sasson, *Sheva HaShanim BeEretz HaMitzrim* [Seven years in the land of the Egyptians] (Tel Aviv, Yediot, 1992), 133.

34. Zvi Gabai, *MeBaghdad LeNetivei HaDiplomatia* [From Baghdad to the pathways of diplomacy] (Jerusalem, Academic Association of Iraqi Jews, 2013), 131.

35. Dowek, *Ktzarim Diplomati'im*, 142.

36. Ibid., 143.

37. Ibid., 150.

38. Sultan, *Bein Kahir VeYerushala'im*, 27.

39. Ibid., 28.

40. Dowek, *Ktzarim Diplomati'im*, 150.

41. Dowek, *U-Vekhol Zot Shalom*, 151.

42. Ibid., 389.

43. Sultan, *Bein Kahir VeYerushala'im*, 41.

44. Ibid., 42.

45. Dowek, *Ktzarim Diplomati'im*, 161.

46. Sultan, *Bein Kahir VeYerushala'im*, 115.

47. Shamir, *Aleh Taraf*, 2.

48. Sultan, *Bein Kahir VeYerushala'im*, 19.

49. Sasson, *Sheva HaShanim BeEretz HaMitzrim*, 133.

50. Ibid.

51. Meir Amit, "The Battle over Peace," *Ma'arakhot* 269 (June 1979): 2–7.

52. Dowek, *Ktzarim Diplomati'im*, 153.

53. Ibid., 233.

54. Ibid., 198.

55. Oron, "Yakhasei HaShalom Bein Israel LeMitzra'im," 77.

56. Dowek, *U-Vekhol Zot Shalom*, 174–75.

57. Stein, "Continuity and Change," 307.

58. Dowek, *U-Vekhol Zot Shalom*, 232.

59. *Ynet*, March 26, 2009.

60. Interview with Smadar Peri, *Yediot Akhronot*, May 9, 2014.

61. *Ynet*, March 23, 2017. Haim Koren, a former Israeli ambassador in Egypt, recently defined the bilateral relations between the two states as "strategic cooperation and civilian detachment." *Kivunim*, November 2018.

62. Cabinet meeting on Golan Heights Law, December 14, 1981, via Israel State Archives, http://www.archives.gov.il/tag/%D7%97%D7%95%D7%A7-%D7%A8%D7%9E%D7%AA-%D7%94%D7%92%D7%95%D7%9C%D7%9F.

63. Sasson, *Sheva HaShanim BeEretz HaMitzrim*, 18.

64. Shlomo Gazit, "Heskem HaShalom Israel-Miztra'im: Ma Nishtana BiKhlof 30 Shana?" [The Israeli-Egyptian peace treaty: What has changed after thirty years?], *Idkun Astrategi* 12, no. 1 (2009): 69.

Epilogue: From Lake Success to Oslo

Realpolitik

On November 29, 1947, the United Nations, then based at Lake Success in New York, adopted UNSCOP's recommendations for the partition of Palestine west of the Jordan River into two states, Jewish and Arab, as well as international territory. The resulting UN resolution created an international basis for the establishment of the State of Israel and marked the starting point of official Israeli foreign policy, the foundations of which had been laid over a century earlier. From the outset, the Zionist movement was an international player par excellence in terms of potential and actual influence. Its effectiveness stemmed from two permanent features of the movement, on which there was near-total internal consensus: its ideology, which defined the movement's prime objective as the establishment of a national homeland for all Jews; and its own weakness, which necessitated continuous international support. As such, this book's title reflects a time-defying existential reality. The long historical process of state building entailed centripetal forces that had a unifying effect as well as centrifugal forces that divided the people. The latter included constant internal disagreement over the demographic, geographic, social, economic, religious, and ideological identity of the future national home, which carried over into statehood and became particularly salient after the Six-Day War, with Israel's seizure of the West Bank, Sinai, and Golan Heights.

From a retrospective viewpoint of more than half a century, therefore, we may safely conclude that Israel's foreign policy was intended to promote objectives that correlate with realpolitik, alongside others that may be termed "idealpolitik" and were based on what Shmuel Sandler described as "ethnonational" perspectives.[1] Raymond Cohen proposed a different typology for Israel's foreign policy objectives, using the terminology of "realism" and "unrealism" and concluding, "Had the Zionist movement simply restricted itself to realism, it is doubtful whether there would now be a thriving Jewish state of five million people. For Holocaust survivors to settle in Palestine, declare a state, and then withstand a thirty-year siege, called on remarkable reserves of blind courage and faith. A judicious blend of realism and unrealism has stood Israel in good stead for much of its existence."[2]

Be that as it may, in this book I have opted to employ the first of the above classifications. A basic argument presented here is that given the degree of political consensus surrounding these centripetal forces, they have always been a key factor in determining the existential needs of states in general, despite growing academic and public attention to other motives. The manner in which I have chosen to present the history of Israel's foreign policy might appear unconventional to some readers because it does not focus on issues of war and peace despite their indisputable and enduring salience, which stems from the hostility and violence that have always surrounded Israel's existence. Accordingly, I propose focusing on the question of how the state navigated its way through these difficult surroundings in matters of the economy, demographics, arms and oil supplies, and the rescue of Jews—all of which were supreme objectives intended to ensure the establishment and fortification of Israel. State building was without a doubt the most important goal of Ben-Gurion, Sharett, Eshkol, Meir, Begin, Shamir, and Rabin, Israel's successive prime ministers during the period under review here. Such a historical analysis extends beyond the prevailing conception of Israeli foreign policy, which is limited to the Arab-Israeli conflict and war and peace between the parties. In my opinion, based among other factors on a review of dozens of transcripts of cabinet meetings and meetings of the ministerial Economic Affairs Committee over the course of four decades, these wars and agreements ultimately constituted a means to a much more important operational end. The unremitting energy devoted on a daily basis to advancing the aim of state building through other means (such as the effort to end Israel's political isolation) attests to the importance of these means. We have examined some of Israel's realpolitik objectives, although others (the concerted effort to attract foreign investment, for example) are beyond the scope of this book.

Key elements of this story were the focus of previous chapters, and it is therefore not necessary to analyze them again chronologically. Nonetheless, it is appropriate to highlight them in the context of this epilogue, which seeks to draw thematic conclusions regarding the means employed over time by the architects of Israel's foreign policy. These means explain some of the successes as well as the failures of the policy in relation to its aims. Such an analytical approach might also contribute to comparative perspectives on the subject.

The main characteristic of that policy in the cases discussed here, and others as well, was Israel's strategic and uncompromising adherence to the concept that building, fortifying, and protecting the state were of supreme and vital importance. This goal was consistently accompanied by a great deal of tactical pragmatism in all matters related to its realization. It was a direct legacy of the Herzlian diplomatic history of the Zionist movement, which predated World War I and manifested in internal debates surrounding the Balfour declaration in 1917, as well as the movement's position on the British partition plan twenty years later and its willingness to accept the UN Partition Plan about a decade after that. In each case the movement was able to achieve increasingly significant results, thanks also to its willingness to make painful compromises, primarily on the matter of borders, shortly before 1948. It adhered to the principle that politics is the art of the possible while also refusing to concede on the ultimate strategic goal. In practical terms this approach informed the Zionist movement's decision, before and after May 1948, to rely on and participate in the diplomatic apparatus of the United Nations, despite the significant risks entailed. It also explains the movement's overall pragmatic internal strategy during the Mandate era—namely, creating a national home through what was termed "goat and chicken diplomacy" or "an acre here and an acre there." Studies on this subject have confirmed the claim that the domestic and foreign success of the Zionists was also due in part to the Arabs' very ineffective counterstrategy over the years—namely, the uncompromising "Rejection Front." In retrospect it is evident that the latter approach only enhanced the international success of the Jews' policy. This trend continued through the process of achieving statehood, as reflected in many of the political decisions Israel adopted after gaining independence, prominent among which, as Yemima Rosenthal has highlighted, were decisions on the cease-fire agreements reached in the summer of 1949.[3] The same approach informed Israel's decision to abide by these agreements as an alternative, albeit an inferior one, to peace agreements with the Arabs. The Arab states began to recognize Israel only three decades after the latter's founding, in large part because the above-mentioned Israeli pragmatism was accompanied by a good deal of obstinacy on three divisive issues: Jerusalem, the Arab refugees, and borders. Israel's 1967 conquests gradually led to a willingness to compromise on new borders, which in turn informed a new type of pragmatism that bore fruit twelve years later, when it signed a peace treaty with Egypt.

A willingness to make tactical compromises, on the one hand, alongside an adherence to overriding goals, on the other, also characterized many of Israel's actions in its historical pursuit of the international recognition it so needed. It took a step that was not common practice in international relations when, in early 1950, it agreed to pay the Persian prime minister a substantial bribe to ensure the opening of an Iranian embassy in Tel Aviv. Sharett could have relied on the Arab proverb "necessity is not to be condemned" to justify this step and withstand the moral criticism of some of his colleagues. Nor did Israel shy away from granting authorization (the "Fischer-Chauvel Agreement") for the continued implementation of agreements dating back to the Ottoman era that granted France extraterritorial rights in Palestine, thus undermining its own jurisdiction for the sake of securing French recognition. Indeed, Israel often had to make difficult decisions regarding whom to recognize. Three such cases forced it to weigh considerations of realpolitik against moral principles, and its decisions shed light on this aspect of Israeli foreign policy. Most notable was the decision to recognize the Federal Republic of Germany, as an inseparable part of the reparations agreement it signed with the latter in 1952. Israel had to weigh the memory of the Holocaust against material needs (among others, the absorption of immigrants and large foreign currency payments for oil and armaments) and the fear that for some unexpected reason Germany could suspend the reparations agreement before fully executing it, which ultimately tipped the balance. Other political constraints were at work in the case of the People's Republic of China, whose recognition in the context of an overall moral strategy would have threatened Israel's vital relations with Washington. As we know, Israel chose the United States. In the case of Spain, there were no such constraints or material and strategic enticements when Israel decided to take the moral path, honor historical memory, and refuse to recognize Franco's regime.

Another foreign policy issue that sparked an internal clash over material considerations versus moral principles was Israel's clandestine search for Nazi war criminals. It began this practice toward the end of World War II and continued it for several decades. The capture of Adolf Eichmann and his trial in Jerusalem in 1961 marked the first public expression of this policy, and from the publicity surrounding this event we know that in this instance Israel prioritized justice and morality over considerations of realpolitik stemming from its diplomatic relations with Argentina and its ties with that country's large Jewish community. The revelation (through Yad VaShem, Israel's official Holocaust museum) in September 2017 of an internal report by the Mossad sheds further light on the incident. This comprehensive report, written a decade earlier and comprising several hundred pages, disclosed that the Mossad had carried out the operation under government orders.[4]

For obvious reasons, Israel feared for its sovereignty. At the same time, it could be flexible when necessary, which led to a number of important strategic successes. Notable in this context was its conscious relinquishment of control over its own energy economy during its first decade. This concession ensured a fuel supply but also extended the monopoly that Britain and international corporations had enjoyed since the beginning of the Mandate era, allowing them to maintain control over Israel's fuel economy after 1948. Israel's policy on aliyah revealed no less, and perhaps more painful, flexibility. In the early 1950s, Ben-Gurion, Sharett, and their governments agreed to refrain, for more than a decade, from concerted efforts aimed at promoting Soviet Jewish immigration, so as not to endanger the massive aliyah from Eastern Europe during those years.

In addition, the state required many diverse and concrete means of advancing its foreign policy objectives. Let us mention some of the more prominent ones. Despite its economic weakness, Israel was often able to exploit its relatively superior standing—in the form of a financial "carrot"—to influence a considerable number of other countries. It made extensive use of this instrument for the sake of aliyah from Eastern Europe, North Africa, Ethiopia, Iraq, and Iran. It also used its own surplus weapons supplies to advance its interests through its ties with sub-Saharan African states.

The arms in Israel's possession also helped the state tremendously in establishing important, long-term strategic ties with the Federal Republic of Germany in the area of intelligence. Beginning in 1956 it engaged in military confrontations that posed the Western weapons in its hands against Soviet weapons that had reached Egyptian and Syrian hands. The Soviet weaponry that fell into Israel's possession proved to be an invaluable asset in cultivating its military ties with Germany. Of particular note, these confrontations (information about which was shared with the United States as well) included the smuggling of a MiG-21 and its pilot from Iraq to Israel in 1966, in a sensational operation code-named "Bluebird." Israel also made massive political use of its intelligence findings on the Soviet bloc, systematically gathered from immigrants from this region, whom it had brought to the country in an operation code-named "Hoard"; it began sharing this information with the CIA in the early 1950s. Details of that operation were recently revealed in Yair Spiegel's official biography of Amos Manor, the third chief of Israel's Shin Bet (General Security Service).[5]

Another important and enduring goal of Israeli foreign policy was to prevent an arms balance that favored the Arab states. Toward this end Jerusalem made a point of repeatedly underscoring its relative weakness to international arms suppliers. There were, however, two instances in which its demonstrable military power actually served it well. The assessment in Paris, for example, of Israel's impressive military prowess vis-à-vis Nasser was a crucial aspect of the two states' strategic relationship in the 1950s. A decade later Israel decisively demonstrated that it was a regional military power when, during one week in the summer of 1967, it defeated the opposing Arab armed forces, thus providing a critical argument in its political campaign to forge a strategic political alliance with the United States.

Significantly, this bold relationship was one of the most important instruments of Israeli foreign policy, even when it was illusory. The image of US-Israeli ties as unshakable and efficacious was quite common, especially in the third world, despite what was often a different reality and very much so until the late 1960s. Thus Israel often came across assessments by third-world leaders that the way to reach Washington, if they wanted to achieve their aims, specifically in the financial sphere, was through Jerusalem. Soviet leaders evidently shared this view, especially during the late 1980s, as then–finance minister Yitzhak Moda'i discovered when the Soviet Union requested his assistance in securing an immediate loan of several billion dollars from the United States.[6] Accordingly, Israel's foreign ministers regularly instructed their diplomats not to correct this impression.

Finally, Israel often relied on Jews across the world to open their hearts, doors, and wallets. In 1952 then–finance minister Levi Eshkol successfully recruited the assistance of Rudolf Goldschmid Sonneborn, a Jewish businessman, who agreed to purchase an American oil company that had succumbed to the Arab boycott and was about to pull out of Israel. The Israeli politician formulated his request as follows: "Like many of us, you wear 'two hats' and you are familiar with our inescapable need to finance our operations from largescale borrowing and charitable funds. Therefore, a foreign oil supplier who is loyal to the State of Israel must seek a modus whereby his operations will be conducted on strict business lines, but at the same time should enable the economy of the State of Israel to obtain cheap energy supplies" (Bialer 1999, 204). Five years later Eshkol described the oil firm that Sonneborn eventually purchased (entitled Sonol) as "a Jewish company."[7] Jewish help had also been considerable in coping with armaments procurement. One aspect of that reality was bluntly explained by General Israel Tal (known for leading the development of Israel's Merkava tank), who in an interview in 2000 said that "until the Six Day War it was the Jewish people who secured our military existence as we paid in cash for our arms bought [mainly] in France. . . . [It is thus clear why we claimed then] that Israel had two or three million inhabitants but also 11 million tax payers in the world. . . . [However,] since [that time] we survived because of the US support as the Jews had not been able to pay the new exorbitant price [of the weapons]."[8]

One of the conditions for a successful foreign policy is the ability to exploit opportunities. Israel was not exceptional in this regard. Nonetheless, a few examples are worth citing. Israel took advantage of the 1954 transnational agreement that put an end to the conflict over oil between Iran, on the one hand, and Britain and the United States, on the other, in order to form ties with small international companies covered by this agreement (IRICON) and achieve a meaningful breakthrough. One of the contributing factors was Israel's willingness to invest in Iran by paying above-market prices over the course of a decade for fuel purchased from NIOC, which was facing hardship under the circumstances, a willingness that yielded immense strategic benefits. Likewise, in 1950 Israel exploited Britain's entangled negotiations with Iraq over oil production and sales, warning of a potential threat posed by Iraqi plans to nationalize the refineries, and once again the dividends for Israel were most impressive. So too was the case with the 1967 blockade of the Suez Canal, which Israel fully exploited in the negotiations with Iran that led to construction of the Eilat-Ashkelon pipeline. And of course one cannot overlook the historic opportunity resulting from Egypt's conflict with Britain and France, which paved the way to Israel's participation in the Sinai Campaign.

In hindsight there can be no doubt that Israel's efforts to realize many of its realpolitik goals (including but not limited to those we examined), which required intensive foreign policy investment, were most fruitful. At the same time, Israel's diplomatic approach was not always successful. To illustrate and explain some of its failures, let us briefly address two cases we have not yet discussed: its relations with the European Common Market during the late 1950s and early 1960s, and the Oslo Accords of 1993. These examples effectively illustrate the two diplomatic tracks Israel took in an effort to minimize the ongoing political isolation it faced as a result of the Arab-Israeli conflict. The first entailed activities beyond the Middle East, while the second focused on reaching political agreement directly with the Arabs.

The Not-So-Common Market

A fundamental and existential economic factor for Israel throughout its history was the threat posed by a negative trade balance. During its early years in particular, Israel had to import nearly all of its food supplies from foreign, primarily European, sources. In 1956, for example, imports totaled $560 million, while exports reached only $170 million. Its economic dependence on Europe also resulted from its directing one-third of its exports at the European Common Market established in 1957. The probability of Britain joining this market, and therefore its former African colonies joining as well, would have meant that no less than 60 percent of Israel's exports would be directed at this European bloc. Many in Jerusalem therefore concluded that cultivating a relationship with the European Economic Community (EEC) was essential, second in importance only to Israel's security needs. The underlying motives went beyond the economic sphere. Many in Israel regarded such ties as a means of breaking the state's political isolation and therefore as having far-reaching strategic value. Moreover, relations with the EEC correlated with the self-image of many in the Israeli leadership. Above all, as he explained it to the Cabinet in January 1960, ties with Europe were "the only way to guarantee the resources needed for Israel's survival."[9]

Israel also expected that joining the Common Market would enhance its international image as a modern Western state—a Jewish European state as envisioned by Herzl. As such, what means were available to Israel at the time to advance this highly ambitious and complex aim? Having explored this question, Gadi Heimann found that Ben-Gurion expected Israel's historic and cultural ties with Europe to bolster its diplomacy in this regard.[10]

In concrete terms, Israel hoped to receive support from the Federal Republic of Germany on the basis of moral considerations. It also hoped it could rely on Europeans in Asia and Africa to promote its economic interests. Finally, Israel expected its strategic ties with France to elicit Paris's support toward this end. Beginning in 1958, therefore, Israel invested much effort in this area. The disappointment that awaited it should not be underestimated. In 1961 it became undeniably clear that Israel's seemingly dependable allies, France and Germany, like other EEC members, objected to Israel's membership. They regarded Israel as a Middle Eastern state and feared far-reaching repercussions if the community strayed from its European foundation. In hindsight, Israel's failure to assess the European arena correctly might be attributable to other factors as well. Evidently there had at the time been the possibility of a limited economic relationship with the Common Market, but Jerusalem's high hopes made it very difficult to climb down from the "tall tree" it had scaled in seeking full economic relations. Failure was thus inherent and inevitable. As such, this was an instance in which Israel had strayed from purely pragmatic considerations, and it paid a steep and painful price as a consequence. The country would have to wait another thirty years before it could conclude the 1995 Association Agreement with the European Union.

Oslo: Accords in Flame

Three months after Egypt and Israel signed the treaty, the Mossad chief addressed the question of "true peace" in a journal for IDF officers.[11] In Amit Meir's view, widely accepted across the political and military leadership at the time and presented here as a basic premise, peace is only one of the elements of national security. Other pillars include military capability, a strong civilian foundation, a strong and functioning citizenry, territory, time (particularly for its deterrent potential in terms of the state's material and human resources), dependable foreign contacts, and a regional environment that includes peace, war, and everything in between. Peace along these lines therefore constitutes only one layer of security—important also because it allows for concessions in other areas, including military and territorial. In this respect, for many at the time, the Oslo Accords represented one of Israel's greatest achievements; for others, one of its resounding failures.

Peace talks between Israel and the Arab states, with participation by Palestinian representatives, officially began after the first Gulf War, in October 1991 in Madrid. After a fruitless year and Yitzhak Rabin's election as prime minister, a clandestine negotiating channel opened between Israelis and Palestinians, later known as the "Oslo process" after the city that hosted the pivotal meetings. The Israeli team included Yossi Beilin, deputy foreign minister; Ron Pundak, a Mossad man; and Yair Hirschfeld, a professor of Middle Eastern studies at Haifa University. The talks bore fruit in September 1993, when the parties agreed on mutual recognition and a Declaration of Principles (DOP) establishing a phased process for Palestinian autonomy in five years within the framework of a final agreement. In exchange the Palestinians would publicly renounce violence as a means to political ends and be permitted to begin a phased process toward establishing a governing authority. The parties agreed to address the core issues—borders, settlements, Jerusalem, refugees, and final security arrangements—during the next phase of negotiations, to begin three years after signing the DOP.

Between 1993 and 1999, Israel and the Palestine Liberation Organization (PLO) signed a series of interim agreements. During the Rabin administration (1992–1995), these included the 1994 Cairo Agreement on implementing autonomy in the Gaza Strip and the Jericho area (of the West Bank) and the September 1995 Interim Agreement (Oslo II) dividing the West Bank into areas under direct Palestinian control (area A), civilian Palestinian control (area B), and Israeli control (area C, including settlements and self-defined "security zones"). During the Netanyahu administration (1996–1999), they signed two follow-up agreements to the Interim Agreement of 1995: the 1997 Hebron Protocol dividing the city between Israelis and Palestinians and the 1998 Wye Memorandum. Finally, under the brief Barak administration (1999–2001), they concluded the Sharm El Sheikh Memorandum in September 1999, stipulating the terms and timetable for final status negotiations. The Oslo process came to a halt after the failure of the Camp David summit in July 2000, the outbreak of the second intifada in late September 2000, and the failure of the Taba talks in January 2001.

This dry chronology obscures a complex story with twists and turns and much drama, as well as the optimism of Israel's leaders as they prepared to sign the DOP. In Rabin's words to Arafat on the White House lawn,

> Let me say to you, the Palestinians: We are destined to live together on the same soil, in the same land. We, the soldiers who have returned from battle stained with blood, we who have seen our relatives and friends killed before our eyes, we who have attended their funerals and cannot look into the eyes of their parents, we who have come from a land where parents bury their children, we who have fought against you, the Palestinians. We say to you today in a loud and a clear voice: Enough of blood and tears. Enough. We have no desire for revenge. We harbor no hatred towards you. We, like you, are people who want to build a home, to plant a tree, to love, to live side by side with you in dignity, in empathy, as human beings, as free men. We are today giving peace a chance, and saying again to you: Enough. Let us pray that a day will come when we all will say: Farewell to the arms.[12]

On September 21, 1993, Prime Minister Rabin called on Knesset members to "give us this great chance. . . . Let the sun rise." Foreign Minister Peres predicted that all the children would inherit "a new Middle East," and Minister Shulamit Aloni felt "as if it were November 29 [the day the UN partition plan was adopted]. . . . We knew we were headed towards days of glory."[13] These hopes were dashed during the two decades that followed the celebrations and signing of the DOP. The Right in Israel, which had never believed the agreement was viable, regarded the Oslo Accords as "one of the greatest disasters of the Israeli-Palestinian conflict ever" and "Israel's most terrible and severe strategic mistake throughout its history."[14] The agreement's supporters, though politically weakened during the two decades after the White House ceremony, were determinedly positive, as Yossi Beilin reflected in an interview with *Ma'ariv* on August 12, 2013:

> In Oslo, the two national movements—Zionist and Palestinian—recognized each other for the first time in history, as a result of which the Palestinian Authority was established, finally freeing us from the heavy burden of daily engagement with the occupation. It led immediately to agreement on the DOP and peace with Jordan, to the end of the Arab boycott, and to diplomatic relations with most Arab states. Transnational corporations, Phillips and others, stood in line to invest in Israel, which increased economic growth and allowed us to double our own investment in education and infrastructure. I don't think these facts can be described as "failure."

That same year Ron Pundak framed the matter as follows:

> In my opinion, the entire political process from the outset, as well as peace itself, represents only interim steps. The overriding goal was and remains safeguarding the full establishment of the State of Israel, a process that began on November 29, 1947, with the UN resolution on partition. The two great achievements of the Oslo Accords were the historic mutual recognition between two national movements—the Zionist movement in the form of the State of Israel and the national Palestinian movement in the form of the Palestine Liberation Organization (PLO), which had been waging war against each other in a zero-sum game where success for one meant defeat for the other—and their agreement that the foundation for a resolution was Security Council Resolution 242 (land for peace), or in other words, the division of Eretz Israel (the Land of Israel) into two political entities—Israeli and Palestinian.[15]

Today we know that in time the two parties, having signed the accords as they interpreted their terms and time frame, then turned their back on the Oslo process. Current literature has found that the attitudes and conduct typical of Israel and the Palestinians during the process included misunderstanding, suspicion, manipulation, and deliberate sabotage. In hindsight we can say that both sides bear responsibility. Beyond the narrow historiographic field, these narratives also provide a basis for a better understanding of the past as well as the future options on both sides.

Another theme in the literature, in addition to differential responsibility for Oslo's failure, is reflected in Pundak's formulation:

> There are three possible answers, representing three different perspectives, that might tell us why the Oslo process failed. The first answer is that peace between Israel and the Palestinians has never had and will never have a chance, and so the Oslo Accords were destined to fail from the outset. The second answer holds that peace is the only option and that to achieve it requires painful concessions. According to third answer, which is close to my heart, there is a chance, and the time is right, but the problem lies in each side's

misinterpretation of the other's real interests, in mismanagement of the process and its implementation, and now also in the lack of Israeli leadership.[16]

An important background factor is that Israel never developed a strategy for
peace with the Palestinians. Shlomo Gazit, former head of Military Intelligence
and one of the architects of Israeli policy on the 1967 territories, explained this in
his authoritative book *Trapped*: "Many Israelis believed that the Palestinians did
not pose a political problem as such because they had no political aspirations of
their own; that their only goal was to see the destruction of Israel; and therefore
that they could not be a negotiating partner. At best Israel could discuss their
problems with another party such as Jordan, Egypt, or even the United States.
This thinking created a mental block [until the 1987 intifada] that prevented any
discussion of the territories or their inhabitants."[17]

The same gap would have existed on the Palestinian side. Studies examining and apportioning blame between the Israelis and Palestinians fall into two
categories: the first focuses on the parties' lack of readiness and the second on
the obstacles and mistakes associated with the process itself. Regarding the first,
Avraham Sela posed a number of questions to which he found the answer was no,
reaching a firm conclusion:

> To what extent were the Israeli and Palestinian communities ripe for undertak-
> ing painful compromises and seeing to their implementation when their leaders
> signed the Oslo Accords? To what extent did Israeli and Palestinian policymak-
> ers exercise political legitimacy within their own constituencies? Moreover, to
> what extent have they been ready to deepen and expand the "official" peace by
> follow-up activities aimed at building social, economic, and psychological bases
> for a "culture of peace"? Have they sought to bolster and perpetuate a peaceful
> relationship by encouraging grassroots social and economic cooperation, revis-
> ing images and perceptions of self and other—"de-victimization" of self and
> "de-demonization" of the other—and seeking reconciliation through reformed
> narratives in the media and the educational curriculum? The decades . . . since
> the 1993 Oslo Accords clearly indicate that the parties have been insufficiently
> ripe for such far-reaching commitments due to social-psychological cognitive
> reasons rooted in their separate yet joint histories from time immemorial.[18]

Of particular note in this context are the conclusions of about twenty Israeli
policy makers who had taken part in the Oslo process, both its initiation and its
implementation. In 2002 researchers at the Hebrew University's Leonard Davis
Institute, including the author of this book, interviewed them. The question
posed was simple, simplistic even: What went wrong with Oslo? The answers
were wide-ranging, complex, diverse, multilayered, and multifaceted, justifying
the study's title—*Rashomon in Jerusalem*.[19]

One of the prominent themes that emerged was the approach on both sides
toward the policy-making process, which apparently included frequent, even

decisive, mistakes that affected the final outcome. (It is worth underscoring here that the Israeli side has been the subject of far more extensive and wide-ranging retrospective historical analysis than the Palestinian side.) Among Jerusalem's shortcomings and failings, the study identified the following: failure on the part of Rabin and Peres to take into account skeptical assessments by military intelligence, which eventually proved to be correct, regarding the limitations of possible Palestinian concessions; lack of negotiating experience among the teams at Oslo and the absence of any mechanism for professional assistance; differences in understanding between the negotiating teams and the prime minister; allowing the Palestinians—given the covert nature and clandestine channels of the talks—to overestimate the flexibility of Israel's position; and a sense of urgency on Rabin's part stemming from the high population growth rate among Palestinians and domestic as well as international pressure to make political progress. Another factor was that until now, negotiations with Palestinian representatives of the 1967 territories had been devoid of any real substance. Shifting the center of gravity to the PLO broadened the scope of representation from about two million residents of the territories to some six million Palestinians worldwide. For the Palestinians this required a far more comprehensive set of objectives, which for the Israelis seemed impossible. Furthermore, the step-by-step process and start-to-finish approach, deferring the core issues until much later while addressing issues of far less importance over the course of eight long years, reinforced differences and obscured the key principle.[20]

During this phase the asymmetry in terms of concession was striking, as exemplified by Israel's agreement to a phased, permanent withdrawal from the territories as early as the interim stage (thus losing its main bargaining chip well in advance of final status talks) with no reciprocal action or agreement required of the Palestinians. Also striking in this context was the "settlements' paradox"— the internal contradiction between Israel's agreement that the IDF would gradually withdraw from significant portions of land during the interim phase, on the one hand, and its insistence on permitting all the settlements to remain, on the other. It is apparent today that Israel overestimated the ability of its negotiating partner to fulfill the agreement, nor did it sufficiently account for the latter's character as a national liberation movement rather than a sovereign state, with all the attendant implications. Moreover,

> We did not correctly assess the determination of opposition to the agreement on both sides. We looked at the surveys that predicted a large majority in support of a political agreement on both the Israeli and Palestinian sides, and we thought that was enough. We predicted that there would be violence, but we thought it would come primarily from the Palestinian side and that it would be comparable to the first intifada. We did not predict the suicide attacks by Hamas and extremist Islamic groups, nor did we look into our own camp.

Even after the massacre at Hebron by Baruch Goldstein we never imagined that someone from our midst would assassinate the Prime Minister.[21]

Thus, there was a misguided minimization, at least on the part of Israel's prime minister, of the vital importance of convincing the Israeli public of the benefits that would follow from the accords.

Whether mistakes could have been prevented throughout the process had there been greater awareness of these and other factors, and whether the course of events might have taken a positive turn toward peace between Israel and the Palestinians—these questions inevitably remain open, especially as the subject suffers from a dearth of documentation in terms of historiography, both Israeli and especially Palestinian, which remains classified and perpetuates the fog still surrounding Oslo. We can say with absolute certainty, however, that the historical event effectively illustrates the depth of the problem that Israel has had to face—rejection by those living in its own neighborhood. Although enormous energies have been invested in trying to alleviate and even resolve this issue, the continuing rejection of Israel demonstrates the intractability of the problem.

Two final remarks are in order. The first is substantive: failure to achieve peace with the Palestinians left Israel facing "nonrecognition islands"—blocs of states around the world that did not recognize it—making it hard for the state to advance other foreign policy objectives such as those examined above. These islands and the fierce discord within Israeli society over political pacts with the Palestinians will ensure that the question of peace remains front and center in Israeli life. The second observation is personal: if such peace is achieved in the future, it will of course necessitate revision of this epilogue as well as major portions of the book. But such future peace will provide further justification for the title, *A People Shall Not Dwell Alone*, as a matter of actual fact. May it come to pass.

Notes

1. Shmuel Sandler, *The State of Israel, the Land of Israel: Statist and Ethnonational Dimensions of Foreign Policy* (Westport, CT, Greenwood, 1993).

2. Raymond Cohen, "Israel's Starry-Eyed Foreign Policy," *Middle East Quarterly* (June 1994). https://www.meforum.org/221/israels-starry-eyed-foreign-policy. For a periodic approach toward analyzing Israel's foreign policy using concepts of state, ethnonationalism, and globalization as analytical tools, see Aran Amnon, "Israeli Foreign Policy in Historical Perspective: State, Ethno-Nationalism, Globalisation," in *Israel's Clandestine Diplomacies*, ed. Clive Jones and Tore Pettersen (London, Hurst, 2013), 13–30.

3. Yemima Rosenthal, ed., *Teudot LeMediniyut HaKhutz Shel Medinat Israel, Kerekh 3: Sikhot Shvitat HaNeshek Im Medinot Arav, Detzember 1948–Yuli 1949* [Documents on the

foreign policy of Israel, vol. 3: Armistice negotiations with the Arab states, December 1948–July 1949] (Jerusalem, Israel State Archive, 1983).

4. Yossi Chen, *Nesi'im VeRuakh VeGeshem Ein* [As clouds and wind without rain] (Jerusalem, Yad VaShem, 2007). On Israel's relations with Latin American states, see Carlos Escude, "Israeli–Latin American Relations, 1948–2010," in *The World Facing Israel—Israel Facing the World*, ed. Alfred Wittstock (Berlin: Frank and Timme, 2011), 189–208.

5. Yair Spiegel, *Yemei Amos* [Days of Amos] (Tel Aviv, Ministry for Defence, 2017). On Israel's sharing its experience about fighting Soviet-made weapons with the United States, see Guy Laron, "When the U.S. Used Israel to Test Out a Weapon—and Dragged It into War," *Haaretz* 7 (September 2019).

6. Personal source.

7. Uri Bialer, *Oil and the Arab-Israeli Conflict, 1948–63* (London, 1999), 204; minutes of the Ministerial Committee for Economic Affairs, December 8, 1957, via Israel State Archives.

8. *Iyunim Bitkumat Israel* 10 (2000), 35–36, 63. For Jewish help in the field of nuclear weapons, see Yitzhak Mualem, "Diaspora in the Service of State: The State of Israel, Jews and the Dimona Nuclear Project," *Diaspora Studies* 12, no. 1 (2019): 79–98, doi.org/10.1080 /09739572.2018.1485236.

9. Cabinet meetings minutes, January 17, 1960, ISA.

10. Gadi Heimann, "The Need to Be Part of Europe: Israel's Struggle for an Association Agreement with the EEC, 1957–1961," *Israel Studies* 20, no. 1 (2015): 87.

11. Amit Meir, "The Battle over Peace," *Ma'arakoht* 269 (June 1979).

12. Address by Prime Minister Yitzhak Rabin on signing the Israeli-Palestinian Declaration of Principles, Washington, DC, September 13, 1993, http://www.rabincenter.org.il /Items/01100/signingoftheDeclationofPrinciples.pdf.

13. Shmuel Even, "Esrim Shana LeHeskemei Oslo: Lekakhim LeIsrael" [Twenty years after the Oslo Accords: Lessons for Israel], *Idkun Astrategi* 16, no. 2 (2013): 75–76.

14. Efraim Karsh, "Ason Oslo" [The Oslo disaster], *Iyunim BeBitakhon HaMizrakh HaTikhon* 123 (2016). Karsh is a professor of political science at Bar-Ilan University and a political analyst in Israel and abroad.

15. Ron Pundak, "Oslo Esrim Shana Akharei—Mabat Ishi VeHistori" [Oslo twenty years later—a personal and historical perspective] (Tel Aviv, 2014), 7.

16. Ibid.

17. Shlomo Gazit, *Peti'im BeMalkodet* [Trapped] (Tel Aviv, Zmora Bitan, 1999), 31.

18. Avraham Sela, "Difficult Dialogue: The Oslo Process in Israeli Perspective," *Macalester International* 23, no. 11 (2009): 105–138.

19. Arie Kacowicz, "Rashomon in Jerusalem: Mapping the Israeli Negotiators' Positions on the Israeli-Palestinian Peace Process, 1993–2001," *International Studies Perspectives* 6, no. 2 (2005): 252–73.

20. Even, "Esrim Shana LeHeskemei Oslo."

21. Yossi Beilin, "Hatzlakhot Oslo" [The Oslo successes], *Haaretz*, September 17, 2013. Baruch Goldstein was an American Israeli physician, religious extremist, and mass murderer who perpetrated the 1994 Cave of the Patriarchs massacre in Hebron, killing 29 Palestinian Muslim worshippers and wounding another 125.

Further Readings

Introduction

Bialer, Uri. "Rewriting History: The Cold War and the Beginning of Israel's Foreign Relations" [in Hebrew]. In *From Vision to Revision: A Hundred Years of Historiography of Zionism*, edited by Yechiam Weitz, 219–34. Jerusalem, Shazar Institute 1997.

———. "Top Hat and Tuxedo beside the Cannons: Israeli Foreign Policy from 1948 to 1956 as a Field of Study." *Israel Studies* 7, no. 1 (2002): 1–80.

Karsh, Efraim. *Israel: The First Hundred Years*. Vol. 4, *Israel in the International Arena*. London, Routledge, 2005.

Lazovik, Yaacov. "State Archivist Report on Archival Declassification" [in Hebrew]. Office of the Prime Minister Office. Via Israel State Archives, January 15, 2018. http://www .archives.gov.il/wp-content/uploads/2018/01/state_archivist_report_2018.pdf.

Chapter 1

Avineri, Shlomo. *Herzl: Theodor Herzl and the Foundation of the Jewish State*. London, Weidenfeld & Nicolson, 2013.

———. "Statecraft without a State: A Jewish Contribution to Political History?" In *Kontexte der Schrift—Ekkehard W. Stegemann zum 60. Geburtstag*, edited by Gabriella Gerladini, 403–19. Stuttgart, Kohlhammer Verlag, 2005.

Bar-Chen, Eli. "Two Communities with a Sense of Mission: The Alliance Israélite Universelle and the Hilfsverein der deutschen Juden." In *Jewish Emancipation Reconsidered: The French and German Models*, edited by Michael Brenner, Vicki Caron, and Uri R. Kaufman, 111–28. Tubingen, Mohr Siebeck, 2003.

Bartal, Israel. "From Shtadlanut to 'Jewish Diplomacy'? 1756–1840–1881." *Simon Dubnow Institute Yearbook* 14 (Jerusalem, Dubnov Institute, 2015): 109–30.

Dekel-Chen, Jonathan. "Philanthropy, Diplomacy, and Jewish Internationalism." In *Emancipation: The Cambridge History of Judaism*, edited by Mitchell B. Hart and Tony Michels, 477–504. Cambridge, Cambridge University Press, 2017.

Frankel, Jonathan. *The Damascus Affair: "Ritual Murder" Politics and the Jews in 1840*. London, Cambridge University Press, 1997.

Friedman, Isiah. "Theodor Herzl: Political Activity and Achievements." *Israel Studies* 9, no. 3 (2004): 46–79.

Green, Abigail. "Rethinking Sir Moses Montefiore: Religion, Nationhood, and International Philanthropy in the 19th Century." *American Historical Review* 110, no. 3 (2005): 631–59.

Guesnet, François. "Textures of Intercession: Rescue Efforts for the Jews of Prague, 1744–1748." *Simon Dubnow Institute Yearbook* 4 (2005): 355–77.

Gutwein, Daniel. "The Politics of Jewish Solidarity: Anglo-Jewish Diplomacy and the Moscow Expulsion of April 1891." *Jewish History* 5 (Fall 1991).

Kouts, Gideon. "The Sokolov Document: The First Propaganda Strategic Working Paper of the Zionist Movement" [in Hebrew]. *Kesher* 41 (Winter 2011): 64–77.

Levene, Mark. *War, Jews and the New Europe: The Diplomacy of Lucien Wolf, 1914–1919.* Oxford, Littman, 2009.

Sagi, Avi, and Yedidia Z. Stern, eds. *Herzl Then and Now: "The Jewish State" in the State of the Jews* [in Hebrew]. Jerusalem, Keter, 2008.

Sandler, Shmuel. *The Jewish Origins of Israeli Foreign Policy: A Study in Tradition and Survival.* New York, Routledge, 2018.

Shimoni, Gideon. *The Zionist Ideology.* Waltham, MA, Brandeis University Press, 1995.

Vital, David. "Diplomacy in the Jewish Interest." In *Jewish History: Essays in Honor of Chimen Abramsky,* edited by Ada Rapoport-Albert and Steven Zipperstein, 683–95. London, Peter Halban, 1988.

——. *The Origins of Zionism.* Oxford, Oxford University Press, 1975.

——. *Zionism: The Crucial Phase.* Oxford, Oxford University Press, 1987.

——. *Zionism: The Formative Years.* Oxford, Oxford University Press, 1982.

Chapter 2

Almog, Shmuel, ed. *Zionism and the Arabs: Essays.* Jerusalem, Shazar Center, 1983.

Halamish, Aviva. *From National Home to a State in the Making: History of the Jewish Community in Palestine between the World Wars* [in Hebrew]. 3 vols. Tel Aviv, The Open University, 2004; Raanana, The Open University, 2004; Raanana, The Open University, 2012.

——. "'Selective Immigration' in Zionist Ideology, Praxis and Historiography" [in Hebrew]. In *Idan ha-Tziyonut,* edited by A. Shapira, J. Reinharz, and J. Harris, 185–202. Jerusalem, Shazar Center, 2000.

Horowitz, Dan, and Moshe Lissak. *Origins of the Israeli Polity: Palestine under the Mandate.* Chicago, University of Chicago Press, 1978.

Lavie, Ephraim, ed. *Nationalism and Morality: The Zionist Discourse and the Arabic Question* [in Hebrew]. Jerusalem, Magnes, 2014.

Lissak, Moshe, ed. *The History of the Jewish Community in Palestine since 1882: The Yishuv in Eretz Israel since the First Aliyah—the Mandate Period* [in Hebrew]. Jerusalem, The Bialik Institute, 1993.

Metzer, Jacob. *The Divided Economy of Mandatory Palestine.* Cambridge, Cambridge University Press, 1998.

Radai, Itamar. *Palestinians in Jerusalem and Jaffa, 1948: A Tale of Two Cities.* London, Routledge, 2015.

Shapira, Anita. *Land and Power: The Zionist Resort to Force, 1881–1948.* Oxford, Oxford University Press, 1992.

Shlaim, Avi. *The Politics of Partition, King Abdullah, the Zionists and Palestine, 1921–1951.* Oxford, Oxford University Press, 1988.

Stein, Kenneth. *The Land Question in Palestine, 1917–1939.* Chapel Hill, University of North Carolina Press, 1984.

Yegar, Moshe. *Czechoslovakia, Zionism and Israel* [in Hebrew]. Jerusalem, The Bialik Institute, 1997.

Chapter 3

Ben Natan, Asher, and David Shiff, eds. *The Briha from Europe to the Land of Israel, 1945–8* [in Hebrew]. Tel Aviv, Ministry for Defence, 1998.

Brenner, Michael. *In Search of Israel: The History of an Idea.* Princeton, NJ, Princeton University Press, 2018.

Cohen-Shani, Shmuel. "The Political Department of the Jewish Agency and 'The School for Diplomats': Building the Institutions of a New State." *Zionism* 19 (1995): 325–44 [Hebrew].

Friling, Tuvia. *Arrows in the Dark: David Ben-Gurion, the Yishuv Leadership, and Rescue Attempts during the Holocaust.* Madison, University of Wisconsin Press, 2005.

Gelber, Yoav. *Shorshei HaKhavazelet: HaModiin BaYeshuv 1918–1947* [Growing a Fleur-de-Lis: The intelligence services of the Jewish Yishuv in Palestine 1918–1947 (Tel Aviv, Ministry for Defence, 1992).

Halamish, Aviva. "Illegal Immigration: Values, Myth and Reality." *Studies in Zionism* 9, no. 1 (1988): 47–62.

Jensehaugen, Jorgen, Marte Heian-Engdal, and Hilde Henriksen Waage. "Securing the State: From Zionist Ideology to Israeli Statehood." *Diplomacy and Statecraft* 23, no. 2 (2012): 280–303.

Kochavi, Arie. *Post Holocaust Politics: Britain, the United States, and Jewish Refugees, 1945–1948.* Chapel Hill, University of North Carolina Press, 2001.

Roger, Louis William, and Robert Stookey, eds. *The End of the Palestine Mandate.* Cambridge, Cambridge University Press, 1987.

Segev, Tom. *Ben Gurion: A State at All Costs* [in Hebrew]. Jerusalem, Keter, 2017.

Sela, Avraham. *The Decline of the Arab-Israeli Conflict: Middle East Politics and the Quest for Regional Order.* New York, SUNY, 1998.

Shapira, Anita. *Ben-Gurion: Father of Modern Israel.* New Haven, CT, Yale University Press, 2014.

Yegar, Moshe. *History of the Jewish Agency Political Department* [in Hebrew]. Jerusalem, The Bialik Institute, 2011.

———. "Moshe Shertok (Sharett) and the Jewish Agency's Political Department—Precursor to Israel's Ministry of Foreign Affairs (Part I)." *Israel Journal of Foreign Affairs* 11 (2017): 79–90.

Yizhar, Tal. "The Declaration of Independence" [in Hebrew]. *Law and Government* (2002): 551–90.

Chapter 4

Ben Dror, Elad. *Ralph Bunche and the Arab-Israeli Conflict: Mediation and the UN, 1947–1949.* London, Routledge, 2016.

Ben Dror, Elad, and Assaf Ziedler. "UN Resolution on the Internationalization of Jerusalem of 9 December 1949" [in Hebrew]. *Iyunim* 29 (2018): 162–81.

Ben Eliezer, Uri. *The Emergence of Israeli Militarism, 1936–1956* [in Hebrew]. Tel Aviv, Dvir, 1995.

Biger, Gideon. "The Boundaries of Israel—Palestine Past, Present, and Future: A Critical Geographical View." *Israel Studies* 13, no. 1 (2008): 68–93.

Caplan, Neil. "Oum Shmoom Revisited: Israeli Attitude towards the UN and the Great Powers, 1948–1960." In *Global Politics*, edited by Abraham Ben Zvi and Aharon Klieman, 167–98. London, Routledge, 2001.

Frank, Haggai, Zdeněk Klíma, and Yossi Goldstein. "The First Israeli Weapons Procurement behind the Iron Curtain: The Decisive Impact on the War of Independence." *Israel Studies* 22, no. 3 (2017): 125–52.

Freilich, Charles. *Israeli National Security: A New Strategy for an Era of Change*. Oxford, Oxford University Press, 2018.

Gelber, Yoav. "The Israeli-Arab War of 1948: History versus Narratives." In *A Never Ending Conflict*, edited by Mordechai Bar-On. London, Praeger, 2004.

———. *Israeli-Jordanian Dialogue, 1948–1953: Cooperation, Conspiracy, or Collusion?* Sussex, Sussex Academic Press, 2004.

———. *Palestine 1948, War Escape and the Emergence of the Palestinian Refugee Problem*. Portland, Sussex Academic Press, 2001.

Greenberg, Itzhak. *The Israeli Reserves Army: Laying Down the Foundations, 1949–1950* [in Hebrew]. Be'er Sheva, Ben Gurion Heritage Institute, 2001.

Loeffler, James. *Rooted Cosmopolitans: Jews and Human Rights in the Twentieth Century*. New Haven, CT, Yale University Press, 2018.

Maoz, Zeev. *Defending the Holy Land: A Critical Analysis of Israel's National Security and Foreign Policy*. Ann Arbor, The University of Michigan Press, 2006.

Morris, Benny. *The Birth of the Palestinian Refugee Problem, 1947–1949*. Cambridge, Cambridge University Press, 1988.

———. *Israel's Border Wars, 1949–1956: Arab Infiltration, Israeli Retaliation, and the Countdown to the Suez War*. Oxford, Oxford University Press, 1993.

Penslar, Derek. "Rebels without a Patron State: How Israel Financed the 1948 War." In *Purchasing Power: The Economics of Modern Jewish History*, edited by Rebecca Kobrin and Adam Teller, 171–91. Philadelphia, University of Pennsylvania Press, 2015.

Tal, David. *Israel's Day-to-Day Security Conception: Its Origin and Development, 1949–1956* [in Hebrew]. Be'er Sheva, Ben Gurion Heritage Institute, 1998.

———. *War in Palestine, 1948: Strategy and Diplomacy*. London: Routledge, 2003.

Chapter 5

Abadi, Jacob. *Israel's Quest for Recognition and Acceptance in Asia: Garrison State Diplomacy*. London, Frank Cass, 2004.

Alperovitch, Lior. "Balancing Traditional Diplomacy and Jewish Norms: Foreign Policy toward Germany in Israel's Nascent Years." *Israel Journal of Foreign Affairs* 11, no. 1 (2017).

Avineri, Shlomo. "Ideology and Israel Foreign Policy." *Jerusalem Quarterly* 37 (1986): 3–13.

Bialer, Uri. "Facts and Pacts: Ben Gurion and Israel's International Orientation." In *Ben Gurion: Politics and Leadership in Israel*, edited by R. Zweig, 216–35. London, Frank Cass, 1991.

———. "Horse Trading: Israel and the Greek-Orthodox Ecclesiastical Property, 1948–52." *Journal of Israeli History* 24, no. 2 (2005): 203–14.

———. "Israel and Nostra Aetate: The View from Jerusalem." In *Nostra Aetate: Origins, Promulgation, Impact on Jewish-Catholic Relations*, edited by A. Melloni and Y. Lamdan. Berlin, LIT Verlag, 2007.

———. "'Our Place in the World': Mapai and Israel's Foreign Policy Orientation, 1947–1952." *Jerusalem Papers on Peace Problems* 33 (1981).

———. "The Road to the Capital: The Establishment of Jerusalem as the Official Seat of the Israeli Government in 1949." *Studies in Zionism* 5, no. 2 (1985): 273–96.

———. "Sterling Balances and Claims Negotiations: Britain and Israel, 1947–1952." *Middle Eastern Studies* 28, no. 1 (1992): 157–77.

Caplan, Neil. *Futile Diplomacy—a History of Arab-Israeli Negotiations, 1913–56.* New York, Routledge, 2015.

Carenen, Caitlin. *The Fervent Embrace: Liberal Protestants, Evangelicals, and Israel.* New York, NYU Press, 2012.

Fink, Carole. *West Germany and Israel: Foreign Relations, Domestic Politics, and the Cold War, 1965–1974.* Cambridge, Cambridge University Press, 2019.

Levey, Zach. "Israeli Foreign Policy and the Arms Race in the Middle East, 1950–1960." *Journal of Strategic Studies* 24, no. 1 (2001): 29–48.

Mualem, Yitzhak. "Between a Jewish and an Israeli Foreign Policy: Israel-Argentina Relations and the Issue of Jewish Disappeared Persons and Detainees under the Military Junta, 1976–1983." *Jewish Political Studies Review* 16, nos. 1–2 (2004).

Pinkus, Benjamin. *Special Relationship: The USSR, Its Allies and Their Relations with the Jewish People, Zionism and the State of Israel, 1939–1959* [in Hebrew]. Sede Boker, Ben Gurion Heritage Institute, 2007.

Podeh, Elie. "The Desire to Belong Syndrome: Israel and Middle Eastern Defence, 1949–1954." *Israel Studies* 4, no. 2 (1999): 121–44.

Shaolian-Sopher, Efrat. "Israel Foreign Policy towards Iran, 1948–1979: Beyond the Realist Account." PhD diss., London School of Economics, 2017.

Sharfman, Daphna, ed. *A Light unto the Nations: Israel's Foreign Policy and Human Rights* [in Hebrew]. Tel Aviv, Hakibbutz HaMeuchad, 1999.

Sheffer, Gabi. *Moshe Sharett: A Biography of a Political Moderate.* Oxford, Oxford University Press, 1996.

Siniver, Asaf. *Abba Eban: A Biography.* New York, Oxford University Press, 2015.

Sufott, Zev. *A China Diary: Towards the Establishment of China-Israel Diplomatic Relations.* London, Frank Cass, 1997.

Waage, Hilde Henriksen. "How Norway Became One of Israel's Best Friends." *Journal of Peace Research* 37, no. 2 (2000): 189–211.

Yegar, Moshe. *Malaysia—Attempts at Dialogue with a Muslim Country* [in Hebrew]. Jerusalem, Magnes, 1996.

———. *On the History of Israel's Foreign Information Campaign* [in Hebrew]. Herzeliya, Lahav, 1986.

Chapter 6

Alexander, Zvi. *Israel's Covert Efforts to Secure Oil Supply.* Jerusalem, Gefen, 2004.

Bialer, Uri. "Delek: The Formative Period of Israel's National Oil Company." In *A Comparative History of National Oil Companies*, edited by Alain Beltran, 291–304. Bern, Peter Lang, 2010.

———. "Oil from Iran: Zvi Doriel's Mission in Tehran, 1956–1963" [in Hebrew]. Pts. 1 and 2. *Iyunim Bitkumat Israel; Studies in Zionism, the Yishuv and the State of Israel* 8 (1998): 150–80; 9 (1999): 128–66.

———. "The Power of the Weak: Israel's Secret Oil Diplomacy." In *Israel's Clandestine Diplomacies*, edited by Clive Jones and Torre Petersen, 67–84. London, 2013.

Brkai, Haim. *The Beginning of the Israeli Economy* [in Hebrew]. Jerusalem, The Falk Institute, 1990.

Cohen, Erez. "Development of Israel's Natural Gas Resources: Political, Security, and Economic Dimensions." *Elsevier Resources Policy* 57 (2018): 137–46.

Cohn, Margit. "Fuzzy Legality and National Styles of Regulation: Government Intervention in the Downstream Oil Market in Israel." *Law and Policy* 24 (2002): 51–88.

Gendzier, Irene. *Dying to Forget: Oil, Power, Palestine and the Foundation of U.S. Policy in the Middle East*. New York, Columbia University Press, 2017.

Greenberg, Yitzhak. *Pinchas Sapir* [in Hebrew]. Tel Aviv, Rasling, 2011.

Lavi, Bezalel. *The Black Gold in Eretz Israel* [in Hebrew]. Jerusalem, Carmel, 1999.

Lenczowski, George. *Oil and State in the Middle East*. Ithaca, NY, Cornell University Press, 1960.

Levkovitch, Zeev. "Oil Supply during the War of Independence: The Problem, Constraints and Solutions" [in Hebrew]. *Ma'arachot* 304 (1986): 16–23.

Painter, David. *Oil and the American Century: The Political Economy of US Foreign Oil Policy, 1941–1954*. Baltimore, Johns Hopkins University Press, 1986.

Rivlin, Paul. *The Israeli Economy from the Foundation of the State through the Twenty-First Century*. Cambridge, Cambridge University Press, 2012.

Rubinovitz, Ziv, and Elai Rettig. "Crude Peace: The Role of Oil Trade in the Israeli-Egyptian Peace Negotiations." *International Studies Quarterly* 62, no. 2 (2018): 371–82.

Shwadran, Benjamin. *Middle East Oil: Blessing and Threat* [in Hebrew]. Tel Aviv, Am Oved, 1975.

Venn, Fionna. *Oil Diplomacy in the Twentieth Century*. London, Palgrave, 1986.

Chapter 7

Arbel, Andrea S. *Riding the Wave: The Jewish Agency's Role in the Mass Aliyah of Soviet and Ethiopian Jewry to Israel, 1987–1995*. Jerusalem, Gefen, 2001.

Doron, Avraham, and Howard J. Kargar. "The Politics of Immigration Policy in Israel." *International Migration* 31 (1993): 497–512.

Gat, Moshe. *The Jewish Exodus from Iraq, 1948–1951*. London, Frank Cass, 1997.

Govrin, Yosef. *Israel's Relations with Eastern Europe States*. Jerusalem, Magnes, 2009.

Hacohen, Dvorah. *Immigrants in Turmoil: Mass Immigration to Israel and Its Repercussions in the 1950's and After*. Syracuse, NY, Syracuse University Press, 2003.

Halamish, Aviva. "Zionist Immigration Policy Put to the Test: Historical Analysis of Israel's Immigration Policy, 1948–1951." *Journal of Modern Jewish Studies* 7, no. 2 (2008): 119–34.

Kimche, Ruth. *Zionism in the Shadow of the Pyramids: The Zionist Movement in Egypt, 1918–1948*. [in Hebrew]. Tel Aviv, Am Oved 2009.

Klor, Sebastian. *Between Exile and Exodus: Argentinian Jewish Immigration to Israel, 1948–1967*. Detroit, Wayne University Press, 2017.

Kochavi, Noam. "Idealpolitik in Disguise: Israel Jewish Emigration from the Soviet Union and the Nixon Administration, 1969–1974." *International History Review* 29, no. 3 (2007): 550–72.

Lazin, Fred. *The Struggle for Soviet Jewish Emigration in American Politics: Israel versus the American Jewish Establishment*. Lanham, MA, Lexington, 2005.

Levine, Zachary Paul. "Concealed in the Open: Recipients of International Clandestine Jewish Aid in Early 1950s Hungary." *AHEA: EJournal of the American Hungarian Educators Association* 5 (2012): 1–18.

Meir-Glitzenstein, Esther. *The "Magic Carpet" Exodus of Yemenite Jewry: An Israeli Formative Myth*. Sussex, Sussex Academic Press, 2014.

Naim, Asher. *Saving the Lost Tribe: The Rescue and Redemption of the Ethiopian Jews*. London, Ballantine, 2003.

Oren, Neli. "Israel's Legation in Warsaw, 1948–1951: On the Question of Israel's Relations with Poland and Polish Jews" [in Hebrew]. *Shvut* (2004–2005).

Peretz, Pauline. *Let My People Go: The Transnational Politics of Soviet Jewish Emigration during the Cold War*. New Brunswick, NJ, Transaction, 2015.

Pinkus, Benjamin. *The Jews of the Soviet Union: The History of a National Minority*. Cambridge, Cambridge University Press, 1988.

Roi, Yaacov. *The Struggle for Soviet Jewish Emigration, 1948–1967*. Cambridge, Cambridge University Press, 1991.

Shimoni, Gideon. *Jews and Zionism: The South African Experience (1910–1967)*. Oxford, Oxford University Press, 1980.

Spector, Stephen. *Operation Solomon: The Daring Rescue of the Ethiopian Jews*. Oxford, Oxford University Press, 2005.

Toktaş, Sule. "Turkey's Jews and Their Immigration to Israel." *Middle Eastern Studies* 42, no. 3 (2006): 505–19.

Waxman, Dov, and Scott Lasensky. "Jewish Foreign Policy: Israel, World Jewry and the Defence of 'Jewish Interests.'" *Journal of Modern Jewish Studies* 12, no. 2 (2013): 232–52.

Chapter 8

Bar-on, Mordechai. *Etgar VeTigra: HaDerekh LeMivtzah Kadesh, 1956* [Challenge and defiance: The road to the 1956 Sinai Campaign] (Jerusalem, 1991).

———. *The Gates of Gaza* [in Hebrew]. Tel Aviv, Am Oved, 1994.

———. *Moshe Dayan: Israel's Controversial Hero*. New Haven, CT, Yale University Press, 2012.

Bialer, Uri. "The Czech-Israeli Arms Deal Revisited." *Journal of Strategic Studies* 8, no. 2 (1985): 307–15.

Brower, Kenneth. "The Israel Defense Forces, 1948–2017." Begin-Sadat Center for Strategic Studies, Bar-Ilan University, Mideast Security and Policy Studies no. 150 (2018).

Crosbie, Sylvia. *A Tacit Alliance: France and Israel from Suez to the Six Day War*. Princeton, Princeton University Press, 1974.

Golani, Motti. *Israel in Search of War: The Sinai Campaign, 1955–1956*. Brighton, Sussex Academic Press, 1998.

Greenberg, Yitzhak. *The Calculation of Power: The Defence Budget from War to War, 1957–1967* [in Hebrew]. Tel Aviv, Ministry for Defence, 1997.

Hadari, Ze'ev Venia, *Second Exodus: The Full Story of Jewish Illegal Immigration to Palestine 1945–1948* (New York, Vallentine Mitchell, 1991).

Heimann, Gadi. "A Case of Diplomatic Symbiosis: France, Israel and the Former French Colonies in Africa, 1958–62." *Journal of Contemporary History* (2015): 1–20.

Hershco, Tslila. "France and the Partition Plan, 1947–1948." *Israel Affairs* 14, no. 3 (2008): 488–98.

Levey, Zach. *Israel and the Western Powers, 1952–1960.* Chapel Hill, University of North Carolina Press, 1997.

Rosenthal, Yemima, ed. *Yitzhak Rabin, Prime Minister of Israel, 1974–1977, 1992–1995.* Vol. 1, *1922–1967* [in Hebrew]. Jerusalem, Israel State Archive, 2005.

Sagi, Nana, ed. *Documents on the Foreign Policy of Israel: The Sinai War, the Political Battle, October 1956–March 1957* [in Hebrew]. Jerusalem, Israel State Archive, 2009.

Siman Tov, David, and Shai Hershkovich. *Military Intelligence Comes to Light: The First Decade* [in Hebrew]. Tel Aviv, Maarachot, 2013.

Tal, David. *The 1956 War: Collusion and Rivalry in the Middle East.* London, Cass, 2001.

Troen, Selwyn I., and Moshe Shemesh, eds. *The Suez-Sinai Crisis, 1956: Retrospective and Reappraisal.* London, Routledge, 1990.

Zamir, Meir. *The Secret Anglo-French War in the Middle East: Intelligence and Decolonization, 1940–1948.* London, Routledge, 2015.

Ziv, Guy. "Shimon Peres and the French-Israeli Alliance 1954–9." *Journal of Contemporary History* 45 (2010): 406–29.

Chapter 9

Abessira, Yael. "Israel's Rural Cooperation Programs in Africa: Retrospective and Analysis (1958–1977)." Master's thesis, Hebrew University, 1998.

Amir, Shimeon. *Israel's Development Cooperation with Africa, Asia, and Latin America.* New York, Praeger, 1974.

Bar-Yosef, Eitan. *A Villa in the Jungle: Africa in Israeli Culture* [in Hebrew]. Tel Aviv, HaKibbutz HaMeuchad, Jerusalem, 2013.

Butime, Herman. "Shifts in Israel-Africa Relations." *Strategic Assessment* 17, no. 3 (2014).

Chazan, Naomi. "Fallacies of Pragmatism: Israeli Foreign Policy towards South Africa." *African Affairs* 82, no. 327 (1983): 169–99.

Decalo, Samuel. *Israel and Africa: Forty Years, 1956–1996.* Gainesville, Florida Academic Press, 1998.

Gelber, Yoav. *Attrition: The Forgotten War* [in Hebrew]. Modiin, Kineret Zmora Dvir, 2017.

Mooreville, Anat. "Eyeing Africa: The Politics of Israeli Ocular Expertise and International Aid, 1959–1973." *Jewish Social Studies* 21, no. 3 (2016): 31–71.

Neuberger, Benyamin. *Israel's Relations with the Third World (1948–2008).* Tel Aviv, The S. Daniel Abraham Center for International and Regional Studies, Tel Aviv University, 2009.

Peters, Joel. *Israel and Africa: The Problematic Friendship.* London, Cambridge University Press, 1992.

Tsoref, Hagai, Amnon Lammfomm, and Louide Fischer, eds. *Israel–South Africa Relations, 1961–1967 (Documents on the Foreign Policy of Israel).* Jerusalem, Israel State Archive, 2014.

Yacobi, Haim. *Israel and Africa: A Genealogy of Moral Geography.* London, Routledge, 2015.

Yegar, Moshe. *The Long Journey to Asia: A Chapter in the Diplomatic History of Israel* [in Hebrew]. Haifa: Haifa University Press, 2004.

Chapter 10

Ben-Zvi, Abraham. *From Truman to Obama: The Rise and Early Decline of American-Israeli Relations* [in Hebrew]. Tel Aviv, Yediot, 2011.

Cohen, Avner. "Israel and the Evolution of US Nonproliferation Policy: The Critical Decade (1958–1968)." *Nonproliferation Review* (Winter 1998): 1–19.

Ganin, Zvi. *An Uneasy Relationship: American Jewish Leadership and Israel, 1948–1957.* Syracuse, NY, Syracuse University Press, 2005.

Gazit, Mordechai. "The Genesis of US-Israel Military-Strategic Relationship and the Dimona Issue." *Journal of Contemporary History* 35, no. 3 (2000): 413–22.

Hahn, Peter. *Caught in the Middle East: U.S. Policy toward the Arab-Israeli Conflict, 1945–1961.* Chapel Hill, University of North Carolina Press, 2004.

Heller, Joseph. *The United States, the Soviet Union and the Arab-Israeli Conflict, 1948–67: Superpower Rivalry.* Manchester, Manchester University Press, 2016.

Kochavi, Noam. "The Benefits of Adaptive Diplomacy: Israel Consolidation of Special Relationship and the Conservative Turn in the American-Israeli Partnership, 1967–1973" [in Hebrew]. *Cathedra* 163 (2017): 191–222.

Levey, Zach. "The United States, Israel, and Nuclear Desalination: 1964–1968." *Diplomatic History* 5, no. 1 (2015): 904–25.

Levin, Geoffrey. "State of the Field Essay on Culture, Communities, and Early U.S.-Israel Relations." H-Diplo Essay no. 160, July 18, 2018. http://tiny.cc/E160.

Manor, Ehud. "'An Infantile Judgement'—Dayan, Alon, Nuclear Ambiguity and the Debate over Israel's Place in the Region" [in Hebrew]. *Politika* 27 (2018): 76–103.

Maoz, Zev. "The Mixed Blessing of Israel's Nuclear Policy." *International Security* 28, no. 2 (2003): 44–77.

Marsden, Lee. "US-Israel Relations: A Special Friendship." In *America's "Special Relationships": Foreign and Domestic Aspects of the Politics of Alliance*, edited by Jon Dumbrell and Axel Schafer. London, Routledge, 2009.

Mart, Michelle. *Eye on Israel: How America Came to View Israel as an Ally.* New York, SUNY Press, 2006.

Rabinowitz, Or, and Nicholas Miller. "Keeping the Bombs in the Basement: U.S. Nonproliferation Policy toward Israel, South Africa, and Pakistan." *International Security* 40, no. 1 (2015): 47–86.

Rosenthal, Yemima, ed. *Levi Eshkol: The Third Prime Minister, Selected Documents, 1895–1969* [in Hebrew]. Jerusalem, Israel State Archive, 2002.

Shindler, Colin, ed. *Israel and the World Powers: Diplomatic Alliances and International Relations beyond the Middle East.* London, Tauris, 2014.

Stein, Kenneth W. "US-Israeli Relations, 1947–2010: The View from Washington." In *The World Facing Israel—Israel Facing the World*, edited by Alfred Wittstock, 159–76. Berlin: Frank and Timme, 2011.

Tal, David. *The American Nuclear Disarmament Dilemma, 1945–1963.* Syracuse, NY, Syracuse University Press, 2008.

Chapter 11

Abadi, Jacob. "Egypt's Policy towards Israel: The Impact of Foreign and Domestic Constraints." *Israel Affairs* (2006): 159–76.

Almog, Orna. "Unlikely Relations: Israel, Romania and the Egyptian-Israeli Peace Accord." *Middle Eastern Studies* 52, no. 6 (2016): 881–96.

Bar-Joseph, Uri. "Last Chance to Avoid War: Sadat's Peace Initiative of February 1973 and Its Failure." *Journal of Contemporary History* 41, no. 3 (2006): 545–56.

Bar Siman, Tov. *Yaacov Israel and the Peace Process: In Search of Legitimacy.* New York, SUNY Press, 1994.

Cohen, Raymond. *Culture and Conflict in Egyptian-Israeli Relations: A Dialogue of the Deaf.* Bloomington, Indiana University Press, 1990.

Gat, Moshe. *In Search of a Peace Settlement: Egypt and Israel between the Wars, 1967–1973.* London, Palgrave, 2012.

Karawan, Ibrahim. "Sadat and the Egyptian-Israeli Peace Revisited." *International Journal of Middle East Studies* 26, no. 2 (1994): 249–66.

Meital, Yoram. "Perceptions of Peace: Israel, Egypt and Jordan." In *The World Facing Israel—Israel Facing the World*, edited by Alfred Wittstock, 29–38. Berlin, Frank & Timme GmbH, 2011.

The Middle East Institute Viewpoints: The Legacy of Camp David. Washington, DC, 2009. www.mei.edu.

Moomen, Sallam, and Ofir Winter. "Egypt and Israel: Forty Years in the Desert of Cold Peace" [in Hebrew]. *Strategic Assessment* 20, no. 3 (2017).

Navon, Emmanuel. "From Kippur to Oslo: Israel's Foreign Policy, 1973–1993." *Israel Affairs* 10, no. 3 (2004): 1–40.

Oren, Michael. "Secret Efforts to Achieve Egyptian-Israeli Peace Prior to the Suez Campaign, 1952–1956." *Middle Eastern Studies* 3 (1990): 351–70.

Rabinovich, Itamar. *Waging Peace: Israel and the Arabs, 1948–2003.* Princeton, NJ, Princeton University Press, 2004.

Stein, Kenneth. *Heroic Diplomacy: Sadat, Kissinger, Carter, Begin, and the Quest for Arab-Israeli Peace.* London, Routledge, 1999.

Steinberg, Gerald, and Ziv Rubinovitz. *Menachem Begin and the Israel-Egypt Peace Process: Between Ideology and Political Realism.* Bloomington, Indiana University Press, 2019.

Telhami, Shibley. *Power and Leadership in International Bargaining: The Path to the Camp David Accords.* New York, Columbia University Press, 1990.

Vanetik, Boaz, and Zaki Shalom. *The Nixon Administration and the Middle East Peace Process, 1969–1973: From the Rogers Plan to the Outbreak of the Yom Kippur War.* Sussex, Sussex Academic Press, 2013.

Weitz, Yechiam. "From Peace in the South to War in the North: Menachem Begin as Prime Minister, 1977–1983." *Israel Studies* 19, no. 1 (2014): 145–65.

Index

National Religious Party, 203; nuclear weapons, 63–66, 210–212, 218, 219, 221, 250, 257, 260–284; oil acquisition, 2, 5, 49, 67, 77, 82, 109–135, 155, 231, 294, 310, 311, 315, 321, 323, 325; Old City, 36; peace agreement with Egypt, 5, 88, 291–317, 322, 327; peace agreement with Jordan, 37, 250, 303, 329; recognition of, 53, 77, 89, 91–92, 95, 101, 102, 105, 233, 243, 294, 295, 300, 327, 328; relations with the Christian world, 2, 4, 50, 81, 101–106, 199–202, 205; reprisal policy, 83, 86, 88, 89, 93; Shin Bet, 3, 48, 84, 324; state archive, 85, 129, 144, 164, 200; wars: war of independence (1948 war), 56–76; Sinai war (1956), 212–214, 216, 218, 250, 261, 293; 1967 war, 2, 4, 57, 65, 83, 85–87, 93, 106, 115, 117, 124, 125, 128, 154, 182, 189, 204, 209, 210, 215, 220, 221, 233, 234, 238, 243, 245, 246, 252, 256, 260, 261, 280, 282, 293, 294, 315, 320, 322, 325; "War of Attrition" (1967–1970), 241, 243, 294; Yom Kippur War (1973), 1, 78, 220, 224, 243, 282, 293, 294
Jewish Agency, 21, 22, 24, 28, 30, 31, 33–36, 39–49, 56, 57, 87, 100, 101, 102, 138, 143, 150, 151, 155, 161, 163, 167, 169, 172, 191, 192, 194, 200; political department, 21, 33, 39, 40, 45, 46, 56, 84, 85, 191
Jewish Anti-Fascist Committee, 176
Jewish Diaspora, 10, 15, 26, 53, 67, 68, 73, 74, 136, 145, 156, 158, 161, 166, 167, 180, 192
Jewish diplomacy, 4, 9, 11; banishing Jews from Prague (1744), 12–13; the Damascus affair, 12, 13–18; international Jewish organizations, 13, 138, 182
Jews of Silence (book), 181
Jezreel Valley, 28
Jinnah, Muhammad Ali, 225
Johnson, Lyndon B., 256, 276–280
Jones, Clive, 40
Jordan River, 32, 34, 80, 320
Jordan Valley, 28, 32
Judean Desert, 34

Kadima organization, 161, 164
Kafr, Kanna, 58
Kahane, Shamai, 94

Kalev, Henriette, 161
Karni, Nahum, 239
Kassa, Kebede, 173
Kassa, Ras Asrate, 240
Katz, Emily Alice, 257
Katz, Katriel, 149
Kedmi, Yaakov, 139
Kenya, 228, 231–234, 237, 239, 241, 243, 246, 249
Kennedy, John Fitzgerald, 64, 254, 256, 259, 269, 270–274, 278, 282, 283
Kenyatta, Jomo, 239, 249
kesoch (Ethiopian spiritual leader), 166
Kfir (jets), 248
Khartoum, 171, 172
Khomeini, Sayyid Ruhollah Mūsavi, 134
Khrushchev, Nikita, 152, 181
kibbutz galuyot (the ingathering of exiles), 65, 66
Kibbutz Galuyot (ship), 151
King Abdullah, 31, 79, 81, 85
King David Hotel, 4
Kinkel, Klaus, 155
Kirkuk, 110
Kiryat Gat, 171
Kissinger, Henry, 249, 281
Klieman, Aharon, 15
Klor, Sebastian, 136
Kohn, Father Leo, 104
Kol, Moshe, 161
Kol Zion LaGola (the Voice of Zion to the Diaspora), 180
Kollek, Teddy, 40, 48, 235, 236, 268
Korean War (1950), 69, 96
Kosloff, Israel, 120
Krzyzanowski, Lukasz, 142
Kumaraswami, P. R., 3
Kuwait, 115

Labour Party, Britain, 24
Lampson, Miles, 25
Laskov, Haim, 219
Latin America, 181, 221, 228, 236
Lausanne, 69, 79, 80, 88
Lavi (jet and project), 248
Lavon Pinhas ("Lavon affair"), 97, 269–271, 286n45

URI BIALER is Emeritus Professor of International Relations and holds the Maurice B. Hexter Chair in International Relations–Middle Eastern Studies at the Hebrew University. He is author of *Cross on the Star of David*.